DIGITAL ACTIVISM AND CYBERCONFLICTS IN NIGERIA

DIGITAL ACTIVISM AND SOCIETY: POLITICS, ECONOMY AND CULTURE IN NETWORK COMMUNICATION

The *Digital Activism and Society: Politics, Economy and Culture in Network Communication* series focuses on the political use of digital everyday-networked media by corporations, governments, international organizations (Digital Politics), as well as civil society actors, NGOs, activists, social movements and dissidents (Digital Activism) attempting to recruit, organise and fund their operations, through information communication technologies.

The series publishes books on theories and empirical case studies of digital politics and activism in the specific context of communication networks. Topics covered by the series include, but are not limited to:

- the different theoretical and analytical approaches of political communication in digital networks;
- studies of socio-political media movements and activism (and 'hacktivism');
- transformations of older topics such as inequality, gender, class, power, identity and group belonging; and
- strengths and vulnerabilities of social networks.

Series Editor

Dr Athina Karatzogianni

About the Series Editor

Dr Athina Karatzogianni is an Associate Professor at the University of Leicester, UK. Her research focuses on the intersections between digital media theory and political economy in order to study the use of digital technologies by new socio-political formations.

Published Books in this Series:
Digital Materialism: Origins, Philosophies, Prospects by Baruch Gottlieb

Forthcoming Titles:
Nirbhaya, New Media and Digital Gender Activism by Adrija Dey

DIGITAL ACTIVISM AND CYBERCONFLICTS IN NIGERIA: OCCUPY NIGERIA, BOKO HARAM AND MEND

BY

SHOLA ABIDEMI OLABODE
University of Hull, UK

emerald
PUBLISHING

United Kingdom – North America – Japan – India – Malaysia – China

Emerald Publishing Limited
Howard House, Wagon Lane, Bingley BD16 1WA, UK

First edition 2018

British Library Cataloguing in Publication Data
A catalogue record for this book is available from the British Library

ISBN: 978-1-78756-015-4 (Print)
ISBN: 978-1-78756-014-7 (Online)
ISBN: 978-1-78756-016-1 (Epub)

Printed and bound by CPI Group (UK) Ltd, Croydon, CR0 4YY

ISOQAR certified Management System, awarded to Emerald for adherence to Environmental standard ISO 14001:2004.

ISOQAR
REGISTERED
Certificate Number 1985
ISO 14001

INVESTOR IN PEOPLE

Contents

List of Figures

List of Tables

About the Author

Shola Abidemi Olabode completed his PhD in Media Studies at the School of Social Sciences, University of Hull, UK. He also holds a Master of Laws (LLM) in International Law, BSc (Hons) in Mass Communication from the University of Hertfordshire, UK, and a Diploma in Mass Communication from the University of Jos, Nigeria. He has served as a Tutor of Media Movements and Radical Politics at the University of Hull. His main research interests are in digital activism and cyberconflicts.

Preface

Developments in media, culture and society have been an area of growing interest in the last few decades given the rapid developments in digitisation infrastructure. The critical role of media (old and new) for political development and the wave of conflict that has been evolving across the globe motivated my curiosity to understand and advance fresh thinking on the intersection between information and communication technologies (ICTs) and conflict. In Nigeria, conflict has been an integral part of political life and has served as a catalyst for a progressive Nigerian society from the pre-colonial era to the current period of democratisation. As in other countries on the continent, dissident movements, social movements, civil society organisations and radical movements in Nigeria have found a voice in conflict and continue to harness various media technologies in their quest to influence government programmes, policies, reforms and changes in Africa's most populous country. In all this, the media has served as a tool and resource for dissident movements who use the medium as a means to achieve their goals.

This monograph is a product of my doctoral dissertation carried out at the School of Social Sciences at the University of Hull. The thesis has been revised in part to broaden its scope to include snapshots of recent conflicts in sub-Saharan Africa. Nonetheless, its primary focus remains the same: the use of information and communication technologies in the Occupy Nigeria, Boko Haram and the Movement for the Emancipation of the Niger Delta conflicts. The three distinct cases provide a lens for examining mobilisation among contemporary movements in Nigeria in one single study and allows for perspectives to be offered on digital activism and cyberconflicts from a developing non-western context.

There are some people to whom I am most thankful for their support, inspiration, assistance and kindness during the length of this research. I acknowledge the inspiration and the strong guidance provided by my supervisor, Dr Athina Karatzogianni, who exposed me to her wealth of experience in the field of research and believed in my work. I am particularly thankful for the opportunities for professional development, her encouragement and support throughout my doctoral programme. I owe my second supervisor, Dr Julia Holdsworth, my sincere appreciation for offering me her valuable support, assistance, suggestions and supervision. I also thank Dr Bev Orton and Dr Anastasia Kavada for their insightful recommendations.

I am grateful to all the interviewees from Nigeria who agreed to be part of this project and contributed to this research. All of the interviewees, veteran activists, civil society actors, academicians and ordinary Nigerians played a significant role in the protests and as such offered profound insights for this research. I am most grateful for the unwavering love, patience, understanding, sacrifice and support shown by my mother Mrs Taiwo Caroline Olabode, my brothers Dr Abayomi Olabode, Dr Mayowa Olabode and Mr Tosin Olabode and my sister Miss Kemi Olabode throughout this research. I thank them for their patience, prayers, encouragement and support. I dedicate this book to the memory of my father, Dr Atanda Olayinka Olabode, who would have been joyful to see me tail his path as a scholar. I am grateful to Mr Wale Ojo and his family for their support during different phases of my academic and professional development.

I wish to thank members of the Amazing Grace Chapel of the Redeemed Christian Church of God (RCCG) in Hull for their prayers. I appreciate all my friends and acquaintances: Dr Ernest Darfour, Dr Eghosa Ekhato, Dr Emmanuel Ubuo and Mr Segun Sokan to mention but a few. I appreciate their valuable contributions morally and spiritually. Finally, I am most grateful to God, in Him whom all things are possible, for the grace and the gift of life to complete this project.

Chapter 1

Introduction

The last few decades have witnessed new waves of socio-political and ethnoreligious conflict across the globe even in particular national contexts hitherto expected. These events have, coinciding with developments in digital media technologies and corresponding applications of the internet, ignited new discussion, debates and heightened the need for a reconsideration of our understanding of conflict in computer-mediated environments. In the present context, the uses of 'conflict' allow for a broad depiction of activities of social movements and insurgency movements (encompassing radical and non-radical movements). Not only has conflict become crucial in debate within political, media and scholarly circles in recent times, but the thrust of such debate has also focused on the impact of networks of Information and Communication Technologies (ICTs) on the new waves of social movements, civil society and insurgency movement protests across the globe. Digital media and ICTs are used interchangeably to follow Diamond's (2010) theorisation of digital ICTs. According to Diamond, digital ICTs refer to 'the computer, the Internet, the mobile phone, and countless innovative applications for them, including "new social media" such as Facebook and Twitter' (Diamond, 2010, p. 70) and YouTube. These technologies offer access to information and increase the socio-political and economic autonomy of individuals to take part in governance.

Drawing on conflict within global civil society, a new wave of socio-political and ethnoreligious conflict is emerging within cyberspace. In sub-Saharan Africa, the expansive developments in digital media infrastructure in the last two decades have led to new uses and audiences which Williams and Mano (2017) argued required critical research more than ever, given the rapidly developing media environment on the continent. Conflict movements in Nigeria provide an illustrative empirical basis for understanding new digital cultures particularly as it relates to youth engagement and contentious politics. Like with most countries on the continent, contentious politics have been a crucial element of Nigerian politics, one that has shaped the political environment through the different phases of the Nigerian political development. Conflict served as machinery for keeping an eye on the democratic institutions, with civil society, the media, social movements and independent activists as protagonists, as will be demonstrated in the empirical chapters.

Nigeria provides a lens to examine the role of ICTs in the activities of non-institutional actors engaged in conflict with the state. Scholarly discussion about the potential impact of ICTs when employed by activist networks during protests has risen in the last few years (Castells, 2001; Garrett, 2006; Karatzogianni, 2006a, 2006b, 2009, 2012a, 2012b, 2012c, 2013; Kavada, 2010a, 2010b, 2012, 2015; Morozov, 2011a, 2011b). However, the reality is that far too little attention is paid to support these claims in the context of low-income earning countries as in sub-Saharan Africa (Obadare & Willems, 2014; Mano, 2017; Mutsvairo, 2016a, 2016b; Shepherd & Shanade, 2016). Therefore, this study aims to explore the role of ICTs in the Nigerian context juxtaposed with empirical cases in sub-Saharan Africa and across the globe. This book is also timely and crucial for several reasons. First, it is worthy to mention that the notion of digital activism and cyberconflict (CC) is a developing area in the African context as in the Nigerian case. Similarly, no study considers the role of ICTs in the activities of socio-political and ethnoreligious conflict movements in a single study in Nigeria. Therefore, examples of Occupy Nigeria, Movement for Emancipation of the Niger Delta (MEND) and Boko Haram contribute to improving knowledge by bridging the gap in the literature with regard to digital activism and CC as a field of study, an examination of the use of digital media in three political movements of various ideological underpinnings in a single country and considering these examples in a developing non-western context. Second, by considering the role and influence of ICTs and the internet on the mobilising structures of political conflicts in Nigeria, this study highlights the barriers and benefits of the uses of new media. The discussion will be useful for understanding the challenges confronting dissident communities in their struggles for social reform, resource control, revolution and political change in Nigeria. Third, the findings of this thesis could prove useful to civil society as a guide for understanding the uses of ICTs for conflict.

A clear distinction needs to be made on the two dynamics, digital activism and CC, that underpin this study. In this context, digital activism is used herein to denote 'political participation, activities and protests organized in digital networks beyond representational politics' (Karatzogianni, 2015, p. 1). Essentially, groups involved in digital activism share a common political attribute that involves the struggle for 'reform or revolution' with non-state players and emergent socio-political establishments, including social movements, protest groups, individuals and civil society groups, as protagonists in such conflicts. Similar to digital activism, CC refers to conflicts in computer-mediated environments involving non-state actors. 'It involves an analysis of the interactions between actors engaged in digital activism to raise awareness for a specific cause, struggles against government and corporate actors, as well as conflict between governments, states and corporations' (Karatzogianni, 2015, p. 1).

The research question does draw from the literature review, but in particular, from the CC framework developed by Karatzogianni (2006a, 2006b). The analysis includes a consideration of the role of ICTs on (1) mobilising structure, (2) opportunity structure and (3) the framing process of conflict movements and activist's repertoires during a protest against the Nigerian state.

1.1. Analytical Framework

As Garrett (2006) rightly pointed out, although the multiplicity of views demonstrated by theorists has enhanced the literature and provided a plethora of perspectives for examining political protests, protest movements and ICT users, nonetheless, this diversity and/or plurality of perspectives could be an impediment to adequately articulating the phenomenon. The challenge has been that very few 'works are commonly cited across the field, and most are known only within the confines of their discipline' (Garrett, 2006, p. 2) from media studies and communications studies to political science, sociology and conflict studies, to mention a few. Conversely, the deficiency in establishing a unified theoretical framework that cuts across such boundaries posed a complexity in articulating the links between the diverse perspectives advanced by theorists (Garrett, 2006, p. 2). Only a unified technological theoretical framework of political protest and/or an analytic framework that will underpin the assessment of the impact of ICTs, the internet and other everyday social media networks on the nature of political protest mobilisation, organisation, collective action and resistance can instruct our understanding of the contemporary Nigeria context.

As early as the 1960s, in view to grasping a full understanding of factors that motivate protests and contentious movements, one school of thought came up with what Breuer (2012) described as 'traditional grievance or relative deprivation models' (Block, Haan, & Smith, 1968; Braungart, 1971; Fendrich & Krauss, 1978; Gurr, 1970; Lewis & Kraut, 1972; Thomas, 1971). The underlying assumption held by this school of thought is rooted in the belief that certain psychological attributes inspire social resistance, political activism and contentious activities. Corroborating this point, Muller and Jukam (1983) explained that individuals participate in acts of civil disobedience, or that political violence are dissatisfied about certain things within a given polity. 'The underlying psychological mechanism at work is that unfulfilled material expectations cause anger, frustration and resentment that manifest themselves in an individual propensity to protest' (Breuer, 2012, p. 4).

In addition, the relative deprivation theorist also extended the psychological perspective. They argue that dissent emerges as a product of three factors: accelerated social change, mobilisation of new groups into politics and a political atmosphere filled with unfulfilled economic anticipation and/or a failed institution of governance (Huntington, 1968, p. 4). Although, this point stresses the importance of material grievances, contemporary studies of the same phenomenon have given more consideration to emotional drives which border on societal expectations (Aminzade, 2001; Goodwin, Jasper, & Polletta, 2001; Jasper, 1998; Jasper & Poulsen, 1995; Oliver & Johnston, 2000). From this perspective, Breuer (2012) explains that moral indignation may serve as a catalyst for contentious activities within a given society. In essence, individual action is determined by an emotional response to an unconducive state of affairs. Intense 'reactive emotions such as anger, moral outrage, or confusion' could be the stimuli and mobilise factors in the same scenario (Jasper & Poulsen, 1995; van Laer, 2011).

The attributes captured by both schools of thought are crucial in the context of contemporary protest in Nigeria especially when considering the underlying factors and motivations for contentious activities. In reality, as demonstrated in various cases, while new ICTs have undoubtedly opened up vistas of opportunities for communication and conflict mobilisations, there still exists constraints on the capacity of dissenting groups to channel their motivations and dissent into collective action. In particular, this is due to government monopoly and their direct or indirect hegemonic influence over the mass media, as seen in authoritarian systems. As Breuer (2012) succinctly puts it, within such contexts, the government controls the national narrative through a blend of censorship, intimidation and persecution to suppress information on economic malperformance, human rights violations, corruption or any other issue which may negatively reflect on the state (p. 5). Ultimately, the mobilisation of dissent and participation is weakened not curbed.

The rational choice approach to contentious activities, unlike the other previous perspectives, reduces the importance of emotions and grievances in the dynamics of political protests in favour of subjective, independent or personal beliefs. For instance, Tullock (1971) asserts that the notion of grievances is non-consequential to the choice individuals make to participate in contentious activities especially where such a person or individuals have personal interests. In this context, participation is essentially a product of individual judgements and more so when based on the benefit or importance of such activity to each participant. In other words, individuals are more likely to participate in an event based on the benefits to them. A major drawback of the rational choice approach is that, like the other perspectives described, it falls short of explanations with regard to conventional impact and uses of ICTs, everyday social media and the internet on the mobilisation of social resistance among dissenting communities. More so, the rational choice approach is also deficient because it predicts 'excessive abstention'; in other words, the model contests the existence of protests (Breuer, 2012, p. 5), whilst the reality is that empirical evidence continues to demonstrate the existence of protest and conflict across the globe (p. 5).

Over the years, however, a few theorists in their approach to this subject have made stringent efforts to develop various integrated theoretical models to explain the phenomenon of the effect of ICTs on political protests in contemporary times and the general workings of political protest movements. Various theorists including McAdam, McCarthy and Zald (1996) and van de Donk, Loader, Nixon and Rucht (2004) in their studies of social movements have attempted to explain the emergence, development and outcomes of such movements by addressing the following three interconnecting features: (1) mobilising structures, (2) opportunity structures and (3) framing processes. These features provided the mechanism with which the Garret (2006) framework assesses the relationship between ICTs and political protest movements (new social movements). According to him, developing a review within this parameter will aid 'conversations across the field around common issues of concern, highlighting connections between scholars and research agendas that might otherwise be difficult to discern' (p. 2).

1.2. The Cyberconflict Theoretical Framework

In an effort to bridge the gap among the diverse works on the subject of conflict in computer-mediated environments and the influence of ICTs on such conflicts, Karatzogianni's (2006a, 2006b) theoretical framework provides a more in-depth study. Although Garret's framework considers the socio-political dimension of dissenting movements, his analysis does not take account of the ethnoreligious (conflict) and media elements. A more integrated approach is considered in *The Politics of Cyberconflict* by Karatzogianni (2006a, 2006b) which extends the analytical tools by developing an analytical framework that considers CC by combining elements of social movement (resource mobilisation theory (RMT) and new social movement theory), conflict analysis and media theories in examining the impact of ICTs on conflicts and political protest movements across the globe. Karatzogianni's comparative and integrated framework for understanding the connection between ICTs and political conflicts makes it particularly suitable for understanding political protests in the Nigerian context. As such, the present study will build upon the theoretical models developed by Garrett (2006) and Karatzogianni (2006a, 2006b) to advance the perspective this study seeks to uphold.

In its original formation, the CC framework was developed as an analytical approach for examining conflicts aided by ICTs, and/or occurring in virtual space, during the pre-social media era (pre-Facebook (FB) 2004, YouTube 2005 and Twitter 2006) of digital media development. In other words, the framework considered political protests that were transferred from real-life settings to cyberspace and vice versa between 2000 and 2005 (Karatzogianni, 2012a, 2012b, 2012c, p. 3). Nevertheless, it subsequently proved useful for understanding protests and conflicts in the social media era. The notion of CC is situated within the principle of computer-mediated communication (CMC; Karatzogianni, 2006a, 2006b, p. 94). The trust of the framework is rooted in a consideration of how ICTs are used as either resource or weapon in both online and offline propaganda wars by the state and political protest movements (Karatzogianni, 2012a, 2012b, 2012c, p. 1). For a succinct exposition of the contentious activities, the CC approach situates the discourse on contentious politics in cyberspace around two broad categories of conflicts that occur in the global landscape: socio-political and ethnoreligious.

The former, that is, socio-political protests, can be explained in terms of political action against authorities. In this context, the protagonist is usually social movements, civil society and radical insurgency groups. While the opposition are the state and/or institutions that represent the state. Socio-political CC encompasses such conflicts or political protests as in the case of anti-globalisation, anti-capitalist and anti-war movements (social movements) and the effect of ICTs and the internet on their mobilisation processes. The struggles of such movements are usually characterised by socio-political and economic inequalities, as well as the abuse of civil and political rights. The Zapatista movement of Mexico, the anti-globalisation movement and Occupy Wall Street (OWS) movement are classic cases that provide illustrative examples of socio-political CC.

The Zapatista movement emerged in the state of Chiapas in southern Mexico. This movement typically exemplifies a group motivated by socio-economic and political grievances. According to Taylor and Jordan (2004), the Zapatista movement actors demanded for health, welfare and citizen rights during the uprising. But what is equally crucial is that the internet provided the impetus for communicating their grievances. 'In this struggle, the Internet functions as a medium through which the demands for these rights and the struggles around these 18 rights can be communicated' (Taylor & Jordan, 2004, p. 94). The struggle started originally as an insurrection guerrilla warfare style but rapidly mutated and decreased into a mediatised conflict. Following the commencement of the North American Free Trade Agreement (NAFTA), which introduced the free trade zone, Zapatista movement actors occupied a part of the Chiapas region in Mexico in protest. The intervention of the army forced movement actors to retreat into the rainforest. Karatzogianni (2006a, 2006b) argued that movement actors innovatively engaged with media tools to the extent that the Mexican authorities were compelled to negotiate to evade the conflict mutating into a full-blown war. Jordan (1999), corroborating this point explained that the Zapatistas were only able to archive such degree of success owing to the unimpeded flow of information which the internet champions. For Ronfeldt, Arquilla, Fuller and Fuller (1998), the innovative uses of new media at the time was unconventional especially when set against the backdrop of the norm (in regard to tactical repertoire) during such kinds of conflict. Movement actors used media tools and the internet to mobilise Mexican civil society to participate in the struggle for social, economic and political change, while calling on the international community to observe the conflict (Ronfeldt et al., 1998, pp. 2–3).

A decade later, the OWS movement like the Zapatista movement is another seminal example of a socio-political movement. In addition, while Zapatista mutated between radical and non-radical conflict strategies, OWS emerged more or less as a peaceful movement. OWS emerged in 2011 in New York in response to what protesters believed was socio-economic inequality and the dominance of a few hands who controlled the means of production. According to the OWS website, the struggle was against'the corrosive power of major banks and multinational corporations over the democratic process, and the role of Wall Street in creating an economic collapse that has caused the greatest recession in generations' (Occupy Wall Street, 2011).

What is however crucial about this movement is their innovative uses of ICTs, the internet and contemporary social media tools. The uses of everyday networked social media (FB and Twitter) was the main highlight of this movement in concert with various physical occupations that were staged by dissidents. Movement actors combined both online and offline tactics in there mobilisation, making it easy for them to communicate with each other and circumvent limitation (Castells, 2001, pp. 171–178; Kavada, 2015).

For the other kind of protest or conflict which Karatzogianni (2006a, 2006b) identifies as ethnoreligious CC – these are mainly ethnic, religious and/or culturally motivated associated groups in conflicts with the state or opposition movements. In the CC contexts, such contestations are carried out in virtual spaces as they are in everyday real-life setting (Karatzogianni, 2006a, 2006b, p. 5). The idea is that similar to their socio-political counterpart, the struggle could occur in real-life settings and have a spill over into cyberspace and vice versa. It is crucial to state that the use of the phraseology 'ethnoreligious' does not necessarily mean that the struggles of such movements are on the whole ethnically and/or religiously motivated. While such affiliations exist, the interests, struggles and motivations of such movements could also be sociopolitical and/or economic.

Israeli vs Palestinian, Indian vs Pakistani conflicts and the Arab upspring are good illustrations of ethnoreligious CCs. In the first two cases, the conflict was essentially carried out in cyberspace with either sides engaging in reprisal cyberattacks. Websites of both parties in each individual case were targeted with defacements and denial of service (DOS) attacks, thereby imbedding the uses of ICTs. For instance, in the India vs Pakistan case, perceived Pakistani intelligence operatives had taking over the Indian Army's only website, posting alleged images that depicted torture of Kashmiris by the Indian security operatives (Karatzogianni, 2006b, p. 348). A short while after, the Pakistanis responded by defacing 600 websites and temporarily taking over government and private computer systems (Karatzogianni, 2006b, p. 348). Although their actions were mostly virtual, it represented a spill over from offline conflict.

As noted earlier, in articulating the uses of the internet and ICTs by sociopolitical movements, and since majority of the social groups discussed previously employ these tools as resources to facilitate their activities, both frameworks put forward by Garrett (2006) and Karatzogianni (2006a, 2006b) employ the RMT to understand the emergence, expansion and consequences of social movements. The focus is on a consideration of the effect of the internet, ICTs and corresponding applications on three interconnecting dynamics: mobilising structures, opportunity structures and framing processes. Before going into an examination of these using the CC theoretical framework, a brief consideration of the motivations of contentious movements is crucial.

Following the RMT perspective, Dalton and Van Sickle (2005) argue that rich and less restrictive societies offer a more encouraging atmosphere for contentious politics and political protests to flourish. While different theories have attempted to understand dissidents of particular communities participating in conflict, RMT helps to demonstrate how new ICTs, 'fits largely within the resource mobilisation perspective as one means for aggregating grievance, building networks and communicating strategies for opposition to the regime' (Breuer, 2012, p. 6). The CC theory takes this further by harnessing the components of the RMT, media and conflict theory in view of the influence of the internet, ICTs and social media. What follows is a brief discussion of the influence of ICTs on the components (mobilising structure, opportunity structure and framing process) of the RMT.

In order to therefore provide a lucid exploration of the subject of the present study, the analysis that follows draws on the Karatzogianni 2006 CC framework. Drawing on the CC framework, any consideration of conflict movements must starts with an examination of the environment of conflict. This allows for an assessment of the online (virtual) and offline (real world) component of the conflict. The framework will then draw on elements of social movement and mobilization, conflict and media theories to understand the activities of contemporary conflict groups.

Accordingly, in relation to the environment of CC, the Karatzogianni (2006a, 2006b) framework puts forward the reversal argument that ethnoreligious CCs represent loyalties of hierarchical apparatuses while socio-political CCs are empowering network forms of organisation. Furthermore, actors engaged in ethnoreligious CC need to operate in a more network fashion if they are fighting network forms of terrorism or resistance, while actors in socio-political CC need to operate in a more organised fashion and more conscious of the rest of their hosting network if they are to engage with the present global political system.

Second, the CC framework looks at socio-political CCs and the impact of ICTs on (1) mobilising structures (network style of movements using the internet, participation, recruitment, tactics and goals); (2) framing processes (issues, strategy, identity and the effect of the internet on these processes); (3) political opportunity structure (the internet as a component of this structure); and (4) hacktivism. For ethnoreligious CCs, the focus is on (1) ethnic/religious affiliation, chauvinism and national identity; (2) discourses of inclusion and exclusion; (3) information warfare, the use of the internet as a weapon (hacking), propaganda and mobilisational resource; and (4) conflict resolution, which depends on the legal and organisational framework, the number of parties and issues, the distribution of power and the content of values and beliefs.

The third aspect of the CC framework considers media components which include (1) analysing discourses (representations of the world, constructions of social identities and social relations); (2) control of information, level of censorship and alternative sources; (3) Wolsfeld's political contest model among antagonists, which involves the ability to initiate and control events, dominate political discourse and mobilise supporters; and (4) media effects on policy (strategic, tactical and representational) (Figure 1.1).

1.3. Methods and Materials Used

Research design and data collection are an essential component of any research process. The question of how the researcher intends to collect relevant data among a research population is a crucial question that forms the essence of a given study. Hence, the importance of methodology, which is a fundamental foundation of researching into the 'how' and 'why' of a phenomenon. Bryman (2012) explained that the assumption and perceptions of how research should be carried out affect the research process. The methodology prescribes a set of principles and guidelines through which the research objective will be attained.

There are two methodological paradigms of inquiry in social research: the qualitative and quantitative paradigms. Quantitative methods deal

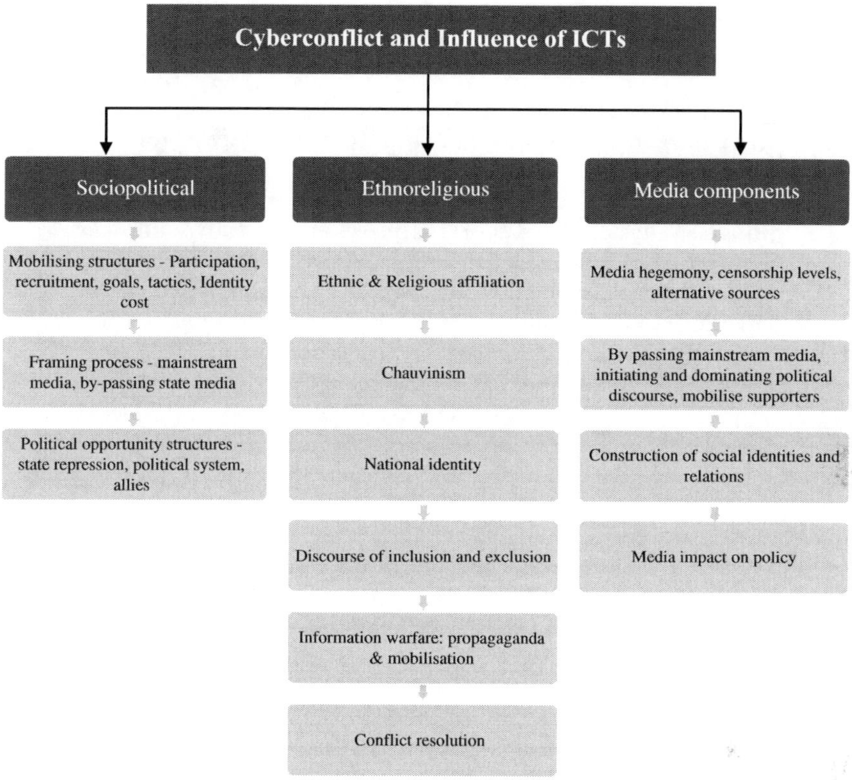

Figure 1.1. Visualising the Elements of the Karatzogianni (2006a, 2006b) Cyberconflict Theoretical Framework. *Source*: Karatzogianni (2006a, 2006b).

with quantity – an evaluation or interpretation of events using numeric measurements and statistics to access relationships (Janićijević, 2011; Pandey, 2009; Žydžiumaite, 2007). The advantage of the quantitative research approach is that it provides a platform for capturing a large proportion of a study population. Besides the size of the study population, Janićijević (2011) further argues that the approach also affords a platform for generalisation and quantification of results. The shortfall of this approach, however, is that data analysis is mostly reduced to evaluation of numbers through questioners and surveys. The numeric values and statistics form the basis for hypothesising and the generalisation which Janićijević referred to earlier. The qualitative paradigm is a direct contrast of the quantitative approach. The qualitative approach as a tool of inquiry is multi-method in nature, issue oriented and involves a natural way of deducing or understanding a phenomenon (Anderson et al., 1998; Berg, 2001; Dabbs, 1982; Denzin & Lincoln, 1998).

The approach involves descriptive connotation of an event using a narrative approach. According to Creswell (2014):

> Qualitative research begins with assumptions and the use of interpretive/theoretical frameworks that inform the study of research problems addressing the meaning individuals or groups ascribe to a social or human problem. […] the collection of data in a natural setting sensitive to the people and places under study, and data analysis that is both inductive and deductive and establishes patterns or themes. The final written report or presentation includes the voices of participants, the reflexivity of the researcher, a complex description and interpretation of the problem, and its contribution to the literature or call for change.
>
> p. 44

Furthermore, 'qualitative research involves the studied use and collection of a variety of empirical materials-case study, personal experience, introspective, life story, interview, observational, historical, interactional and visual texts that describe routine and problematic moments and meanings' (Denzin & Lincoln, 1998, p. 3).

The method is interpretive since it encompasses an exploration of in-depth understanding from the population of study. It therefore allows the researcher to explain events in the context of their existence. While both paradigms (qualitative vs quantitative) can function independently, yet depending on the subject of inquiry, the two paradigms can be harnessed to yield specific results (Blake, 1989; Creswell & Plano Clark, 2007; Greene, Caracelli, & Graham, 1989, Rossman & Wilson, 1991). The last decade witnessed a surge in contentious politics involving protests, activism, insurgency and violent militancy groups across the globe. In view of these conflicts, a number of studies have attempted to explain the developments in connection to ICTs, the internet and social media using various approaches. While some explore a wholly qualitative or quantitative paradigm, others harness the components of the two paradigms to achieve their aim.

For instance, Lui (2012) employs a wholly qualitative paradigm in his analysis of how Chinese dissidents use mobile phone to engender change in politics and democracy. Lui's research therefore employed a multiple case study approach and draws on participant observation and interviews as the principal technique for data collection. In a different study, Miere (2011) harnesses quantitative and qualitative analyses in examining whether ICTs empower states as against civil society or vice versa. The approach unites statistical findings with the findings from a qualitative approach in a comparative discussion of multiple case studies. For the researcher, the main objective is ensuring that the approach is appropriate for the domain and purpose of inquiry (Janwoski & Wester, 1991, p. 46).

The current study aims to explore in-depth meanings of events that would yield comprehensive understanding. In order to achieve this aim, the inquiry considers attitudes, personal experience and opinions of individuals. Jensen's point above on the 'how' and 'what' and 'why' serve as a guiding principle in exploring the phenomenon conflict in the Nigerian context. Specifically, the study investigates the influence of ICTs on the mobilisation of dissenting socio-political and ethnoreligious groups in Nigeria. The study takes into cognisance the use and benefits of new ICTs (in particular mobile phones, the internet and everyday social media networks). It is noteworthy to state that the generalisability of research on the influence of new ICTs on political protest and conflict in the Nigerian context is problematic. Morover, the discussion offered in this study will draw a cross-comparison between the socio-political movement and ethnoreligious movements under examination. This makes the present study crucial, especially in the context of contributing to existing knowledge in the literature on protests and conflict in Africa's largest economy.

1.4. Collecting the Data

A single data collection technique will fall short of the desired expectations due to certain factors including variations in the structural dynamics and orientations of the different case studies. As such, the study harnessed different approaches under the qualitative paradigm to fully achieve methodological proficiency, rigour and relevance. Berg (2001) argues that the implication is 'a better, more substantive picture of reality; a richer, more complete array of symbols and theoretical concepts and a means of verifying many of these elements' (p. 4). In the present context, the use of mixed techniques is mainly to bridge the gap created by the structural differences between the movements, which include issues of accessibility and security concerns. Second, the mixed method approach ensures rigour and replication of perspectives, especially in the second case study (ethnoreligious movements) (Figure 1.2).

In the first case involving Occupy Nigeria, a combination of ethnographic interviews was the principal data collection technique. Although there are

Figure 1.2. Data Collection Techniques Explored in the Study.

different ways to administer interviews including email and telephone interviewing, the interviews were administered face-to-face in the field to fulfil some of the characteristics of ethnographic interviewing. For instance, one-to-one interviews in the field enabled the researcher to contextualise the issues raised by respondents against the backdrop of their natural settings. Hammersley and Atkinson (1995) considered ethnography in terms of participation. However, this is not necessarily in terms of being actively involved with the activities of the studied group. Drawing on the point advanced by Hine (2000), the approach enabled the researcher to benefit from the interactive characteristics of ethnographic research that allows the researcher to not only observe (as a non-participant observer) the phenomenon and the context within which the event happens, but also interact with participants to gain much deeper insights into certain characteristics exhibited by the researched population. Besides the ethnographic interview approach, the discussions and perspectives of participants are also considered alongside secondary sources including audio-visual material broadcast by dissidents and the media through online media during the protests. As one commentator noted:

> The data of qualitative inquiry is most often people's words and actions, and thus requires methods that allow the researcher to capture language and behaviour. The most useful ways of gathering these forms of data are participant observation, in-depth interviews, group interviews, and the collection of relevant documents.
>
> Maykut & Morehouse (1994, p. 46)

1.5. Semi-structured Interviews

There are different types of interviews that the research can employ as part of the research design. This includes the structured, semi-structured and unstructured interview techniques. Lussier (2009) explained that in structured interviews, all interviewees are asked the same questions from a pre-planned list, while the unstructured interview is the direct opposite of a structured interview in that there is no list of questions or pre-planned list of topics (p. 240). The third interview technique, the semi-structured interview, falls in-between the first two. Here the researcher has a list, but does not necessarily follow the list to the letter and will often ask unplanned questions and probe responses (Lussier, 2009, p. 204). The researcher's choice of a particular interview technique for a study depends on the objectives, goals and what the research aims to achieve. Consequently, for this study, semi-structured interviews were selected as the main technique of inquiry.

Other mixed methods (under the qualitative approach) were employed in order to 'increase accuracy of research findings' (Gilbert, 2008, p. 127). The choice of the semi-structured interview is because it conforms to the overall aim of collecting in-depth perspectives of participants. As a consequence, interviews are able to also tell their stories. Another benefit for the researcher is that the semi-structured interviews enabled a series of probes, which helped to yield clarity on issues put forward by interviewees. Interviews can be administered in a number of ways, but the more familiar approaches include face-to-face and/or one-to-one interviewing; other methods include conventional approaches like mailed or self-administered questionnaires, email and telephone interviews (Denzin & Lincoln, 2003, p. 48) and more recently video conferencing interviews. That said, the different techniques are harnessed in order to manage and fully maximise the potential of the method. The benefit of using various techniques is that it helps to manage the challenges of insufficient data and the lack of accessibility to a study population.

1.6. The Case Study Method

Having chosen the qualitative paradigm, the researcher determined the case study method as the best approach that expresses the technique explored in the study. Besides case studies, there are other qualitative research designs. For instance, we have the biography, phenomenology, ethnography and grounded theory research designs. However, for the sake of the present study, the focus is on the case study approach. Case studies have a rich history of being well explored and embedded in clinical research (Crowe et al., 2011) and widely used in social science research (Amerson, 2011; Creswell, 2014; Crowe et al., 2011). According to Creswell (2014), the scope of the case study method also extends to legal and political science research. Case studies could be explained as a qualitative approach useful for examining issues in a real-life setting, a current case or numerous cases in a time frame using in-depth data collection techniques (Creswell, 2014, p. 97).

Baxter and Jack (2008) identified different types of case study research designs. Drawing from their theorisation, a case study can be explanatory. According to Yin (2003), the explanatory case study is employed to provide answers to studies that attempt to expound on causal links in real-life conflicts between two parties. For Yin, the usefulness of the explanatory design hinges on the difficulty of other methods like the survey or experimental strategies to provide deep insights into the intricacies and complexities of real-life issues. According to Yin (2003), 'In evaluation language, the explanations would link program implementation with program effects' (cited in Baxter & Jack, 2008, p. 547).

Besides the explanatory case study design, other types of case studies include the exploratory design. Yin (2003) explained that this type of research design is used to explore circumstances in which the case being evaluated provides no clear or particular set of outcomes. There is also the 'intrinsic' case study approach, which helps the researcher to better understand a given case, and the'instrumental' case study design, which is used to shed insights regarding an issue and could be instrumental in redefining a given theoretical framework. Furthermore, and particularly crucial for the current study, Yin (2003) also identified the descriptive and multiple case study designs. Yin explained that the descriptive approach is used to provide a lucid account of a phenomenon and the context in which it exists, while the multiple case study provides a comparison platform for the research to engage in a cross-comparison between different cases under examination. For Yin (2003), the objective of the multiple case study is to duplicate findings across the case examined. The research can then predict parallel occurrences across the cases, or inconsistent findings across the cases and in reference to theory. Hence, the present study draws on the multiple case study and descriptive methodological designs. The choice of the research design approach is decided by the nature of the case studies.

1.7. Selecting Case Studies

Having identified the objective of the study, that is, a consideration of the influence of ICTs on conflict mobilisation in Nigeria, it served as the initial starting point of the research phase. The choice of subject was decided by crucial changes in the nature of the activities of dissenting mobilisations in Nigeria since the democratic transition emerged and especially in the wake of the technological revolution which emerged concurrently. A study of conflict in computer-mediated environments in the Nigerian context is useful for understanding the general workings of movements engaged in conflict, as well as the uses or influence of ICTs on groups engaged in conflict in Nigeria. Undertaking this study provides a platform to contribute to improving knowledge by bridging the gap in the literature with regard to digital activism as a field of study, an examination of ICTs in three political movements of various ideological underpinnings in a single country and considering the study in a developing non-western context.

In order to therefore obtain a succinct understanding of the dynamism of conflict in Nigeria, two types of conflict were identified between 2006 and 2014: one socio-political and the other ethnoreligious. Since the study considers conflict movements that take root in both socio-political and ethnoreligious dimensions, a multiple case study approach (see Yin, 1994, 2009; Yin & Moore, 1988) in concert with a descriptive method provides a platform for a lucid description of events and a comparison across the different cases. The choice of the multiple case study approach was arrived at by a consideration of three movements (Occupy Nigeria, Boko Haram and MEND) with distinct orientations. The method provides a platform for a cross-comparison between the three cases under examination. By comparing the three cases, the researcher is able to identify common trends, generally shared traits and differences between the different cases being studied. This approach enables the researcher to have a platform to consider a 'contemporary phenomenon within its real-life context' (Yin, 2009, p. 18).

While Nigeria has a huge population and an enormous geographical landscape, therefore the concept of multiple cases helps to avoid over generalisation of conclusions. One case study will not be sufficiently representative of the huge population of Nigeria, especially where questions of 'why' individuals use ICTs, their motivations or 'how' new ICTs are being deployed are raised, just to mention a few of the issues that did arise in the course of the study. Therefore, the multiple case study design addresses such complexities and divergence, which will in turn ensure replication of findings and comparison across contexts.

Ultimately, by considering cases of ICT-mediated protests (radical and non-radical) happening concurrently, engineered by different movements and within a different geopolitical setting in Nigeria, the study is able to provide cross-comparative conclusions. Hence, a research approach using multiple case studies, as espoused here, is crucial for an informed explanation of computer-mediated forms of conflict in Nigeria.

The focus of the present study is on contemporary cases of conflict in Nigeria within the period of democratisation (post-1999 era), a period which spans over a decade. For the present study, however, it will be a herculean task to consider all cases of conflict that have emerged within this period. Since the study's focus is on socio-political (non-violent) and ethnoreligious (mostly violent militancy and insurgency) conflict movements, the study choose the most contemporary cases of conflict to reflect both dimensions of conflict within the time frame. Occupy Nigeria movement provides an example of a socio-political movement. Jamā'at Ahl as-Sunnah lid-Da'wah wa'l-Jihād (People Committed to the Prophet's Teachings for Propagation and Jihad), popularly known as Boko Haram, and MEND are examples of ethnoreligious movements.

The selection of these cases was guided by the following criteria. First, these cases represent novel, most recent and ongoing cases of conflict. All three cases occurred between 2006 and 2014 and some are ongoing. More importantly, these cases specifically reflect computer-mediated forms of conflict and demonstrate the influence of ICTs on the mobilisation and organisation of contentious activities within the period being examined. It is noteworthy to note that these cases represent mediated forms of conflicts; however, there are also differences in terms of their orientation. The latter two cases (Boko Haram and MEND) take on a violent militancy and insurgency orientation, and the former (Occupy Nigeria) takes on a peaceful social movement type of orientation. Yet one could observe common trends and comparative dynamics across the three cases. Chapter 7 addresses the cross-comparative dynamics across the three cases. The contemporary nature, currency and ongoing activities of some of these cases provided a platform for an examination of the issues in their real-life context.

The next step which involved interviewing participants allowed the researcher to obtain in-depth opinions of actors in the protests. The semi-structured interview only applied to the socio-political case study involving Occupy Nigeria and served as the principal data collection mechanism. The researcher therefore embarked on fieldwork. Interviews were undertaken in Nigeria, where the perceptions and opinions of individuals who participated in the January 2012 Occupy Nigeria protest were collected. What follows is a description of the processes involved in the interview phase of the data collection.

1.8. Constructing the Interview Questions

As highlighted earlier, one of the benefits of the semi-structured interview method is that, unlike the unstructured approach, it allows the researcher to develop a set of questions that mostly serve as a guide for the interviews.

A second benefit, unlike the structured approach, is that the researcher can often probe the interviewee on certain interesting points that could yield novel findings. For the present study, the research questions were broken down into sets of interview questions to serve as a guide for the interviewer and a means for facilitating the interviews. The interview questions were informed by the Karatzogianni 2006 CC theoretical framework. In particular, the questions were constructed based on the socio-political components of the framework. Note that the socio-political component of the CC framework considers the effect of ICTs on the mobilising structures, opportunity structures and the framing activities of conflict movements. Thus the interview question is categorised according to the socio-political dynamics mentioned earlier.

There were three main sections. First, the mobilisation section with questions about the influence of ICTs on conflict mobilisation during the Occupy Nigeria protests. The second section takes on the opportunity structure, with questions on the political opportunities for contentious activities and the effect of the ICTs on such opportunities for bypassing censorship and shaping public opinion, just to mention a few. The third section involves the framing activity of the movement. Here, questions were raised about the role of the media (traditional mainstream) and the influence of ICTs in countering the narrative of the state and the media. The list of questions under each section served as a guide for facilitating the interviews and a useful means for organising the data, both for transcription and analysis. At different intervals, a series of probes were introduced as a means of eliciting deeper insights from interviewees of issues raised. These probes were later captured under the relevant sections. Ultimately, the essence of the interview question guide and the series of probes that followed was to ensure that interviewees touched on crucial areas of the study. In order to build rapport with interviewees following phone conversations, each interview commenced with an introduction, which provided the interviewees with a brief data on the researcher, the research and the structure of the interview.

1.9. Identifying Participants

For the first case study (Occupy Nigeria movement), which employed interviews chiefly as the main data collection techniques, a total of nine semi-structured expert interviews were conducted between November 2013 and January 2014 during fieldwork in Nigeria. These included face-to-face interviews with the exception of one interview, which was obtained through email. Although the interview population may seem small, nonetheless (Mark, 2010) this is not an uncommon characteristic in qualitative studies. As Mark (2010) explains, there is a point where more data do not necessarily produce more information. More so, the in-depth nature of semi-structured interviews means that, as in the current context, the researcher can collect a rich and comprehensive information about the phenomenon under study. The interviews achieved saturation, given that a careful evaluation showed no generation of significantly new data from the ninth interview. The interviews lasted between 40 minutes to about an hour each. Given the scope, effectiveness and impact of the government's policy change, which resulted in the Occupy Nigeria movement protest in January 2012, the outrage that ensued started from Nigeria with Nigerians as its main protagonists. These included a culmination of both formal and loose civil society groups, Nigerian workers, independent activists, students and various other civil society organisations including the clergy from different religious settings and ordinary men and women. As such, this study carefully identified and selected key civil society actors and activists who participated in the protest. For one, these actors were selected based on their role and their level of participation in previous protests and contentious activities.

In order to achieve rigour and reflect the diversity of the Occupy Nigeria movement, selected participants included a traditional member of Labour Congress. The Nigerian Labour Congress represents a coalition of 43 professional workers unions. The selected member of the Nigerian Labour Congress actively participated in the protests, using ICTs to mobilise and influence public opinion. The labour union has a rich history of being at the epicentre of political protests, collective action and political action in Nigeria and beyond. Members of the union played a seminal role in the Occupy Nigeria protests in January 2012, including organising strike actions, boycotts and participating in the negotiations with the government. Besides, participants were also drawn from other civil society organisations with elements and characteristics of contemporary social movements. These organisations and individuals also have a rich history of involvement in political struggles in Nigeria, dating back to the anti-military and democratic struggles in Nigeria. Their involvement contributed to the emergence of the present democratic culture. To reiterate, through respondent-driven sampling (RDS), participants were selected based on the role they played prior to, during and after the Occupy Nigeria protests, their uses of ICTs and their expert opinions given their rich antecedent of participating in collective action and protests. Participants were drawn from the United Action for Democracy (UAD), Medical and Health workers Union of Nigeria (MHWUN) and the Joint Action Front (JAF). Although participants were drawn from these organisations, nonetheless they spoke independent of the organisations they represent, narrating their roles in the Occupy Nigeria protests, why they participated and the influence of ICTs. Other participants included independent activists, including journalists, as well as ordinary Nigerians.

Due to confidentiality reasons and the need to fulfil ethical considerations, names and identity of participants are anonymised. These methods have gained wide reception and legitimacy within social science and humanities research (see Denzin & Lincoln, 2003, p. 48). That said, these different techniques were harnessed to manage and fully maximise the potential of the method being explored. For instance, initial communication with participants was done via telephone and email; subsequently, participants were met individually having agreed a date and time to be interviewed. The availability of various techniques helped to manage the limitations. As part of the data collection process and to effectively manage the data elicited from participants during the interview, note-taking practices in concert with audio recording were employed, given prior consent of participants.

To locate participants, the snowball sampling and RDS methods were employed. As we may already know, the identification of participants during protests and conflict can be a difficult task. Due to the sensitive nature of contentious politics, getting access to key actors within such networks can become difficult. Both techniques, snowballing and the RDS, bridge the gap by providing an alternative and easier way to access difficult to reach research populations in society and key movement actors (Heckathorn, 1997, 2002; Salganik & Heckathorn, 2004; Wejnert, 2009; Wejnert & Heckathorn, 2008). In Nigeria, like any other political setting whether democratic or dictatorial, citizen participation and engagement in contentious activities (protests and conflict) comewith high risks. In the past, we have seen how the state uses its security apparatuses to witch-hunt civil society activists. In particular, the state does so through arrests, detention, torture and even extra-judicial killings, which have become prevalent instruments used by the authorities as a repercussion for dissent and conflict especially during military dictatorships.

In environments of conflict, one can reasonably expect that actors can become difficult to access especially in an attempt to get them to speak on issues relating to their activities. By this token, civil society activists, including other conflict movement actors in the present, are qualified as hidden population due to their usual hesitation to expose their identities (Heckathorn, 1997, p. 174) for fear of scrutiny from the state. In the Nigerian context, there was a general reluctance among some participants to have a discussion about individual roles during the protest for the fear of exposing their identities. The RDS therefore provided a platform for bridging the difficulty involved in accessing key civil society and movement actors who participated in the Occupy Nigeria protest. RDS is similar to other chain-referral methods like the snowball sampling approach. The central idea is that one informant who is an insider of a particular conflict movement volunteers or is recruited by the researcher. The informant becomes the link to other members of the movement unknown to the researcher. According to Heckrathorn (1997), the RDS contrasts the snowball sampling in the sense that the latter relies on an incentive for participation. The RDS advances two incentives for the participant. For one, the interviewee's benefit from being interviewed, and second, the interviewee has the leverage of suggesting, nominating or recruiting other key participants in the study (Heckrathorn 1997, p. 178). In the Nigerian context, the researcher sets out a criterion to avoid interviewees from suggesting participants who could divert the research direction. For one, interviewees were properly briefed on the research direction, including the aims and objectives of the study. Second, interviewees were requested to suggest participants based on the role played by such participants in the Occupy Nigeria movement.

The RDS approach is also crucial for the Nigerian context due to the huge population of participants that attended the January 2012 protests. While a number of participants when contacted declined to be interviewed, out of the few that offered to be interviewed, an initial participant in the protests was identified to serve as an informant. The informant was chosen based on his/her involvement in the protests in Abuja. This informant later produced the contacts of other key participants. The informant being an insider means that he/she had the necessary link, individual relationship, inter-organisational relationship and trust of other participants, which the researcher leveraged upon. This leads to criterion sampling, which best explains the scenario between the informant and his/her links to other participants. In criterion sampling, the researcher selects his/her interview population based solely on their involvement in the event. As Creswell (2014) theorised, 'the criterion sample works well when all individuals studied represent people who have experienced the phenomenon' (p. 155). The benefit of relying on eyewitness accounts for the study is that it can guarantee that the researcher obtains first-hand information, which further impacts positively on verification of facts and validating claims.

The informant and interviewees were then interviewed as part of a process to check the accuracy and clarity of the proposed interview technique. Prior to this, an informal interview was carried out with four other volunteers to ensure that the research questions were clear. Having interviewed the first interviewee, he was also given the opportunity to suggest other key actors in line with the objectives of the study. The process is repeated with other interviewees. The main interview comprised of participants identified by the informant and others suggested by interviewees who met the criteria for the study. The research benefited from the trust and bond formed between the informant (as an insider) and some other participants on in the Occupy Nigeria movement protests. The recommendation from the insiders (informant) made it easy for participants to offer access and bond with the researcher. More so, some of the participants interviewed also suggested other key participants in line with the direction of the research.

1.10. Administering Interviews

Interviewees were then asked to confirm their details which included names, vocation and age group. This was followed by some questions to confirm participant's involvement in the conflict (in particular the Occupy Nigeria protest) and their use of ICTs (which ones and for what purposes). Having established their familiarity with ICTs, the next session involved the three sections structured according to the framework. The interviews were conducted in Abuja, the Federal Capital Territory and the seat of power. The choice of Abuja is for a number of reasons: (1) although the uprising spread across major Nigeria cities (Ilorin, Ibadan, Lagos, Kano and Kaduna, to mention a few), Abuja represented the main centre. The Capital also serves as a miniature Nigeria with a good representation of the diverse population and culture and religion that embodies the spirit of the country. (2) The main negotiations between dissidents, civil society and the Nigerian government took place in Abuja. (3) Abuja is concentrated with key civil society organisations, social movements and their head offices. It is noteworthy to state that political commentaries on the Occupy Nigeria movement were collected and studied. These included blogs, social media and in particular various online news media reports. This was helpful especially for providing sufficient information to respondents, clarifying issues and probing their response during the interviews. The in-depth nature of semi-structured interviews meant that the researcher was able to probe the perceptions of the interviewees on the influence of ICTs during conflict in computer-mediated environments.

In the long run, the semi-structured interview approach gave interviewees a free hand to narrate and demonstrate their experience and opinions freely with regard to varied facets of ICT uses for collective action and political protests. During the fieldwork in Nigeria, the researcher only had the opportunity of interviewing participants once. As such, it was crucial for the interviewer to use the avenue to probe interviewees on the main issues by asking a series of sub-questions and rephrasing some questions to validate claims made by interviewees. The series of probes that followed fell within the confines of the interview guide which was structured according to the CC framework. Depending on the participant and in order to ensure that they understand the issues, the interview questions were seldom asked word-for-word. The original questions were employed as a general guideline for the thesis (Table 1.1).

1.11. Secondary Data, Audio-Visual and Textual Data Online

The Occupy Nigeria case study also draws on secondary data, including audio-visual and textual material online. This included data from social media including FB, Twitter and YouTube. Others included online news media materials that included political commentaries on the Occupy Nigeria movements at it unfolded during the protests. While interviews were used as the principal tool for collecting data in the Occupy Nigeria case study, other sources including social media data and online news data complemented the interview data. Social media is particularly useful for understanding the framing activities of conflict movements. Besides FB and Twitter, the research also drew from 'Nairaland', an online media platform. Like FB and Twitter, the platform provides an avenue for discussions and communication between individuals across the border. Yet the forum mainly targets Nigerians. In 2016, the website of Nairaland recorded roughly over 2 million members online. The social media forum was created and managed by Seun Osewa, a Nigerian. Nsehe (2013) in a Forbes report explained that 'for perspective: In Nigeria, Nairaland gets more visits than Wikipedia'. The forum, such as FB and Twitter pages and groups created by Occupy Nigeria, was crucial for understanding the Occupy Nigeria discourse during the protests. The choice of these platforms is based on the fact that postings are principally made by Nigerians either at home or abroad and as such reflect the sociopolitical, economic and ethnic discourses characteristic of Nigerians.

For the second case study involving Boko Haram and MEND, the study principally relied on secondary online sources. These included online textual and audio-visual materials. The main source of data collection included a selection

Table 1.1. List of Interviews with Individual Participants in Occupy Nigeria.

S No.	Name of the Participant	About the Participant	Date and Location of Interview	Reason for Interviewing
1	Interviewee 1	Educationist/and civil society activitst	Face-to-face interview, 11 December 2013, Abuja	Participated in both online and offline mobilisation of the Abuja protest
2	Interviewee 2	Journalist and activist	Face-to-face interview, 17 December 2013, Abuja	Actively participated in the Occupy Nigeria online mobilisation during the protests
3	Interviewee 3	Veteran activist, lawyer/civil society actor	Face-to-face interview, 20 December 2013, Abuja	Participated in the Occupy Nigeria protest, spoke at rallies and contributed to online media (audio-visual) commentaries during the protests and social media
4	Interviewee 4	Official of the labour union	Face-to-face interview, 1 January 2014, Abuja	Participated in the online mobilisation of Occupy Nigeria protests. Contributed to online media commentaries during the protests including social media
5	Interviewee 5	Official of social movement organisation, member of labour union	Face-to-face interview, 6 January 2014	Veteran activist, participated in the Occupy Nigeria protest. Member of the Labour Civil Society Coalition and striking committee. Participated in the negotiations with the government during the protests. Contributed to online media commentary including on social media

Table 1.1. (*Continued*)

S No.	Name of the Participant	About the Participant	Date and Location of Interview	Reason for Interviewing
6	Interviewee 6	Individual participant	Face-to-face interview, 11 January 2014, Abuja	Civil society activist, participated in the Occupy Nigeria protest. Contributed to online media commentaries during the protests. Actively participated in online and offline mobilisations
7	Interviewee 7	Civil society actor/civil rights activist	Face-to-face interview, 15 January 2014, Abuja	Participated in the Occupy Nigeria protests. Actively involved in the online mobilisations during the protests and contributed to online media commentaries
8	Interviewee 8	Veteran activist, educationist, conveyner of social movement and civil society organisation. Member of labour union	Face-to-face interview, 15 January 2014, Abuja	Activity participated in the Occupy Nigeria protests, member of the Labour Civil Society Coalition and striking committee. Contributed to online and offline media commentaries in both local and global media and social media
9	Interviewee 9	Student	Email interview, 29 April 2014, online	Participated in the demonstrations, rallies and occupation in Lagos

Table 1.2. Main Sources of Secondary Data Collection Online News Media Surveyed.

Main Online Nigerian Newspapers	**Major Global Media Online**
Premium Times, Nigeria (online)	*BBC News* (online)
Vanguard, Nigeria (online)	*The Guardian*, UK (online)
Sahara Reporters (online)	*New York Times* (online)
Daily Times, Nigeria (online)	*Global Bulletin* (online)
The Nigerian Guardian (online)	And others

of online news reports from mostly Nigerian online news media and a few global media sources online (see Table 1.2). The choice of mainly Nigerian media sources was based on the fact that media organisations are mostly based in Nigeria and they provided a diverse array of perspectives, interviews and opinions on the movements. This included commentaries from movement actors, the government, civil society stakeholders, security experts and ordinary Nigerians. More so, media reports examined also provide up-to-date information and insights into the activities of the concerned movements. In total, five main Nigerian newspapers online were identified and selected for analysis. Across these 5 online media portals, 75 reports focusing on the Boko Haram and MEND were selected and examined to cover the period between 2006 and 2014. This specific time frame was chosen to reflect the structural dynamics in the origins, development and advances of the respective movement and due to a number of important events that took place in these periods, most importantly the mutations in the movement's tactics and strategy.

In addition, the study collected other audio-visual data online, including documentaries and political commentaries on the ethnoreligious movements. The data collected also comprised journal entries and publications on the movements published by Nigerian and global researchers. Harnessing all these sources provided a platform for validating claims and replication in line with the principle of triangulation. Journal publications on the movements provide relevant data for cross-comparison across the groups, yet there is a general discrepancy on the origins of the ethnoreligious movements. The data generated and discussions that follow will attempt to shed new insights and perspective on these movements, especially in view of the influence of ICTs, the internet and social media on the general working of these political protests or more aptly conflict movements. In this context, the ethnoreligious components of the CC framework were the basis for the analysis of the secondary data. The data collection technique used in the case study is sensitive to the peculiarities and structural dynamics of each case in the sense that, since the study considers both radical and non-radical political protest groups, the technique deployed is dependent on the case study and other socio-political considerations. For instance, in this context, a consideration was whether the political environment was conducive enough at the time for data collection. Put differently, the case study determined the data collection instrument employed. The next section provides a general discussion of the analysis of data collected.

1.12. Thematic Analysis

The study used thematic analysis against the backdrop of software-assisted computer technology for coding and structuring the research documents for the analysis. Over the years, several social researchers employing qualitative approach have employed such software. In this case, NVivo was employed as the principal technology-assisted software.

The use of computerised software packages to aid data analysis is not a new phenomenon in research. In fact, these systems have benefitted researchers within the quantitative paradigm for some decades. For instance, software packages like SPSS have been used by researchers as an analytic tool to measure surveyed opinions of participants in quantitative research living out qualitative research. But in more recent times, software packages for data analysis within the qualitative paradigm have also emerged, greatly impacting the way and manner through which qualitative researchers make sense of their data and fieldwork notes. According to Bazeley and Richards (2000), these tools have become recognised and integrated within research in academia.

Although these softwares have been developed with the researcher in mind, it is noteworthy to clearly state that the role of computer-assisted programs and/or better still CAQDAS, as it is popularly called, in research is limited to facilitating the data analysis process in contrast to such software doing the data analysis in itself. In other words, 'such software does not carry out the analysis for you – unfortunately, this is still the domain of humans, who must inject their imaginative reflection into the data' (Bryman, 2002, p. xix). Nonetheless, the software enables the research to get familiarised with the data while also providing a platform for the researcher to adequately organise, store and structure his/her data. Much of the analytic responsibility relies on the interpretation, creativity and knowledge of the researcher.

In the context of the present study, the NVivo software, which has become the most popular qualitative assisting data software and developed by QSR International, was employed strictly to organise and structure the data in a process of identifying and coding the data collected during the data collection process. This process applied to both interviews conducted with Occupy Nigeria actors, other materials collected and in the two other cases, Boko Haram and MEND. The analysis process began with an initial process of transcription following the interview sessions with respondents. The next step was to import into NVivo all the transcripts. The same process was applied to the other case study; although in this context there was no need for transcription, online news materials were simply imported into the software.

The software was particularly useful for storing transcripts while also serving to organise initial views, concepts and thoughts in the various interviews. The process involved a step-by-step creation of nodes and sub-nodes or better still categories which reflect new trends and associations within the transcriptions. Memos are also used to store important ideas that could impact on the final analysis or serve as a link to important ideas. Interestingly, the tools also provided a platform for editing and proofreading materials and documents that had been imported. The software also facilitated an in-software transcription of video files imported into the package. In other words, once the video was imported into the software, while listening to the video one could also target specific segments within the video and transcribing them.

By documents and materials, this chapter refers to data that have been imported into the NVivo software for the purpose of analysis and coding. In the present context, imported documents included interviews, videos and news articles and political commentary on blogs as shown in the diagrams later. These documents, with the exception of the interviews, which require transcription and computer imputation are usually in the form of 'rich text files' or 'proxy representing files' which made it easy to simply upload such files into the software directly from the internet site. Each interview and document is imported into NVivo independently. Similarly, with online texts, the researcher captures and imports web pages and their content directly into the software using a feature in NVivo 'NCAPTURE'. Having collected all the data in software, the interactive interface allowed for various tasks to manage the document including editing, proofreading, copy and pasting between documents, folders and files. The software's benefits which aids data storage and the platform it for coding helped in the analysis of the data collected during fieldwork. The thesis benefited immensely from this process. Nevertheless, much of the analytic construct is a product of independent thought, reflection, personal construction and in-depth interpretation of events based on the data. In other words, the researcher plays a central role in dissecting the components of the data to reveal new ideas and thoughts.

In order to fully grasp the intrinsic ideas embedded within the data, researchers harness the components of specific qualitative analytic tools and or established methods of analysis. In this case, a thematic analytical framework succinctly fits into the objective of the current study and is therefore employed in the computerised software to provide an interpretation of the data collected across the socio-political and ethnoreligious case study. The essence of an analytic tool in a methodological context is for the researcher to make sense of the data, and likewise for the relevant audience. Before going on to establish the step-by-step procedures of the thematic analysis, especially as employed in the current study, it is first useful to establish what exactly the concept of thematic analysis entails. According to Greg (2011) and Bryman (2012), thematic analysis is one of the most explored forms of analysis within social research. It is a process through which the researcher identifies recurring patterns, themes, topics and relationships across data collected during fieldwork for final analysis.

The researcher, through a careful reading of data collected during fieldwork, will be able to identify the most important themes that make up the data. The entire process revolves around what has been described by Holloway and Todres (2003, p. 347) as 'thematising meanings' (cited in Virginia & Victoria, 2006, p. 4), in other words, the extraction of themes and their meanings from data gathered during a research process. In terms of the process and procedures involved in the thematic analysis, it is difficult to delineate this approach from other analytical approaches for data analysis (Boyatzis, 1998; Ryan & Bernard, 2000). In fact, Ryan and Bernard (2000) argue that the thematic approach follows similar practices with other analytical frameworks like the grounded theory. The crucial point is that the different frameworks all pursue coding in view to identifying unique characteristics across studied texts. The thematic approach nonetheless focuses on identification of themes.

The analysis here refers to the process of reporting findings, juxtaposing findings with the literature, raising questions and putting forth a theoretical framework. This process cuts across all forms of data sources collected from interviews to the analysis of media reports, documents and audio-visual material. It is with these in mind that the computer-assisted software becomes relevant, especially as a facilitator of the processes described. The thematic analytic process began with data collection. Once the data were collected, then in the case of interviews, the next phase was the transcription of the audio into text. 'In the case of the research by Jones et al., once the transcripts had been incorporated within the software, the authors say they conducted a thematic analysis' (Bryman, 2012, p. 13).

In the present context, the thematic process began with a careful examination of transcribed interviews and other collected data. Having examined the documents, the next phase included computerisation of the interviews and other online documents collected for the ethnoreligious movements being considered. By computation, what is meant is the process of transferring data to the NVivo software. This stage is particularly important as it also facilitated easy accessibility and retrieval of such documents as the analysis progressed. Once the documents had been transferred to the computer program, the software facilitated some word frequency queries as seen in Figure 1.3. The word frequency provided a platform for examining the different issues participants were discussing. It also enabled a check across the interviews and other documents to see the most commonly used phrases among respondents or across the other documents, thereby exposing the most recurring themes in all the interviews and other documents.

The use of the word frequency allowed the researcher to familiarise himself/herself with the issues being raised and discussed amongst participants. But more specifically, the word search also revealed major hints on, for instance, motivation of the group, ideological orientation, issues, challenges and other structural dynamics like the highlight of the movement's activities. For instance, from Figure 1.3 'Boko Haram' stands out in the image, which points to the text as the central issue or main point of discourse; the use of Nigerian, Nigeria, Africa and the north are also key indicators of the groups' location and target. However, 'Islamic', although minutely reflected in the images, tells of the group's identity and ideological orientation. This pointer became useful during the analysis, especially in identifying key codes (Figure 1.4).

Figure 1.3. A Word Frequency Search in NVivo.

Next, in other to identify trends and particular themes, a second and more thorough reading of each interview transcript and secondary data collected online was carried out within the software. This time, the first set of codes are generated and highlighted using the NVivo software to organise the codes usually in nodes. Several nodes are generated and organised based on prior research questions and theoretical instruments. The idea at this stage is to identify connections, repetitions, reprises and replications, inter-connections across the data and conceptual assumptions on ICTs and contentious activities. These initial codes generated and organised are then reduced by harnessing key thoughts and ideas with shared commonalities or characteristics across the interviews and other documents examined in each case study.

This process of reduction allowed for the generation of the first set of themes that are more defined compared to the broadly generated codes. A further careful consideration allowed for more streamlining of similar themes under one principal theme so that a principal theme could have sub-themes and categories for easy understanding of causality and relationships. These final themes become the unit of analysis. In other words, the themes become analysed to represent new

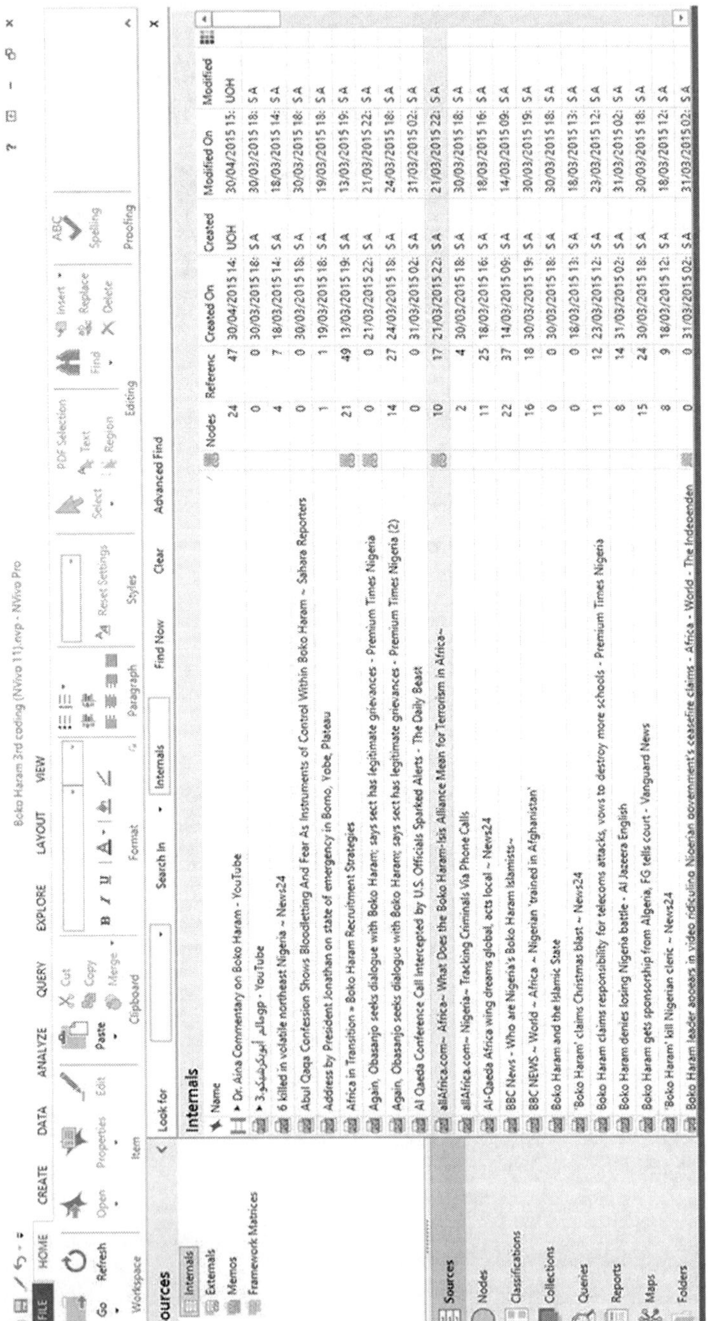

Figure 1.4. Screenshot 1: Example of Document Imported into NVivo Using N-Capture.

thoughts and ideas in the study. The reduction process helps to break down the large data that have been collected into 'parts' and or fragments to ease analysis and understanding. With these processes, Bryman (2012) explains that data are being managed since transcripts are being made more manageable through the process of reduction; the coding process that follows get the research more acquainted with the data (s)he seeks to understand and the data are simultaneous being interpreted in connection with the research question, theory and literature. The Nvivo software facilitates these processes with several inbuilt structures for reducing, merging codes (nodes) and managing huge data (Figure 1.5).

In contrast to other data interpretative strategies, the thematic analysis is not a method of inquiry that has a distinguishable or particularly unique custom or that has been delineated in relation to distinctive cluster of techniques (Bryman, 2012, p. 578). In other words, it is not a straight jacketed methodical approach with a much pre-determined set of structures. The main focus here is on a consideration of thematic preoccupations (which are important ideas within a data set) and theme generation as the tag 'thematic analysis' suggests. Nonetheless, as is the culture of several analytic techniques, identification of themes and coding are a generalised component of most if not all qualitative and quantitative data analyses. In other words, the thematic analysis is not an exception. In essence, although there is no clear-cut approach or set of techniques set out as identifiable guidelines or principle as some schools of thought argue (Bryman, 2012, p. 578), yet, there are similar practices in the design and procedure for analysing data across the different analytical approaches. In simple terms, the thematic approach follows the general principles of data analysis (Figure 1.6).

The thematic analysis is employed to understand the main issues across the socio-political and ethnoreligious movements despite the differences between the three cases examined. In the ethnoreligious case study, since data relied principally on secondary sources, in particular online news materials and videos, the sources for both cases (Boko Haram and MEND) were carefully selected based on their coverage of the activities of the movements. These included mainly Nigerian online newspapers and a few other global online media organisations. The use of mainly secondary sources is due to the limitations highlighted elsewhere. More so, data in this context are rather easily accessible on the internet. In addition, the internet provides an archive of both text and video data from the insurgency groups that will be useful in analysing the ethnoreligious and likewise the socio-political dimensions of their activities. Some of the main Nigerian online media sources identified include *Vanguard Nigerian*, *Premium Times*, *Sahara Reporters*, *BBC* online, *New York Times* online and *Global Bulletin* to mention but a few of the notable ones.

1.13. Book Structure

Moving on from this chapter and following the rational of the CC framework, Chapter 2 sets out a discussion mapping the environment of conflict. The analysis considers the political landscape, media landscape and the development of

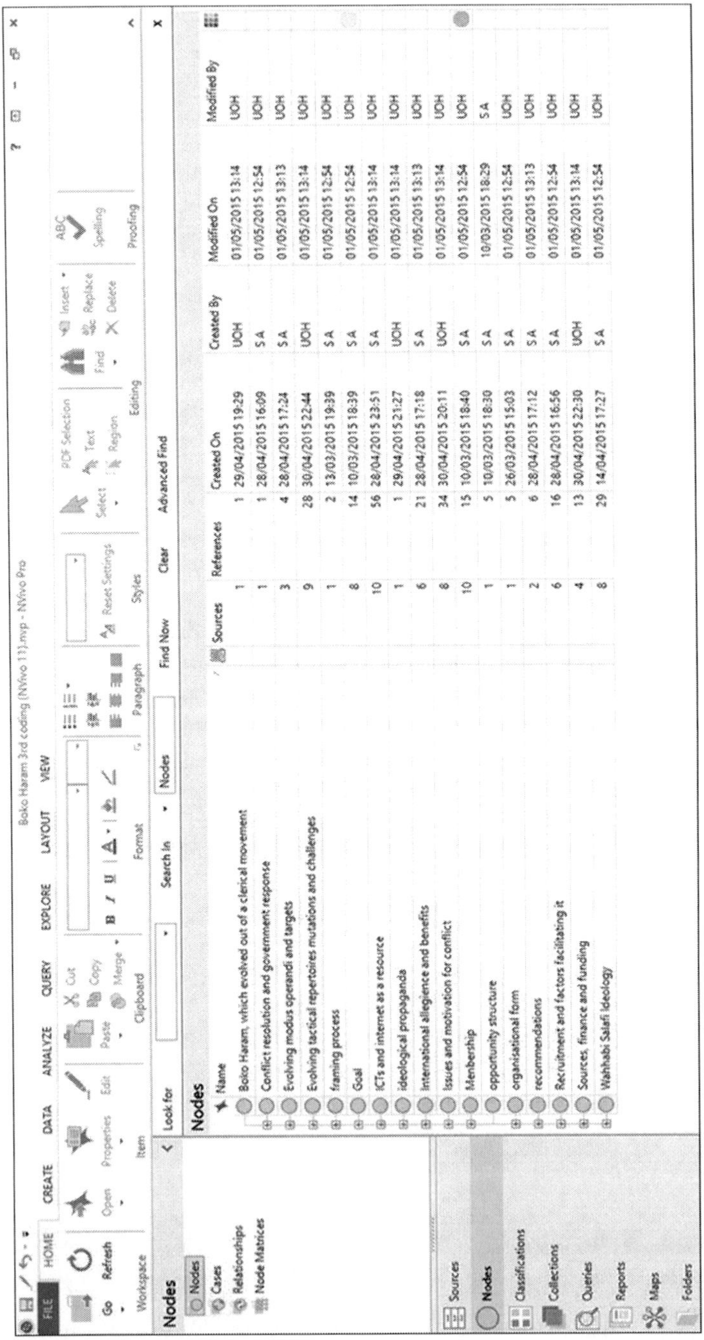

Figure 1.5. Screenshot 2: Developing and Reducing Themes in NVivo.

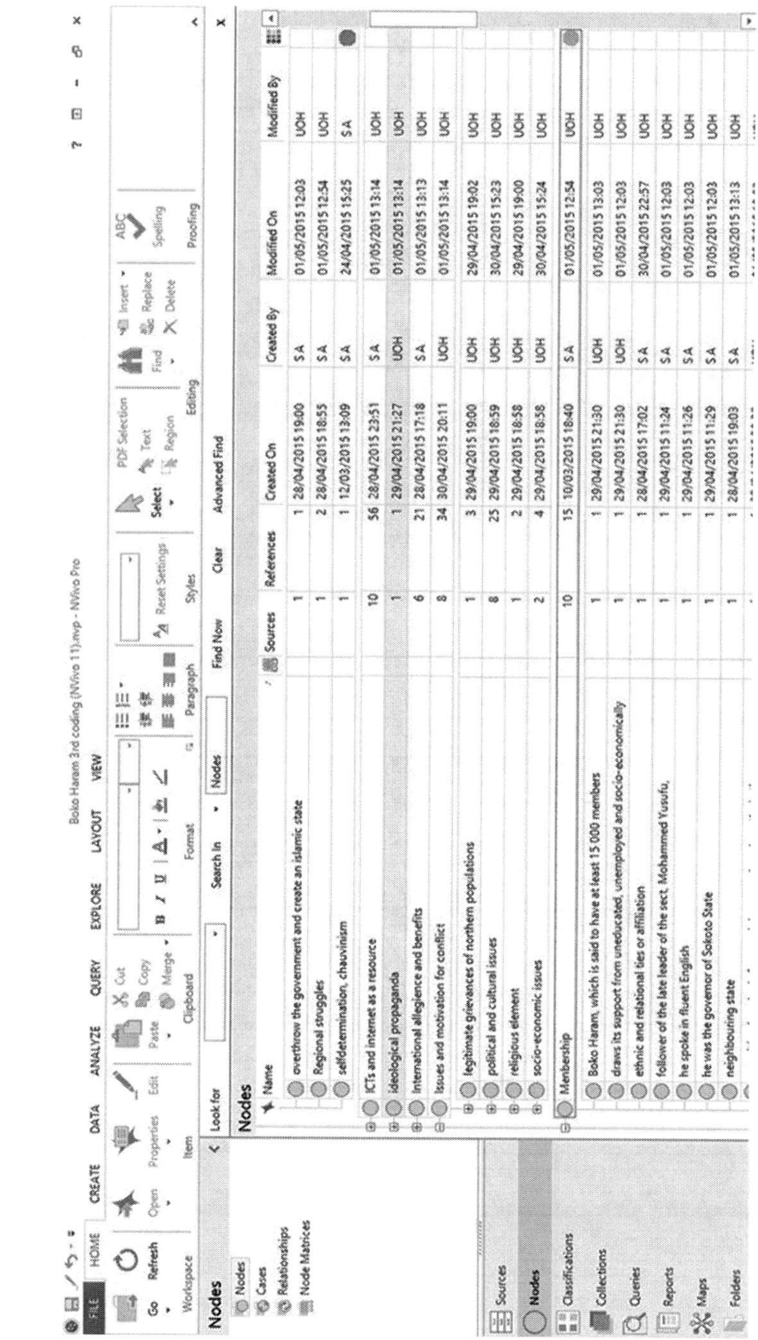

Figure 1.6. Screenshot 3: Example of Themes and Sub-themes in NVivo.

ICT infrastructure from a historical perspective. The aim is to situate modern conflict in Nigeria within broader historical influences. The discussion provides a foundation for understanding the discourse in the empirical chapters and provides an overview of the developments in ICT infrastructure. This section argues that gradual advances in media opened the environment to participation and an inclusive culture. Chapter 3, relying on empirical cases, undertakes a review of essential debates on ICT uses in computer-mediated environments and looks at youth engagement and digital activism in sub-Saharan Africa and across the globe. The discussion in this section uses empirical evidence to underscore the significance of communicative technologies for contentious politics. It then reflects on the limitations of ICT in contemporary conflicts.

Chapter 4 sets out a discussion on the Occupy Nigeria movement. This chapter explores the role of digital media in mobilising structures, opportunity structure and framing during the January 2012 protest. The focus turns to Boko Haram in Chapter 5, where the discussion considers the role of digital media in the movement's conflict. The study examines the mobilisation, opportunity structure and framing processes of the movement and other parts of the ethnoreligious CC framework. Following the same rationale, Chapter 6 looks at the role of digital media in activities of MEND. The ethnoreligious and socio-political elements of the CC framework also provide a mechanism for the mapping the activities of MEND. In Chapter 7, the study concludes by re-examining the use of digital media in conflict and highlights key findings acrossthe study and recommendations for future research.

Chapter 2

Mapping the Political Economy of Media Industry and ICT Infrastructural Development in Nigeria

2.1. Contextualising the Socio-economic and Political History

Any discussion about conflict against the backdrop of ICTs (whether new or old) would be incomplete without an account of the environment of conflict. The discussions must consider such dynamics as the political, socio-economic, media and technological context within which conflict takes place. The chapter takes a historical approach to understand the political economy of communications as a prelude to understanding the conflict in present-day Nigeria. This section consists of four parts. First, this chapter sets out an empirical discussion on the political and economic landscape. The chapter then engages in a debate about the media and communication environment. The next section sets out a focus on the development of digital and technological communication infrastructure. The final part concludes by summarising the key arguments of this chapter. By engaging discussions on the political environment of conflict, I lay the foundation for understanding the factors that underpin the dialectics, dynamics and motivations of dissenting communities, social movements, civil society and insurgency movements in Nigeria. The focus is on those socio-political and ethnoreligious undertones, which catalyse conflict in Nigeria.

The large population, ethnoreligious diversity and the vast natural resources that include oil and gas are some of the characteristics that have placed Nigeria on an international spotlight since independence in the 1960s. These features have also been a primary source of internal conflict and have therefore played an important role in attracting bad press, tensions, political debate and scrutiny from Nigerians and non-Nigerians across the globe. The last population census in 2006 put the Nigerian population figures at about 140 million (National Population Commission, 2006). However, different indices including the World Barometer and the World Factbook put the current population as at 2016 roughly above 180 million, making the country Africa's largest and most populous nation. Nigeria's population spreads across 36 states including the Federal Capital Territory, with approximately 250 ethnic groups divided across six regions (National Bureau of Statistics, 2015).

The structure of Nigeria's multilingual diversity encouraged the use of the English language as the official language in Nigeria. Thus English is the official language used to communicate during formal gatherings and occasions in schools, offices and other similar activities. Nonetheless, if one is to follow a structure of the most dominant languages widely spoken by Nigerians daily, pidgin English (a localised Nigerian form of Creole) closely follows the English language in its use on a day-to-day basis (National Population Commission, 2002). Drawing on the National Population Commission report, Hausa, Yoruba and the Igbo ethnic groups account for about 60% of the total Nigerian population and represent the dominant section of the country's population. This ethnic dominance is reflected in Nigeria's first three republics since it gained independence in 1960. During this period, political power revolved around the three dominant groups in the country until the fourth republic when in 2010 (the incumbent president at the time) Dr Goodluck Jonathan emerged as president from an ethnic minority group.

2.1.1. Socio-economic and Political Historical Context

The formation of what has come to be known as Nigeria is a product of an amalgamation of two independent colonies under British control as far back as 1914. These territories included the northern and southern protectorates. The Hausa-Fulani ethnic group was dominant in the northern region that they had occupied, while the Yoruba ethnic group dominated the southern part. The amalgamation was problematic right from its birth through the pre-independence period and the military dictatorships to the subsequent civilian-led governments that followed the independence in 1960. The major problem was the merger of two distinct and independent colonies. These colonies had different cultures, norms, religion and political practices that were unique to their existence. The merger, therefore, created ethnic and political tension between the diverse groups. Fabiyi (2014) explained that the amalgamation caused mixed feelings about whether the move was a huge mistake. According to him, the fusion resulted in an entrapment within the same country of ethnicities that would not have considered a union with one another. Nonetheless, the merger served the purpose of its creators, fulfilling and serving the interests of the colonialists at the time, which was to gain full control in their administration both in a socio-economic and political sense (Olusegun & David, 2010, p. 6). The large population that emerged because of the amalgamation is one reason for the multi-ethnic and religious diversity that resulted in what is today Nigeria.

Since gaining independence in 1960, the country's socio-economic and political history has revolved around conflict of ethnic, religious, socio-economic and political dimensions. These have become intertwined with the political culture of Nigeria. Before 1963, when Nigeria gained full independence and became a republic (the 1960 independence declaration was partial), there was a united anti-colonial struggle that was led by civil society organisations. These included student organisations, women associations, youth movements, activists and workers (professionals and unskilled) (Momoh, 1996, p. 154). Similar to other colonial territories, resistance and protests characterised the pre-independence period discussed further in the following paragraphs. As in the struggles of the pre-independence era, the post-independence period experienced similar conflicts. The political battles of the post-independent Nigeria period can be seen through the lens of the four republic transitions between 1960–1979, 1979–1983, 1993–1999 and 1999– the present era. The republics represent the different periods of transitions and regime change from independence. Not only does the different period represent political transitions between regimes (military or civil), it also reflects critical moments of conflict, resistance and protests in Nigerian history.

Following the political transition from colonial rule to independence, the newly independent Nigeria mirrored the political system of the colonial era, taking both form and shape of the British parliamentary system. The belief among political commentators and liberal scholars across the globe was that of optimism that the newly created democracy would thrive in Nigeria. Ihonvbere and Vaughan (1995) argue that their confidence came as a result of the emerging Nigerian elites schooled in the Western, rising urbanisation, the many natural resources embedded in the country and the growing consumer culture. The 'high hopes' served as a significant sign of the Nigerian democratic mood at the time.

However, the much-shared optimism of a prosperous democracy was short-lived. Political differences and socio-economic drawbacks continued to serve as a motivation for conflict. Oduko (1987) explained that early effort to build a democratic political entity, one that will reflect the multi-ethnic diversity of the Nigerian state, resulted in conflict, intertribal distrust and religious tensions. Nolutshungu (1990) argues the post-independence era became marred by extreme ethnic and regional rivalries with successive conflicts between political parties, regions and other elements interested in power. There was a political dilemma of who or which ethnic groups would qualify to spearhead governance of the new democracy following the 1960 independence. This problem represents one issue that has thrived in the four decades since the colonialist relinquished power. The political strife continued to threaten peace and stability in contemporary times as will be seen throughout the rest of the thesis and demonstrated in the concluding chapter. For one, Nigeria has never come together along the lines of ethnicity and, without a political resolve, power continued to revolve around the three dominant ethnic groups given their prevailing percentage of the total population. Minority groups have been relentless in expressing their outrage while there have been tensions between the three dominant groups (Rose & Auwal, 2014, p. 89).

Perhaps the most significant conflict during the first republic (1960–1979) was the Biafra conflict that lasted from 1967 to 1970. The Biafra conflict or more aptly the Nigerian civil war is an illustrative example of the distrust, ethnic tensions and rivalry that characterised the post-independence period (Anugwom, 2000; Diamond, 1983; Korieh, 2012; Okpaku, 1972; Perham, 1970; Uche, 2008). The conflict represented the socio-political struggle for ethnic leadership and political inclusion. The tensions also expose struggles for dominance among the three dominant ethnic groups, the eastern bloc dominated by the Igbos and the coalition of the predominant Northern Hausa-Fulani and the South-western Yorubas. Given the growing ethnic and political rivalry, the south-eastern block (mainly Igbos) made attempts at secession from the newly independent Nigeria. The struggles for self-determination resulted in a bloody civil war lasting about three years (Somide, 2001, pp. 19–30). During this conflict, approximately 2 million members of Biafra, which represented the predominantly Igbo Eastern region, were estimated to have died (Somide, 2001; Uzokwe, 2003). One can safely argue that the dreadfulness of the Biafra war further inspired mistrust, suspicion and division between the eastern region and the North.

Together with the brewing ethnic tensions as epitomised in the Biafra war also came religious distrust, suspicions and conflict which became predominant in the northern region as will be seen in Chapter 4. A notable example of a religious crisis in the post-1960 independence period is the Maitatsine conflict between 1980 and 1985. The Maitatsine was a radical insurgency and jihadi movement with anti-state and anti-establishment political orientation led by Mohammed Maruwa. The post-1999 transition period has seen a sharp rise in ethnoreligious conflicts from recurrent clashes between Muslims and Christians in Kaduna State and Jos, Plateau State to the conflict led by Boko Haram in the last decade and a half which in many respects is similar to the Maitatsine. Chapter 4 of this study captures the Boko Haram movements discourse in greater detail. Nonetheless, it is noteworthy to mention that some of the ethnoreligious conflicts including the Boko Haram have traits that predate contemporary times. In other words, the activities of the groups and indeed other disputes that have roots in Northern Nigeria are symptomatic of the general tensions that emerged since the amalgamation and have stayed in post-independent Nigeria till contemporary times.

The parliamentary style adopted at independence experienced irregularities. According to Gould (2012), these abnormalities emerged because of grievances in the leadership of the country. He argued that during the period leading to independence in 1960, the state was under the control of the British, the northern elite and their coalition partners. Following independence in 1960, the northern upper-class and the well-to-do continued to dominate the political scene. Thus, despite the democratic system in place, elections were marred by fraud with the lot falling to the northern elite. The growing northern political control had created a general feeling of frustration among individuals and groups who aspired inclusion in governance and top leadership positions in the country. The eastern bloc's displeasure and grievance towards the growing control of the North led to calls for secession, which ended in conflict at the time with critical historical continuities in the present age. For instance, over four decades, since the Nigerian civil war, the ethnic divides still pervade, with the resurgence of a Biafra agitation resurfacing around issues of neglect, exclusion and marginalisation in 2015. Their goal remains to fight for self-determination (see Attoh, 2015).

The leadership struggles that followed independence paved the way for the military to interfere with the democratic structure that was in place. Diamond (1988) explained that the army seised power under the guise of a failing constitution and growing ethnic and regional hostility. The new democracy abruptly ended in a bloody coup precisely six years after independence in 1966. These events left a permanent impression on the nation's politics as it gave room for the military to exact influence and hold sway of power in much of the country's history. Nolutshungu (1990) noted the negative impact military incursion had on 'the possibilities of alternative forms of mobilisation and representation of interests' in Nigeria (p. 80). Following the *coup d état* in 1966, the government remained under military rule for the next three republics between 1966 and 1999 with brief spells of civilian rule during this period. As Ojo (2009) aptly put it, 'anti-colonial struggles, crisis, coups, counter-coups, and a thirty-month agonising civil war between 1967 and 1970' (Ojo, 2009, p. 2) characterised the Nigerian political landscape. The different military regimes that held power between 1960 and 1999 neither achieved success in promoting ethnoreligious cohesion nor did they deliver economic growth (see Lewis, 1996, pp. 79–103).

The period between 1993 and 1999 is of particular significance especially for political, civil liberties and media freedoms. According to Olukotun (2002a, 2002b), this period is the most gruesome and hideous in the Nigerian political history for repression of the press, widespread dissent, civil liberties, freedom of expression and the press (p. 317). The lack of socio-political, economic development, contests for political power, ethnic and religious divides catalysed civil society conflict. The Nigerian Labour Congress (NLC), the umbrella organisation representing trade and worker's union, championed and led such conflicts. Their grievances were against issues of governance, human rights, the economy, democracy, poverty and the increasing levels of corruption. The protests that ensued resulted in stiff repression from the military regime. Resistance and repression greeted protests emerging from civil society, pro-opposition media, political activists and other non-institutional groups from the military (Amuwo, Bach, & Lebeau, 2001; Ihonvbere & Vaughan, 1995; Lewis, 1996; Olukotun, 2002a, 2002b). For example, the regime sought different means to inhibit all legitimate forms of communication and express dissent through legal and illegal means including censorship. On the one hand, laws were enacted to circumvent freedom of expression, and on the other hand, the use of coercion became a central approach of the military.

For instance, in separate accounts, Olukotun (2002a) and Ihonvbere and Vaughan (1995) argue that contentious activities experience difficulties due to the arrest of civil society actors, murder and assault on newspaper houses, independent activists and opposition figures. In addition, the dictatorial regime banned traditional labour groups and other civil society actors, for instance, the NLC, the Nigerian Bar Association (NBA), the National Association of Nigerian Students (NANS), Women in Nigeria (WIN) and the Academic Staff Union of Universities (ASUU). In the 1990s, the consensus was that Nigerian political situation degenerated into a form of military dictatorship, ignoring the arrangement of previous military governments between 1970 and 1980, in favour of coercion and state violence (see Lewis, 1996, cited in Olukotun, 2000b, pp. 137–138). The general mood of the military regime is by no means a surprise as it conforms to the general attitude of the military towards civil society dissent in autocratic systems. For instance, Breuer (2012) explains that under dictatorial regimes, organising and mobilising political protest is more complicated since the dictatorial regimes employ persecution, repression and manipulation to shut down dissent.

In the face of repression, Olukotun (2002b) pointed out that civil society pressed on, often relying on alternative communication platforms to communicate dissent. For instance, the hostile situation towards media freedoms, civil liberties and political rights led to several underground press outlets and a pirate radio station, 'Radio Kudirat' emerging. Civil society actors, opposition forces, activists and independent activists worked together to establish and operate the underground media organisations from unknown destinations. Although a local pirate radio station, a 2015 Immigration and Refugee Board of Canada report explained that Radio Kudirat broadcast worldwide on shortwave frequency. The clandestine media had a local (national) and global reach. 'It was in this context that [...] the media, drawing on a tradition of activism [...] invented guerrilla tactics to oppose the military' (Olukotun, 2002b, p. 318).

The stiff opposition on activists and the media by the dictatorial regimes did not dissuade the media in Nigeria from fulfilling their role as the 'watchdog' in society. As Odugbemi and Norris (2009) pointed out, the media also provided checks on various sectors of society and the leadership, whether private or in a public capacity. The media play an essential role in safeguarding public interest against low-level performance, corruption and misinformation and propaganda. While the media is an avenue of contestation to dominate political discourse, the state under the dictatorship exerted its leadership by enforcing control on the media. However, activists (Professor Wole Soyinka and General Alani Akirinade to mention but a few notable actors) continued to show resilience by confronting the state and disclosing the corrupt practices of the dictatorial government using the underground channels. Subsequently, following the death of the military head of state in 1998 and the general elections that followed in 1999, a democratic government emerged.

2.1.2. The Post-military Era

The change in the political system to become a democratic culture in 1999 is considered as a milestone in Nigerian political history. Besides the transition to a democratic culture, the 1999 development marks the most extended and uninterrupted civil rule the country has enjoyed since gaining independence in 1960 (Nitya, 2011; Ojo, 2009; Olukoyun, 2004). As with the 1960 independence, the transition to democracy in 1999 brought feelings of joy, high expectations and renewed hope for a better society. According to Jega (2015), it led to beliefs and expectations that the new government would ensure better governance that would satisfy the necessities and desires of ordinary Nigerians. There were also doubts in Nigeria and abroad on whether the principles of liberal democracy would be enjoyed, strengthened and consolidated by the new administration. For instance, a report by *The Economist* in 1999 explained that the new president (Olusegun Obasanjo) would face a difficult task and questioned whether the president was up to the task (The Economist, 4 March 1999). The mixed reaction is by no means a surprise in light of the autocratic attributes and the tendencies experienced during the military regimes, especially between 1993 and 1999.

The new democratic regime began to demonstrate an indication of socio-economic and political reform epitomised by the degree of openness, participation, civil liberties and media freedoms. The Human Rights Watch report for 2003 revealed that advances in 'freedom of expression and civil liberties were among the immediate gains of Nigeria's transition to civil rule' (Human Rights Watch, 2003, p. 2). The new political terrain encouraged citizen participation and engagement through elections and free association. The government led transformative initiatives with spells of development in different sectors especially in the areas of ICTs (mobile phone and telecommunications). For Nolutshungu (1990), despite the optimism for development heralded by the transition, the reality often motivated the deepest doubts about the chance of any progress in either development or democracy. For one, this point is significant especially when considered against the backdrop of the subsequent decrease in the standard of living, widespread insecurity, unemployment and ethnoreligious and socio-politically motivated conflicts that continued to weaken the Nigerian democracy ethos. The principle of a liberal democracy rooted in the ideology of civil liberties and political rights (see Bratton & Walle, 1997) continued to decline in the country's nascent democracy.

It appears that some of the tendencies of the post-military regimes continued, although in a subtler form. For instance, following the transition, there have been alleged cases of assault, arrests andtorture of activists, journalists and protesters. These actions have followed attempts by consecutive governments to subdue political protests and popular dissent, thereby employing anti-democratic attributes (Freedom House, 2009, 2011, 2012; Human Rights Watch, 2003a, 2003b, 2007, 2008, 2010). Similarly, under democratic dispensation, the pace of development has been somewhat slow, owing to the deficiencies of good governance and the government failing to promote democratic ethos. The 2012 Freedom House index report (the organisation surveys civil liberties and political rights democracies across the globe) corroborates this point on the pitfalls in governance in Nigeria.

As per the 2012 report, Nigeria scored 4.5 for media freedoms and civil liberties, representing a below-average score that represented the country's democratic status in poor light. The score proves that not much has changed in the country over one decade of democratisation. In fact, the index further revealed that media freedoms and civil liberties decreased between 2011 and 2012 in comparison with previous years. A 2014 Freedom House report revealed between 1999 and 2014 low levels of freedoms and unpopular perception on political rights since the transition. These rights (civil and political rights and media freedoms) have remained below average with little development.

In the Freedom House, 2014 report on press freedom, the seminal organisation attributes scores using three variables, the legal environment, the political atmosphere and the economic environment. Out of 100%, Nigeria again scores an average point of 51%, which underscores the unstable and partially free atmosphere for media freedoms. On democratic gains and losses in democracies across the globe, the Freedom House (2014) report also portrays a Nigeria with a negative perception of democratic gains. The trend reveals a situation with minimal or no change. Drawing on a point made by Bratton and Walle (1997), there is a direct connection between the low level of change in Nigeria and the continuous recycling of leaders, which is a common trend in Africa and across the globe.

For instance, the 1999 elections witnessed a former military Head of State, General Olusegun Obasanjo, contest and win the general elections on the platform of the People's Democratic Party (PDP), thereby returning to head the state as a civilian president. Olu Falaye, the 1999 presidential candidate of the opposition party, the All Peoples Party and Alliance for Democracy, set the tone with his famous phrase 'a soldier in civilian disguise'. Widespread claims of electoral malpractice and fraud greeted the PDPs electoral victory. Even so, the phenomenon was repeated in the 2003 elections when the retired general, now President Olusegun Obasanjo, was again elected for another four years. The scenario above was yet another event that created significant debate and protests both abroad and across Nigeria. Although the electoral dissent in Nigeria revolves around the issue of electoral malpractice and fraud, one can argue that such grievances are elements of ethno-nationalist struggles among different ethnic and religious groups.

In the Transparency International Corruption Index for 2012, which scores different countries on corruption from 0 (very corrupt) to 100 (very clean), Nigeria and other countries, Azerbaijan, Kenya, Nepal and Pakistan, achieved a rating of 27. Demonstrating a poor and below-average perception of corruption. This position has remained the same with slight changes in the last decade and a half. For instance, the 2013 index reflected a decrease from 27 to 25, ranking 144 out of 177. Three years in a row, the trend continued to indicate a below-average score for Nigeria's corruption index. The instability in governance and government's failure to tackle corruption opened a window of opportunity for socio-political protests, conflict and crime which is the subject of the empirical chapters.

The second cluster of issues involves an increasingly growing surge of radical insurgency conflict (including terrorism-related insurgency) and other socio-political crisis, which has left the country in constant turmoil. Indeed, the last decade has witnessed an enormous trend of militant and insurgency-related conflict (Boko Haram, MEND) that has further deepened the socio-political, ethnic and religious divide in the country. These conflicts undermined the fragile Nigerian democracy and other aspects of business and life in the country. These events have meant that the full potential of democratisation has not fully manifested. The thesis here is not to suggest that there have not been notable democratic achievements. The point is that the process has been short-lived due to instabilities that in turn continue to fuel a new form of socio-political, ethnic and religious conflict epitomised in ongoing dissent and protests widespread in Nigeria (see discussions in the empirical Chapters 3–5).

In the past, the labour unions and pro-opposition media championed protests focusing on economic issues, such as oil price increases, and political problems, such as election abnormalities. Following the democratic transition in 1999, more of such groups have emerged including social movements, women movements and youth organisations. In theory, the current political system is open to freedom of expression, as well as civil and political rights including the press. Nevertheless, the political environment for traditional media and civil society action remains unconducive. In addition to the government's direct and indirect interference with the political rights described earlier, other challenges relate mainly to insecurity concerns associated with insurgency activities. For instance, a significant event in 2011, as reported by Freedom House, was the murder of a journalist by the radical Islamic group, Boko Haram (Freedom House, 2012, p. 1).

Before going further with the discussion on the media environment, it is relevant to consider the socio-economic climate as necessary in the socio-political trajectory of protests and conflicts in Nigeria. In fact, the two go hand in hand. In their seminal piece, 'Can Nigeria's nascent democracy survive?' Ojo and Adebayo (2009) explained there is a causal link that exists between the economy and democracy. These theorists believe that a 'broad-based economic prosperity sustains democracy, whereas widespread poverty and ignorance undermine it' (Ojo & Adebayo, 2009, p. 2). Although, Nigeria is Africa's biggest economy, yet in practice, key indices reveal alarming rates of poverty and lack of development. Agriculture is one source of income for many Nigerians, given that more Nigerians live in rural areas compared to urban areas. Farming and other similar agricultural-related activities are normal practices in such areas. Nonetheless, developments in the oil industry negatively affected the agricultural sector.

In the 1960s, agriculture accounted for 65–70% of total exports; it fell to about 40% in the 1970s and crashed to less than 2% in the late 1990s. The decline in the agricultural sector was largely due to rising crude oil revenue in the early 1970s (Olajide, Ojo Akinlabi, & Ojo Tijani, 2012, 105).

Beyond agriculture, the country has other natural resources including gold, limestone, tin and columbite among others that remain mostly underexploited (Gabriel et al., 2015).

Nigeria has relied mostly on an exploration of petroleum right from the 1950s. Petroleum later became the mainstay of the Nigerian economy even though there are current efforts to diversify the economy. According to the Nigerian National Petroleum Corporation website, the Nigeria oil industry ranks sixth in the world for its producing capacity and is the largest in Africa. According to Onigbinde (2015), petroleum accounts for about 80% of the Nigerian government's revenue. Over the years, the heavy reliance on the oil industry further dented any prospects for developing the agricultural sector. In spite of the enormous wealth that came with oil and gas exploration, the country remains mostly poor because of corruption in the industry. Also, the growing levels of corruption and failing institutions of governance negatively affected the economy and by implication the standard of living of the average Nigerian. For instance, a 2012 BBC report stated that poverty rose to nearly 61% with over a 100 million people living on less than US$ 1 a day (BBC, 13 February 2012). One commentator explained that Nigeria's oil wealth and the revenue derived from the industry over the decades have not manifested in improving infrastructural development, wealth generation, poverty reductions and appreciation in living standard for the majority of Nigerians (Luqman & Lawal, 2011, p. 60). They explained that:

> The failure of economic policies in Nigeria have manifested in stagnation of the nation (sic) economy, over-dependence on a

> single commodity for export and revenue, the neglect of the agricultural sector, decaying infrastructure and poor delivery of social services [...] compounded by mirage (*sic*) of other problems [...] the crisis of political instability and the horrendous level of corruption [...]. These challenges have given rise to a steady decline in virtually all indexes of human development in Nigeria over the years.
>
> Luqman and Lawal (2011, p. 60)

Besides relying mainly on the oil sector, the discovery of oil also provoked a new form of resource control with vested interest only in the hands of a few controlling the means of production. In other words, the oil and gas sector continued to be monopolised mainly by elites. Monopoly is symptomatic of the capitalist system, where the rich enjoy more benefits and dominance due to their economic advantage. The unequal spread and distribution of such resources and the benefits accrued in concert with weak governance structure have subsequently become another source of conflict in contemporary Nigeria. According to Charles Soludo, a former Governor of the Central Bank of Nigeria, the principles of democracy has not been consolidated in Nigeria. For him, this is because the economic numbers did not add up. 'Democracy and indeed any form of government must deliver tangible economic benefits to the generality of the citizenry to be credible and sustainable' (Soludo, 2005, cited in Ojo & Adebayo, 2009, p. 3).

To better encapsulate the points raised, several factors continue to underpin the conflict that has evolved over the last decade and a half in Nigeria, the principal of these dynamics can be contextualised broadly regarding socio-political shortfalls, ethnoreligious divides and socio-economic drawbacks. These three dynamics are interconnected and may not be necessarily separated. For instance, a sorry state of the economy in itself could be a vector provoking socio-political tension and ethnoreligious divides. An illustrative example of the interplay between these dynamics is apparent in the events surrounding President Goodluck Jonathan's emergence as Nigerian President.

Following the completion of the two-term tenure (eight years) of President Olusegun Obasanjo (between 1999 and 2007) of Yoruba descent (one of the dominant and major tribes), power transferred through elections to President Umaru Musa Yar Adua, of the Hausa/ Fulani descent. President Yar Adua succeeded the former under the flagship of the PDP. As with his predecessor, Yar Adua electoral victory faced dispute and criticism among political commentators at home and abroad. Yar Adua's death in 2010 gave room for the Vice President, Dr Goodluck Jonathan from the south–south geopolitical region to emerge constitutionally as president of Nigeria through succession.

One can safely suggest that the penetration of the (so-called) minority south–south ethnic group created an inclusive space for 'the others' that is (those who had formerly been excluded from the presidential politics) to be part of the political process. On the subject of ethnic minorities, over the years, issues of representation, participation and inequality have generated debate and conflict within the polity (see Suberu, 1996, pp. 66–79). For instance, the scuffle for equality and representation is evident in the struggles of the people from the Niger Delta, who for many years had engaged the state through a series of fundamental conflict, protests, militancy and insurgency. With an incumbent vice-president, Goodluck Jonathan, who hails from the region, relative peace emerged between the insurgents and the government. Jonathan's ascension to the office of president brought about more stability in the region. The phenomenon represents a hallmark event given that for the first time an ethnic minority occupied the office of the President of the federal republic. Nonetheless, the dominant ethnic groups (especially the northern region) greeted the development with mixed feelings. Aye (2012) explained that Goodluck Jonathan's emergence in 2011 was marked by disbelief in more than a few quarters (p. 106).

To further demonstrate the issue of ethnic and cultural tensions, following the death of President Yar'adua, a large section of the northern part of Nigeria believes that a northern candidate should have been sought to complete the tenure of the late President, as he was also from the North. On the one hand, one could trace some elements of sentiments of bias and ethnicity. On the other hand, some northern critics argue on the basis of a constitutional clause that is unique to the ruling PDP. The clause provides for zoning and rotation of power. Enshrined in Article 3 (C) of the party's constitution, the clause states among other things that 'The Party shall pursue these objectives by [...] adhering to the policy of the rotation and zoning of the party and elective public offices in pursuance of the principle of equity, justice and fairness'. Political power was meant to be distributed on a rotational basis among the different geopolitical regions. A condition that would violate and undermine the provisions enshrined in Section 146 (1) of the constitution of the Federal Republic of Nigeria states that: The Vice President shall hold the office of President. If the office of President becomes vacant by reason of death or resignation, impeachment, permanent incapacity or the removal of the President from office for any other reason in accordance with Section 143 of this Constitution (Constitution of the Federal Republic of Nigeria, 1999 s 146 (i)).

The concept of rotation of power enshrined in the constitution of the People's Democratic Power unveils strides to promote political inclusiveness and equal representation between the different geopolitical zones. But at the same time reproduces ethno-nationalist tensions and struggles for political participation.

The constitutional clause explains the outrage, insistence and contestation of the northern faction of the PDP to continue to hold on to power following the death of the former president. There is a conflict between the Nigeria constitution and the PDP constitution. Despite this conflict, one would reasonably expect that where party constitution conflicts with the law of the federal republic of Nigeria, the former would be set aside. More so, the conflict continues to expose deeply entrenched ethnic and religious divides within Nigeria, one that predates the present situation. Nigeria had never been united along ethnic and religious lines, and this has been one of the crucial motivations for conflict in the country's four republics since independence. The idea of zoning political power has both positive and negative consequences. With a zoning policy, political power would be shared between the different zones on a turn-by-turn basis.

That way, members of each zone will wait for their turn to take on public office. Nonetheless, the zoning of political power in itself could also undermine fair play. In that, the process does not necessarily mean that every section of society within the different states that make up each zone would get adequate representation. As such, some segments of society may still be underrepresented particularly where one ethnic group is dominant in the region.

2.2. The Political Economy of the Media Industry

In the debate on the struggles for socio-political, democratic, ethnic and religious emancipation, the mass media have played a crucial role. From the pre-colonial era and independence to the present democratic regime, the platform of the media has had a significant role in society. The media has played a crucial role in promoting discussion, providing information, serving as an independent check on government and serving as the public eye. For example, for conflict, the media has the potential of boosting communication and interaction, as well as promoting diverse opinions and perspectives. It is, therefore, no surprise the media has been a significant tool of contestation between various political contenders across the globe (Gamson & Meyer, 1996; McAdam, McCarthy, & Zald, 1996). The media serves as a vector carrying opinions that could influence socio-political change, resistance and propaganda.

The unstable political landscape that characterised much of the Nigerian political history played a crucial role in shaping the economy of communications and the media in Africa's most populous nation. In discussing the constraints on mass media policies in Nigeria, Mogbejume (1991) succinctly identifies three factors that have shaped the economy of media and communications in Nigeria. These are constitutional instabilities, constant political complexities and the pattern of media ownership. These factors continue to decide the fate of the mass media in contemporary Nigeria.

The constant political flux affected the structure of the media, ownership and monopoly in Nigeria. The mass media here refers to traditional media, that is, print, newspapers and magazines including electronic broadcast media that is, television and radio. On the one hand, the current socio-political climate played a significant role in advancing the media in Nigeria. At the same time, the socio-economic dynamics have also been influential in shaping the media. Unsurprisingly, given the predominantly authoritarian political system in pre-democratic Nigeria, the state monopolised almost all mass media and channels of communication. Private media was mostly under scrutiny and censorship. These allowed the state to control public knowledge broadcast through the media. At the same time, it provided the government with a platform to exert its influence and propaganda. The media and communications sector remained a critical subject because of state control and censorship. State control of the media can be traced as far back as the colonial era; post-independence, the tradition continued through military dictatorships to the few spells of civilian regimes (see Agbaje, 1992; Bush, 2008; Sani, 2014, p. 6256).

Media monopoly at the time allowed for a one-way pattern of communication, whereby communication was controlled by the ideologies and perceptions of the state. For instance, Adeleke (1988) explained that although Iwe Irohin, the first newspaper printed in Abeokuta Ogun State, had a missionary background, nevertheless it was a political weapon for the articulation, propagation and defence of imperialist ideologies in the Yoruba-dominated region of Southwestern Nigeria. It served to reinforce colonialist ideologies between 1859 and 1867 when the pioneer newspaper collapsed. Ibrahim (1997) argued that Iwe Irohin was principal to mobilising the minds of the masses to recognise and accept capitalist principles and tradition.

The mass media continued to enjoy similar forms of repression and suppression during successive governments in post-independent Nigeria. This is particularly true throughout the first three republics, which was characterised by military dictatorship coups and counter *coup d'états*. In the face of repressive environment, the media during this time adapted an activist-like culture, exposing the ill deeds of state actors and bad governance, which made the dictatorial regimes uncomfortable and more aggressive. Before 1992, when the Nigerian Broadcasting Commission (NBC) Decree 38 was promulgated, 'all legal and constitutional instruments in force in the country effectively made broadcasting an exclusive preserve of the federal and state governments' (Oketunmb, 2006, p. 3). Decree 38 brought about the liberalisation of broadcast media in Nigeria, which in essence meant that private individuals could now own their broadcast media from 1992. Before 1992, government (military and civilian) exercised significant control over information flow through its regulations and censorship.

The Nigerian government's struggles to control information and communications media platforms shows the importance and power of the media as a tool and resource. In particular, the significance of the media is in relation to shaping public opinion and the implication for stimulating protests and conflict, when harnessed as a resource for social change and engineering. The potential influence of the media explains why the different regimes explored different options, regulation and force to control the media. The media in Nigeria have been at the forefront of ensuring government accountability by mounting surveillance to monitor government's activities to stem an inherent disposition towards excesses (Oseni, 1995, p. 3). The contestation over the tools of communication also displays the importance of the communication machinery of every generation for advancing change. The printing press enjoyed both private and public ownership patterns right from the historical foundations of the Nigerian media in contrast to electronic broadcast media. Nonetheless, as in the case of its electronic counterpart, Olukotun (2002a, 2002b) explained that the printing press, especially those that were critical of the activities of the state, were subject to censorship and repression from the government.

This form of government opposition to the press was prevalent in the 1970s and mid-1980s. For example, some newspapers were shut down by the government, such as Newbreed in 1977; the Tribune was also closed down in 1984, and Newswatch was censored in 1988. Among others, these newspaper organisations were affected due to their critical stance towards the government. Not only was printing press media shut down, but individual journalists and media personnel were also harassed (Olukotun, 2002a, 2002b, p. 324). For instance, according to the Press Reference Online (no date), Minere Amakiri, a reporter with the Nigerian Observer, was detained in 1971 for an article he published on the plight of teachers and the ills of the education system. Similar actions of the government during this time had wide-reaching implications for the entire industry and civil society. The repressive measures imposed directly and indirectly made it difficult for the press to fulfil its responsibilities.

As a tool and resource, both civilian and military regimes and civil society exploited the media to propagate their cause and for their gains and benefits. Oduko (1987) explained that the media were used and abused by politicians to manipulate and win supporters in elections. Some of the popular titles were owned and founded by the same politicians. The Concord Group is a classic example. Founded by Moshood Abiola, it was employed principally to advance its owner's candidature, as well as party's political interest and agenda. State control on other media platforms was an instrumental factor and motivation for setting up such news media.

The motivation for the suppression of dissent and the hegemony over the media was in view to controlling debates on government activities in a society. The action of the state incentivised further revolts and protests. For instance, various decrees were promulgated to regulate the operations of the media and civil society. Examples of such proclamations are the Offensive Publications Decree Nŏ. 35 of 1993 and the Newspapers Decree No. 43 of 1993. According to Ojo (2009), the latter is arguably the most oppressive media laws promulgated in Nigeria. Section 7 of the Decree makes it a crime for a person to own, publish or print a newspaper not registered under the Decree, carrying a punishment of a fine of N250.000 or imprisonment for seven years or both. Besides the media regulations, media operators were also subject to other decrees not directly targeted at the media.

Some of the general decrees used against journalists are the State Security (Detention of Persons) Decree No. 2 of 1984 as amended and the Treason and Other Offences (Special Military Tribunal) Decree No. 1 of 1986 (Ojo, 2009, p. 202).

Olayiwola (1991) explained that it was the general belief of civilian and military regimes that free dissemination of information and communication could constitute a threat to the state. Therefore, they promulgated decrees to restrain the press. Thus, a few independent media (especially the press) outlets that surfaced during this time did so at their peril, given that any publication the regime considered a threat attracted severe sanction from the state. The period leading to the 1999 democratic transition is of particular significance. A Human Rights Watch (2003a, 2003b, p. 3) report found that a ruthless suppression of dissent characterised this period. Joseph (1997) upheld that the period was marked by arbitrary arrests and detentions, extrajudicial killings, harassment of journalists, democratic activists and arson attacks on media houses. The perceived threat of the media to the state which Olayiwola mentioned earlier, particularly for exposing the ills of the government, served as the primary motivation for the hugely repressive attitude of the authorities.

For instance, Abiola, the 1993 presidential candidate under the Social Democratic Party (SDP), was arrested and later died in detention. The National Union of Petroleum and Natural Gas (NUPENG) and the Natural Gas Senior Staff Association (PENGASSAN) were proscribed. Also, pro-democratic activist Wale Osun was detained in 1995, and Ken Saro-Wiwa, a media practitioner and activist, was arrested and later killed in 1995. The same year, newspaper houses were closed down including The Guardian, Nigeria, Concord group and the Punch. The Concord Group was owned by Abiola, a former presidential candidate in the 1993 general elections. Despite the restrictive environment, civil society actors and media stakeholders remained determined in their protest for socio-political and economic reform (Olukotun, 2002a, p. 317).

The exclusive preserve held by the state and the federal government over broadcast media ended in 1992 following a decree that brought about liberalisation of broadcast media by the Ibrahim Babangida's regime. The decree also established the NBC, whose mandate is to regulate both public and private broadcasting and issue licences in Nigeria. The NBC replaced the Nigerian Television Authority (NTA), which was born out of Decree 24. By this decree, the NTA took over all existing broadcast stations founded by state governments at the time. In 1979, the return to democratic rule and the introduction of the constitution set aside the decree and paved the way for all parties that is, the government, state governments and private individuals, to own broadcast media. However, the right of ownership of such media was at the discretion of the President. According to the NBC, the emergence of the NBC in 1992 led to the issuance of radio, television and cable broadcast licences in 1993 to individual operators for the first time in the history of broadcasting in Nigeria.

In his work on the deregulation of the broadcasting industry in Nigeria, Enemaku (2003) argues that liberalising the broadcast sector became essential as the state-owned media failed to satisfy the communication and information needs of civil society adequately. Although from 1992 onwards private operators could gain a broadcast licence, the full benefit of liberalisation was not immediately evident until the transition to democracy in 1999. The return of military dictatorship between 1993 and 1999 extended repression of media freedoms and political rights. One can safely suggest that the transition to democratic rule in 1999 had a positive influence on private media ownership. As one would reasonably expect, the political environment was less repressive after 1999 in contrast to the military dictatorship eras.

Liberalisation of broadcast media allowed for more private ownership of broadcast media in Nigeria thereby ending the long years of the monopoly enjoyed by federal and state government. In the aftermath of the liberalisation, there have been developments in private, independent broadcast media in Nigeria. In 2010, Ariye recorded the most recent figures for broadcast media organisations: there were 13 independent television broadcast media operators, while roughly 22 private radio stations were broadcasting across the country and beyond with more media outlets emerging (see Ariye, 2010, pp. 415–423).

Although these are small numbers, it is not a surprise, especially when considering the cost of owning and running such forms of media. Private media operation in Nigerian broadcasting was greeted with the optimism that the independent media will provide a platform for genuine and independent news to develop while encouraging a free atmosphere for pluralistic views and civil society to engage with political actors. Although the availability of privately owned broadcast stations lessened government monopoly and manipulation of media channels for propaganda, nonetheless, several factors continue to challenge the smooth functioning of private outlets.

Taking a cue from this point, Olukoyun (2004) explains that the regulatory atmosphere in which privately owned broadcast media now functioned foil their effort of being critical. This position is crucial, mainly because of sanctions that were issued continuously against some private broadcasting media outlets between 1999 and 2005 under the auspices of the NBC. Some privately owned broadcast houses had their licence suspended for acting in a non-partisan manner, and in opposition to the government. For instance, following the 2005 Belleview plane crash in Nigeria, the perceived propaganda in the reportage of state-owned broadcast media of the event surrounding the crash prompted a counter-reportage by some privately-owned media stations. An example of this was the African Independent Television (AIT, the privately owned broadcast media outlet with national and international reach). AIT sought to set the record straight by broadcasting real images and details on the wreckage. The government received AIT's actions with mixed feelings which then resulted in the suspension of the media outlet's licence.

Eventually, because of protests from the media and civil society, the government subsequently retracted its decision. Besides the illustration earlier, there have also been spells of confrontation and intimidation of media practitioners, media organisations and vendors. An illustrative example is a raid carried out by the Nigerian army in June 2014 on newspaper outlets and media houses. The military had claimed that it was a routine exercise based on an intelligence report of suspected transport of bombs by Boko Haram through the newspaper distribution chains. Citizens including media organisations and civil society actors protested the acts of the security agents. According to a BBC report, 'newspapers said their delivery vans had been searched, and vendors questioned across the country, and copies of the papers destroyed' (BBC news online, 7 June 2014). The general belief among civil society actors was that the government was making attempts to repress and censor the media. Such forms of subtle or direct control on the media have adverse effects on broadcasting. For instance, it could affect the quality of reportage, communication and output of broadcasters, who for fear of sanctions and coercion may tread with caution and impose self-censorship.

The NBC and other media regulators that existed before the NBC enjoyed government funding and reported directly to the president. According to the NBC website, the president must personally approve recommendations and applications for licences. Under the NBC's category, 'obtaining licensee', the document reads: 'the application is processed by the Commission, recommended through the Honorable Minister of Information, to the President and Commander-in-chief of the Federal Republic of Nigeria for further consideration' (NBC). What this means is that despite the broadcast liberalisation, some control is still administered by the government, although indirectly through its set up media regulators. Adeleke (1988) expounded that since the state and a few capitalists own the media, they bring to bear significant levels of influence on the cultural workmen who are supposed to follow strictly and comply with the philosophical inclinations of their owners.

These forms of control continue to weaken the constitutional provisions for freedom of expression and press freedom. One could reasonably assert that the politically unstable atmosphere and the patterns of ownership have been too rigid to allow the media to fulfil their responsibilities in society. Besides, the nature of old media under both private and public ownership does not allow interactivity for political communication, citizen engagement and participation to thrive within civil society. Much of the use of the media under successive regimes has been one-sided, in favour of the state, which puts civil society and other non-state actors at a disadvantage. Adeleke (1988) argued that with the structural limitations of old media, the masses are expected to 'accept docily' whatever the authorities say (p. 47). Ultimately, with the influence of the state on the media, epitomised largely through the regulations and the repressive political atmosphere, the four republics of Nigeria's political history witnessed decreasing trust and reliance on old media under both public and private ownership.

2.3. Digital Economy, Media Infrastructure and Development

The challenges faced in the traditional mainstream media dispensation, especially with the limitations of access to civil society, low citizen engagement and participation dramatically changed with ICT development. The ICT revolution occurred concurrently with the transition to democracy in 1999. Interestingly, the last few years in Nigeria have witnessed an array of protests and rising conflict engineered by non-state actors including civil society and insurgency movements. The crucial thing to note is that new ICTs (the internet, social media, mobile phones and other tools) are playing a considerable role in mobilisations and other spheres of life in Nigeria. ICTs are gradually reversing the covert and overt limitations meted on traditional media during the pre-democratisation period. According to a 2012 Freedom House Report, the online media has reasonably been free from such constraints as censorship. The internet in concert with the rise of ICTs and other social media networks has brought significant advances in transforming political communication, in particular by advancing socio-political change and democratic reforms. These advances especially as it relates to the conflict are discussed in Chapters 3–5.

Nigeria like other countries on the African continent did not immediately tap into the benefits of the technological innovation. In Nigeria, the benefits of new ICTs and digital media was mostly felt in the aftermath of the democratic transition in the fourth republic from 1999. This period also marked the boom of mobile telecommunications and other ICTs. At this stage, the Nigeria digital infrastructure and ICT environment had undergone a gradual but steady growth and development with significant strides since the 1999 democratic transition. However, the socio-political and economic climate of the instability of the time emerged as a considerable obstacle. For instance, access to such ICTs was limited to those with means, that is, the political and economic elite. The economic inequality meant that only the rich and powerful in society could afford the luxury at the time, re-enacting the digital divide and digital inequality debate about access to ICTs (Hassani, 2006; Hilbert, 2010, 2013; Mossberger, 2003). As a result of the socio-economic gap, doubts emerged on the potential of new media technologies as tools for democracy, social reform and political change. The concern raised was whether any genuine transformation is possible without a shift in the long-standing digital gap (Obadare, 2006, pp. 95–96). This limitation meant the masses remained at a disadvantage since their economic background impeded them from enjoying the benefit of the innovations of ICTs.

At first, there was a steady increase in the rise of Cybercafés, which was the first point of access to the internet for Nigerian dissidents across various cities in Nigeria at the time. Again, a significant obstacle was the expensive tariffs that cybercafé owners charged, and connections were slow. The subsequent introduction of internet access by mobile phone service in 2004 dramatically increased access to the internet and its users in Nigeria (Freedom House, 2012, pp. 1–2). As at June 2000, following the transition, the Internet World Statistics (IWS) recorded an estimate of about 200,000 internet users. By June 2015, IWS recorded over 92 million internet users in Nigeria, which represents roughly over 51% of the total population which demonstrates that there have been significant developments between 2000 and 2015. Nigeria remains the hub for Internet use in Africa. With a surge in mobile phone use in the last 10 years, the Open Society Foundation (Akoh & Jagun, 2012, p. 17) report reveals that mobile phones are the primary medium of internet access in Nigeria.

Government's radical reforms in this area, especially introducing the internet on mobile phones, opened new platforms of communication for civil society, activists and individual political groups. Similarly, different group's can communicate dissent and advocacy aimed at impelling sociopolitical and economic development. Unlike traditional media, which has had covert and overt control before 1999, the state has not been able to exact similar patterns of censorship and control over online media. On the use of ICTs and online media, Karatzogianni (2006a, 2006b) explained that the avenue provides new opportunities for political actors once denied access to traditional mainstream means to punch above their weight.

Consequently, civil society and conflict groups in Nigeria have been taking advantage of ICTs (especially through the mobile cellular technology) for political communication and technological activism (communicating dissent, political mobilisation, whistle-blowing and for mobilising civil society) among other uses. With the uses of ICTs especially for facilitating mobilisation and collective action, the decrease in advocacy and dissent that resulted from the dictatorial period is being replaced with a positive spirit and opportunities to participate in political activity in Nigeria.

It is now much easier than in the pre-internet age to make information available online that would otherwise have been censored by traditional media. Hence, there is a general rise in whistle-blowers targeting classified information, rumours and sometimes innuendoes (Akoh & Jagun, 2012, p. 41).

As the empirical chapters will demonstrate, dissident movements using ICTs have become more aware of the privileges afforded by access to information provided through the internet and ICTs. To this extent, there is a new wave of resistance, protests and conflict brewing in cyberspace and within society in real-time. The technological revolution in contemporary Nigeria opened a new paradigm to civil society groups together with other political protests groups, including insurgency groups to bypass the restrictions of traditional mainstream media. Also, they can exploit online media and digital platforms as resources and weapons for the struggles for socio-political change, democratic reform and political communication in Nigeria. Resistance and protests have been on the rise in both online spaces and off-line spaces, with some form of interconnection between the former and the latter. What is particularly significant is how digital media technologies are shaping the nature of conflict in ways that were previously impossible.

The steady growth of the internet in Nigeria as the report of the International Telecommunication Union (ITU) revealed is also crucial for understanding user activity and penetration over the years. It further indicates a trajectory of a gradual shift from traditional mainstream media to online media by civil society in Nigeria. The ongoing change to ICTs has influenced a move towards convergence among conventional mainstream communication media. At least, all major newspaper organisations also own an online version of its newspapers and the electronic broadcast media including television and radio.

To conclude, the socio-political and economic drawbacks of the Nigerian political historical developments unveil the dynamics that underpin the dialectics of contentious activities emergent in contemporary Nigerian society. The instability in Nigeria can be located historically going as far back as the pre-colonial era and the colonial days to the brief spell of the civil rule at independence, to the dictatorial regime that followed to the current democratic dispensation. As demonstrated in this section, the mass media has been at the centre of contestation between civil society on the one hand and the opposition (in the case the state and government) on the other. The lot fell in favour of the authorities, given its ability to exercise control over traditional mainstream media, using both legal instruments and illicit means (by using force, arrests and torture).

The impact of repression was felt directly within civil society. Contentious activities, protests, rallies, demonstrations and conflict increasingly declined in the period leading to the democratic transition in 1999. In fact, there were no major contentious activities between 1993 and 1999 during a period characterised by the most repressive military dictatorship in the Nigerian political history. The wave of extrajudicial killings, arrests and torture increased, shutting down civil society and sending many activists, media stakeholders and pro-opposition forces into exile for been too vocal and critical of the government (Olukotun, 2002a, 2002b). One example of a political commentator who embarked on exile at the time is Professor Wole Soyinka, the Nobel Laureate in literature often described as Nigeria's national conscience. Interestingly, in exile, many Nigerians in the diaspora continued their advocacy, research on which I have conducted elsewhere (Olabode, 2016).

For fear of censorship, many media houses became the mouthpiece of the state carrying government propaganda and activities. As a result, they deviate from their role as the 'watchdog' of society. To this end, Nigerian conflict groups (civil society, social movements and insurgency movements) are seizing the opportunity availed by ICTs and other communication paraphernalia in contemporary Nigeria for advocacy. Chapters 4 to 6 address the use and role of digital media in conflict and other issues. This section has using a historical lens traced the developments in the political economy of communications in Nigeria. Ultimately, the unstable political history and economy are a prelude to the modern character of conflict in the Nigerian society. The motivations for conflict in modern Nigeria can be captured under three categories: sociopolitical, ethnoreligious and economic dimensions.

Chapter 3

Empirical Accounts of Digital Activism and Cyberconflicts

3.1. ICTs, Activism and Conflict

In the last few decades, youth engagement and activism have been rife across the globe even from developed to developing countries and in authoritarian contexts where protests were hitherto thought impossible. Recent events in sub-Saharan Africa also demonstrate an increasing trend in this phenomenon and a new wave of participation in politics among youths and dissident movements especially in national contexts where protests and conflict of any sort were hitherto thought impossible. While conflict has been integral to many successes in political struggles on the African continent, from the pre-independence and post-independent struggles to the dictatorial era and the current democratic transitions, nonetheless, the developments in ICT infrastructures have reignited debate and discussion on the role and uses of such new media tools. Williams and Mano (2017) explained that studies on African media audience and users are particularly crucial in the present time due to the strides in media developments on the continent in the last few decades. This chapter uses empirical evidence in an international context to underscore the debate on the use of ICTs as tools for youth engagement and activism using empirical cases. The chapter demonstrates the role played by ICTs in the struggles for socio-political reform and change from sub-Saharan Africa to examples from across other parts of the globe including in sub-Saharan Africa and in the light of the Karatzogianni 2006 CC framework. The discussion in this chapter is particularly crucial for the subsequent understanding of the notion of computer-mediated forms of communication (CMC) and conflict in Nigeria.

Information and communication technologies are those communicative tools and machinery that allow for two-way interaction between two or more groups. This includes the uses of computers, the internet, mobile phones and countless innovative applications for them, including 'new social media' such as FB and Twitter (Diamond, 2010, p. 70). Over the years, such communicative tools have become integrated into the activities of conflict movements. The intersection between ICTs and conflict attracted various terminologies, from notions of technological activism and digital activism to online activism, cyber protests, cyberactivism and CC (see Karatzogianni, 2006a, 2006b; Laer & Aelst 2010; McCaughey & Ayers, 2003; Meier, 2011; Van de Donk, 2004). While these terminologies are employed to imply conflicts facilitated by the use of ICTs, the internet and other everyday social media networks, in the present context, the study will draw on the CC concept. The concept of CC describes forms of protest emerging from real-life settings but are then transferred to cyberspace and vice versa (from cyberspace to real-life everyday setting). Using CC also helps to clear the ambiguities between peaceful protests and militarised insurgency and radical conflicts. Both dimensions are no new phenomenon, considering that such disputes have been on the increase across the globe since the beginning of the twenty-first century (see Garrett, 2006; Karatzogianni, 2009, 2013, 2015; Kavada, 2013, 2015; Meier, 2011; Morovoz, 2011a, 2011b).

Uses of technologies during conflict have a long history going back to the development of various communication media technologies that is electronic and print media. An illustrative example as demonstrated in the previous chapter is related to the struggles of the Nigerian media and civil society. Given the role of the media as a watchdog of society, they pressed for socio-political and economic reforms from the colonial era and various military regimes, to subsequent civilian administrations. In this regard, the media served as catalysts for change and reform in Nigeria. Media outlets and independent activists for advocacy and activism innovatively employed traditional communication media, in particular the printed press and radio, especially in the republic period between 1993 and 1999. Media advocacy and civil society activism during that period caused uneasiness on the part of the military leadership and contributed to the eventual pressure on the government to relinquish power. It is this perception that outlined Grosheck's (2010) exposition that advances in technologies of communication had given rise to the crucial tools and instruments of democracy (p. 142).

For Schudson (1999), the importance of communication tools for democracy dates as far back as the printing press and the role the medium played in enhancing democratic movements of the past. The same applies to similar communicative technologies of the past. For instance, radio was perceived as a potential tool for improving development as far back as 1899. Susan Douglas, a historian, wrote about radio in 1899; she explained that 'It was not at all clear how, or even if, corporations could own or manage [it]. It seemed that [this medium] might be the truly democratic, decentralised communication technology people had yearned for, a device each individual would control and use whenever he or she wanted, without tolls' (cited in Hargittai, 2001, p. 51).

Douglas shows optimism about the potential of the radio as a democratic platform, free from the autonomy of the state at the time. Radio was perceived as returning autonomy to the people, as an empowerment tool and a liberating technology.

Consequently, the notion of conflict movements (which include social movements and radical insurgency and militant movements), utilising new ICTs, the internet and other everyday social media as a resource or tools in contentious politics, is articulated as an extension of a long tradition of technological activism. The use of ICTs in conflict scenarios is amplified by the development of new technological innovations of communication media. Over the years, expansion of ICTs (such as cell phones, email and the World Wide Web) continued to attract discussion amongst various theorists on the role played by these technological innovations during conflicts. The debate over the role of ICTs in conflict has incrementally developed in the wake of the last decade where ICTs have either served as resources or weapons of warfare in conflicts and protests from Europe and the Arab world to different parts of Africa. For example, in the Arab world, the last decade has been characterised by computer-mediated conflicts in Bahrain, Syria, Lebanon, Libya and Tunisia to mention but a few countries where dissidents challenged authoritarianism (Castells, 2001; Karatzogianni, 2013; Kavada, 2015; Meier, 2011; Morovoz, 2011a, 2011b).

Despite these developments and their perceived effects on the nature of conflicts, a critical survey of the empirical evidence, journals, literature and ongoing discourse reveals different paradigms on the subject. As will be demonstrated, ICTs are playing a crucial role as tools for conflict movements in their struggles with the state, while at the same time, state authorities are increasingly using ICTs in conflict scenarios. The state can now more than before impedethe activities of conflict movements using ICTs to achieve their goals. It is, therefore, crucial to assess the role of ICTs during conflict, especially in view of the CC theoretical framework and recent movement activities across the globe (from Asia and Europe to the Middle East and Africa). This will provide the basis for understanding how these tools are empowering new forms of collective action and the role ICTs play in the activities of civil society actors, social movements, independent activists and armed insurgency conflict.

3.2. Youth Engagement and Digital Activism in Sub-Saharan Africa

In Africa, rapid digitalisation infrastructural developments in the last decade are inspiring a new form of youth engagement in politics mainly through digital activism. Although on the continent, issues of access still raise concerns, social media and in particular FB and Twitter are becoming more frequently used as a tool to advance the goals and activities of different groups in society. The latest Internet World Stats record showed an estimate of about 453,329,534 internet users on the continent in December 2017. The statistics also showed that Nigeria, Egypt, Kenya, Uganda, Ghana and South Africa to mention but a few are in the top ten internet user countries on the continent with mobile phones serving as the main access point for users.

Widespread conflict across Africa is in part connected to the developments in ICTs together with socio-political and economic dynamics that motivate conflict. As will be seen, there are commonalities in the underlying modus operandi of various youth-led movements on the continent, although with varying impacts. To understand the current conflicts on the continent, it is crucial to comment on the period of development in the ICT infrastructure on the continent that coincided with youth activism. For one, Mano (2017) explained that most African countries had experienced spectacular growth in access and availability of both mass media devices and digital technologies in the last few decades. This development in mobile telephony which now serves as the primary access point for citizens accessing the internet, social media and indeed traditional mainstream media including radio and television advances our understanding of the rapidly spreading youth engagement in politics albeit through activism in recent years on the continent.

Mano (2017) argues that the growth in internet access is mainly because of affordances in internet-enabled mobile phones. Similar factors are engendering new forms of digital cultures and youth engagement, that is, one informed by ICTs. Several indices and statistics demonstrate the growth in information and communication technologies over the last two decades and the quest by users to be online. Such an index shows youths on the continent at the forefront of internet users not only in Africa but also across the globe. The 2017 International Telecommunication Union report put the percentage of youths accessing the internet between the age of 15 and 24 at 71% which is considerably more significant than the rest (48%) of the entire population using the internet. In Africa, 'at the end of 2015, 46% of the population in Africa subscribed to mobile services, equivalent to more than half a billion people' (GSMA, Mobile Economy Africa, 2016, p. 2). According to the GSMA (2016) report, Egypt, Nigeria and South Africa are the three principal markets in the region and account for about a third of the region's overall subscriber base.

There has also been a sharp rise in the number of mobile internet subscribers in Africa. This has tripled in the last five years to 300 million in the last quarter of 2015 (GSMA, 2016, p. 3). The rise in internet figures has also led to increase in social media uses on the continent with roughly 11% of the population, which represent about 125 million people, subscribing to FB in the last quarter of 2015 (Mano, 2017). The expansive developments in digital and other ICT infrastructure explain the rise in digital activism and as a result increased youth engagement on the continent. This section takes us through some instances of activism against the backdrop of ICTs in sub-Saharan African countries, the aim being to demonstrate how the ICT tools are serving as tools for promoting social reform and change.

3.2.1. Mobilising Structures and ICTs

Mobilisation is an essential element of conflict movements whose core objective includes the formation of networks encompassing groups of individuals who share a common goal (Caramani, 2014, p. 269). Usually, these goals will consist of organising and mobilising political action within a community with the specific aim of enforcing socio-political and economic reform or change through collective action (Caramani, 2014, p. 269). McCarthy (1996) explained that RMT helps in articulating how mobilising structural forms develop, as well as how they are selected, combined and adopted by social movements activists. Mobilisation structure, therefore, refers to a deliberate attempt by an individual, group or movement to put in place a system to facilitate conflict.

According to McCarthy (1996), such mechanisms include social structures and tactical repertoires. Another commentator explains that the mobilisation structure is targeted at creating movement's structures, preparing and carrying out conflict actions (Rucht cited in McAdam, McCarthy, & Zald, 1996, p. 186). From Brown's (2000) point of view, the process entails one actor gaining the support of another, thereby enhancing their resource during the conflict. It is a mechanism drawn to facilitate citizen engagement in view to drawing a passive group into a contentious political event (cited in Karatzogianni, 2006a, 2006b, p. 59). The literature suggests that ICTs and similar technologies play a role in mobilising structures and likewise in the opportunity structure and the framing process of movements, as will be demonstrated in succeeding paragraphs. As pointed out by Karatzogianni (2006a, 2006b), the role played by ICT is encouraged by the open, decentralised, non-hierarchical nature of new social movement (NSM) which makes them ideal for internet communications. To adequately assess the role of ICTs and corresponding applications of social media networks on the nature of mobilisation, the CC framework further divides mobilisation structures into sub-categories including organisation, participation levels, recruitment, tactics and goals.

With regard to participation levels, there is a definite correlation between ICTs and participation levels during conflict events. In other words, ICTs play a crucial role in increasing participation levels in both socio-political and ethnoreligious conflicts. The literature and empirical evidence have demonstrated how in the technological revolution era, the relatively low cost of participation owing to the availability of ICTs has had an effect on participation levels during conflicts (Della Porta & Mosca, 2005; Diani, 2000; Garrett, 2006; Karatzogianni, 2006a, 2006b; Kavada, 2012; Meier, 2011). Participation here refers to the level of support, physical involvement and engagement in movement activities. With access to ICTs and the internet in both developed and developing countries, conflict movements are able to more efficiently create and manage a decentralised network which allows those who are connected to virtual networks communicate dissent, resistance and carry out advocacy whilst also mobilising a cyber or real-life community of dissidents (Karatzogianni, 2006a, 2006b, p. 61). According to Karatzogianni (2006a, 2006b), political organisations that are vast and resource-rich, including being well connected to party and government politics, may rely on internet-based communications mostly to strengthen and lessen the cost of already established communication practices (p. 61).

Speaking further on the effect of the low cost of ICTs on participation levels, the impact is felt more by smaller conflict movements with limited resources and less money. ICTs have proven useful for such groups especially in the attempt to mobilise and organise individuals to participate in their struggle for change. Ordinary citizens are empowered to surf the web, manage sites, find information and contribute to the political discourse on issues that affect them. The process is less complicated and technical than traditional mainstream media except of course in cases of very low literacy and digital exclusion. Shirky (2008) explained that besides the cost-lowering effect of ICTs, the tools advanced by these innovations make them better, more productive for innovative uses and more flexible and easier to manoeuvre in comparison to traditional communication media (television/radio/newspapers). Consequently, more conflict groups have found an alternative ground to participate in the political process by organising collective action, before which, only more affluent, more powerful and formal organisations could afford the tools (Shirky, 2010b). Boncheck (1997) also advocates that the decreased costs of communication and coordination of ICTs encourage group formation, recruitment and retention, and at the same time movement effectiveness is enhanced. Regarding recruitment, conflict movements are benefiting from the lower cost of ICTs. Just as new ICTs have employed 'millions of new consumers, ICTs present an important recruitment mechanism for social movements—one that is not addressed in the traditional literature' (Meier, 2011, p. 38). For instance, from the Tunisia revolution of 2010, 2009 Iceland protests and Egyptian revolution of 2011 to the 2011 Indignados in Spain and 2011 Occupy Wall Street protests, ICTs played a crucial role in the mobilisation and recruitment of participants throughout the affected countries.

3.2.2. *The Arab Uprising*

The 'Arab Spring' provides us with the most recent account of computer-mediated conflict on the continent. 'Arab Spring' is a phrase used to define a movement that swept across parts of the Middle East and North Africa between 2010 and 2013. The movement marked a defining moment in the specific context of digital activism not just on the African continent, but also across the globe. The starting point for the Arab uprisings was in Tunisia when, in protest, Mohamed Bouazizi, a 26-year-old trader, set himself ablaze following a brawl between him and security operatives over trading permits. Bouazizi's protests subsequently ignited widespread protest within the Tunisian society. A report by the National Public Broadcasting Inc (2011) pointed out that Bouaziz's protest reverberated spontaneously with dissidents across the country. The protest moved from what began as a revolt against the coercive approach of security operatives to demands for the resignation of President Zine El Abidine and his regime. 'About a month later, he fled' (National Public Broadcasting Inc, 2011). The Tunisia protest became an incentive for protests that erupted across the region and beyond (Egypt, Libya, Syria, Yemen, Algeria, Jordan, Morocco, Iraq, Kuwait and Oman). In Egypt, 'the Egyptian revolution' as it has come to be known internationally started on 25 January 2011 and spread throughout the Egyptian society. The 18 days protest forced the Hosni Mubarak regime out of power. 'The Egyptian revolution was dramatized, in the wake of the Tunisian example, by a series of self-immolations [...] to protest the rise of food prices that left many hungry' (Castells, 2011, p. 54). Nonetheless, multiple issues culminated into what became the Egyptian revolution. Egyptians were tired of the endemic oppressive culture that permeated the political fabrics that made up the Egyptian society. These included decades of 'oppression, injustice, poverty, unemployment, sexism, mockery of democracy, and police brutality' (Castells, 2011, p. 53). Similar situations also influenced the widespread anger and dissent that ensued in the Tunisian revolution. But more importantly is the fact that in all the other conflicts that emerged in the 'Arab spring' region, similar factors were also responsible for the grievances and subsequent demand for system change or complete overhauling of regimes. In the period preceding much of the conflicts in the regions, the region had been under authoritarianism and absolutism (Castells, 2011, p. 1).

In the affected Arab countries, social media applications including FB, Twitter and YouTube, were deployed innovatively by movement leaders to make calls for action, as well as provide and distribute information, which in turn provided impetus and the desired drive for citizen participation in the events. In Tunisia for example, movement actors disseminated videos of protests and police brutality over the internet and made calls to action in strategic locations around the country (Castells, 2001, p. 23). There was an immediate response to the calls to action with solidarity formed and protestors staging various occupations across the country (Castells, 2001, p. 23).

In the Egyptian as in the Tunisian case, the tremendous outpouring of citizens onto the streets and the protests that led to the occupation of Tahrir square cannot be detached from the use of ICTs, the internet and social media. In the Egyptian revolution, various solidarity networks were also formed around social media to build momentum for the revolution. Notable among such networks on social media include the FB group which amassed about 70,000 followership and the FB group 'We are all Khaled Said' (Castells, 2001, p. 54). Abroad, networks of solidarity were formed online by Egyptians to support Egyptians at home, from the 'Voice of Egypt Abroad' to the 'Egyptians Abroad in Support of Egypt' and 'New United Arab States' (Eltantawy & Wiest, 2011, p. 1217). These networks of solidarity formed in real life (offline) subsequently transferred to online networks, with dissidents physically occupying various strategic areas. Protesters used ICTs and online media to generate support for the movement by circulating audio-visual images of police harassment. A point in the case was the murder of a protestor who had broadcast an audio-visual material exposing police exploitation (Iskhandar, 2010). According to Castells (2001), the FB groups and several other groups that emerged online during the uprising called for their sympathisers and supporters to join in the protest. Movement actors called on dissidents to protest in front of the Ministry of Interior and show dissent against the inhumane activities of the Egyptian security operatives. For fear of government surveillance, other movement actors circulated pamphlets anonymously educating dissidents on how the authorities were monitoring their online activities, dissuading them from using online media and using the same platform (leaflets) to provide information on planned protests (see Black, 2011).

ICTs have also played a crucial role in the empowerment of forms of engagement with the state and among networks. It is not particularly surprising that civil society groups, social movements and other conflict movements (insurgents) have a long-standing role in engaging the government through political debate, raising public opinion and advocacy: 'many are new and exist because the Internet has facilitated the interaction and organization of like-minded citizens' (Howard, 2010, p. 140). Mario Diani (2000) reiterates that as a result of the affordability of new ICTs, a broad base of inactive publics in society is provided with a low-intensity space in cyberspace to interact, thereby reinforcing their sense of collective identity and loyalty with particular movements (cited in Meier, 2011, p. 38). In a different account, Howard explained:

> The disruptive use of ICTs in repressive environments is no longer the unique provenance of isolated, politically motivated hackers. It is instead deeply integrated with contemporary social movement strategy and accessible to computer and mobile phone users with only basic skills: it is a distinguishing feature of modern political communication, and a means of creating the élan that marks social change.
>
> Howard (2010, p. 11)

Another interesting point to observe in connection with mobilising structures and the role of ICTs is that the latter inspires the formation of communities in cyberspace, one which is reflective of real-life settings. Besides the reduced cost of participation which is crucial for conflict movements using ICTs, Garrett (2006) also describes the promotion of collective identity and creation of community in what can be described as the role availed by ICTs during conflict. In this context, interaction between activists, resistance and protest movements are fostered 'through automated mailing lists that distribute announcements, online discussion forums such as chat rooms, message boards, text/instant messaging, and links to the webring of affinity groups with like-minded objectives' (Chen et al., 2008, p. 135). This point connects with the strategies of conflict movements, and aptly reflects the practices of protesters during the Arab uprisings, Occupy Wall Street and other examples cited in previous paragraphs. For instance, in the 2009 Iranian election, contestants and opposition parties were said to have employed FB to create a sense of community and inclusion for their followers (Howard et al., 2011, p. 41). The high tariffs that normally come with a subscription to mainstream communication media (Television/Radio and Newspapers) make them expensive and mostly unaffordable for individual activists, civil society and social movements to afford such media in concert with other issues such as media affiliation and censorship. For instance, the cost of running and managing 'Radio Kudirat' contributed to the subsequent demise of the former radio station (Olukotun, 2002a, p. 326). Similarly, as demonstrated in Chapter 1, in restrictive environments (dictatorial regimes), access to such media would be even more difficult.

Moreover, some studies conjecture that ICTs and Web 2.0 make it possible to harness and connect transnational networks (Brainard & Siplon, 2000; Elin, 2003). Although some theorists have contended this perception, for Hampton (2003), even everyday social networks providing only feeble connections encourage contentious politics and political protests (Garrett, 2006, p. 209). According to Karatzogianni (2006a, 2006b), ICTs may not necessarily alter the very logic of collective action. However, they affect the structure of political mobilisations. With networks, Tormey (2004) demonstrated that the onus is on engagement. Networks encourage the formation of momentary associations, coalitions, agreements and interaction between proponents in a conflict. In his words, 'a network consists of chains of allegiance and intersection or what are sometimes called nodal points; where there is convergence to act in support of some group or cause' (Tormey, 2004, p. 159).

A sense of community in a contentious political situation is a particularly significant factor, without which some participants, independent activists and individuals will feel insecure to partake in political protests. Meier (2011) explained that 'social ties' is an essential feature for 'recruiting and catalysing a movement engaged in high-risk activism' (p. 46). The importance of this element in the mobilisation process is not unconnected to the idea that individuals would be more likely to demonstrate loyalty to and join particular movements with an existing personal connection like friends and families who are already members of such movements or cause (Meier, 2011, p. 46). Gladwell's (2010) seminal study of an Italian terrorist group of the 1970s 'Red Brigades' revealed that 76% of participants enlisted into the movement had a friend who was in the group before their involvement. Moreover, the literature suggests that 'collaborative communities never get off the ground without a core group of leaders who establish the vision and community values, help manage group interactions, championing the cause, and attract more people to the ecosystem' (Tapscott & Williams, 2010, p. 301).

The role played by ICTs in the tactical repertoire of conflict movements during the mobilisation process is another 'key issue to focus on when analysing mobilisation structures in NSM' (Karatzogianni, 2006a, 2006b, p. 62). Thus, the question is whether or not the presence of ICTs has altered popular tactics of protest movements and how new media is revolutionising these. The tactical repertoire is conceived as how (the mechanism employed) political dissidents 'mobilising supporters, neutralising and transforming mass and elite publics into sympathisers'. The influence of ICTs on the tactics of movements is not particularly a new phenomenon. It is a continuation of a normal trend. For instance, about the information revolution that was heralded by the printing press, one commentator explained that the innovation of the printing press played a crucial role in the intellectual and political chaos in Europe which ended in the 1600s (Shirky, 2008, p. 73). Also, Ronfeldt and Varda (2008) asserted that 'the printing press and later technologies, like the telephone and radio, did not prevent new and even worse forms of autocracy from arising' (p. 12).

In modern times, we have seen across different contexts how ICTs play different roles in mobilisation. Howard et al. (2011) with regard to Kyrgyzstan's Tulip Revolution of March 2005 explained that mobile phones were again used to organise activists to join the protests at critical moments, thereby helping democratic leaders build a social movement with sufficient clout to oust the president. Kuwait's women's suffrage movement was much more successful in 2005 than it had been in 2000, in part because it was able to use text messaging to call younger protesters out of school to attend demonstrations (Howard et al., 2011, p. 3). In Egypt, Tunisia and Kazakhstan, dissenting movements that were affected by state repression (censorship) simply transferred their online activities to servers in other countries. In Turkey and Malaysia, polls revealed the role of blogging in cementing democratic organisations. Some opposition candidates who used blogging as an integral element of their strategy during the campaign trail triumphed over candidates belonging to the government of the day who downplayed the potential of the online tools (see Howard, 2010; Meier, 2011).

Rheingold (2003) and Shirky (2010a, 2010b) in separate accounts also commented on the role of ICTs during the conflict that resulted in the ousting of President Estrada of the Philippines in what has come to be known as a 'Coup de Text'. This is an illustrative example of how numerous text messages were employed innovatively in mobilising both public opinion and protests that subsequently led to the ousting of the president (cited in Meier, 2011). The benefits of ICTs (mobile phone in this case) were felt strongly such that using the medium of text messaging for advocacy helped to generate support and urged the political upper class (the ruling elite) to act in desired ways that the dissenters intended. Another interesting scenario illustrated by Rheingold (2003) and Shirky (2010a, 2010b) in supporting the idea that ICTs play a seminal role in the political landscape highlighted the Madrid bombing case of 2004. The literature suggests that a reasonable part of the organisation of the protests in Madrid emerged through the uses of text messaging via SMS. The efficient use of the medium eventually accelerated the exit of the Spanish Prime Minister at the time.

Half a decade after the organising and advocacy of SMS, the emergence of social media network applications once again demonstrated a continuous drive by social movements and activists to adopt newer technologies of communication and the applications that accompany them to enhance their mobilisations. In Moldova, Shirky (2010a, 2010b) explained that immense protests were organised and coordinated with SMS and contemporary online media networks, including FB and Twitter, following the purportedly rigged elections in 2009. As in the example earlier, individuals and activist have a habit of reverting to digital online media and communication paraphernalia to express their grievances and organise political protests, more so because of the failing trust in traditional mainstream media due to limitations (imposed and inherent) on the medium. During the Madrid protests in 2004, the now widely predominant technological innovations and social media networks were not in as much force at that time. These explain the reason for the widespread uses of SMS (via mobile phones) in the Madrid conflict. Five years later, in the event of the Moldovan protests, we see ICTs' continuities. Everyday social media and new ICTs in concert with Web 2.0 play a central role in the protests. The use of social networks such as FB and Twitter together with SMSs characterised the Moldovan protests. The implication was huge as seen in the increase in participation and the mobilisation of a massive conflict in the country.

More recently, the events surrounding the Arab uprisings further affirmed the notion of the perceived role of ICTs and online media networks as a resource and weapon for contentious politics. In his article on the 'Twitter revolution: how social media helped the Arabs spring', Kassim (2012) found that social networking was pivotal to activist roles during the conflicts. In the 'Cyberconflict analysis of the "Arab Spring" uprisings', Karatzogianni (2012a, 2012b, 2012c) reveals that 'digital networked everyday media and social media networks were used in creative ways to connect the protest both internally and externally […] and to plan and accelerate protest mobilisations' (p. 2). Indeed, these digital networks were particularly crucial in Jordan, Yemen, Egypt and Tunisia, where FB and Twitter were prominent during the protests. One commentator who was involved in the Arab Spring echoes this point. He explained that they used FB to schedule the protests, Twitter to coordinate and YouTube to tell the world about an Arab Spring uprising from Egypt (Shearlaw, 2016 citing Rashed, 2011). His statement reflects how social movements utilise ICTs and other online media for advocacy, protests, resistance and activism. Karatzogianni's (2013) citing the Arab Social Media Report (2011) explained that during the period following January–April, the use of social media networks such as FB within the Arab region tremendously increased, and on some occasions, the use of such platforms doubled the average trend.

Huang (2011) succinctly captures the aforementioned position. In his exploration of the peak usage of Twitter and FB in the region at the time, Huang found that almost all Egyptians and Tunisians interviewed argued that they used FB to plan protests or disseminate information in view to creating awareness about the events. In Egypt, Libya and Bahrain, tweets relating to protest were found to be the most prevalent tweets coming from the Arab region during the period (between January and March 2011) of revolt (see Huang, 2011). FB and Twitter contributed to the call to action and the day-to-day activities of the movement. Huang (2011) explained that among the bulk of roughly 200 individuals surveyed during the uprising, 88% Egyptians and 94% Tunisians revealed that they became aware of the protests because of information shared through social media. Huang (2011) report revealed that the information on social media outstripped information that was been obtained from other traditional mainstream media sources. For instance, information received through nongovernmental local media was put at 63% in Egypt and 86% in Tunisia while for foreign media 57% in Egypt and 48% in Tunisia. The awareness generated by ICTs reflects the increasing shift from traditional mainstream media (television, newspapers and radio) to new ICTs and the growing importance of ICTs. As one would expect in contentious situations as in the present case, the affected governments attempt to repress information by blocking social media sites during the uprisings is indicative of the perceived influence of ICTs. Such attempts failed and added momentum to the protests as people became more active, especially in finding alternative ways to communicate and organise their activities (Beaumont, 2011; Channel 4, 2011; Howard et al., 2011; Huang, 2011).

Nonetheless, as Kassim referring to the Arab uprising pointed out, social media did not stimulate cause. However, it was pivotal in facilitating the revolution. Ultimately, these theorists advocate the view that ICTs and social media networks offer an alternative channel for mobilising political protests, communicating dissent and instigating social change in dictatorial and democratic settings. For instance, Hands (2011) explained that in response to widespread protests in Iran in 2009, following allegations of electoral fraud, the 'Twitter Blog' on Monday, 15 June 2009 suspended its planned closure for maintenance. The perceived role of ICTs, the internet and corresponding applications such as Twitter in facilitating communication and protest events at the time formed the basis for the decision of the government. As the *New York Times* revealed, Iranians were blogging, posting to FB and mostly coordinating their protests on Twitter (Stone & Cohen, 2009, cited in Hands, 2011). Social media facilitated instant broadcast of events including reportage of:

> Unrest, street protests and images of youth thronging the streets, chanting demands for election results to be fairly recognized and taking on the phalanxes of armed police, were, were flashed around the world. The tagline of the story, in tune with increasing awareness of the social networking phenomenon of Twitter, was the notion that this was a radically new kind of protest, coordinated online in real time and producing a new kind of collective intelligence.
>
> Hands (2011, p. 1)

3.2.3. *From #RhodesMustFall to #FeesMustFall – South Africa*

The momentum garnered in the Arab uprising continued to inspire the rise of similar movements across sub-Saharan Africa. Not only did the Arab protests serve as a stimulus, but it also ignited protests rooted in digital cultures. Dissident youth movements in different African countries have also taken to ICTs and in particular social media as a means for activism on issues relating to socio-political reform and change within their respective national contexts. The #RohodesMustFall (hence #RMF) and #FeesMustFall are South African movements that sprung on university campuses in South Africa between 2015 and 2016. In the first case, that is, #RMF, the protest started when students at the University of Cape Town demanded the removal of the erstwhile British colonialist, Cecil John Rhodes, from the Cape Town University Campus. The student-led movement sought to challenge the issue of racism which is an institutionalised (Bosch, 2016, pp. 1–4) problem within the South African society. The apartheid struggles of the late 1980s to the 1990s bear testament to the complexities around the issue of racial divides in the country. This kind of protests is not a surprise given the country's political history; it is more surprising that collective action around racism has not been more recurrent (Bosch, 2016, p. 2). The #RMF protest subsequently moved beyond institutional racism to broader social and political issues that affected ordinary citizens. The #FeesMustFall movement also took a cue from the #RMF protests, as it emerged within the same period between 2015 and 2016. The protests had a clear cause that indicated a struggle against the increased cost of tuition fees in South African universities and the increasing plight of the ordinary citizens. Again, it was a student-led protest, only that it was more extensive and included civil society (broadly defined). Student protests against an increase in tuition fees in post-apartheid South Africa are not unusual (Langa, 2017, p. 6), similar to other parts of the continent. However, Langa (2017) explained that traditional mainstream media seldom reported such events. In the present case, however, the student-led protests gained momentum and quickly spread throughout the country (Langa, 2017, p. 6).

The two cases provide an illustrative example of how social media can shape contemporary activist activities. Although South Africa enjoys a broad appeal to social media, that is Twiter, FB and YouTube, in the present context, Twitter was the main rallying point for activists in the #RMF and #FMF protests as it played a crucial role. Twitter allowed the conversation to develop among activists in the #RMF protests. 'Debates and discussions about the removal of the monument took place in several online and offline spaces, but at the height of the debate, social networking sites became central to the organisation of the campaign' (Bosch, 2016, p. 3). Such discussions were coordinated using the hashtag #RhodesMustFall. The platform was instrumental in galvanising local and national support for the cause in both online and offline spaces.

> Social media discussions on Twitter specifically and the resultant emerging networked public of #RMF successfully set the agenda for public debate in other virtual and real-world spaces including campus workshops and meetings, as well as mainstream print and broadcast media; and that the Twitter discourse also played a key role in public perception of the movement.
>
> Bosch (2016, p. 2)

Turning to the #FMF, Twitter was also the central tool in the student-led movement employed to advance their cause. As in the #RMF protests, Bosch (2016) explained that students adopted the medium as a means for organising the demonstrations as an avenue for nation-wide deliberations and discussions around broader issues. Quintal (2015) argued that messages about the protest were circulated via social networking sites including on FB: 'a message started doing the rounds on social networking site Facebook threatening a total shutdown at Rhodes University in Grahamstown' (Quintal, 19 Oct, 2015 Mail and Guardian online). Such messages served as a stimulus for students to participate, and in doing so, created the momentum for the movement that quickly became national. Pictures and other audio-visual images were also disseminated on social media to establish their grievances. For instance, during the protests, a trending picture which circulated on social media was a placard reading 'Our parents were sold a dream in 1994 [...] and so we are here for a refund' (Maringira & Gukurume, 2017, p. 38). Other placards disseminated on social media carried wider issues and concerns (corruption, inequalities and police brutality prevalent in the South African Society, to mention but a few). Besides the #RMF and #FMF, there have also been other notable protests organised around hashtags in the country, that is, #ZumaMustFall protest, #Paybackthemoney protest and #SaveSaProtests, to mention but a few.

The use of ICTs in the two contexts proved useful for students to organise and mobilise collective action online, one that impacts on offline physical occupations. The rise of youth engagement in South Africa, mainly through activism in the wake of ICTs and other ICT developments, shows the growing importance of ICTs for pushing development in transitioning democracies. van Eeden Taljaard and Borchardt (2013) traced increasing youth engagement in the country to the advent of the adoption of the .za domain. They argue that social media experienced growth on an unprecedented level mainly due to rapid advancement in internet development and access. Hence, advances in ICTs infrastructure have been responsible for new forms of digital cultures in the South African society, one that is inspiring a youth consciousness and involvement in the polity in the last decade. As Sternberg (2014) points out, the innovative uses of ICTs are carving out spaces of freedom and moments of free communication. This point is crucial especially against the backdrop of controls of traditional mainstream media. With ICTs, '[...] youth [...] articulate their consciousness of their social, cultural and political world' (Sternberg, 2014, p. 56).

3.2.4. Congo Protests and Social Media

Other parts of Africa have also been witnessing waves of protests and other forms of youth engagements shaped around social media in the last decade. This protest also has social, political and economic undertones, and the antagonist has been authorities in government. For instance, in Congo, the National Public Radio (online) news headline in 2016 read 'Congo to Block Social Media Sites Ahead of Protests against the President' (Kennedy, 2016). According to Kennedy (2016), the government under the auspices of President Joseph Kabila had perceived the influence of social media and had therefore instructed service providers to block access to sites such as FB, Twitter, YouTube, Skype and LinkedIn. The contention was over Kabila's failure to relinquish power after 15 years in power. Mvemba Phezo Dizolele of the Johns Hopkins School of Advanced International Studies stated 'the Constitution only allows him two terms, five years each. And now he's trying to wiggle his way to stay for longer' (National Public Radio, Online, 16 December 2016). A momentum of dissent had been developing on social media, and the only way this could be stopped from translating into a full-blown national crisis was to curb the people's access to information and ability to mobilise, shape and influence public discourse. It was not the first time the government would take such action. 'During violent riots in January 2015, the authorities ordered a total 48-hour shutdown of the internet, but the measure completely paralysed the economy, mainly because banks were unable to complete transactions' (Daily Mail Online, 15 December 2016). Congo is not the first country to block social media during protests; in fact, it is a popular tactical strategy of government authorities in computer-media environments.

In 2016, Gabonese authorities blocked the internet and by implication corresponding applications including social media. The blockade followed the conflicted presidential election that saw the reflection of President Ali Bongo Odimba's incumbent government (Searcey & Barry, 1 September 2016, New York Times, Online). Also, Matfess (2016) argued that in Ethiopian's, Chadian's, and Ugandan's, there have been a crackdown on social media and users particularly during elections. Similarly, the use of force by security apparatuses of the state during conflict is not a new phenomenon. Governments in both developed and developing societies have explored the use of coercion as an approach to silence dissent. In the current case, protests went ahead in different parts of the country in spite of the clampdown of social media and subsequent use of coercion by the security apparatuses of the state.

3.2.5. Ousting Zimbabwean Mugabe

The fourth quarter of the year 2017 saw the ousting of one of Africa's longest serving presidents, Robert Mugabe, who had remained in power since the transition from the British colonialists for a total of about 37 years. Several factors contributed to terminating the ambitions of President Robert Mugabe from continuing to rule the southern African country. For instance, decades of economic downturn, political instabilities and other social problems (repression and suppression of dissent and attack on political rights and civil liberties) contributed to the anger and outrage of Zimbabweans over Mugabe's relentless efforts to exercise rule in the alienated country. David Seddon in a blog article for the *Review of African Political Economy* succinctly captures the socio-economic and political issues that culminated in the present crisis. For instance, in spite of the burgeoning economy Mugabe inherited at independence, 'Zimbabwe is the region's crisis point'. In 2009, Zimbabwe's currency deteriorated into hyperinflation that made the country adopt the dollar as its primary means of exchange. About a recent (2017) study by Research Advocacy Unit (RAU), David Seddon explained that most prominent was a pattern of violence and intimidation that became exposed under President Robert Mugabe. Therefore, following the military incursion in November 2017 in what has come to be known as 'a coup that was not a coup':

> The reaction from the public was immediate and almost universally joyful. There were celebrations from the crowds in the streets, and it seemed clear that whatever their status or political persuasion, the people of Zimbabwe were pleased to see 'the old man' go, and looked forward to a new era of change.
>
> David Seddon, *Review of African Political Economy*, 11 January 2018

Social media played a crucial role during the protests especially in spreading information. In an article for inews.co.uk, Dr Winston Mano, Director of the Africa Media Centre at the University of Westminster, explained that social media was used to disseminate the military's activities and 'bold challenge to their leader and ruling party' to a local and international audience. Zimbabwean dissidents were also able to debate, discuss and negotiate meaning to the message of the military on Twitter, FB and WhatsApp, which provided an alternative platform for public opinion to rise in the milieu of repression and control of traditional mainstream media in the country. Mano explained that:

> The […] the political crisis in Zimbabwe has witnessed a dramatic shift in how the county's citizens access information during crisis.

> […] there was an absence of state media coverage of the Zimbabwe national army address in which the army stated that it was not going to 'hesitate' to intervene.
>
> Winston Mano, inews.co.uk, 17 November 2017, referring to the subsequent 'coup that was not a coup'

In 2014 the public demonstrated outrage through protests, mainly led by youths and civil society in Burkina Faso following attempts by President Blaise Campore to amend the constitution to favor another tenure in office after 27 years in power. The 'Burkinabe Protests' as it was called at the time quickly spread throughout the society (David Seddon, Review of the African Political Economy). According to the Guardian African Network, hundreds of thousands of people participated in the protests which forced Campore to jettison his plans to amend the constitution for a further three terms in office. In the ensuing conflict, Harsch (2015) explained that President Campore fled into exile. The vacuum that had been created in government led to the subsequent formation of a National Unity Government. The situation in Burkina Faso is not very different to the scenario in the previous cases examined. The main source of contention revolves around the sit-tight attitude of some presidents on the continent in the midst of economic woes and political instabilities. Social media and the internet also played a role in the protests. #Burkina, #lwili and #faso were a popular choice of hashtags deployed during the protests as a means of forming collective identity and organisation. The internet and social media provided a platform for sharing and obtaining information in the Burkinabe uprising.

> Followed on Twitter by journalists and protestors, and with live reports streaming on Radio Omega FM Ouaga's online station, this 'revolution 2.0' has been called a victory by the Burkinabè opposition.
>
> Guardian African Network (*The Guardian*, Online, 30 October 2014)

The government also saw the importance of ICTs and made efforts to relate to citizens via social media mainly to calm protestors. For instance, the president at the peak of the protest tweeted 'Chers Compatriotes Burkinabè, je lance un appel au calme et la sérénité', which was a text appealing to Burkina Faso citizens to remain calm during the protests. Similarly, following the cancellation of the proposed amendments to the constitution which would have seen the electoral law amended, the Communication Minister, Alain Edouard Traore, shared the news via social media.

> The Government informs the entire population of the cancellation of the examination of the draft law amending the Constitution. #cnn
>
> @Burkina24

In April 2015, dissidents in Burundi also revolted instigated by President Pierre Nkurunziza's attempt to seek re-election for a third term in office. This incident started protests with a ripple effect across the country. According to David Seddon, the protest lasted for about three weeks. The conflict saw both peaceful protests and riots in different parts of the country. Again, the influence of the internet and social media was felt strongly across Burundi. Like in South Africa, Seddon explained that social media platforms were influential in the mobilisation, even though the issues motivating protest were different in the two countries. While in South Africa, racial matters ignited the protests followed by socio-economic and political concerns, in the present case, the main problems as with Zimbabwe, Congo and Burkina Faso are in relation to socio-political and long-held economic grievances. Dissidents, especially the youths in Burundi, used social media as a means for sharing information and mobilisation. Given the impact of the media, Yusuf (2015) explained the reason for the Burundian government's shutdown of traditional mainstream media, that is, privately owned radio station, Radio Publique Africaine, and restricted access to social media websites used to organise and mobilise protestors against the president's ambition to continue for a third term.

> Patrick Wasso, RPA's presenter and producer, said he is angry he can no longer do his work. 'I feel sad today I cannot speak to my listeners and the public. I cannot go to the field to collect news and tell people what is happening around them', Wasso said.
>
> Yusuf (2015, Voice of Africa News (Online), May 3)

The benefits of ICTs cut across protest and insurgency conflict movements. Despite the repressive attitude of the Chinese authorities towards media freedoms, Yang (2009) found that 82% of 129 civil society organisations surveyed in China were at the time connected to the internet including 65% hosting their website. As a result, he asserted that the increasingly growing presence of the ICTs and internet connectivity expedite the activities (including interactivity) of the surveyed civil society groups. This is crucial for dissident movements that emerged to challenge authoritarianism in the Arab world. The reason has been that the affected 'countries were in different stages of digital development' (Karatzogianni, 2013). The burgeoning digital infrastructure in the affected Arab countries further inspired mobilisations. However, Karatzogianni (2013) already points to structural factors such as neoliberal adjustment policies, precarious labour processes, the role of the military, the fragmentation of grievances, ethnic cleavages and weak support for regimes as the actual causal factors for revolutions; at the same time, the uprisings failed to affect social change and resulted in regime change in most cases.

Speaking further on the benefits of ICTs for mobilisation, Howard (2010) argues that ICTs have played a seminal role in the organisation of radical youth movements which by employing innovative protest tactics were able to destabilise dictatorial regimes. An excellent example of this can be demonstrated in the Arab uprisings from Tunisia, Egypt, Libya, Jordan and Bahrain, to mention but a few.

The Arab revolution provides an illustrative example of how interconnection between ICTs, social movements and protests informed system change in the Arab world and North Africa between 2010 and 2012. Arquilla and Ronfeldt (2001) shed more light on the discourse, explaining that new tactics exploited by protest movements display 'several shared characteristics that derive, at least in part, from their reliance on loosely coupled networks of individuals and groups, which are made more feasible by new ICTs' (p. 2). Furthermore, Tilly (1978) demonstrates how it takes such macro-historical factors as the rise of the nation-state and the emergence of new communication technologies to engender novel forms of protest. The benefit of such an approach is that the new protest approach and innovative uses that come with the new ICTs can quickly catch the state off guard, thereby creating a severe political effect in comparison to previous protest tactics (cited in Nikolayenko, 2009, p. 9).

Empirical studies have shown how the qualities of new ICTs and Web 2.0 (including speed and swift nature) have made them suitable for mobilising publics. As Garrett (2006) explained, with these qualities, the tools can be harnessed to produce a swarm-like effect by taking multiple actions at the same time in different locations. Leizerov (as early as 2000) suggested that ICTs have the prospect to enhance the flow of political information. Consequently, ordinary individuals in society who have access to smartphones and similar technologies are more likely to get access to the internet and the benefits it affords for participation. The internet has always been seen as holding the potential to correct the decreasing political participation culture and declining civic engagement prevalent in societies due to stiff opposition and repression from the state (Ayres, 1999; Barber 1996; Shirky, 2010a, 2010b; Walker, 2007). The 2010 riots in London provide a classic example of the aforementioned point. Meier (2011) explained that student protestors employed Google Maps through their mobile phones in London to coordinate and organise their activities. This savvy use of technology has been tagged 'cyberactivism' in that the combination of both tools (ICTs and the application) facilitated on-the-go tactical mapping for protest swarming (Meier, 2011, p. 51). Consequently, we can assert that there is an effect because of ICTs and corresponding applications on the tactical repertoire and conflict movements, independent activists and movements engaged in contentious activities. These benefits extend to both violent and non-violent movements alike. Also, there is an increase in citizen engagement and participation in politics (directly and indirectly). As Howard (2010) explains, states, where internet tariffs are cheap, have witnessed a surge in the usage of the platform, including a significant increase in the number of political groups who now rely on the internet to map and execute their activities. In his own words, 'some groups are long-standing contributors to civic discourse; many are new and exist because the internet has facilitated the interaction and organisation of like-minded citizens' (Howard, 2010, p. 140).

Also, the literature and empirical studies have enlisted hacktivism and electronic civil disobedience as other instances that demonstrate the role ICTs and other online media applications play with regard to tactical repertoire of conflict movements and independent activists (Karatzogianni, 2006a, 2006b; Meier, 2011). The definition of hacking and hacktivism is subject to individual understanding, ideological and legitimacy discourses and context-specific (Karatzogianni, 2006a, 2006b, p. 215). Taylor (1999) succinctly captures the context-specific difference in the interpretation of hacking; a novice may have an exaggerated meaning of the expression, often tied to a contrary belief of bad uses of ICTs among computer experts. However, Taylor explains that computer enthusiasts may conjure up linked images in the theatrical and superficial drama in the movies and other modern genres. For the computer systems analyst, the term may denote programming that strictly relies on a depth of skills and professionalism.

Following Taylor's explanation, for computer security and industry experts, the phrase hacking may set the pointers in the direction of contempt usually associated with 'electronic vandals' (see Taylor, 1999, p. xii). Indeed, the interpretation of hacking has progressed from the the uses of professional programming to a more contemporary meaning affiliated to unlawful computer incursion or meddling (Taylor, 1999, pp. 13–14). It is this part of illegal computer incursion and meddling that this study draws on that has been the subject of both socio-political and ethnoreligious CC and warfare across the globe. Following this trail, 'electronic vandals' or better still hackers have exploited ICTs and the internet as a means of resistance. 'The concept most commonly used to connect IT and the military is information warfare. What this means is that the object of conflict is no longer territory or resources, but information' (Karatzogianni, 2006a, 2006b, p. 224). This could involve unlawful intrusions and actions of parties in a conflict engineered to exploit, corrupt or destroy the enemy's information and its functions in view to achieving information superiority (Crumm, 1996; cited in Gupta, 2009; Karatzogianni, 2006a, 2006b; Meier, 2011). Although, much of the work of a hacker is illegal and unauthorised, nonetheless, Karatzogianni (2006a, 2006b) pointed out that in the present day and age, hacking, for its protagonists, has become an instrument used to fight for more explicit political goals.

The more societies depend on ICTs, Denning (2001), Reilly (2003) and Edwards (1998) argue that the more the potential for ICTs to be employed for such disruptions. Over the years, we have seen other dimensions of conflict and protest, for instance, conflict movements adapting cyberwarfare tactics involving electronic disobedience and hacktivism in both developed and developing societies in their struggle for socio-political and economic reform and change. Prominent examples of ICT/cyber-based conflicts range from the United States vs China and Israel vs Palestine to the Indian vs Pakistan and the Kosovo vs Serbian cyber attacks. In the highlighted cases above, adherents engaged each other via disruption to each other's computer systems using electronic defacements, denial of service attacks including the dissemination of propaganda during the conflicts (Karatzogianni, 2006a, 2006b, pp. 154–160).

In the Serbian case, in 1998, hackers affiliated to the Serbian terrorist movement were believed to have hacked Kosovo's websites. The Crna Ruka (Black 42 Hand, as they were known) posted images containing Serbian nationalist symbols in both English and Serbian: 'welcome to the Web page of the biggest liars and killers […] Brother Albanians, this coat of arms will be in your flag as long as you exist' (BBC Online 25 October 1998). Similarly, following failed reconciliation and negotiation deliberations in 2000, Palestinian and Israeli hackers engaged in a cyberwarfare, causing service disruption, defacements and denial of service attacks on each other's online services. Similarly, in the Indian vs Pakistan case, 'sympathisers on both sides of the Kashmir conflict (in north-eastern India) used cyberattacks to disrupt each other's computer systems and to disseminate propaganda' (Karatzogianni, 2006a, 2006b, pp. 341–353).

Conversely, not only social movements but civil society also has demonstrated the role ICTs play in their tactical repertoires. The same theory applies to the tactics of radical and insurgency movements. According to Karatzogianni (2006a, 2006b), in modern times, the majority of radical movements depend on the internet to enlist new members. 'Terrorist groups rely increasingly on the internet chat rooms, more anonymous than traditional websites' (p. 160). Kavada (2010a, 2010b) also argues that communication in cyberspace is interactive, anonymous and offers a global platform. These characteristics fit succinctly into the covert strategy of militant (terrorist and insurgency) groups. The effect of ICTs and Web 2.0 on the structure of such movements is therefore felt strongly and is seen in the increasingly growing presence of insurgency-related websites over the last two decades. Gabriel Weimann, an Israeli professor at the University of Haifa, in his research on terrorist-related websites moved from his initial finding of 12 to over 4,500 as at 2004 (cited in Karatzogianni, 2006a, 2006b, p. 160). This figure would have doubled today (Mantel, 2011, p. 129). For instance, by 2009, Mantel (2011), citing Gabriel Weimann, explained that 7,000 sites were monitored. The platform advanced by cyberspace offers radical groups a suitable option to fulfil their objectives. In essence, the web provides a haven for adherents of the insurgency to conceal their identities, carry out multiple actions across multiple locations and in doing so catch the state off guard and escape state sanctions.

The other dimension to the point above is cyberterrorism, which involves 'computer-based attacks intended to intimidate or coerce governments or societies in pursuit of goals that are political, religious or ideological' (Denning, 2001). Also, Denning explains that such attacks should be damaging enough or unsettling enough to instigate terror and anxiety tantamount to what is applicable in real-life acts of radical insurgency. This type of conflict could result in death or be capable of causing physical harm, electrical blackouts, plane crashes and water pollution, including other socio-political and economic losses. Note that although the earlier context referring to cyberterrorism is capable of physical consequences that would usually result in conflict between affected communities in both offline and online circles, the action taken is nonetheless in virtual space.

ICTs also play a crucial role in safeguarding movement actors, in particular by helping to avoid unnecessary exposure of themselves to security apparatuses of the state prosecuting the dissidents responsible for the war. For instance, Karatzogianni (2006a, 2006b) explained that adherents of radical tactics seldom use their personal computers. Instead, they are fond of operating from cyber cafes and other discrete options available to them. The seemingly shapeless structure of the web and 'disregard for national boundaries and ethnic markers fits exactly with bin Laden's original vision for al-Qaeda, which he founded to stimulate revolt among the worldwide Muslim [...] community of believers' (p. 161). The 11 September 2001 attackers were believed to have methodically employed the internet to organise the 9/11 attacks. This has also become a common practice among insurgency movements and terrorist organisations since the 9/11 attacks. Mantel (2011) explained that the attackers use the internet to research flight schools and to organise their activities (pp. 140–141). A former head of the CIA counter-intelligence unit argued that 'Internet communications have become the main communications system among al-Qaeda around the world because it's safer, easier and more anonymous if they take the right precautions, and I think they are doing that' (cited in Karatzogianni, 2006a, 2006b, p. 161). Ultimately, it's argued that ICTs, the internet and everyday social media provided a relatively cheaper avenue for activists and political movements to mobilise, and for citizen participation and engagement in political discourse in the Nigerian context of contentious activities.

3.2.6. ***Framing Process and ICTs***

The framing process is the second element in the development of social movement along which the Garrett (2006) and Karatzogianni (2006a, 2006b) frameworks examined the relationship between ICTs and conflict movements. To be clear, Garrett (2006) defines the framing process as a deliberate effort to construct, broadcast and challenge the narrative repertoire used to portray a dissenting movement. Accordingly, Zald (1996) argues that the principal aim of the framing process may not be unconnected with the need to validate the claims upheld by protestors and encourage or inspire collective action via ethnically shared values (cited in Garrett, 2006, p. 4). During conflict there is always a contest between different parties to dominate the media in which case the government and those belonging to the highest class in society (Howard, 2010, p. 103) the 'cultural elites' may enjoy more control.

The aforementioned scenario means an exclusion of the vast array of the public from their rights to partake in debates and shape public opinion during conflicts. However, with the present structure of new ICTs, individuals are contesting and developing public discussion using ICTs and platforms availed by the internet. As one commentator explained, 'now there are mechanisms [...] allowing [...] contrasts and divergence of opinion' (Howard, 2010, p. 103). Howard made this inference about the widespread presence of Web 2.0 and new media tools such as mobile phones. Consequently, both the elite and the general public can influence public opinion to enjoy the freedom of unmediated communication in the Web 2.0 era. The public and dissenting communities can now set the record straight, setting the agenda for public discourse and news media, when the need arises. Accordingly, frames (framing) are those particular 'metaphors, symbolic representations, and cognitive cues used to render or cast behaviour and events in an evaluative mode and to suggest alternative modes of action [...]. Symbols, frames, and ideologies are created and altered during contestation' (Zald, 1996, p. 262).

Conflict groups can connect established cultural frames to specific concerns, make clear and boost a frame that bears on such concerns, and by implication increase the scope of political protest groups to incorporate more participation and perceptions through the process of 'frame bridging', 'frame amplification' and 'frame extension' (Karatzogianni, 2006a, 2006b, p. 151). The media are the centrepiece of such operations, hence the competition among the parties in a conflict for the platform. With the limitations usually imposed by the state on traditional media, the interesting thing to note is that ICTs have made it a lot easier for the framing processes highlighted earlier to be achieved, having taken the monopoly of media institutions from the hands of a few in society. In other words, contemporary social movements can more readily, using the tools provided by new ICTs, amplify their cause, shape public opinion, counter opposing narratives in the media and engage in propaganda. 'Now there are mechanisms for at least allowing some contrasts and divergence of opinion. The Internet and mobile phones, in some modest respects, have freed public opinion from being narrowly constituted as the opinion of a small elite' (Zayani, 2008, cited in Howard, 2010, p. 103).

In an attempt to explain the changing dynamics of communication Castells (2011) describes a process he tagged 'mass-self communication' and in his most recent work on *Networks of Outrage and Hope* (2012) he identified the concept of 'autonomous Communication'. Both concepts are used similarly to affirm that the individual activist and social movement actors, relying on the decentralised nature of Web 2.0, have more autonomy and control over the communication process. As such, they can initiate and self-direct their messages to their target audience free from most restriction. Ultimately, the alternative platform afforded by new communication technologies is crucial for the participation of these actors in public discourse and propaganda. Eventually, that one-sided dominance is lessened by the availability of ICTs' corresponding applications of Web 2.0.

Drawing from McAdam et al. (1996), Karatzogianni (2006a, 2006b) succinctly sums up the essential constituents of the framing process. The framing process involves: (1) the cultural toolkit available to would-be insurgents; (2) the strategic framing efforts of movement groups; (3) the frame contests between movement and other collective actors – principally the state, and counter-movement groups; (4) the structure and role of the media in mediating such contests; and (5) the cultural impact of the movement in modifying the available toolkit (McAdam et al., 1996, p. 19, cited in Karatzogianni, 2006a, 2006b, p. 150). In the Nigerian case, the most important thing to note is the role played by ICTs and, in particular, the internet during the Occupy Nigeria protest and how dissidents used the tools to construct their narratives. Also, bypassing traditional mainstream media limitations, contesting the language of the media and the state were crucial components of the framing process during the January protests.

For Snow and Benford (1988), the whole framing process involves a purposeful construction and preservation of meaning by movement actors directed towards other parties, in this case, the state and multinational oil companies. Both sides, the protagonist and the antagonist in conflict, equally benefit from the framing process. In essence, whether it is the state against conflict movements or one movement against another, the significance of ICTs means that both parties in conflict make strides to shape and control the perception on the actors in the conflict via ICTs. Thus, drawing from Snow and Benford (1988), the framing exercise allows for an interpretive process that involves the creation of meaning. The objective has been 'to mobilise potential adherents and constituents to garner bystander support, and to mobilise antagonists' (Snow & Benford, 1988, p. 198). In essence, such frames are meant to make the targeted public act in such ways as desired by the protagonist. Accordingly, Benford and Snow (2000) argue that collective action frames represent a set of principles and meanings that enthuse and appropriate or justify the activities and advocacy of conflict groups.

Snow and Benford (1988) and Benford (1993) also extend their perception, arguing that there are two essential categories of framing, which are: (1) the core framing tasks which ties to the action-oriented function of such frames and (2) are those shared, discursive processes that attend to the core framing tasks and thus produce collective action frames. To illustrate their point, Benford and Snow (2000) explained that collective action frames emerge as dissidents in a conflict and try to identify the issues and apportion blame, proffer an alternative cause of action and provide the necessary stimuli for individuals to act. Accordingly, Snow and Benford (1988) classified this process as diagnostic, prognostic and motivational framing. For Klandermans (1984), framing activities boil down to two objectives: (1) consensus mobilisation and (2) action mobilisation. 'The former fosters or facilitates agreement whereas the latter fosters action, moving people from the balcony to the barricades' (Benford & Snow, 2000, p. 615).

Benford and Snow (2000) described 'motivational framing' as another dynamic in the framing process of movements. Like the phraseology sounds, this characteristic has to do with the frames used by movement leaders to motivate individuals to act on the issues identified by the movement. As Benford and Snow argued, this third phase 'provides a "call to arms" or rationale for engaging in ameliorative collective action, including the construction of appropriate vocabularies of motive' (Benford & Snow, 2000, p. 617). The central idea of the motivational framing can be attributed to the desire to stimulate response and effect change having fulfilled the other criteria of the framing tasks. One can assert that there is a trail of interconnectivity between the three dynamics. In essence, the three cannot be separated. To understand the motivational framing dynamic and how movement actors engage in this activity during conflict, Benford (1993) describes four basic types of lexical tools of motive exploited by such actors: severity, urgency, efficacy and propriety (cited in Benford & Snow, 2000, p. 617). The idea is that, if efficiently harnessed, such frames as described by Benford and Snow earlier hold the potential of being persuasive and mobilising with regard to grabbing the support of activists, sympathisers and bystanders and revitalising and upholding their membership.

In the same context of framing, in the previous chapter, it was demonstrated that a significant drawback with traditional mainstream media is with regard to the capacity for the state to covertly and overtly enforce censorship which can undermine the framing process and public opinion on particular events (Best & Wade 2005, p. 78). Groshek (2010) further explained that despite the predominant presence of mass media tool, the media (in particular state-run media) are known to align with the ideological disposition of the state, while non-state media enforce self-censorship depending on the level of state influence. These limitations pose significant challenges, considering that the mass media are articulated as the principal machinery through which frames are broadcast and reframed (Karatzogianni, 2006a, 2006b, p. 68). For Gitlin (1980) and Ryan (1991), a further implication of the hegemony of the cultural elite is that the authorities and those belonging to the high class in society would exploit the 'status quo' for propaganda and propagate more of their ideologies through the mass media at the expense of ordinary citizens in a society.

However, conflict movements can now bypass these limitations to participate in political discourse and shape public opinion from different alternative points aided by the innovative uses of new ICTs and through what has been described as 'horizontal communication networks and mainstream media to convey their images and messages, these increases their chances of enacting social and political change – even if they start from a subordinate position in institutional power, financial resources, or symbolic legitimacy' (Castells, 2011, p. 302).

For instance, Morovoz (2011a, 2011b) argues that instead of advocating the view that everyday social media networks such as FB were mainly employed as a tool or resource for mobilising political protests in Morocco which engendered the democratic process at the time, on the contrary, the tools' major influence may be attributed to its role in 'pushing the boundaries of what could or could not be said in the conservative society' (p. 212).

The innovative uses that come with ICTs have a considerable effect on the framing process during the political protest and on the nature of dissident movements, civil society groups and other protests groups, as in the case of insurgency or terrorist movements. These tools allow for activists and protestors to respond to and correct misconceptions about movement activities. In doing so, these actors can innovatively bypass the rigours of state scrutiny through the alternative channels provided by ICTs. Similarly, as it has been demonstrated through empirical studies and in literature, the medium allows for the creation of a common understanding and shared identity among the members of such movements. Also, a direct effect of ICTs on the framing process is the crop of citizen-based media and the rise of citizen journalists, which includes activists and ordinary individuals using social media to broadcast news and images during particular events or a given phenomenon, thereby shaping public opinion on the event in question. As a direct consequence, Garrett (2006) makes clear that activists who provide information in a format that is easy-to-use and easily verified are [...] likely to have their views and interpretations presented alongside those forwarded by elites' (citing Ryan, 1991, p. 223; Vegh, 2003).

> To be sure, activists using the Internet in repressive states have been able to frame how local events have been reported and discussed. In Iran, the Mousavi opposition leveraged ICTs precisely because he was barred from accessing state-run television and newspapers.
>
> Meier (2011, p. 75)

In addressing the London European Forum (ESF) of 2004, Kavada (2012) considered the growing importance of the internet and its uses in the Global Justice Movement (GJM). Her finding further sheds some insights into the significance of the internet for the activities (organisation and communication) of conflict groups. For instance, in addressing the communication culture, a commonly shared trait and character can be seen in their use of email lists. According to Kavada, the Horizontals employed the email list as a means to deliberate on their grievances. Similarly, Kavada (2010a, 2010b) in her examination of the GJM explained that the use of email list helps movement actors to maintain divergence, diversity and individual autonomy. Beyond mobilisation which is aided by the internet including the uses of email list by dissident movements, an added advantage is that the same tools facilitate communicative cultures of dissident movements by giving them a free hand to shape their communications internally and externally. Kavada (2012) explained that these new media tools allow movement actors access to networks and a channel to transmit their messages to the members of pre-existing social networks. 'I like these words of Chairman Mao "The world is ours, we should unite for achievements. Responsibility and seriousness can conquer the world and the Chinese Communist Party members represent these qualities". These words are incisive and inspirational' – Bo Xilai, Communist Party chief (Page, 2011). The extract earlier represents the Chinese 'red texting' example mentioned in the previous paragraph. Morovoz (2011a, 2011b) explained that 13 million mobile phone users in the city of Chongqing received the above text message that was disseminated by the city's communist party's secretary Bo Xilai. The message was subsequently re-sent 6 million times by dissidents. The well-composed text message and the uses of mobile phone technologies to disseminate it does not exist in a vacuum. According to Morovoz (2011a, 2011b), Bo Xilai had been at the centre of speculation of higher political interests within the party. Going by the speculation, one can argue that the text may have been composed with the intention to garner publicity, or at least legitimate his plans.

Conflict movements irrespective of their orientations exploit ICTs innovatively to construct or craft various forms of identities around the notion of 'us against them' or 'us versus them'. For instance, in reference to the Israeli-Palestinian CC, which involved elements of hacktivism (hacking as a form of resistance, protest and retaliation), 'we see the use of national symbols when hacking websites, such as the Israeli flag, Hebrew text and even a recording of the Israeli national anthem on the Hezbollah home page. This explicitly urges us to look at issues of national identity, nationalism and ethnicity' (Karatzogianni, 2006a, 2006b, p. 378). Interestingly, the use of ICTs in ethnoreligious CC is further translated into some form of warfare. Essentially, this included both parties, as in the case of the Israelis and the Palestinians, sending a threat and intimidating emails to the 'other' and spreading information on how to destroy the opponent's website.

There was a similar scenario during the Indian vs Pakistan CC. There was extensive use of the internet, in this case as a propaganda mechanism and weapon. Propaganda in the sense that the internet was used to manipulate and shape public opinion, albeit negatively on both sides. For instance, Karatzogianni (2006a, 2006b) explained that the Indian military's website 'was set up as a propaganda tool, and hacked pictures of alleged tortures of Kashmiris by Indians were placed on the site, in a similar propaganda tactic' (p. 198). Similarly, as a warfare instrument, the internet was exploited to send viruses to the opponent. An illustrative example of this was when Indian hackers spread the Yaha worm to execute denial of service attacks on Pakistani websites in 2003 (Karatzogianni, 2006b, pp. 158–159). The Yaha worm was allegedly sent as retaliation to similar Pakistani cyberattack which included defacement of Indian websites. 'Yaha.Q attempted to launch a Denial-of-Service attack against five Pakistani sites, changing user settings on infected machines and containing a number of messages directed at Pakistani hackers, other virus writers and an anti-virus researcher' (Karatzogianni, 2006b, pp. 158–159).

In the Indian vs Pakistani ethnoreligious CC, actors tailored their discourse and messages in a manner that will attract sympathisers, build a sense of community and a shared grievance. Actors carefully create frames around the issue of inclusion and exclusion. According to a BBC 2008 report, a supportive Indian sympathiser's statement reads, 'A whole-hearted salute for my brothers fighting for our country with a religious maverick enemy' (Karatzogianni, 2006a, 2006b; Nuttall, 1998). '[W]e wish that our Muslim brothers given the right to choose, as was promised them [...]' (cited in Karatzogianni, 2006a, 2006b, p. 379). A similar practice is observable in the Kosovo–Serbia case: 'We will hate China forever and will hack its sites' (US–China), 'Down with Japanese militarism, Kill all Japs' (China–Japan) and 'Welcome to the web page of the biggest liars and killers, Long Live Serbia' (Karatzogianni, 2006b, p. 379). The kind of frames used in the first example demonstrates a sense of belonging (inclusiveness) on the part of Indian sympathisers who use online media to show support for the activities of Indian hackers. About the issue of national identity and the notion of exclusion and inclusion, religious themes are employed by actors. This use of religion displays the movements' religious affiliation and can be an instrument delineating its membership structure. Individuals outside such groups are by this token restricted from joining. Similarly, the use of frames or themes such as 'brother' and 'our country' in the text draw on the notion of collective identity and solidarity. Collective identity is in the sense of their ethnic and religious affiliations. For instance, 'brother' is not used in the genetic sense. In the Serbia–Kosovo case and US–China contexts, different adjectives are used to construct and embed discourses of national identity, and themes relating to the 'other'.

The first scenario is the Indian vs Pakistani ethnoreligious CC, while the second situation captures the US–China and Kosovo–Serbia conflicts. In all these cases, we can see how the internet can be very instructive in shaping identities of communities in contention, the uses of the platform to create narratives that demarcate such identities, create the other, propaganda and also instigating notions of national identity, although in these cases, the idea of national identity is embedded within a chauvinistic perspective. Various frames and phrases are the units of analysis, given that the discourse is embedded in the language used.

One can see a trait in the role played by the internet and ICTs on the mobilisation of the ethnoreligious movements as seen in the cases earlier especially in terms of the internet capacity for creating new forms of conflict online. A more recent scenario can be seen in the speech and discourse of members of the Islamic state, in particular, the spokesperson, whom intelligence agencies have tagged as Jihadi John. These groups have exploited the benefits of the internet to construct their identity, 'us vs them' notion and propaganda. The following is a transcription of a video posted by ISIS and published by *Daily Mail* newspaper online in which Jihadi John speaks before murdering his victims.

> I am back Obama, and I am back because of your arrogant foreign policy towards the Islamic state, because of your insistence and continuous bombing of the Islamic state […] despite our serious warning. You Obama has yet again for your actions […] another American citizen. So as far as your missile continues to strike our people, our knives will continue to strike the neck of your people. You have entered this evil alliance with the Americans against the Islamic State to back of and leave our people alone […] You have been at the forefront of the aggression against the Islamic state, and you have plotted against us and gone far out of your way to find reasons to interfere in our affairs. Today your military is attacking us daily in Iraq, your strikes have caused causalities amongst Muslims, you are no longer fighting against an insurgency, we are an Islamic army and a state that has been accepted by a large number of Muslims worldwide so efficiently any aggression towards the Islamic state is an aggression towards Muslims from all works of life who have accepted the Islamic caliphate as their leadership. So any attempt by you Obama to deny the Muslims their right of living in safety under the Islamic caliphate, will result in the bloodshed of your people.
>
> Webb (2014)

In the passage earlier, religion is mentioned, thus establishing the religious affiliation hypothesis. Also, the use of phrases such as the Islamic state is suggestive of a form of national identity perhaps with some inclination towards self-determination drawing upon principles of international law. Others include 'Islamic caliphate' (national identity/ethnic/religious affiliation), the phrase 'we are an Islamic army and a state that has been accepted by a large number of Muslims worldwide' and 'our people' (indicative of collective identity and solidarity). 'Obama' is constructed as the 'Other' also symbolic of Americans, the West and perhaps Europe.

Given the widespread uses of ICTs by conflict movements during recent conflicts in Nigeria, namely the Occupy Nigeria, Boko Haram and MEND, ICTs, the internet and everyday media were instrumental in constructing and broadcasting activists' frames to a global audience, whilst also being used as a means to set the record straight, as Chapter 5 utilising these insights demonstrates in great detail.

3.2.7. Opportunity Structure and ICTs

The opportunity structure is another factor in the development of movements that is believed to connect the notion of ICTs and other online media applications to political movements. In this context, the opportunity structure is considered as those dynamics that either enhance or hamper the activities of dissident movements and the media in the event of a contentious political situation. These factors are crucial for dissident communities, political protest movement and activists to consider for any successful and effective coordination of contentious activities. This is important since these dynamics form the basis for the events that take place during contentious political situations (Garrett, 2006, p. 17). McAdam et al. (1996) classify four such dynamics to be considered by movement actors, including whether or not the political system is accessible to extra-institutional actors (civil society organisations, social movements and other political protest movements), the unity or division among elitist groups, the existence of elite supporters or allies and the power of individual states to impede political activities such as protests and demonstrations through repression and/or suppression of dissent (cited in Garrett, 2006, pp. 17–18). The opportunity structure can be further divided into sub-categories to enable a succinct understanding of the perception being advocated here. The Garrett (2006) framework describes two main categories that include the political structure and the economic structure within a given political environment, which can either facilitate or constrain movement activities.

Garrett (2006) explains that each countries' opportunity structure is shaped by alliances and events and activities taking place in other countries and worldwide. As such, a particular phenomenon in a country can be linked or attributed to past events or similar activities happening elsewhere. The ability of one conflict activity influencing another can be seen in the spread of the Arab uprisings from Tunisia to the countries in the Arab league. In Meier's (2011) seminal work on 'Liberation Technologies', he describes a process of 'information cascades'. Following Meier's analysis, each actor, relying on the annotations of others, alters their personal information to opt for the same option as the other. 'Less formally, an information cascade demonstrates the power of peer pressure – many individuals will choose actions based on what they observe others doing' (Drezner, 2010, p. 40, cited in Meier 2011, p. 61). Meier (2011) however explained that the process of information cascade could be affected by other events such as an external shock (natural disasters and elections).

The media has been the link connecting society to global/transnational events, which as suggested influences activities taking place in other national contexts. In another perspective, Karatzogianni (2006a, 2006b) posits that media spotlight, for instance, also provides support for the actions of contentious movements, and makes such movements, and its political actors involved, key stakeholders in the struggle for political reform and social change. What this suggests is that 'the opening and closing of media access and attention is a crucial element in defining the political opportunity for movements' (Karatzogianni, 2006a, 2006b: citing Gamson & Meyer, 1996, p. 285). In a similar trail of thought, Kielbowicz and Scherer identify three ways through which the media influence the activities of dissident movements; they argue that the media serve as a principal channel for getting to a particular target audience, in view to acquiring their support and mobilising them to participate in contentious activities; the media also serve as a link between various movement networks and stakeholders, whilst also serving as a psychological base to elicit support for movements (cited in Karatzogianni, 2006a, 2006b, p. 69). It is impossible to detach the media element when discussing the political opportunity structure. 'The media form a component of the political opportunity structure with both structural and dynamic elements' (Karatzogianni, 2006a, 2006b, p. 69). Also, they suggested that the media is crucial in that it forms an avenue for a competitor to contest their claims during contentious events (Karatzogianni, 2006a, 2006b citing Gamson & Meyer, 1996, p. 289). The implication is that the public is left to make or create their meaning of the events, judge and decide what side to support.

The idea is that the media is that channel which society employs to measure political activities and events. This could have the effect of influencing a community to support specific campaigns, for advocacy or to stimulate the desire to participate in protests and conflict in a contentious atmosphere. It is not a surprise therefore that the medium is subject to contestation between, on the one hand, dissident movements who want to exploit the medium for mobilising support for advocacy, disseminating information and exposing state excesses, and on the other hand, the state, who also want to exploit the avenue for the same purpose. Both sides' uses of the media are centred on propaganda. Consequently, McAdam et al. (1996) argue that the media become a platform that supports extra-institutional actors in one context, while in another enhance the activities of institutional actors (cited in Karatzogianni, 2006a, 2006b, p. 69).

As it has been documented in literature, and empirical evidence further confirms, in both dictatorial and democratic settings, the state has always demonstrated the capacity for repression in different ways, from regulations and decrees to extreme use of force including kidnap, murder, imprisonment, destruction of properties and through other coercive means; in doing so, they inhibit the opportunity structure for political participation, public opinion and contentious activity. Nonetheless, it is believed that new ICTs are changing the paradigm by influencing the opportunity structure of movements engaged in contentious activities. For instance, Ayer (1999) asserts that ICTs, in concert with universal economic practices, promote transnational cooperation – the collective action including in contentious situations. Such activity arguably 'influences national-level political opportunity structures' (cited in Garrett, 2006, p. 18). Also, given the transnational nature of ICTs, Schulz (1998) and Vegh (2003) explain that dissident movements have better opportunity to discover major 'elite allies' and divided state elites and their global equivalents.

As sequel to the earlier point, Scott and Street (2000) and Kidd (2003) suggest that new ICTs, especially the internet, offer individuals, movements and groups in contentious politics an approach to communication which principally defies the rigours of regulation usually imposed upon mainstream media by the state. As an alternative platform, new ICTs offer movement actors room to control the general flow of information and monopoly over their political communication (cited in Garrett, 2006, p. 18). For instance, the interconnected and interactive nature of new ICTs offers an alternative platform to circumvent the limitation meted on other mainstream channels. As a result, Garrett (2006) explained that if these factors are considered, it becomes difficult to thwart a communication from reaching its destination 'by controlling the data flow across an arbitrary node on the network' (p. 18).

As may have been observed, the majority of the discussion so far has tended to focus on the impact of ICTs on social movement and civil society mobilisation relying on the resource mobilisation models. The CC framework successfully integrates elements of the RMT in its consideration of the impact of new communication technologies. The preceding discussion is a deliberate effort to treat each dimension of the CC framework independent of the other to enable a detailed analysis. The three inter-related variables used in understanding the impact of ICTs on the modus operandi of socio-political movements are also crucial for our understanding of how groups in the ethnoreligious dimensions mobilise and organise their activities. This includes boosting participation, recruitment tactics, framing issues and identity. Also, the framework helps us understand the opportunity structure which can aid or limit activities of such conflict movements in the ethnoreligious dimension, in particular, the effect of ICTs, the internet and everyday social media on those processes. 'This type of political activity is not sufficiently explained by social movement theory. Instead, an approach is needed that is capable of capturing the sources and nature of the ethnoreligious conflict, as well as its global context' (Karatzogianni, 2006a, 2006b, p. 165).

While the socio-political elements of the CC framework are useful for understanding the activities of ethnoreligious movements with regard to mobilisation, framing and opportunity structure, Karatzogianni (2006a, 2006b) also identifies specific dynamics that can aid our understanding of ethnoreligious movements, their motivations, issues and challenges. Again, these elements may not be necessarily limited to the understanding of ethnoreligious movements, the components of both socio-political and ethnoreligious movements in the CC framework are intertwined and are crucial for considering the general workings of conflict movements. As the name suggests, ethnoreligious CCs are mainly ethnic, religious and culturally motivated groups in conflict with the state or opposition movements. Interestingly, socio-political movements could also demonstrate such identities and affiliations. In the CC contexts, such contestation is carried out in virtual spaces, as they are in standard real-life setting (Karatzogianni, 2006a, 2006b, p. 5). The idea is that similar to their socio-political counterpart, the struggle could occur in real-life settings and have a spillover into cyberspace and vice versa. It is crucial to state that the use of the phraseology 'ethnoreligious' does not necessarily mean that the struggles of such movements are on the whole ethnically and religiously motivated. While such affiliations exist, the interests, conflicts and motivations of such movements could also be socio-political and economic.

The Israeli vs Palestinian and Indian vs Pakistani conflicts are excellent illustrations of ethnoreligious CCs. In the first two cases, the conflict was carried out in cyberspace with either side engaging in reprisal cyberattacks. Websites of both parties in each case were targeted with defacements and DOS attacks thereby limiting the uses of ICTs. For instance, in the India vs Pakistan case, perceived Pakistani intelligence operatives had taken over the Indian Army's only website, posting alleged images that depicted torture of Kashmiris by the Indian security operatives (Karatzogianni, 2006b, p. 348). A short while after, the Pakistanis responded by defacing 600 websites and temporarily took over government and private computer systems (Karatzogianni, 2006b, p. 348). Although their actions were mostly virtual, it represented a spillover from offline conflict.

The CC framework also integrates those dynamics that facilitate or inform our understanding of ethnic and religious (ethnoreligious) conflict groups. One such quality is the issue of ethnic and religious affiliations, the idea that organisations engaged in this paradigm are usually tied to ethnic and/or religious orientations. Karatzogianni (2006a, 2006b) makes an astute point that such conflicts are founded on concerns of ethnic, religious and national attraction embedded in a robust sense of identity. According to her, 'ethnic affiliation provides a sense of security in a divided society, reciprocal help, and protection against neglect of one's interests by strangers. Ethnic divisions reaffirm rather than undermine fixity and closure' (Karatzogianni, 2006b, p. 170–171). Essentially, this component of the CC framework can be said to provide an incentive and motivation for becoming a member and participation in such movements of dissent or resistance. For Horowitz, '[i]n deeply divided societies ethnicity – in contrast to other lines of cleavage, such as class or occupation – appear permanent and all-encompassing, predetermining who will be granted and denied access to power and resources' (cited in Karatzogianni, 2006a, 2006b, p. 171). The implication for the present context is that the uses of ICTs enhance such identities, the internet and social media networks as they are today, which could lead to the stability and cohesion of such conflict groups (Karatzogianni, 2006b, p. 171).

The other tools useful for our understanding of the ethnoreligious CC include a discourse of inclusion and exclusion, how groups in this paradigm use the internet as a tool for propaganda and mobilisation and conflict resolution resource. The discourse of inclusion and exclusion is embedded around the construction of identities of contentious movement. Conflict movements are used deliberately to capture both socio-political movements and ethnoreligious movements because conflict as a term cuts across both dimensions of protest and resistance.

To sum up the discourse between socio-political and ethnoreligious movements in relation to ICTs, the CC framework argues that actors in socio-political CC need to function in a more systematised/cognisant manner (more organised fashion) especially if such actors are productively or positively engaged with the present global political system or segments of the polity. 'Conflict resolution will only be possible when hierarchical apparatuses become more networked, and rhizomatic groups become more conscious of the rest of their hosting network' (Karatzogianni, 2006a, 2006b, pp. 202–203). Karatzogianni argued that 'actors in ethnoreligious CC need to operate in a more networked/multitudinal fashion if they are fighting network forms of terrorism or resistance, or they are clandestine networks attempting to influence the global political environment' (Karatzogianni, 2006b, p. 202).

The ethnoreligious component also has a third dynamic, conflict resolution. This feature attempts to consider how the internet can be used as a mechanism for resolving crisis and conflicts (Karatzogianni, 2006b, p. 380). By extension, this can also apply to the socio-political component of the framework. In this context, Karatzogianni argues that the onus rests on 'community-based diplomacy, interfaith dialogue (which reflects the importance of exchanging ideas reflecting the common beliefs of different religions), and building a positive relationship as a platform for resolution' (Karatzogianni, 2006b, p. 380).

However, the thrust of the debate here is about the impact of the internet, ICTs and other everyday online media networks on the processes and conflict resolution dynamics aforementioned. The final section considers the media component of the structure. This takes a look at the internet as a platform for (1) analysis discourses of representation, construction of social identities and social relations (2) assessing controls of information, level of censorship and alternative sources (3) its ability to create and dominate public discourse and (4) media effects on policy.

3.3. Limitations of ICTs for Cyberconflict

States and respective authorities are reacting to the technological revolution given the role of ICTs in conflict scenarios. Given this, one can posit that some limitations still exist that could curtail the crucial role played by ICTs for conflict movements. Morovoz (2011a, 2011b) explains how states too can exploit new ICTs for propaganda purposes, as a vector for coercion and under the guise of patriotism to attract support from dissidents. As the literature demonstrates, 'non-democratic regimes heavily regulate the use of new ICTs as means new to disseminate propaganda' (Meier, 2011a, 2011b, p. 84). Howard (2010) argues that in such countries, new media technologies are closely regulated, if not banned or directly owned by ruling families or administered by the state. This effectively excludes other sources of cultural and political authority from any mechanism of disseminating news, information or other cultural content (Howard, 2010, p. 122). On the uses of new ICTs and social media for propaganda by the states, China's text messaging also known as 'red texting' and Saudi Arabia's usage of ICTs and online media to brand itself as the centre of Islam are few, but are illustrative examples of how states are adjusting to new communication technologies, and their role and response to the technological struggles (Howard, 2010, cited in Meier, 2011, p. 84; Morovoz, 2011a, 2011b).

Similarly, in the Saudi Arabia example in the previous paragraph, Howard (2010) asserts that the monarch uses ICTs to safeguard its hegemony over politics and the economy.

In his seminal piece, *The Net Delusion: How Not to Liberate the World*, Morovoz (2011a, 2011b) attempted to draw a balance between the discourse of whether or not the benefit of the internet and ICTs about conflict has gone more in favour of the public at the expense of the state. Drawing attention to the one-sidedness of such propositions that ICTs favour dissidents, which he tagged 'cyber-utopianism', he argued that such perception constitutes a 'naïve belief in the emancipatory nature of online communications that rests on the stubborn refusal to acknowledge its downside' (Morovoz, 2011b, p. xiii). This oversight in considering the response of authorities in both dictatorial and transitioning democracies created a lacuna since these regimes also enjoy access to the same communication technologies. 'Cyber-utopians did not predict how useful it would prove for propaganda purposes, how masterfully dictators would learn to use it for surveillance, and how sophisticated modern systems of internet censorship would become' (Morovoz, 2011a, 2011b, p. xiv). Also, these technologies do not necessarily necessitate greater involvement but may help facilitate it. Meier (2011) postulates that in the event where the usage of a certain tool (ICT) turns out to be extreme or aggressive, 'challengers' (the state/opposition) can be deprived the right to use such resources. Alternatively, particular features of that medium can be customised to make it obscure to its users.

> Most cyber-utopians stuck to a populist account of how technology empowers the people, who, oppressed by years of authoritarian rule, will inevitably rebel, mobilising themselves through text messages, FB, Twitter, and whatever new tools that come along next year.
>
> Meier (2011, p. xiv)

Contrary to the widespread 'utopianism' on the emancipatory role played by ICTs and the internet, many states (governments/authorities) have developed technologies and found ways to clamp down on protesters (Meier, 2011; Morovoz, 2011a, 2011b; Ronfeldt & Varde, 2008). An example that is illustrative of how these technologies can serve as propaganda tools for the state can be seen in the Green Movement protests in Iran. The Green Movement protest as it was widely called was a conflict that emerged in Iran following the 2009 electoral victory of President Mahmoud Ahmadinejad. Protesters called for the removal of Ahmadinejad. Morovoz (2011a, 2011b) explained that few months after calm had returned to the streets, the Iranian authorities constituted a team of cybercrime experts with the mandate to fish 'insults and lies' on the Iranian websites. A search emerged spearheaded by security service for photos and videos in cyberspace especially on social media networks to identify individuals who participated in the protests. As of December 2009, Raja News, believed to be a pro-government source, published several photos of protesters. Consequently, some of the highlighted participants in the pictures were identified and arrested.

According to Morovoz (2011a, 2011b), FB and email personal information of Iranian protesters in the diaspora were scrutinised while protesters at home were dissuaded from using any social media networks.

Also, Garrett (2006) paints a scenario whereby, under the circumstance where protesters rely on mobile phones to mobilise the public for contentious activity, cutting off mobile phone service would interrupt their attempt to mobilise or communicate with each other. For example, a 2011 *Guardian* report online during the Egyptian revolt stated that the Egyptian authorities blocked social media websites to curb the unrest (Arthur, 2011). Apparently, the government was responding to the effect of the social media on the mobilisation and organisation of the protests. According to the report, Twitter confirmed the social media obstruction put on affected sites was intermittent. Sites affected by the intermittent cut-off included Twitter and FB. Arthur (2011) explained that online media handles registered within Egypt could not be reached from abroad including Google, YouTube, Hotmail, Baidu, a Chinese search engine, and a proxy service – which provided a platform for individuals to bypass restrictions all perceived to have been blocked at the time. The implication for Egyptian dissenters who relied on social media, in particular, would have been obvious – mainly the inability to communicate with each other. The tools are only useful to the degree to which individuals and movement actors have access. This point is particularly a significant drawback for the political opportunity debate. Garrett (2006) argues that authorities can sustain control over the flow of information by 'altering network protest in an information society architecture such that all information travelling to and from the Internet must pass through controlled gateways, or firewalls, providing a mechanism for screening messages already on the network' (Garrett, 2006, p. 19–20).

An illustrative example is seen in the Chinese context, whereby this strategy is employed by the state to check communication between individuals and activists. For instance, Hermida (2002) argued that while China endorses the internet as a tool for economic uses including advancing the communist governments agenda. The government has made frantic efforts to suppress the internet as a platform for free information and debate. The 'Great Red Firewall' tag in view of China's blocking of access to external websites such as Google, the country's physical control of lines that connect China's internet with the worldwide system to the outside world and the usage of internet filters (software that can obstruct access to particular web addresses) by authorities to restrict accessibility are few notable examples of the government's efforts to silence the medium. According to Karatzogianni and Robinson (2014), the above scenario is archetypal of key occasions in China. They explained that the repressive environment produces a widespread feeling of 'disempowerment, an inability to protest, and even an existential gap between the regime and any possible opposition' (p. 7). It can be argued that despite the massive clampdown on media freedoms, the internet, new ICTs and other everyday social media networks have helped independent activists and conflict movements across the globe to circumvent and bypass the rigours of state regulation and censorship on both private and public mainstream media. These tools arm dissidents with multiple alternative access points for gaining information and disseminating information about ongoing movement activities.

In another event, in May 2010, given the increasingly growing response of the public to social media networking, FB was banned by the government in Vietnam. Subsequently, in view to monitoring and curtailing the activities of its citizens, Morovoz (2011a, 2011b) explained that the authorities launched their social networking site 'GoOnline', 'staffed with three hundred computer programmers, graphic designers, technicians and editors'(p. 156). Unlike FB where individuals or, as in the present context, activists would often deploy pseudonyms to conceal their original identities (although there is contestation with FB cracking down on 'fictional' users), Roughneen (2010) explained that users of the Vietnamese social media application have to register with their official ID information. That way, authorities can keep track of content and activities of users on the site. This action by the state also points to their recognition of the role and effect of new media technologies.

The Vietnamese authorities have a rich history of repression and suppression of popular dissent, with traditional mainstream media being the mouthpiece of the state, with jailing of pro-democracy activists and writers. The anti-social media campaign is therefore not a surprise. Besides banning FB, Mediashift (2013) records a clampdown against bloggers who disapprove of state policies and programmes using DDOs attacks and other regulatory means. In furtherance of its tightened grip on the media, a BBC (2013) report revealed that in 2013 a new regulation came into effect restricting communication on Twitter and FB to exchange personal information. Although what constitutes personal information could be debated, the general understanding is that the government wants to curb publication on the web that could be critical of the state and as such be damaging to the image of authorities. In most state scenarios and especially in the developing countries, mobile phone technologies are the primary source of access to the internet for activists and protesters, given the high tariffs charged by cybercafé operators. Mobile phones serve as an alternative access point and have increasingly become crucial for mobilising protests due to the platform it offers for access to the internet. However, Morovoz (2011a, 2011b) contends that little has been said on the challenges that come with mobile activism.

Ultimately, digital activism (using ICTs for protest) comes with advantages as demonstrated in the cases earlier and other examples as in the 1998 Indonesian protests which led to the ousting of the incumbent government, the 2001 revolution in the Philippines which led to the ousting of President Estrada and the Ukrainian protest of 2004 where the uses of text messaging, the internet and social media contributed to some form of emancipation or liberation. Even so, digital activism and protests mainly relying on new technologies, virtual space or cyberspace has its drawbacks and weaknesses. In the cases demonstrated so far, state hegemony, propaganda, censorship and surveillance have proved to be a significant barrier confronted by civil society and social movements. Belarus, China, Azerbaijan and Moldova further provide an illustration of how the state can impede the uses of mobile networks under circumstances it deems politically necessary. For instance, in the Belarusian case, Morovoz (2011a, 2011b) states that during the purportedly failed colour revolution in 2006, the authorities shut down mobile networks of protesters and demonstrators who had assembled in the open area which obstructed their capacity to network and communicate with each other within and outside the region. The Belarusian conflict emerged as a response to the electoral victory of President Alyaksandr Lukashenka, which was highly contested by the opposition in 2006 (see Marples, 2006, pp. 351–361). The authorities denied claims that networks were shut down, arguing that the widespread use of mobile phones and their corresponding applications during the conflict put unusual strain on the networks which affected mobile network services (Morovoz, 2011a, 2011b). Correspondingly, in 2009, the Moldovan officials shut down mobile networks in the central square of the Moldovan capital. This factor inhibited communication and interaction between activists involved in the revolution which was facilitated by Twitter.

Stepanova (2011) commenting on the 'Arab uprisings' identified another limitation in the role played by ICTs, the internet and other everyday social media networks as agents of change and liberation. Certain structural dynamics can also undermine the uses of the tools. For instance, going by the belief that ICTs are catalysts for protests, third-world countries 'would be excluded from social media activism by default owing to underdevelopment and lack of internet access, such as Iraq and Afghanistan or other countries such as Myanmar and Somalia' (Karatzogianni, 2013, p. 9). Despite the structural inadequacies in low-income earning countries, Stepanova revealed that in both scenarios, that is, countries with high internet access such as Bahrain with an estimated 88% of its population using online media (Web 2.0), a rank above the United States, and in such countries with a relatively low level of access to the internet, such as Yemen, mass protests were experienced (Stepanova, 2011, cited in Karatzogianni, 2013, p. 10). Karatzogianni makes an astute point that 'in cases with low levels of exposure the cell phones, tweets, emails, and video clips were used to connect and transmit protests to the world. Different ICTs were used in different ways, and social media did not outmatch satellite or mobile communications' (Karatzogianni, 2013, p. 10).

For Khonder (2011), the perceived role of ICTs, the internet and its accompanying applications are over-generalised. The commentator argued that some social media networks and Web 2.0 were indeed instructive resources during the Arab Spring. However, mainstream media played a seminal role in disseminating the events to a global audience, which spurred support for the revolution within the international community (Khonder, 2011, p. 677). This is not in any way a motivation to undermine the prospects of ICTs. About the wave of conflicts that swept through Middle Eastern countries between 2011 and 2012, Saletan (2011) succinctly captures this argument. His findings revealed the following. (1) ICTs do not guarantee revolution due to certain factors such as poverty that hinder access to new media technologies. Also, education, technological know-how and other socio-economic and political factors impede access and usage of communication media. (2) The internet can be a vector of repression. (3) There are similar characteristics between offline and online crowd dynamics. (4) Finally, states could employ the online media to identify and resolve conflicts.

Ultimately, this section, using literature, empirical accounts and the CC theoretical framework examined the role of ICTs in conflicts. It identified two kinds of conflicts existing side by side, that is, socio-political and ethnoreligious movements. Further, this section demonstrated the crucial role played by ICTs in the activities of such movements. The core argument here was whether or not movements benefit overall from ICTs as tools and resources during conflicts or state actors limit them too much. In both contexts of conflict, there is no doubt that ICTs have radically changed the way movements actors approach conflicts. Such tools of communication have become integrated into the activities of conflict movements and are playing a crucial role in aiding and facilitating not only mobilisation, but also communication and interaction. Nonetheless, state governments and respective authorities are deploying new technologies as tools and resources for propaganda. There are several limitations that can impede the uses of new media, from issues of accessibility and digital gaps to the ability of authorities to block networks, the use of legislation to impose restrictions albeit indirectly and the use of coercion. These dynamics still pose significant issues and challenges for dissident movements. These debates and contexts would be very crucial for our understanding of conflict activities in a Nigerian setting. It also went further to consider the CC theoretical framework that succinctly captured the debate on the effect of ICTs on the activities conflict movements. This model allows for a consideration of these groups from multiple perspectives, by harnessing the components of RMT, conflict and media theories, respectively. Following on from the discussion offered in this chapter and the previous chapters, Chapter 4 describes and justifies the research methodology employed in this thesis.

Chapter 4

The Occupy Nigeria Protest

4.1. Evolution of Occupy Nigeria

The January 2012 protest emerged as a response to the removal of petroleum subsidy in what came to be known as Occupy Nigeria. The Occupy Nigeria protest is a hallmark event in the history of collective social movement action in Nigeria. However, to provide a clear description of the Occupy Nigeria movement, it is crucial to first give a brief political background on protests ignited by changes to petroleum policies, which have been rife in Nigeria. In fact, constant flux in oil prices, as Figure 4.1 demonstrates, accounts for a significant cause for protests in Nigeria's four decades since independence. The removal of petroleum subsidy in January 2012, which was meant to subsidise the cost of petroleum, led to an immediate surge in the price of petroleum products that more than doubled the normal amount (see Figure 4.1). To be precise, before the removal of the subsidy, petroleum sold at 65 Naira; however, following the withdrawal, the price moved up to roughly to between 138 and 250 Naira, representing

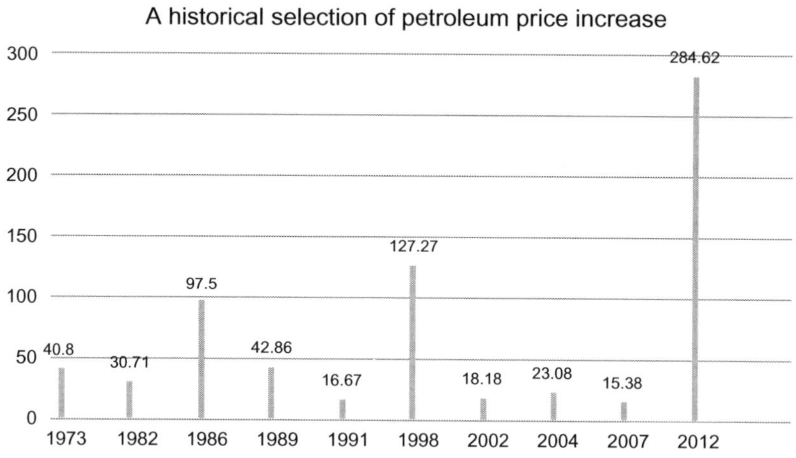

Figure 4.1. Margins for Increase in Oil Prices (1973–2012). *Source*: An analysis based on data provided by Vanguard Nigeria. Available at: http://www.vanguardngr.com/2012/01/fuel-or-fraud-subsidy-war-nigeria-loses-n2trn-in-six-days/

between 112.31% and 284.62% increase. A further effect of general inflation on market goods and services had emerged as a result of the removal of subsidy.

It is not the first time that Nigerians are engaging in political protests on issues relating to the increase in the price of oil (Luqman & Lawal, 2011, p. 71). The labour unions and other traditional trade unions have been at the epicentre of protests and activism relating to increases in the price of petroleum (Adesina, 2000; Luqman & Lawal, 2011; Oyelere, 2014). Strikes and sit-ins became a vital component of the tactical repertoire of these civil society actors in challenging state policies on petroleum considered people unfriendly (Nwoko, 2009, pp. 139–151). Before the current technological revolution, protests usually targeted against the government in Nigeria were often facilitated by the traditional mainstream media (Ikelegbe, 2001, p. 8). These include print media and electronic media. For instance, circulars on strike action would be communicated via television, radio and newspapers including through letters addressed to civil society representatives in various states of the federation (Taiwo, 2007, p. 231). A significant concern, however, was that the state often stalled civil society access to mainstream media through various forms of repression as discussed in Chapter 1 (Nwoko, 2009, p. 147). In particular, the authorities (Government) used censorship and coercion, which often comprised a direct attack on the media, civil society and independent activists. For instance, in an attempt to silence dissent and suppress information during oil-related protests between 2002 and 2003, 'several journalists were beaten by the police during the fuel strike and protests' (Human Rights Watch, 2003a, 2003b, p. 3). In late November 2002, *The Argus*, *The Beacon* and *The Independent Monitor*, three independent newspapers founded in Port Harcourt, had their premises ransacked by the police, and the police detained some journalists for broadcasting stories seen as scrutinised by the state government (Human Rights Watch, 2003b p. 25).

Protests decreased during the dictatorship years, especially during the period leading to democratisation in 1999. Nonetheless, protests have been evolving since the transition to democracy and given the technological developments in the areas of new ICTs that emerged in Nigeria after democratisation. So, the question is what makes the current case of Occupy Nigeria crucial? Occupy Nigeria is a distinctive model for collective action in the contemporary Nigerian context for several reasons. The rest of this section will demonstrate this assertion. However, the most notable of these qualities is the emphasis on the movement's network form of mobilisation and using ICTs, the internet and social media during the protests.

In this regard, 1 January 2012, will go down as a major landmark in the Nigerian history of conflict, the day the Occupy Nigeria movement emerged. For many years, given the country's history of repression, one would have debunked the possibility of mass protests and revolts in Nigeria. The scepticism remained in spite of the shortfall in development and the highly repressive political atmosphere characterises the pre-1999 democratic transition. Nonetheless, the uncertainty was challenged in the wake of 2 January 2012. The Nigerian government had just announced the removal of an oil subsidy policy in favour of a new programme it had adopted on 1 January 2012. Although this is not the first time a policy reform had affected the prices of petroleum products, this time, the impact of the removal of subsidy was much more remarkable (see Figure 4.1). Nigerians responded to the government's new policy through sustained conflict which mainly included protests and dissent across symbolic venues in Nigeria, from the Eagles Square in Abuja, the federal capital territory, and Freedom Park in Lagos to the Liberation Square in Kano, Mokola Roundabout in Ibadan and Murtala Square Kaduna, to mention a few. Soon the Occupy Nigeria occupations and rallies were replicated across the globe. Nigerians occupied strategic locations (Nigerian High Commissions) in major cities of the world, from the United States and the United Kingdom to Switzerland, Canada, Brazil and China, to mention a few, during the 18 days the protest lasted (Emmanuel & Ezeamalu, 2013).

4.1.1. Organisation and Evolution in Leadership of Occupy Nigeria

One of the crucial issues with contemporary movements is regarding the structure of leadership. There were mixed reactions among participants in the Occupy Nigeria protests interviewed when asked questions on how leadership evolved and functioned in Occupy Nigeria. While some argue there was no clear leadership, others explained they initiated the movement and contributed to some form of leadership. Their response is no surprise as it aptly reflects the spontaneous structure of new social movements (NSMs), which suggests that such movements usually have no clear organisation or leadership form. An illustrative example is the seminal Occupy Wall Street movement. Castells (2001) explained that 'there were no leaders in the movement, not locally, not nationally, not globally [...] no traditional leadership, no rational leadership, and no charismatic leadership' (p. 179). Nonetheless, there were leadership roles that were administered via a general assembly which enables all participants to have a say in the decision-making process.

Nonetheless, two perspectives emerged from the view of the interviewees on the leadership form of the Occupy Nigeria movement. In the third quarter of 2011, Nigerian civil society actors got a hint regarding the government's plan to remove subsidy on petroleum from 2012 onwards. Thus, civil society actors had started initiating a direct grassroots mobilisation of civil society actors, activists, ordinary Nigerians and other stakeholders to debate the implication of the removal of subsidy and possibly consult on measures to take to counter the government's decision. All this had been in the stream months before Occupy Nigeria emerged (see Sahara Reporters, 1 December 2011). These stakeholders engaged in various consultations and meetings in which they combined both old and new media tools to achieve their objectives of mobilising civil society for deliberations.

Several town-hall meetings and other consultations were organised where civil society actors were mobilised using ICTs mainly through listserves, emails and mobile phone and the online media (Interviewee 8, 15 January 2014, Abuja). Press releases were also issued during these events and disseminated on social media and independent media and other online portals of Nigerian newspapers. The press releases were used to make a strong case against the government's plans, the socio-economic and political consequences for the ordinary Nigerian and also serving as a platform for calls for mass protests in January 2012. An interviewee stated that 'there were heated, daily, or even hourly discussions' (Interviewee 8, 15 January 2014, Abuja) on FB groups, Twitter and various list servers that emerged during the pre-Occupy Nigeria period. Interviewee 8, narrating his experience, explained that the formal meetings were happening concurrently with informal discussions in places like bars, where new bonds were formed among citizens who had social relations, mutual interests and the common goal of challenging the state as their ultimate objective. 'The interesting thing was that the height of mobilisation was between August and October 2011' (Interviewee 8, 15 January 2014, Abuja), which was before the removal of the oil subsidy. The aim of such meetings organised by civil society coalitions was to put in place mechanisms to counter any eventuality of the government removing the oil subsidy. Some of the civil society organisations/social movements included Action Aid, United Action for Democracy (UAD), Nigeria Labour Congress (NLC) and Legislative Advocacy Centre (CISLAC) (see Sahara Reporters, 1 December 2011). These civil society actors used this period to plan, schedule dates for protests, issue press releases and identify key civil society actors. What this meant was that there was a direct mobilisation effort on the part of civil society actors in pre-Occupy Nigeria.

The other side of the narrative is regarding the Occupy Nigeria spontaneous outburst on 1 January 2012. Interviewees explained that the movement thrived and expanded more or less as a loose, spontaneous movement in the wake of January 2012 (see also Ejiogu, Adejumo, & Szczygiel, 2013; Hari, 2014). The spontaneity came as a direct reaction of ordinary Nigerians who were angered and outraged at the decision of the government on 1 January 2012. To be clear, the spontaneity here refers to the self-motivation or independent effort on the part of many Nigerian citizens who trooped out in large numbers to rallies and demonstrations across Nigeria without any direct or targeted mobilisation attempt by any individual, group or organisation. This also happened concurrently with the dissent that emerged in cyberspace, especially on social media and blogs. In essence, the January 1 outburst comprised loose groups and individuals who were outraged and, therefore, came out to the streets to show resistance and dissent. One participant corroborating this point stated that

> The fightback started on 2 January 2012 as a spontaneous outburst in Lagos, Ilorin and some other places. It was not because the Joint Action Front JAF demonstrated that Mujahedeen was killed in Ilorin on 3 January … as far as Mujahedeen and the people that moved to the post office in Ilorin to protest that day were concerned, a lot of them may not have heard of the Joint Action Forum (JAF) in their life.
>
> Interviewee 8, 15 January 2014, Abuja

Interviewee 8 in the aforementioned statement makes a case for the spontaneous outburst and outpouring of Nigerians to the streets in what became occupations of various strategic locations in Nigeria. These actions according to him were independent of civil society or any targeted mobilisation by any group. Interviewee 5 observed that the coalition of civil society organisations involved in the August to October 2011 consultations, organisation and mobilisation had planned a warning protest action. This had been scheduled for the 3rd of January 2012. However, the January announcement regarding the removal of the subsidy policy by the government caught the coalition of civil society off-guard, and likewise during the spontaneous outburst of Nigerian citizens that ensued offline and online. The coalition of civil society organisations that had been pre-organising and mobilising for a national protest action subsequently joined the spontaneous, loose groups that formed the Occupy Nigeria movement from 3 January 2012 (Interviewee 8, 15 January 2014, Abuja; Interviewee 5, 6 January 2014, Abuja).

Subsequently, based on the personal account of interviewees, a self-styled form of leadership gradually evolved during the protests. On the one hand, the leadership that emerged helped to facilitate negotiation between the government and protestors. While on the other hand, it also helped to stop the protests from degenerating into chaos. According to one interviewee, this leadership was down to two coalitions. The core coalition that was at the epicentre of the Occupy Nigeria protests and negotiations with the authorities was the Labour Civil Society Coalition. It is not exactly clear how many organisations were involved, but the membership of this coalition was drawn from among the leadership of the two traditional labour organisations, the Nigerian Labour Congress (NLC) and the Trade Union Congress (TUC), and two civil society coalitions, the Joint Action Forum (JAF) and the UAD. These civil society organisations were also at the forefront of grassroots organising, mobilising and coordinating deliberations amongst activists, ordinary Nigerians and the government in pre-Occupy Nigeria from August to October 2011. According to the NLC website, the seminal organisation boosts of 37 state councils and 40 affiliate unions with corresponding structures across Nigeria.

Although the government's announcement had caught the Labour Civil Society Coalition off guard, the coalition joined the protest between the 3rd and 9th of January and voluntarily provided some leadership by spearheading deliberations and negotiations among the millions of protesters who had converged on the different rally grounds across the country. For one, it is not surprising, given that these coalitions have had a notable historical antecedent of leading contentious activity, political struggles that predate the Occupy Nigeria movement, in concert with their well-established organisational structures across Nigeria, thereby making it easy for them to correspond with the government. Also, these civil society coalitions had identified relevant stakeholders (affiliates) across the country during their pre-Occupy Nigeria mobilisation. Those identified became useful in the context of coordinating, organising protests, protesters and reporting to the Abuja Coalition from across their respective geopolitical zones. It is pertinent to note that these processes, including their communication, interaction, organisation and mobilisation could not have been possible without ICT, the internet and social media mobilisation as Interviewee 5 observed. This interviewee who has served as a conveyer of different social movements said that:

> In the previous three months before the Occupy Nigeria protest, we had identified people, in the course of the campaigning that if there is a removal of subsidy, there will be protests. We had started identifying people on social media who had also begun to organise in their areas, so some of those people became the pioneers and integral part of Occupy Nigeria across different cities.
>
> Interviewee 5, 6 January 2014, Abuja

The other coalition is the 1 January 2012 movement, which comprises the entire civil society in Nigeria. These were loose groups that pursued similar goals but were not necessarily connected to each other. These included individuals who had responded spontaneously, students, churches, mosques, social movements, market women, associations, institutions and other groups in Nigeria. These were different organisations that came up to be part of the process. This was the spontaneous group that started the Occupy movement on the 2nd of January 2012. These groups that had no formal structures naturally 'subordinated themselves voluntarily to that labour, civil society coalition' (Interviewee 5, 6 January 2014, Abuja) management, especially in serving as the intermediary negotiating between the Occupy Nigeria movement and the government. Several other groups emerged across the country with coalitions of civil society in different states, but they took direction from the Labour Civil Society Coalition without being part of them.

The Labour Civil Society Coalition's principal responsibility was the handling of negotiations on behalf of the people with the government. Therefore, although the Occupy Nigeria movement was leaderless in its original formation as in the case of contemporary and NSMs, some quasi-leadership structure emerged subsequently based on the self-styled dynamic talked upon previously. The leadership was considered quasi- or self-styled because there was no election of any form of representative leadership or appointment of leadership by the Nigeria movement's activist community. The role taken up by the Labour Civil Society Coalition was a voluntary initiative to which the dissidents of Occupy Nigeria were allowed merely since there was no defined leadership. This was necessary for the goal of Occupy Nigeria to be achieved. The coalition set-up a Nigerian striking committee that engaged in direct negotiations with the government on behalf of protestors. Figure 4.2 shows the composition of the 'striking committee' and communication flow based on the perception of members.

Within the NLC striking committee, a further sub-committee was established to ensure some equal levels of representation encourage participation and arrive at some form of consensus among protestors across the country. According to Interviewee 8, there was a secretariat formed for the mobilising committee. The secretariat included individuals in the sub-committees who represented the six geopolitical zones, the South–South (SS), South West (SW), North Central

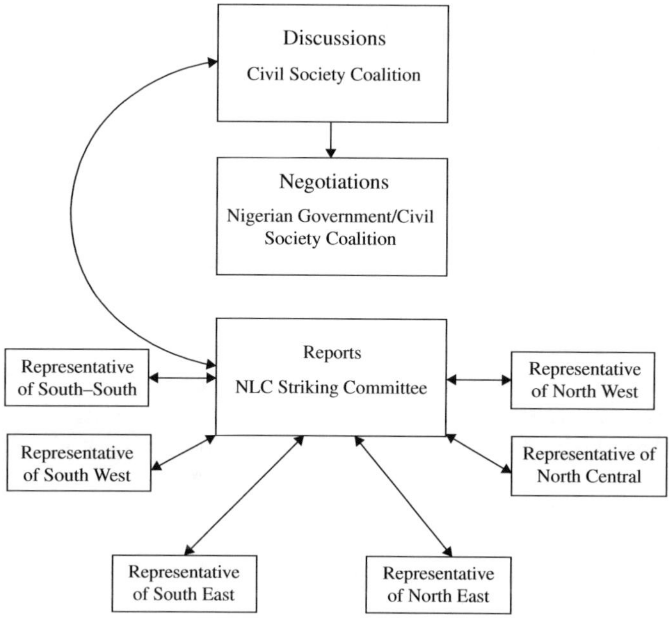

Figure 4.2. Communication Flow and Consensus Chart of Occupy Nigeria Abuja.

(NC), North East (NE), South East (SE) and the North West (NW) zones as represented in Figure 4.2. With the formal structures (sub-divisions) of the NLC in every state of the federation participating in piloting and coordinating Occupy Nigeria protests across the country, the six representatives of the striking committee were responsible for obtaining reports and updates from the different zones they represented. The constituencies as used here refer to, for instance, the designated labour unions in the different zones across the country. Participating civil society organisations, social movements and activist networks provided reports and updates. A member of the NLC striking committee and directly in charge of one of the zones substantiates this point. According to him,

> Every day, our routines was such that after every demonstration, those of us that were assigned to specific zones, six of us that constituted like the secretariat of the mobilization committee, had to get reports from the trade union in each of those states in our zones, but also from activists so that we had a balanced perspective. We then reported back every day the NLC strike committee would meet.
>
> Interviewee 8, 15 January 2014, Abuja

The reports and updates helped the NLC–civil society coalition to monitor developments and better manage and coordinate protestors including resolving issues and concerns. Looking through a more theoretical lens, one could posit that although the Occupy Nigeria movement adopted an informal leadership structure (given that there were no elected/appointed leaders for the movement), including the absence of a properly articulated organisational form that corresponds with the general workings of NSMs, the structure allowed for some participatory democratic culture. While the Labour Civil Society Coalition engaged the government in negotiations and carried along protests, other activist groups, individual activists and other ordinary Nigerians planned, initiated, organised and coordinated protests both offline (real-life settings) and online. In more theoretical terms, a strictly post-modernist perspective of contemporary social movements advocates the notion of a horizontal structure or decentralised network, which Deleuze and Guattari (1987) described as 'rhizomatic' as opposed to hierarchical structures. Occupy Nigeria, however, presents an illustrative example of an interplay between the two dimensions, thereby forming some linear or hybrid structure which combines elements of both the horizontal (rhizomatic) and the hierarchical structure of the organisation. While from the discussion earlier one can see the hierarchical dynamic in the organisational structure of the Occupy Nigeria movement, the rhizomatic aspect of the structure is demonstrated in the role played by ICTs, the internet and social media in diffusing the protests across Nigeria and abroad, thereby empowering and arming dissidents with the necessary tools to control and manage their activities online. As will become clear in subsequent sections of this chapter, the whole process culminating into the Occupy Nigeria movement was aided by the decentralised structure of the internet and digital media that limits state interference and gives autonomy to movement actors.

Thus, given the organisational form explained, when asked how the process of organisation, communication and mobilisation was managed between civil society organisations and individual dissenters, a participant explained that the process was only possible through the uses of ICTs, which were efficiently employed. In his words,

the United Action for Democracy UAD, the Nigerian Labour Congress NLC and Trade Union Congress TUC used ICTs, even now if the NLC had to call a national executive meeting, our National Executive Council (NEC) comprises of all the chairmen and secretaries of all the states of the federation and all the presidents and general secretary of all the unions all over the country … to summon a meeting of such capacity in 24hours, we must have used ICTs (Interviewee 4, 1 January 2014, Abuja).

In this regard, email communication was the most explored in the inter-civil society communication.

4.2. The Role of Information and Communication Technologies

4.2.1. Framing Issues and the Uses of ICTs

Following the CC framework, one component of the resource mobilisation model that ICTs are thought to influence during social movement action is the framing process. Frames as established in Chapter 3 refer to those particular 'metaphors, symbolic representations, and cognitive cues used to render or cast behaviour and events in an evaluative mode and to suggest alternative modes of action [...]'. Symbols, frames and ideologies are created and changed in the process of contestation (Zald, 1996, p. 262). Meier (2011) also shares a similar explanation. According to him, the process involves 'deliberate efforts to craft, disseminate and counter the language and narratives used to describe a resistance movement' (Zald, p. 35). Consequently, the management of such frames is crucial to the success of any mobilisation attempt targeted at individuals by movement actors. Zald (1996) pointed out that the purpose of frames used by actors is to justify claims made by movement actors with the implication of motivating collective action (p. 206).

During the January 2012 Occupy Nigeria protests, many Nigerians in an outburst against the governments' policy took to the streets to participate in the protest. The protest started as a single issue movement with Nigerian dissidents advocating for the Nigerian government to reverse its decision to end the oil subsidy programme that had benefited Nigerians for decades. In this regard, the main focus was around the slogan 'N65 or nothing' which Occupy Nigerian protesters carrying placards chanted as they marched through the streets of major Nigerian cities. This was the manifest issue. Subsequently, other issues confronting the Nigerian state became incorporated into their advocacy. These issues revolved around the central theme that demanded that the government reverse its decision. Banners in demonstrations that took place across major cities in Nigeria contained slogans that included, 'Stop corruption, not the subsidy', 'Kill corruption, not the people', 'Say no to government wastages', 'N65 a litre or revolution now', 'Nigerian say no to removal of subsidy' and 'Remove corruption, not subsidy', to mention but a few slogans used by Occupy Nigeria dissidents. These were the secondary issues that emerged. For instance, the issue of corruption surfacing a lot in the rhetoric of Occupy Nigeria dissidents was a means that protesters used to identify and re-channel the government's focus to what they considered the underlying problem in the down-stream oil sector that needed to be fixed rather than ending the subsidy. These primary and secondary issues existed side by side during the Occupy Nigeria protests. For instance, the majority of participants interviewed identified the demand 'N65 or nothing' as the main theme. Nonetheless, they also highlighted other demands for the government to end the tide of corruption that was ravaging the oil industry and other sectors of the economy, as well as system change that later emerged in the narrative of some protestors. For example, some slogans demanded revolution, 'N65 a litre or revolution now' and another that read as 'Incompetent Jonathan, must go' are notable examples. Other issues included the issue of insecurity and the need to put in place the necessary mechanisms to ensure good governance surfaced within the narrative of protesters. The protest moved beyond the issue of subsidy to incorporate long-held grievances around socio-political and economic injustices epitomised by the issue of corruption and general insecurities caused by the Boko Haram conflict.

Together with FB and Twitter, Nigerians exploited the platform created by Nairaland, an online media forum designed and managed by a Nigerian, Seun Osewa, as far back as 2005. According to Alexa.com, it is a broad discussion forum for Nigerians. It covers numerous subjects from politics and romance to technology, education, business and entertainment, to mention but a few. This platform was used by Nigerians to debate and engage in discussion on the removal of the subsidy during the protests. Like FB and Twitter, the online platforms (Nairaland) allow individuals to hold conversations in real time, making comments and responding to other users, mostly using pseudo-names. In an interview with *CPAfrica,* Seun Osewa demonstrated the national coverage of Nairaland, in the sense that most of the discussions on the platform originate mostly among Nigerians at home which is a direct contrast to the transnational and global coverage of FB and Twitter. A consideration of some of the discussions of participants later examined on Nairaland revealed a divided opinion on the issues of the government's removal of oil subsidy. On the one hand, some members of the forum argued that the movement was a single-issue movement, while on the other hand, others claimed it was a multiple-issue movement involving diverse issues. For instance, one member of the forum explains that Nigerians were merely concerned about returning the subsidy. According to him,

> I have heard a lot of people saying that the Nigerian masses are protesting against corruption. That is a big lie! Nigerian masses want the price of fuel to be returned back to 65 Naira. That is what they are protesting for [...] In essence, they care less about corruption and bad leadership. As long as they keep getting subsidy (awoof) from government, the government can freely steal them blind!
>
> User 1, 14 January 2012, Nairaland

For the aforementioned member of the forum, Nigerian dissidents protesting were oblivious of the level of exploitation the subsidy opened to the rich in the Nigerian society, hence, their concentration on the return of the subsidy. It is apparent that for this participant, the removal of the subsidy will curb the exploitation and corruption in the sector, but the member fails to explain the benefit for the Nigerian dissidents protesting against harsh conditions that the policy change had effected. By contrast, other members of the forum advocated that the issue goes beyond the demand for the return of the oil subsidy. A member of the forum explained that beyond subsidy and corruption, Nigerians were protesting against other issues including

> Boko Haram, negligent of the Niger-delta, killing of Christians [...] this is way beyond subsidy because subsidy has been removed in the past and there have never been a protest like this. Nigerians have had their cup filled and they are venting out their anger on the government.
>
> User 2, 14 January 2012, Nairaland

The understanding here is that there had never been protests on the scale of the January 2012 protests despite many previous attempts by the previous government to remove the subsidy and fluctuation in the prices of petroleum in Nigeria. Commenting on a similar point to the one made by User 2 earlier that the protests that surfaced in January 2012 had been long overdue, an interviewee noted that 'Nigeria was sitting on and is still sitting on gunpowder. People were just waiting for something to ignite the fire' (Interviewee 4, 1 January 2014, Abuja). In this context, the removal of the subsidy created the opportunity for multiple issues (manifest and latent) to emerge. Moreover, on the same point, some other members of the forum also agreed that the issue for which individuals and groups had taken to the streets went beyond the removal of subsidy. This group, however, questioned the continuity of the protests if the government reversed its oil policy by returning the subsidy. One member's narrative is particularly telling:

> If we revert to N65, will the protests continue? Will the movement against corruption, etc. gather more momentum?
>
> User 3, 14 January 2012, Nairaland

> [...] If the prize is reverted back to N65 [...] watch people sing the hallelujah victory song, jugging home gleefully in a victory lap.
>
> User 4, 14 January 2012, Nairaland

Another member of the forum corroborated the initial point made by User 2 that the issues go beyond the removal of subsidy. According to him,

> It is very likely that the strike/protests might end if the price of gas is reversed, but that doesn't mean that the fight was all about gas.
>
> User 5, 14 January 2012, Nairaland

> The present struggle is not just about the removal of subsidy on petroleum. It is also about good governance and also [...] about a fight against the unbelievable level of corruption in government.
>
> Participant 6, 11 January 2012, Save Nigeria Group Facebook

The varied perspectives of members of this forum correspond with some of the views of participants interviewed. Another interviewee simply argued that

> The goal of the Occupy Nigeria movement was to ensure that the government did the needful which was to listen to the cries of Nigerians who were really aware of the issues involved and that the government would revert to the normal price of petroleum. Even if the price was going to increase at least let it be done in a transparent way.
>
> Interviewee 1, 11 December 2013, Abuja

> First is the injustice of the increase in the pump price of fuel and petroleum products, which is the catalyst. But, beyond all of that, it was also an opportunity for citizens to put a resounding voice to the incompetence of the government of the day. So these are the real driving themes.
>
> Interviewee 7, 15 January 2014, Abuja

One can argue that the removal of oil subsidy provided an opportunity for protests to emerge within the Nigerian civil society. As a result, the medium was used for advocacies covering other issues within the already strained and aggrieved population. Hence, this resulted in the emergence of problems relating to corruption, security, economy and regime change, which is a development that had been a major source of struggle in the country's 50 years of independence.

Regarding the framing process dynamic, although partly discussed as a component of the opportunity structure elsewhere, it is essential to consider this dynamic as an independent variable here and in particular whether or not the uses of ICTs influenced the framing of issues, identity and strategy of Occupy Nigeria dissidents. In the framing context, ICTs were crucial, as seen earlier in the activities of Occupy Nigeria online. The influence of the framing process was felt both locally and across the globe. Participants engaged their issues online through political commentaries on weblogs, news releases on various online media platforms and intense discussions on social media (in particular FB, Twitter and Nairaland). Other platforms used include civil society websites, private media and documentaries on YouTube, to mention but a few.

> I was posting on an average, like 2 dozen tweets and on Facebook may be about double of that amount or thereabout. […] I was writing every day and posting on my blog. At the last count, I realised that most of what I wrote was re-blogged or even published in newspapers in 17 different countries […] in different languages.
>
> Interviewee 8, 15 January 2014, Abuja

Interviewee 8 added that his blog posts and write-ups during the uprising were translated and published in German and Greek. The write-ups have also surfaced on Canadian, Australian and United Kingdom online media platforms. These activities are partly responsible for the widespread transnational movement that was formed around Occupy Nigeria. In part, the exposure to information published by Nigerian dissidents at home during the protests enthused action among Nigerians in the diaspora. Veteran civil society actors who participated in the Occupy Nigeria protest explained that various online media instruments shaped movement activities in the 18 days that the Occupy Nigeria protests lasted.

Interviewee 4 taking a similar stance argued that his personal FB pages which he operates are set principally to broadcast information and in particular political commentary to a local and global audience, the media and activists.

According to him, the use of multiple FB accounts was an initiative he had to bypass potential limitations of one been shut down or scrutinised by the state during conflicts. During the protests in January, he explained that his FB pages, which have (all together) roughly 15,000 followers, were relied on among Nigerians for information.

> I got wind of what will happen to petroleum prices so, I wrote an open letter to the president, to Jonathan, which was published that same day 1st of January, so it assisted people with information. It was published in most Nigerian newspapers, and online sites like Sahara reporters, news diary online [...].
>
> Interviewee 4, 1 January 2014, Abuja

Digital media were particularly crucial for Occupy Nigeria protesters and indeed for the wider Nigerian public because of the decreased trust in traditional mainstream media due to limitations of censorship or self-censorship. In particular, because there is an unfair balance that tilts in favour of the state with traditional media. Both public and private media were reluctant to broadcast the protests at the inception of the protests; therefore, bypassing and circumventing such limitations was found to be a priority for Occupy Nigeria protestors if they were to get their messages out to the public. This explains the predominant uses of ICTs among participants who wanted to shape public opinion.

On one hand, while state-run media are perceived as a tool for advancing the propaganda of the government, given the government's direct hegemony and interference over public media in Nigeria, private media, on the other hand, enjoy similar limitations (Oketunmbi, 2006; Oseni, 1995; Olukotun, 2002a, 2002b). Groshek (2010) argued that data that are accessible in cyberspace 'is less likely than other mass media formats to conform to the prevailing national-level ideological and hegemonic structures' (p. 146). Groshek's (2010, p. 146) point which corroborates the findings from the Occupy Nigeria case stems from the belief that because of the structures of ICTs, there are higher chances for almost anyone to take part and contribute in an online environment in contrast to the more traditional media types. The free flow of information that the web structure offers meant that Nigerians who had access to the internet could express their views, constructing their stories on a daily basis and disseminating to the global community. However, the digital gap, income gap and literacy levels between urban and rural areas mean that particular communities of the population of the country are excluded from the benefits of ICTs during protests. Nonetheless, participants argue that the benefits of ICTs especially for getting out information far outweigh the negatives. One respondent noted that:

> On social media your voice is not in the Nigerian context, restricted, you have direct access to the publishing platform, if you want to access the normal traditional media, you will be thinking about first of all getting someone to report your views, it will be competing with several other things that they are trying to

> fit into the newspaper, or into their air time and again, it may not be something they feel is worth being put out there especially when they look at all the things they have. So, social media gives you an easier and more flexible platform that is at your fingertips. You are your publisher.
>
> Interviewee 2, 17 December 2013, Abuja

The hashtag '#OccupyNigeria' on Twitter became the central platform used predominantly by Nigerian dissidents at home and abroad to share information within and outside Nigeria. Blackberry messenger was also used to share information with networks of friends and blogs used to publish political commentary and information (see for instance http://solidarityandstruggle.blogspot.co.uk/). Photo sharing sites including Flickr and Yfrog also provided an avenue for Nigerian dissidents to upload images of events as it unfolded, while video platforms, in particular YouTube, were used to disseminate audio-visual material including news and documentaries to Nigerians at home and diasporic counterparts (see also Ejiogu et al., 2013, p. 222). *Sahara Reporters*, an online media firm owned by a Nigerian in the diaspora also provided a platform for Nigerians to get their message across the globe. One interviewee corroborated this point. According to him:

> We started consciously reporting it as Occupy Nigeria, we started given report on January 3rd, and we had occupied Nigeria day 1 report, Occupy Nigeria day 2 report, so we consciously put that in the minds of the people and by Friday, January 6th that weekend, that Friday 4th, 5th, and 6th, through the efforts of the likes of Sahara Reporters and Kayode Ogundamisi, what was happening in Kano was being streamed online.
>
> Interviewee 5, 6 January 2014, Abuja

The uses of different online media platforms of social media allowed for a balance of perspectives between the stories emanating from the private, public media outlets and Occupy Nigeria dissidents who had the capacity to direct media agendas and set the agenda for their activities including how they wanted to be perceived locally and across the globe (Sowore, 14 January 2013). A significant element of the framing process is also that the platform provided an avenue for legitimatising discourses of parties in a conflict by giving multiple platforms and alternative sources for individuals to evaluate and decide what line of thought is relevant or appropriate for them to follow. As such, the monopoly over the media once held as the exclusive preserve of the state can be argued to be gradually diminishing. A participant noted that in the present age, people are more informed (Interviewee 4, January 2014, Abuja). In his words:

> In the past, it was easy for governments to lie or some political party to lie and misinform the public, but it is difficult now

> because when you lie, individuals would check through social platforms and verify the truth.
>
> Interviewee 4, 1 January 2014, Abuja

The discernment of the truth is one tool of mobilisation because it exposes the lies of the state that give credence to the cause. Issues that individuals raise on the social media platform are particularly very informative. Such matters can produce vital information which in turn influences people's opinion about politics and society. In this regard, it is argued that ICTs increase political consciousness (Mohammed, 2012; Sowore, 2013), a position which conforms with the response of an Occupy Nigeria activist interviewed. In the current context, ICTs have opened up spaces for the Nigerian civil society to increase their social and political awareness on the issues that affect them. Such political consciousness implies that since individuals are equipped with the knowledge of their rights when infringed upon by the state as in the case of Occupy Nigeria movement, they can demand a redress by engaging in collective action.

Besides social media, protesters were able to bypass traditional media limitations by relying on online news media like *Sahara Reporters*, as mentioned earlier. The new media was used to broadcast and publish their stories, pictures and videos during the Occupy Nigeria protests. The online platform granted interviews to participants of the Occupy Nigeria movement via Skype and published such interviews and documentaries on its website and YouTube channel. The *Sahara Reporter*'s platform on YouTube has roughly over 115, 000 subscribers and over 40 million views as at the last time of check-in December 2015. In one video posted by the organisation on its YouTube channel during the protests, it generated over 32, 000 views (see Saharatv, 13 January 2012). Another Occupy Nigeria video posted by *Sahara Reporters* on Day 2 of the protest attracted over 12, 000 views (see Saharatv, 3 January 2012). Besides this, ordinary protestors were sending pictures, images, texts and video to the online media organisation using smart phones, IPads and laptops. These documents were then disseminated on the website *Sahara Reporters* as the events unfolded. Narrating the role played by the online media outlet, Interviewee 3 explained:

> Some of the appearances I made on Sahara Reporters in the cause of the protest were through Skype, some through telephone conversation others through emails. Some of the first images that Sahara Reporters published when Nigerians were attacked at the Eagles Square by security personnel were pictures I posted to my Facebook page and my Facebook wall.
>
> Interviewee 3, 20 December 2013, Abuja

Besides using the *Sahara Reporters* platform, individual postings on YouTube were also rife during the protests, which reflect the benefits of the decentralised nature of Web 2.0 and ICTs especially for getting their message out. A simple search for 'Occupy Nigeria' in YouTube, as at the time of writing in December 2015, revealed over 50,000 results involving videos posted by individual Nigerians, organisations and independent media organisations at home and in the diaspora. Each video is also evidencing several thousand views and likes, too numerous to capture in the present study.

4.2.2. Occupy Nigeria's Core Framing Tasks

The framing process aims to provide impetus and justification for collective action, both of which if appropriately managed by movement actors could have a positive impact on the overall outcome of movement activities. It has been established that ICTs enable movement actors to construct their narratives, stories and shape public opinion (Garrett, 2006; Karatzogianni, 2006a, 2006b; Meier, 2011). For contemporary movements, framing process using new media can help reduce pressures from the state. A careful observation of the narrative repertoire of Occupy Nigeria dissidents reveals specific collective action frames. In particular, while there are several frames employed by Occupy Nigeria activists, an overarching theme is that of injustice. Other frames that emerged are considered here as sub-themes embedded within the injustice frame. Sub-themes on *corruption* and *economic crime*, *minority rights*, and *government responsibility* (responsible government) emerged as frames used by dissidents to communicate their plight. All framing resonates around the injustice of removing the subsidy. These frames were means through which movement actors sought to pursue their collective goal, justify their activities and build impetus for the cause (Benford, 1993; Snow & Benford, 2000).

As the terminology suggests injustice, frames are themes used by Occupy Nigeria dissidents to demonstrate unjust, unfair, inequality and a violation of their rights. These attributes were used to convince bystanders, as well as Nigerians at home and abroad, to participate in the protests. According to Gamson (1982), the motivation to engage in contentious activities hinges on the belief that the action of the authority if left unchecked could lead to injustice. Gamson's explanation was used in a pre-emptive scenario such that dissidents act based on information before actual action being taken by the authority. In this context, however, the injustice frame is used before, during and in post-government action. Going by the discussions of Occupy Nigeria dissidents, injustice frames were used to showcase dissent towards what they perceived as the government's unjust and unfair decision to remove the subsidy which places them at a disadvantaged position. For instance, an interviewee noted that for her:

> I think it was everything coming together, for me it was personal, I was just finishing my NYSC, I have a car which consumes a lot of fuel, and if the price of fuel goes up, it will directly affect everything I do. So it was very personal. It was also about how people were not getting the right service for the amount we were paying.
>
> Interviewee 6, 11 January 2014, Abuja

Speaking further on the injustice frame, a few examples from the official FB posts and Twitter feeds of Occupy Nigeria are particularly telling. It is crucial to note that there was one official Twitter account operated by Occupy Nigeria namely #OccupyNigeria. A few other Occupy Nigeria pages that sprouted up were mostly created by individuals (the details regarding operators and demographics of the other pages are unclear). The same applies to FB. Again different Occupy Nigeria FB pages were set-up by individuals and groups which in most cases reflected the geographical locations where dissidents were domiciled both at home and abroad. Nonetheless, the Occupy Nigeria Abuja page was the official page of Nigeria. The official description of the Occupy Nigeria movement on the official page of the movement on Twitter reads, 'We the 99% need to start action or else 1 day the effect of Corruption and negligence will be in our immediate household. The time is now, and yes, you are needed' (@Occupynigeria Twitter, 2012). The notion of corruption and negligence is symbolic of the many years of exploitation of the wealth of Africa's largest economy. Much of Nigeria's wealth is believed to rest in the hands of the political class in the Nigerian society. Occupy Nigeria dissidents were of the opinion that most of the 'few' have monopolised the natural means of production (land and mineral resources) and continue to perpetuate economic crime, especially within the down-stream sector of the oil and gas industry that accounts for Nigeria's mainstay of the economy. Different indicators of poverty show poverty on the increase in the country with more than half of the population living on less than US$ 1 a day.

> The system we live in is the most irrational thing you can imagine. There is more than enough for everyone to live a good life. But to borrow from one of the metaphors of this period, the 1% have appropriated everything to the detriment of the 99%.
>
> Interviewee 8, 15 January 2014, Abuja

Corruption emerged as a significant theme in the advocacy of Occupy Nigeria dissidents. This topic surfaced in all rallies held across major Nigerian cities at home and abroad and has been one long-held grievance for Nigerians over the years. Not much has changed in this regard as epitomised in the narratives of Occupy Nigeria movement actors. Various indices of corruption have shown no significant change. Although a secondary issue, Occupy Nigerians made a case for negligence on the part of public officials in tackling the situation (see Sahara Reporters, 1 December, 2011). The general neglect has impacted negatively on development in the country as will be demonstrated in case studies in the succeeding chapters. Besides the explicit call to action embedded in the official Twitter text of the movement, there is also an explicit demonstration of the injustice frame in the text of the group account.

The injustice here goes beyond the removal of oil subsidy. Again, the general sense of dissatisfaction spread across all spheres of areas and sectors of the Nigerian economy. This is epitomised by the issue of corruption, which resonated during the Occupy Nigeria protests. It was with this observation that Interviewee 4 explained (mentioned earlier) 'that Nigeria had been and continued to sit on a gunpowder waiting to ignite' (Interviewee 4, 1 January 2014,

Abuja) considering the pain and suffering the Nigerian population has been subjected to owing to what Tanzi (1998) described as misuse of public power for non-public benefits, in this case, for private gains. The Occupy Nigeria advocacy relied heavily on injustice frames as a means to expose the government as an exploitative one, insensitive to the plight of the ordinary Nigerian. The exploitation of injustice frames helped the group to push for support from their target audience at home and abroad:

> Hav u tot about d angle of d few rich enjoying billions at d expense of a larger poor, it's just like in an attempt to kill a scorpion an ant is crushed along […].
>
> Participant 3, 11 January 2012, Occupy Nigeria Facebook

> The people hav borne d cost for long enough. Govt, u shal meet urs. Let me just say dat 'I sori for govt n all d people wey dey there'.
>
> Participant 4, 16 January 2012, Occupy Nigeria Facebook

> 72% recurrent expenditure budget, ASUU on strike, No power, No water, No good roads, still importing fuel, you think it's over? #OccupyNigeria.
>
> Participant 5, 16 January 2012, Occupy Nigeria Facebook

In a similar vein, on the FB pages of the Occupy Nigeria movement, as of 6 January 2012, the official post reads, 'silence is a crime in an unjust society'. The post was made about the same issue of corruption, poverty, lack of development and inequality that characterised the Nigerian society. The removal of subsidy was perceived by Nigerian dissidents as an extension of the exploitative scheme of the rich and well-to-do in the Nigerian society. While the post is used to force momentum, ignite protests and participation from especially bystanders, it also makes a statement about injustice and the sub-themes that emerged from the protests. In the same post, commentators sought to mobilise the minds of Nigerian dissidents to participate. One commentator argued that 'silence isn't just a crime but personal injustice against yourself, personal deprivation, and crime against God himself' (Participant 1, 6 January 2012, Occupy Nigeria Facebook). Another comment stated that that's what Baba Fela referred to as: 'THE CONSPIRACY OF SILENCE'. The idea that Nigerians remained docile despite their worsening political and socio-economic conditions (Participant 2, 6 January 2012, OccupyNigeria Facebook).

> Now is fuel! We no go gree! Is either 65 or notin. Jonathan! U r simply wicked. No job, no Rd, no security, no housing estate.
>
> Participant 9, 12 January 2012, Save Nigeria Group Facebook

> FG should know that Nigerians are not only clamouring for fuel subsidy but also against bad leadership, oppression, corruption, self-centeredness, nepotism, and marginalisation. The voice of the masses is the voice of God [...] My people lets come together under one umbrella and tell it to their face that they can't fool us any longer. Aluta continua!!!
>
> Participant 8, 12 January 2012, Save Nigeria Group Facebook

> Enough is enough for our irresponsible govt!
>
> Participant 7, 11 January 2012, Save Nigeria Group Facebook

> The load is too heavy for the common man to carry. Please our Leaders, take note, we have asked you to look over this policy (Petrol increase) that you are enforcing on our people: Mr President, you cannot enforce 105% petrol increase in a country like Nigeria. In an advance, or growing country, the normal increase takes 2%-10% increase with proper consultation with its citizens: Nowhere in the world do we have petrol increase of 50% talk less of 105%: Please, !!!!
>
> Participant 10, 12 January 2012, Save Nigeria Group Facebook

The use of injustice-related themes or frames as used in the Occupy Nigeria case is similar to the advocacy of transnational social movement (TSM) challenging socio-political and economic inequality.

> #OWS is fighting back against the corrosive power of major banks and multinational corporations over the democratic process, and the role of Wall Street in creating an economic collapse that has caused the greatest recession in generations. The movement [...] aims to fight back against the richest 1% of people that are writing the rules of an unfair global economy that is foreclosing on our future.
>
> https://occupywallst.org/

In this regard, Occupy Nigeria protests could be situated within a broader ideological struggle of the global anti-capitalist and anti-globalisation movements across the globe as in the case of the Occupy Wall Street movement. The aforementioned text from the official web page of Occupy Wall Street shows a similar dissatisfaction towards the monopoly of the world's wealthiest conglomerates with Wall Street considered to facilitate unfair practices in its economic policies. As stated, it is the goal of the protagonists to challenge the unfair (inequality) practices of the capitalist that pose a threat to the future of the economy and future generations. In the Occupy Nigeria context, several frames are used to garner momentum, mobilise participation and shape public opinion on the issue of oil subsidy in view to forcing the Nigerian government to revert her decision and take responsibility for the failings and future direction of the country. Nonetheless, injustice frames are the principal means by which these grievances are expressed.

The sub-themes or sub-frames are used by Occupy Nigeria dissidents also to attribute blame and as a means to redirect the government and the global community to the movement's idea of the underlying problems. For actors online and offline, the government should be tackling the underlying issues rather than imposing more hardship on the population. For instance, Interviewee 5 explained that his conviction was that the arguments for removing oil subsidy were not tenable. He stated, 'my personal conviction is that the country had a problem, and the problem was with corruption with economic crime' (Interviewee 5, 6 January 2014, Abuja). Economic crime was in the sense that the few 1% had abused the subsidy framework by exploiting and accumulating oil benefits for personal use and nothing was done to check the excesses of the system. 'I was convinced about, that there was fraud going on and that it was an attempt to cover the fraud rather than to deal with the fraud' (Interviewee 5, 6 January 2014, Abuja). The other two sub-themes of inequality and government responsibility are by no means exhaustive of the themes that emerged in the narratives of Occupy Nigeria dissidents. However, these themes encapsulate the general sense of injustice and the failing infrastructure of governance. These frames are used to depict the widening economic gap between the rich and the poor and how changes, especially in the context of the removal of oil subsidy places an unfair balance on the poor.

Meier (2011) found that the state can foster patriotism and shape public opinion by using ICTs in contentious situations and, as Morovoz (2011a, 2011b) also argues, authorities have increasingly become technically inclined, and as such, authorities use ICTs to achieve their goals. In the Nigerian context, the government used online media platforms to create acquiescence and agreement by sponsoring various adverts providing information on the benefit of the removal of oil subsidy. Interviewed participants also claimed that the government sponsored individuals on social media to respond to the antagonism, propaganda and advocacy of Occupy Nigeria dissidents online in view to defending the government's decision and providing an excellent public image for the state. While the researcher could not verify this claim, there was a reasonable debate on social media between individuals who supported the government's action and those who did not. This conflict of interests does not necessarily suggest that those who supported the government's decision to remove the subsidy were sponsored. Nonetheless, interviewees did not think the government was efficient in its deployment of ICTs. The benefit of ICTs fell in favour of the protesters. One interviewee explained that although the government is on social media, he never thought the government used social media platforms as much as the opposition. According to him, the government only used online media to 'issue press releases that were not important to protesters' (Interviewee 4, 1 January 2014, Abuja).

4.2.3. Political Opportunity Structure: Bypassing State Limitations during Occupy Nigeria

It is crucial to state that the importance of the framing activities, as described earlier, wouldn't be useful without ICTs, the internet and everyday social media. This is particularly true given the limitations that are associated with traditional mainstream media. Undoubtedly, the state exercises hegemony and control over traditional media. This leads us to the next point on the political opportunity structure: the impact of ICTs, the internet and social media on these and the implications for the framing process. As stated earlier, political opportunity and the framing process are intertwined and cannot be separated, especially when the discussion is set against the backdrop of digital activism. As seen in the previous section, the majority of Occupy Nigeria discussions emerged online using various channels available to them. The following analysis considers the political opportunity dynamic.

The political opportunity as described in Chapter 2 is one of the dynamics of the resource mobilisation theory that ICTs are thought to influence conflict movements. McAdam, McCarthy and Zald (1987) explained that the 'political system, structures the opportunities for collective action and extent and form of same'. Explaining this phenomenon, Garrett (2006) describes the opportunity structure as those characteristics of a social system that aid or constrict a movement's action. The structure of political opportunity is used to describe whether or not the national context is open or closed, and democratic or dictatorial. Certainly, these factors determine whether or not contentious activities will thrive. In a separate account, commensurate with Garret's position, Meier (2011) adds another factor besides the political dimension. Meier (2011) found that the relative economic conditions are another component of the opportunity structure, which could either encourage contentious activities or be a limiting factor. Interestingly, these factors played a role in conflicts in contemporary Nigeria. The question is about the role of the internet, ICTs and everyday social media with regard to the opportunity structure. Garrett's (2006) hypothesis proves useful for explaining the interconnection between ICTs, conflict and opportunity structure. He explains that transnational occurrences, trends and change largely compel a country's opportunity structures. This position which, as will be demonstrated, conforms with the findings from the Occupy Nigeria case study can be succinctly articulated in terms of 'information cascade', which Garrett describes as a state in which dissidents engaged in conflict align their actions based on the previous actions of others.

Following the information cascade theorisation, in the context of Occupy Nigeria, some participants interviewed also connected the mass protests to conflict movement activities across the globe particularly between 2011 and 2012. Interviewees found that the wave of conflict that was ongoing within the global scenery played a role in influencing Occupy Nigerian protesters. ICTs provided the opportunity to view those protests in their real contexts, from the Arab uprising, Tunisia, Egypt and the Occupy Wall Street events. The exposure of Occupy Nigeria dissidents to transnational and global protests and revolutions provided the stimuli and impetus for Nigerians to form collective action. One participant explained that:

> What happened in January 2012 was part of a broader moment in history, and it goes, to borrow from Critical Realism, to confirm the truism about the emergence of revolution in a contemporary capitalist world as an international phenomenon evident in the way upsurge are, were and are still interconnected, how Egypt inspired Wisconsin, and Wisconsin inspired Indignados, Swell Puerto inspired…, and then Greece. These came back to inspire Occupy Wall Street and even within the same narrative, Occupy Nigeria that empty signifier came as an inspiration from Occupy Wall Street.
>
> Interviewee 8, 15 January 2014, Abuja

In other words, TSM conflicts, especially in the Middle East and part of North Africa in concert with the interconnectedness, free space and free flow of information created by ICTs, provided the opportunity for civil society and social movements within national contexts to experience and be exposed to activities of TSMs in other parts of the world. A further implication is that such events essentially become stimuli for subsequent protests being duplicated nationally. This is particularly true in countries where individuals are aggrieved by specific government policies, systems or programmes, but there is not enough momentum for public dissent to emerge. This was a motivation in the Occupy Nigeria protests that evolved on 1 January 2012. In concert with this view, another interviewee noted that the 'metaphor itself, the politics, the praxis […] the narrative all reflect the dialectics of a moment in history' (Interviewee 8, 15 January 2014, Abuja). About the Arab Spring and the Occupy movements in the US and Europe, this interviewee goes on, explaining that:

> There was a sense globally, that resistance was possible, resistance was happening, and that change was possible […]. Three governments had fallen in the Arab world. For many of the younger generation of Nigerians, Occupy Nigeria presented an opportunity for them. It was the first time they were taking independent political action, the first time they were engaged in a movement activity that is other than themselves, outside of their family, out of what they could gain any immediate direct material benefit from and this was what it was for many of them, really reinvigorating.
>
> Interviewee 8, 15 January 2014, Abuja

The influence of globalisation in the context of social movement activities on Nigerian dissidents during the Occupy Nigeria protests goes to confirm the 'social media, acceleration, diffusion and transnationalism hypothesis which is offered relentlessly in the global media landscape' (Karatzogianni, 2011, p. 1). The implication being that the free flow of information given the interconnectivity of the internet, social media and new communication technologies aids transnational exposure of TSM activities, thereby influencing social movement activities across different institutions, as well as national and cultural contexts, as seen in the Nigerian case. This point on the influence of TSM activities is corroborated in other studies on conflict. For instance, in her exposition of the impact of ICTs on the Arab uprisings, Karatzogianni (2013) identified the domino effect, that is, the chain reaction that evolved from one event. A striking feature across the highlighted countries can be seen in the role played by ICTs as it created opportunities especially in terms of facilitating the activities of dissident protesters. The quick spread of conflict across the Arab world could be seen as *a* mutation of events from one country to the other due to the awareness created by ICTs. Such exposures then become replicated across national contexts with shared socio-economic, political and cultural experiences. As Karatzogianni (2013) pointed out, the Arab countries affected in the uprisings shared individual characteristics, including domestic food prices, political repression, social media and youth unemployment (p. 8).

In line with the structures of political opportunity argument, the political system of a given country is another factor thought to influence contentious activities and political action by non-institutional actors. In a democratic setting, one can reasonably expect a more flexible and open system that encourages civil, political and human freedoms including participation. In comparison, in totalitarian contexts, one would reasonably expect a more closed society, one in which those freedoms and rights are limited (Meier, 2011, p. 62). In either case, however, the argument is that the internet, ICTs and everyday social media would create an alternative opportunity structure for civil society actors to advance their case with limited barriers from the state. It is in this context that Meier (2011, pp. 62–63) argues that the relative 'accessibility of the political system in the context of coercive states is by definition highly limited'. Also, he explained that:

> This necessarily reduces the public space for protests and other forms of resistance. For example, accessibility in North Korea is virtually impossible save for the small number of elites. While the political system in Burma is also closed, the regime's information blockade and reign of terror is not as effective but limits access to the political system. The same was true of Egypt before 2011 where the most political action occurs on Facebook rather than on the streets.
>
> Meier (2011, p. 63)

Applying this point in the Nigerian context, members of the Occupy Nigeria movement recognised this dynamic as a crucial component in the 2012 uprisings. The situation in Nigeria at the time 'was mobilising enough to make the average Nigerian youth-conscious of their economic environment' (Interviewee 8,

15 January 2014, Abuja). In other words, the fact that Nigeria operates a democratic system aided the Occupy Nigeria movement protests. Perhaps this also explains the explosive nature of the protests, never witnessed in the history of contentious politics in Nigeria. The interviewee's argument takes note of protests related to oil price increase under the repressive military regimes of the past, as seen in Figure 4.1. Despite the military dictatorship at the time, protests still evolved. For instance, there was the 1989–1991 anti-Structural Adjustment Programme (SAP) riots and the 1998 oil protests. The 1989 anti-SAP protest was a reaction to the Nigerian government's implementation of the SAP suggested by the World Bank and the International Monetary Fund.

The SAP programme was meant to among other things reduce the enormous reliance of the economy on the oil sector and diversify the economy, which will then increase development and growth (Adebanwi & Obadare, 2010, pp. 108–109). Contrary to the promise by the government that the SAP programme will boost economic growth, the economy took a turn for the worst (Adebanwi & Obadare, 2010, p. 109). The worsening economic effect of the programme, and as a result of the increase in the price of petroleum products, there were widespread anti-SAP protests across the country, with traditional civil society organisations, students and associations mobilising the protests. Nonetheless, none of these or the other petroleum-related protests emerged on the scale of January 2012 Occupy Nigeria protests. 'It came to us as a surprise under a civil democratic regime; a civil president could even fathom the idea of removing oil subsidy' (Interviewee 3, 20 December 2013, Abuja).

Consequently, in regard to accessing the political system, all the respondents argued that the use of new communication media including ICTs, the internet and social media during the protests made it generally more comfortable for civil society actors to relate to each other during the protests, 'because some civil society organisations are run by young men and women who are ICT savvy' (Interviewee 3, 20 December 2013, Abuja). Also, there is the dynamic of more access to information which means that with these tools (ICTs and internet) citizens can ensure transparency and verify information. The implication is that 'those Nigerians who sat on the fence had [...] access to civil society portals that had current information, current happenings and some in real time' (Interviewee 3, 20 December 2013, Abuja), given that participants on the ground were recording and broadcasting the events from protest locations. For those who were not initially part of the rallies, demonstrations and actual occupations, being exposed to events and getting access to protest information via ICTs became useful especially for encouraging them to join the protests.

The other issue in the political opportunity and ICT discourse is regarding how non-state actors are using the medium to bypass state censorship and regulation including self-censorship of the media. The media is an essential acme in the political opportunity structure for several reasons. As elucidated upon by Karatzogianni (2006a, 2006b), movement actors need to find ways to balance between extreme political action which attracts media coverage and 'conventionality which, (even if potentially persuasive) is ignored by the media' (Karatzogianni, 2006b, p. 156). More so, the medium is a vital contested arena between the challenged and the challenger, especially since it is a platform for getting society to obtain support, mobilise thought and participants. The media can provide the basis for inter-movement connectivity including with other political and social actors. Other benefits of the media for eliciting sympathy for a cause, as well as legitimising social movement activity as noted by Kielbowicz and Scherer (cited in Karatzogianni, 2006a, 2006b, p. 157; Gamson & Meyer, 1996, p. 285), all highlight the struggle for the contested platform. From this point of view, Karatzogianni (2011, p. 157) observes that the media's openness to social movements is in itself a crucial component of the structure of political opportunity. What is the implication for the Nigerian context? In the discussion later, I discuss these in connection with the Nigerian context.

In contemporary Nigeria, Occupy Nigeria provides a case for examining the openness of the media system. Considering the endemic uses of ICTs, the internet and social media during the Occupy Nigeria protests, two perspectives emerged from participant opinions. Members of the Occupy Nigeria movement interviewed agree that the platform offered by new communication media indeed provides more access to the political system, given that individuals were able to more readily channel and express their grievances and dissent directly to the state using such platforms. As one activist explained, 'One did not have to rely on platforms that were controlled by the government or those sympathetic to the government' (Interviewee 1, 11 December 2013, Abuja), in which case, the free flow of communication may have been impeded via regulation or censorship.

Indeed, there were indications of the state's (government's) attempt to shut down telecommunications and Social Networking Sites (SNS) providers, though this was debunked by the Nigerian Communications Commission (NCC) which regulates and issues licences to broadcasters in Nigeria (Akinbode, 2012). It is not the first time that the government has made attempts to block communication networks. Such efforts were made before, during the Occupy Nigeria protests and indeed after the protests. Notable among these is a draft Lawful Interception of Communications Regulation introduced in 2013, and a purported government surveillance contract with an Israeli company to monitor Nigerian email communications and online communications, both of which were greeted with dissent amongst Nigerians in cyberspace (see Freedom House report, 2013; Omanovic, 20 October, 2014; Vanguard, 22 May, 2013). This, in essence, reveals the dialectics between the different contenders over the public sphere (Gamson & Meyer, 1996, p. 287; Karatzogianni, 2006a, 2006b, pp. 157–158; Klandermans & Goslinga, 1996, p. 319; Rucht, 2004; McAdam, McCarthy, & Zald, 1996, p. 289).

Commensurate with this point, Interviewee 5 explained that traditional media platforms, electronic and especially the print media, are avenues for contestation between the governments and Occupy Nigeria protestors. Interviewee 5 argued that traditional media outlets were divided along three paradigms: pro-government, pro-Occupy Nigeria and neutral. The first was the public media outlets that took a pro-government side, thereby providing limited reportage of the events as they unfolded and offered limited access to civil society actors. The government used such media outlets including state-owned and some private for propaganda purposes. For example, Keita (2012) in his exposition on Occupy

Nigeria news coverage argued that the Nigerian Television Authority (NTA) and African Independent Television (AIT) were accused of providing pro-government coverage of the protests which was full of bias. Protests were therefore targeted at such media outfits. The second category is made up of private media outlets, which are further divided into two groups, those who took a pro-Occupy Nigeria stance, providing reportage and giving access to Occupy Nigeria protestors, and the other that included private media outlets who remained non-partisan and tried to offer a balanced reportage of the protests. For example, Channels Television, *Vanguard* newspaper, *The Guardian*, Nigeria, and *Premium Times*, Nigeria, to mention but a few, provided daily coverage of the protests. Regardless of the perceived implication of the three paradigms and the varied responses from the different media outlet, one participant stated that 'The uses of ICTs broke that barrier, by opening new avenues of intercourse so to say that was not possible previously' (Interviewee 1, 11 December 2013, Abuja).

Ultimately, ICTs, the internet and social media, as participants argue, handled circumventing the highlighted limitations of traditional mainstream media. More so, the presence of independent global media, who's on-ground representatives monitored and reported the events as they unfolded, also contributed to bridging the communication gap. As a participant explained, 'there were quite some independent freelance journalists who also came in from Europe with their cameras, making stories and just selling to any network to broadcast about Nigeria' (Interviewee 5, 6 January 2014, Abuja). These reports made it difficult for reluctant traditional media outlets not to provide coverage since Occupy Nigeria dissidents were already broadcasting the protests via multiple channels including social media (Twitter, FB and Nairaland) and other private media outlets at home and abroad (such as the *Sahara Reporters*, *Aljazeera* and BBC). According to members of Occupy Nigeria, these platforms, besides social media, also provided a window of opportunity for protestors to export their ideologies and stories to an international global audience. Interestingly, before the physical presence of these global media outlets and some Nigerian private media organisations in Nigeria, Interviewee 5 narrated how ICTs and social media, in particular, served as a lens for both global and private media for reporting the Occupy Nigeria protests. 'I think what pushed most of the traditional media was because the event was already live on social media' (Interviewee 5, 6 January 2014, Abuja). Ultimately, all the interviewees advocated that new communication media provided an alternative platform for Occupy Nigeria dissidents to bypass the limitations imposed by traditional media.

In response to whether or not ICTs have created an atmosphere of better access to the political system, participants interviewed had a positive response; the challenge, however, is that there is an unfair balance on the side of the government. As one respondent succinctly put it, since communication is a two-way thing, it is a different thing entirely when you consider the response of the government. 'The government has not been as responsive as civil society, in taking advantage of social media actually to interact with the citizens. So, very often, it is citizens talking to the government and the government, maybe once in a while they reply us' (Interviewee 5, 6 January 2014, Abuja). In other words, the government has not been able to engage with ICTs effectively and as such are not able to sufficiently communicate and engage citizens. ICTs opened up an alternative platform for participants to bypass state hegemony over traditional media and self-imposed limitations on private media by empowering individual participants in the Occupy Nigeria protests, civil society and social movement actors who were exploiting the benefits of the new communication technologies. This echoes the findings of Castells (2001) who found that new technologies of communication empower individuals through a process he describes as mass-self communication (p. 7).

In another context, in spite of the opportunity structure created by ICTs in concert with the politically conducive environment, interviewees also pointed out certain limitations, especially regarding government interference, which they argue persists and remains a major obstacle to civil society action during contentious activities. For instance, interviewees asserted that civil society, independent activists and ordinary citizens continue to face the 'sledgehammer' of the state via its security apparatuses. All of the interviewees also identified government interference during the Occupy Nigeria protests in various ways from direct assault and arrest of activists to censorship and complete shutdown of communication networks. The implication is that political opportunity to engage the state through legitimate action is curtailed while the uses of ICTs further increase ensions between the state and civil society. One interviewee's narrative on the government's interference is telling:

> The uses of ICTs increased conflict between the government and protesters. In terms of governments attempt at disinformation [...]. Eventually, they tried to use draconian methods to stop the protests that instead backfired. Remember the murder in Ilorin which went viral and got more people angered [...] They tried to shut down service providers/ networks during the Occupy Nigeria protests, but service providers were a bit edgy. Maybe in some areas, they did, but it wasn't something service providers embraced wholeheartedly [...]. That is what [...] has now manifested in the shutdown of service networks in Maiduguri.
>
> Interviewee 1, 11 December 2013, Abuja

It was a subject of debate in May 2013 when the Nigerian government instructed relevant authorities to shut down mobile networks in three states (Maiduguri, Yobe and Adamawa) where the Boko Haram insurgents mainly operated (Audu, 2013). The government's ability to enforce a shutdown of networks of mobile communication in the north-eastern states where insurgency activity of Boko Haram was rife confirms the findings of Morovoz (2011a, 2011b), who argues that governments and different authorities have become increasingly savvy in their uses of ICTs and as such can impede the use of digital media. The implication is their increased ability to censor online portals, impose regulations, and shut down networks of communications, including using the same platform as tools to spread propaganda and shape public opinion. As such, the Nigerian government's attempt to control or impede the uses of ICTs during the Occupy Nigeria protests as some participants on social media and interviewees claimed and is reported later is not a new phenomenon. Similar occurrences have been seen in authoritarian contexts across the globe from Asia to the Arab world. In the current context, it reflects the state's continuous resolve to curtail the influence of social movements and independent activist given the potential of the tools. This conforms to global trends in the struggles between the state and its opposition.

> For 4 days the networks shutdown twitter and Facebook. Like me its only today I was able to access Facebook. It's all sabotage.
>
> Participant 11, 4 January 2012, Occupy Nigeria Facebook

> I have been saying so too, if the block it we will find a means to use that same social sites they don't want us use. Yes we can! God be with us.
>
> Participant 12, 4 January 2012, Occupy Nigeria Facebook

> The Federal government Tuesday denied shutting down Blackberry services for two weeks, over the messages that are being exchanged on the recent deregulation of the downstream sector of the economy.
>
> Participant 13, 3 January 2012, Occupy Nigeria Facebook

Other respondents noted that in spite of the state's actions and traditional media's (public/private) response to broadcasting the events, social media, ICTs and the internet provided alternative opportunity platforms for protestors to bypass and circumvent, on the one hand, state limitations (censorship/regulation) on public media, whilst on the other hand, avoid private media biases (including self-censorship). Proponents of this view seem to adopt the same view noted by social, political and communication researchers on the resilience of contentious groups to seek a better alternative mean embedded in ICTs to maintain an advantage over the state (Garrett, 2006; Howard, 2010; Meier, 2011). For one respondent, 'on social media, your voice is not restricted, and you have direct access to the publishing platform' (Interviewee 2, 17 December 2013, Abuja). So individuals, civil society actors and independent activists were able to construct, shape and export the objectives of Occupy Nigeria, including their ideologies, goals, stories, experiences and opinions to both Nigerians at home and a global audience. Besides, Interviewee 2 explained that if you want to access the normal traditional media, first, you will be thinking about how to get someone to report your views that will be competing (threshold) with other things […] they want to fit into the airtime (Interviewee 2, 17 December 2013, Abuja). The challenge is that the newsworthiness of your story is left to editorial decision and as a result, your event might not be reported. Therefore, use of ICTs, the internet and social media:

> Gives people who have a voice a platform to get their voices heard, and then it also reduces the capacity for censorship that exists. There is also the fact that […] if you use it effectively, it can build your stories; you can get your stories or what you want to say in a better way that will elicit a better kind of response […]. Social media gives you an easier and more flexible platform that is at your fingertip. You are your publisher.
>
> Interviewee 2, 17 December 2013, Abuja

Another interviewee noted that there were groups of people who were streaming the protest live on their own and *Aljazeera* was getting stories from such streams. But this was not peculiar, as traditional mainstream media in Nigerian had also relied on those streams on social media, including feeds from FB, YouTube, Twitter, blogs and Skype interviews to make sense of the phenomenon in Nigeria. Interestingly, this trend reflected a reversal of the typical pattern in which individuals and social networks rely on traditional media to report events on their platforms. As an interviewee observed, before 'most people who shared stories on social media had to go to the website of traditional media, pick their stories and share, but now they rely on materials being generated on social media to sell their papers' (Interviewee 2, 17 December 2013, Abuja). Eventually, like traditional public and private media who later joined the protests in Nigeria to broadcast the events, 'Aljazeera sent a unit also to cover the protests in Abuja. Also, there were quite some independent freelance journalists who also came in from Europe with their cameras making stories and selling to any network to broadcast' (Interviewee 2, 17 December 2013, Abuja).

Consequently, because information went out faster, it became difficult for the state to suppress the movement. But does it then mean that old media is being abandoned for new media? This is not the case as one participant explained.

> It was not just social media mobilization, even in bars, like me, I am a very sociable person, in places where people normally drink and talk about fine girls, they were talking about 'ah o ma le gun' (it will be a tough struggle) that dialectic between old media and new media, because even face to face communication in beer parlours is part of the old media in a sense, the way they blended (old and new media).
>
> Interviewee 8, 15 January 2014, Abuja

Interviewee 8 makes a crucial point, considering that Occupy Nigeria combined both word of mouth and the uses of ICTs. The idea of participants communicating, discussing and deliberating on the Occupy Nigeria issues in bars in a face-to-face scenario epitomised a long tradition that dates as far back as the pre-colonial time and is crucial in a media sense, since the media's role is informative. Such avenues become an arena or a hub for information dissemination. Van de Donk (2004) explained that the qualities and characteristics of ICTs could enhance a political protest group's capability, especially regarding putting forward a more coordinated action, including responding more swiftly to outside contest. Such groups could become less reliant on traditional mass media in broadcasting their messages to targeted publics. For another, new media has 'relativised, but has not replaced, the traditional means of both internal and external communication of the movements' (Rucht, 2004, p. 53). Rucht's point reflects the perspective put forward by Interviewee 8 earlier. In the present case, the two mediums (face-to-face and computer-mediated communication) were harnessed to achieve the movement's goals.

4.2.4. *Effect of ICTs on Mobilisation and Demobilisation in Occupy Nigeria*

ICTs are also thought to influence the mobilising structure of contentious movements. The assumption is that contemporary social movements and other political protest groups benefit from the innovative uses of ICTs, the internet and social media during their mobilisation of protests and participants. These movements' networked style in their operational repertoire has defied conventional hierarchical/centralised, top-down model of old media in favour of a more rhizomatic, decentralised and horizontal model of communication which ICTs, the internet and social media continue to facilitate. The implication of the perspective put forward by proponents of this paradigm (Castells, 2001; Deleuze & Guattari, 1987; Karatzogianni, 2006a, 2006b) is that the current structure of the web makes it easy for movement actors to mobilise participants. The web structure essentially provides multiple alternative entry points and helps to circumvent limitations that may be posed by the state as demonstrated in dictatorial or authoritarian systems.

A 'shift to a decentralised network of communication makes senders receivers, producers consumers, and rulers ruled, upsetting the logic of the first media age' (Karatzogianni, 2006a, 2006b, p. 97). What is the implication in the Nigerian context? What is the impact of ICTs on the mobilising structure of movements engaged in protests in Nigeria? Indeed, in the case of contemporary social movements and civil society groups in Nigeria, in particular, the Occupy Nigeria movement provides an illustrative example of the role of networks in movement activities. Traditional Nigerian veterans at the forefront of civil society and social movement activities, who were also active members of the Occupy Nigeria movement, recounted the benefits of new communication media both as a mobilisation and demobilisation tool. Indeed, a majority of interviewees agree that new communication media, ICTs, the internet and social media played a massive role during the January 1 uprising in Nigeria, especially regarding facilitating the protests, fostering inter-civil society relations and information sharing. As one respondent pointed out:

> In every generation, the means of communication and transportation that represent the acme of technological advancement […]

> become tools for the struggles of real living human beings [...]. As such, social media is at best a tool for social movement of this generation [...] the failure of any generation to utilise the communication tools of their time is in itself problematic.
>
> Interviewee 8, 15 January 2014, Abuja

On the impact of ICTs, the internet and social media during the Occupy Nigeria protests, it goes without contest as participants demonstrated that the ICTs provided a ground for contestation and an alternative means for mobilisation. Participants' views agree with the hypothesis that new communication media increases participation in contentious activities. There exists a notion that use of ICTs, the internet and social media to mobilise participants during contentious activities are less expensive in contrast to old media (Meier, 2011, pp. 38–44). As such, the cost barrier is reduced for participation in contentious activities (protests). One interviewee explained it this way:

> The advantage is that it [...] helped us to overcome the problem and challenge of logistics. The major challenge of social movements is that of organising mass meetings were, you have to bring together representation from a wide expanse of an area, the share cost and logistics involved in doing that is such that only structured organisations like labour unions that can do that and even for labour unions the can only do that within structured processes, they cannot just wake up and say that they want to call for such a meeting. But the social media platform enables us to be able to overcome that challenge. So you can be an activist at no cost.
>
> Interviewee 5, 6 January 2014, Abuja

Another respondent also noted the impact of ICTs and other online media applications on participation levels during the Occupy Nigeria protests. Interviewees argued that ICTs, the internet and especially social media played a huge role in the mass character of the movement. One participant noted, 'many people who participated and turned-up would not have' (Interviewee 5, 6 January 2014, Abuja), considering that millions of Nigerians came out to the streets to participate in the rallies and demonstrations. The traditional civil action called by the labour union would probably have ended up in mobilising a particular faction of the populace and would have been restricted to the 36 state capitals of the Federation of Nigeria. Hari (2014) observed that Occupy Nigeria protest called to attention the potential of social media platforms to motivate socio-political engagement to influence social change. One activist recounted, 'at our last count, the uprising had spread to about 55 towns, and cities across the length and breadth of Nigeria with participation for at least a minimum of four days during the uprising. That was mostly down to social media mobilisation' (Interviewee 5, 6 January 2014, Abuja). The reason for this is not hidden, according to one participant, the influence of ICTs on participation level is not unconnected to:

> The proliferation of ICTs, the expansive development of the web structure of the African continent, which is not restricted [...] to Nigeria. If you look at Nigeria, South Africa, Egypt, and Tunisia, we have had significant development of ICT structures in these countries, hence, the wave of protests between 2010 going to 2012.
>
> Interviewee 3, 20 December 2013, Abuja

Attendant to this point, this interviewee explained that:

> Telephone handsets, IPads had become very cheap in this part of the world, where you have all sorts of second-hand technologies coming from Europe, and brand new once coming from China. So you find an average Nigerian youth who is unemployed and can't feed himself having at least three luxurious mobile handsets, an IPhone, Samsung and perhaps multiples of blackberries and an IPad.
>
> Interviewee 3, 20 December 2013, Abuja

Interviewee 3 makes a valid point; it is common practice in Nigeria for individuals belonging to the lower cadre of the economic class to have multiple communication technologies. In the present case, the use of various phones provides a more accurate description of this group. However, for the more technologically savvy youths, and those who belong to the middle class, one will mostly find a combination of different communication gadgets being used for different purposes. Interviewees were asked how they accessed the internet, and one explained:

> I have a laptop which I [...] use for Facebook [...] I have a blackberry, I have a tablet, But the one I use most is my blackberry, because it is small, handy and easily accessible, I have a tablet too which I am charging, I use that when I have to take pictures to send [...].
>
> Interviewee 4, 1 January 2014, Abuja

In the same vein, other respondents narrated similar experiences:

> I use my desktop and my mobile, and that gives you an idea that I access social media most of the time, all day long.
>
> Interviewee 2, 17 December 2013, Abuja

> I seem very handicap when I am not with my laptop, [...] my most convenient, and the one that I use most often would be my laptop. I sometimes use a tablet and sometimes my phone, particularly for twitter it's easier for me to look on twitter on my phone without feeling the inconvenience that I feel, for example to interact on Facebook.
>
> Interviewee 5, 6 January 2014, Abuja

The reduced cost of participation owing to new communication media produced several impacts and implications in the Nigerian context. For instance, the internet and ICTs helped to form solidarity in cyberspace through the community that had emerged in the virtual space around the cause. For example, several listservers, email list, blackberry groups, Twitter accounts and FB pages sprang up in the period leading up to the January uprising in Nigeria (Ejiogu et al., 2013; Interviewee 8, 15 January 2014, Abuja; Olua, 2012). There was the Occupy Nigeria group page on FB and Twitter to other civil society organisation group pages such as 'Save Nigeria Group' (SNG), 'Enough is Enough', the 'Niaraland' forum and individual pages that became an avenue for Occupy Nigeria activities. These platforms provided space for discussions to develop among Nigerian dissidents while also generating debate, organising meetings and eliciting sympathy for the cause. In his words, 'I lost count of those that I was on [...] these were not just groups that were having on and off messages [...] you could have dozens of postings by different people on a daily basis'. For example, there were group pages under the hashtag 'say no to price hike', and 'Nigerians say no to fuel hike prices' (Interviewee 8, 15 January 2014, Abuja). It is important to note that pages created on social media were tailored to specific locations at home and abroad. For example, while there was the Occupy Nigeria New York page, there was also the Occupy Nigeria Abuja, and Occupy Nigeria Community FB page that represented the Occupy Nigeria in London. There was also an Occupy Nigeria app that was feeding dissidents who downloaded the app with information on the protests. According to the description of the app, the medium provided ongoing news, videos, blog posts, live streaming video, local events and Tweets (APK Direct Occupy Nigeria 1.0.0)

These communities created in cyberspace, especially before the Occupy Nigeria movement kicked off in 2012, enjoyed increased participation from the onset. Nigerian dissidents held discussions on the proposed plans of the government to remove the subsidy. The 'say no to fuel price hike' membership shot up from about 8 members the day it started to a 1,000 or 2,000 in less than a week and continued to increase throughout the 18 days of the protests (Interviewee 8, 15 January 2014, Abuja). Subsequently, the cyber-communities that emerged around the movement theme in pre-Occupy Nigeria helped in the development of new bonds of mutual interest among Nigerian online dissidents that later reflected in the offline nodes of the mobilisation process during the Occupy Nigeria protests. As one participant aptly put it, the belief that 'when we unite in our fight, we can win', led to new ties of solidarity being formed and 'the ties of solidarity that emerged in those moments could be called upon for subsequent waves in a circle' (Interviewee 8, 15 January 2014, Abuja). This point tallies with Meier's (2011) argument that community creation is another benefit for political movements using ICTs since the latter facilitates the former. For Chen et al. (2008), the internet and ICTs become useful for creating 'a sense of community, through automated mailing lists that distribute announcements, online discussion forums such as chat rooms, message boards, text/instant messaging, and links to the webring of affinity groups with like-minded objectives' (p. 135).

Corroborating this point, members of the Occupy Nigeria movement argued that ICTs, the internet and social media were particularly useful for distributing and sharing information among Nigerian activists' networks, both home and abroad, including among civil society (intra and inter) and among ordinary Nigerian protestors. The tools provided a platform for delivering updates in real time, from information relating to developments about the protests and plans for rallies and demonstrations to various updates on the direction protests will take, meeting points, tactics and strategies. This information was distributed in real time and helped to shape the nature of the protests on a day-to-day basis during the 18-day period the protest lasted. The following posts on the Occupy Nigeria FB group page are illustrative:

> Spread this to all save nig group that latest news frm abuja now as at 5:20pm that PENGASIM is given red altert to shot down all oil industry.
>
> Participant 14, 11 January 2012, Occupy Nigeria Facebook

> URGENT ALERT [...]
>
> Please take note that #OccupyNigeria Abuja will TODAY hold vigil for Nigerians killed in the Kano attacks and protest against the 'Do nothing' posture of the government. Time 4pm; venue: Ascon Freedom Square, Wuse 2, Abuja. Dress mode: All black. (Via Abdul Mahmud) Others to take a cue from this initiative.
>
> Participant 15, 22 January 2012, Occupy Nigeria Facebook

> ALERT [...]
>
> DEFY THE DICTATOR RALLY
>
> Flash! Activists to hold a DEFY THE DICTATOR RALLY IN LAGOS Thursday Gani Fawehinmi, Freedom Park, Ojota on Thursday, 19th January [...] Prominent Activist and Leaders to March in Lagos Today.
>
> Participant 16, 13 January 2012, Occupy Nigeria Facebook

On how this translated into a useful mechanism for mobilisation, an interviewee suggests, 'ICTs and social media were used to mobilise protestors through such updates, letting them know where they could meet, and letting them know what the issues were [...] even if you were not going on the street, it is important that you show that you were protesting in one way or the other'. The Interviewee, who is also an active member and official of the NLC (Union), added that 'the major social media platforms experienced increased usage during the protest. In fact, a lot of people who eventually got on Twitter got on Twitter during the protests' (Interviewee 4, 1 January 2014, Abuja). Individuals who wanted to join the protests and those already participating got appropriate information about what was going to happen including what their role entailed. Although no actual data are available to indicate the number of Nigerians who joined Twitter during the protests, Figure 4.3 shows that the scale of discussion during the protests are symptomatic of an increase in usage which can be as a result of more participation. The figure shows an incremental rise in tweets (Figure 4.3).

Besides using social media, activists extensively explored text messaging SMS both as a means for communicating within activist networks and as a tool for putting pressure on the labour unions and government officials. 'For instance, before we even entered negotiations, each of us had received 500 text messages on our lines telling us not to compromise, don't do this, and then rumours are already being circulated' (Interviewee 5, 6 January 2014, Abuja). For this interviewee, with the pressure exacted via text messages, it became difficult for the Labour Civil Society Coalition, negotiating on behalf of Occupy Nigeria dissidents, not to stay committed. To confirm the assertion that Occupy Nigeria

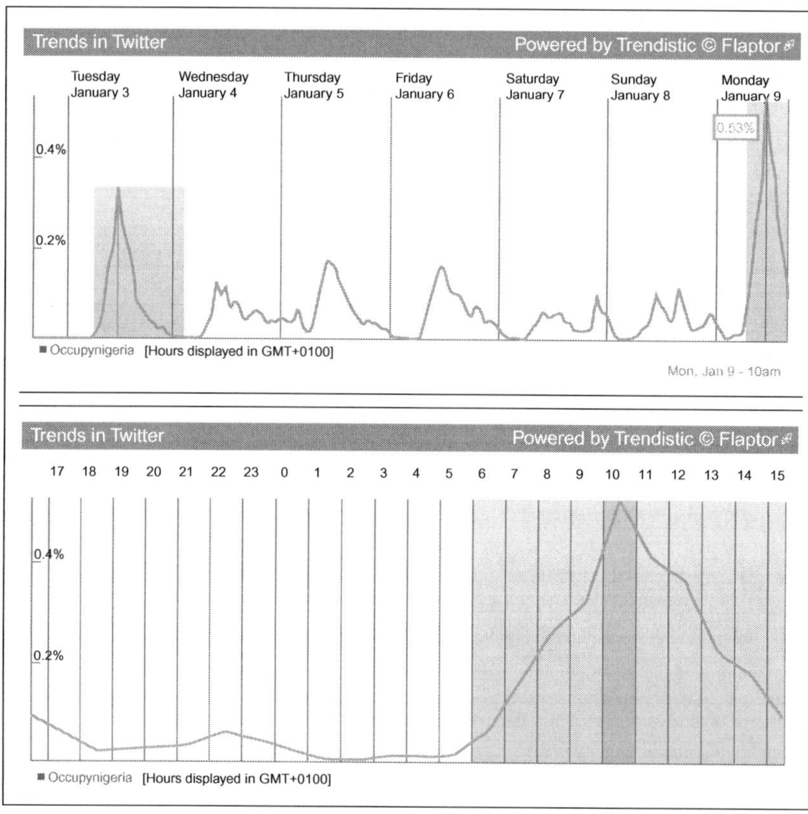

Figure 4.3. A Trajectory of Occupy Nigeria Tweets from 3 January to 9 January.
Source: Techloy.com. Available at: http://techloy.com/2012/01/09/occupynigeria-sees-highest-trend-on-twitter-today-stats/

dissidents pressurised the negotiating team, one post on the FB page of Occupy Nigeria read:

> VERY URGENT [...] TIME TO FLOOD LABOUR BEFORE THE NEXT MEETING
>
> NLC EXECUTIVES: 080xxx, 080xxx, 080xxx, 081xxx, 080xxx. NLC ABUJA: 080xxx.
>
> Participant 17, 13 January 2012, Occupy Nigeria Facebook

The need to put pressure on the Labour Civil Society Coalition became urgent following rumours that emerged that the negotiating team were going to give in to the demands of the government:

> In being forced to refute the rumours, when we go in for the negotiation we had to be very careful. Otherwise the rumours can be confirmed, not necessarily because there was any substance to it, but because you just made a shift without getting back to your constituent. So, that created a lot of frustration for the government during the protests in the sense that they felt we couldn't make decisions immediately, expeditiously and it was advantageous to us because then, we could always say we can't decide without consulting the people.
>
> Interviewee 5, 6 January 2014, Abuja

Similar to the Labour Civil Society Coalition, government officials were also bombarded with text messages from Occupy Nigeria dissidents expressing dissent. On the FB group page of the Occupy Nigeria movement, messages that included the personal details of government officials including mobile numbers were posted urging Occupy Nigeria activists to send messages to such numbers. For instance, one post read:

> VERY URGENT [...] TIME TO FLOOD [...]
>
> Last night [...] Governor [...] played a damaging role in the NLC/TUC/JAF and FGN negotiation. #Occupy his line – 080xxx and that of his media adviser [...] 080xxx. Please share, ASAP.
>
> Participant 18, 13 January 2012, Occupy Nigeria Facebook

While the trigger was the removal of subsidy, the economic implication of the government's decision, which participants saw as repressive, and a display of ignorance on the part of the state towards the increasing hardship and pain of Nigerians played a crucial role. Hence, it was easy for the already tense Nigerian community (owing to the widespread economic difficulties that predate the Occupy Nigeria protest) to push their frustrations into protests. As one interviewee noted, 'you did not need a prophet to tell us that something was capable of happening' (Interviewee 3, 20 December 2013, Abuja). More so, 'consistently, if you look at the protests from 2001 to last year (2012), there have been consistent opposition of Nigerians to the removal of oil subsidy, but why last year's (2012) was different from the previous one of the early part of the decade was that the ICT infrastructure was not as developed as it had last year (2012)' (Interviewee 3, 20 December 2013, Abuja). So, it was easy for youths to click on their FB account, click on Twitter and mobilise not only themselves but also those Nigerian people who had access to the internet. The point is that Nigerian citizens had access to these tools and other online applications, which made it easy for them to mobilise friends and family in that circle.

It is, therefore, safe to suggest that the combination of the multi-functional, multimedia, capabilities of new ICTs in concert with the affordability and low-cost factor all contributed to the mass character of the protests in comparison to the days of traditional communication media. ICTs have established themselves as a credible means of communication and of passing information. As such, individuals engaged in contentious activities are more equipped to discern what information is relevant or not. In considering the Occupy Nigeria protests, it became apparent how ICTs have opened more access to individuals who were hitherto passive and undecided, but may want to participate in the protests, to successfully engage the polity and be involved in one way or the other. More specifically, protestors have the benefit of engaging with those issues that are leading to protests from their comfort zone. According to one interviewee:

> I am sure imperialism will be regretting that the world according to them has been reduced into a smaller global village through ICTs, because I think ICT has been of benefit to the oppressed than to the oppressor, because I can sit down here and organise a protest as we have done in the past, and several countries have done so in Greece, Turkey, Egypt, Syria, and in Libya. There is practically no serious protest in the world that is not powered by ICT. So ICT played I can say 90% role in organising the January action.
>
> Interviewee 4, 1 January 2014, Abuja

More so, there is the general belief that the public, civil society and social movement actors have lost confidence in public media, which they argue are usually under the hegemony of the state. Both mediums, public and private, depending on their degree of alignment are perceived as 'newsletters of the government' to use one participant's phrase. As such, all they (public and private media) can do is to report contentious activities in a negative light taking on a pro-government side. 'Even within the so-called private outlets, the editorial policies sometimes link towards the preservation of the status quo' (Interviewee 7, 15 January 2014, Abuja). Consequently, individuals have not only lessened their dependence on traditional media sources, the interactivity, multimedia capabilities and free-flow structure offered by ICTs encouraged movement actors to rely more on new ICTs during protests. Movement actors can have a monopoly over information they disseminate and a choice over which information or platform to follow.

The presence of social media enabled meetings to be held in cyberspace, with correspondence between activist networks from far and near circumventing the problem of censorship and other state limitations which could put activists at risk. One advantage of this for NSMs as in the case of Occupy Nigeria is that it helps to eliminate in some part that state interference dynamic that is typical of governments that deploy security forces to interrupt, arrest and stop social movement activities and meeting which usually led up to the protest event (Interviewee 1, 11 December 2013, Abuja; Interviewee 3, 20 December 2013, Abuja). 'ICTs can promote communication, political expression and action amongst citizens who cannot meet in person, provided that they can trust the security of electronic media and their integrity against surveillance. It appears, however, that when authorities are monitoring participants with different opinions, then the Information Superhighway's (ISH) potential as a reliable democratic tool is damaged' (Karatzogianni, 2006a, 2006b, pp. 38–39).

A veteran activist who participated in the protests narrated his ordeal during the student-led protest against the political transition programme of the military regime in 1991 and explained that during the process of national mobilisation across Nigeria, he was apprehended in Lagos and held at the maximum security prison (Kirikiri) for several months. His continuous travels for advocacy meetings and protests at the time exposed him to the state and also uncovered the security he had built around him. According to him:

> Perhaps, with my knowledge of ICT today and if we had these infrastructures of ICT in 1991, it would have to take a well-developed national security infrastructure to tail where I was tweeting from [...]. ICT infrastructure opens multiples of handles, and these handles can be managed by different individuals.
>
> Interviewee 3, 20 December 2013, Abuja

On the one hand, interviewees agree that new communication media proved very resourceful for facilitating Occupy Nigeria protests and providing an alternative platform for communication and interaction during the January uprisings. Some respondents found that ICTs do not only promote socio-political mobilisation, but there are also some downsides to using new media technologies in contentious situations that could undermine the essence of the whole process if not properly managed. Interviewees trailing this line of thought identified a research gap with uses of ICTs for mobilisation during political protests especially in the context of the digital divide. For instance, one school of thought explained that 'much as other technologies, the internet has diffused unevenly across countries, raising concerns about a digital divide' (Milner, 2005, p. 2). Note the key word here is 'unevenly', which means that there is a disparity regarding access to ICTs, the internet and social media. Globally, one can reasonably expect that the West has more access compared to other parts of the globe and in particular developing countries as in the present case. On the other hand, one could also consider access from a national point of view, in which case, one would reasonably expect more access to technological tools of communication within urban areas compared to rural areas due to income inequality or technical know-how, or political bureaucracy, in spreading ICTs (see Akoh, Jagun, Odufuwa, & Akanni, 2012; Olatokun, 2009). Regardless, both dynamics can significantly impede uses of new media tools for mobilisation during contentious activities. Milner (2005) added that besides technologies and economy, which are factors usually blamed for the digital divide, other political factors affect access.

In the Nigerian context, interviewees explained that issues of accessibility to ICTs and the internet presented challenges in specific areas during mobilisation. Rural areas were the most negatively affected in this regard. A scenario I described as 'infrastructural poverty' is a concept used to depict the low spread of ICT infrastructure between urban and rural areas across the country. All the interviewees drawing on the infrastructural backwardness in rural areas argued that the digital gap affected the mobilisation message of Occupy Nigeria getting to some parts of the country. Statistics show an increasing penetration of the internet in Nigeria since the transition to democracy with the NCC, reporting a rise in the number of internet users on Nigeria's telecoms networks from 95.37 million recorded in August 2015 to 97.21 million in November 2015 (see Vanguard Report, 10 May 2015). In reality, there remains a wide margin between urban and rural areas (see Figure 4.4). Further to the point on the digital divide and how this affects individual engagement in online activism, Interviewee 7 highlighted a deficit in the people's purchasing power to be able to be online on a sustainable basis. In this regard, economic poverty surfaced as a central problem. Interviewees identified lack of infrastructure and government interference as other fundamental concerns and obstacles during the Occupy Nigeria protests and beyond.

One participant's narrative is telling: 'you find that for some people who come on FB, they are only able to do so once in maybe two months, which

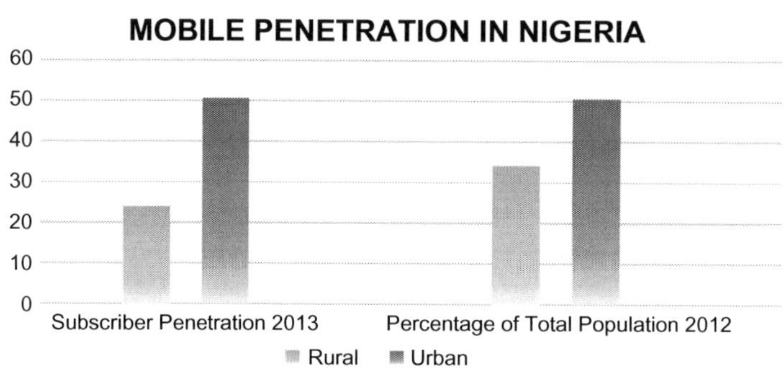

Figure 4.4. Rural and Urban Mobile Penetration in Nigeria. *Source*: Nigeria Bureau of Statistics, GSMA Intelligence. Available at: http://draft-content.gsmaintelligence.com/AR/assets/4161587/GSMA_M4D_Impact_Country_Overview_Nigeria.pdf

simply tells you that that is when he/she can afford it' (Interviewee 7, 15 January 2014, Abuja). On government interference, there was a general belief amongst protestors that the government tried to shut down communication networks during the January 1 uprising such that at particular times during demonstrations and rallies, protesters found it very difficult to upload protest materials and data to the web. 'The Nigerian security intelligence had jammed out web connectivity, so that limited the amount of work those young boys and girls could do' (Interviewee 3, 20 December 2013, Abuja), an interviewee explained.

For some interviewees, neither the digital divide nor the economic and political dynamics highlighted alone constitute a challenge during protest mobilisation. A proponent of this account (Interviewee 3, 20 December 2013, Abuja) argues that the uses of ICTs, the internet and other everyday social media could in itself contribute to socio-political demobilisation. Meaning that the uses of such tools could impede the essence of the mobilising potential of ICTs and the internet for facilitating participation in a call to action. Their argument seems to be influenced by the implications of online advocacy as against real-life demonstrations and protests especially when such online advocacy does not include hacktivism[1]. As opposed to using online media to mobilise protesters, hacktivism empowers a form of protests, which has significant real-life or offline implications. For example, hacking into a power grid network or military hardware could endanger lives and even stimulate war between countries. ICTs, the internet and social media are deployed as a resource for socio-political mobilisation rather than direct action.

Since traditionally the central aim of a protest or demonstration is to get individuals on the streets during contentious activities, not just in virtual space, the fear is that social movement actors could get caught up in the spur of the moment in online or virtual spheres, thereby failing to participate in offline activities. This produces a counter-mobilisation or demobilisation effect such that it negates the manifest intention of real-life occupations. It was within this point of view that Putnam (2000) argued that the tools offered by ICTs hinder dissidents from 'participating in the more effective forms of participation in the activist repertoire that have traditionally been used' (cited in Christensen, 2011, p. 1). How did this play out during the Occupy Nigeria protest? One participant explained that the challenge during the January 2012 uprising was that 'the younger generation of the Nigerian youth that drove the Occupy Nigeria movement saw organisation only from one point of view, that mere presence at the virtual level was enough to drive the political action' (Interviewee 3, 20 December 2013, Abuja). Another respondent identified a similar challenge: 'the action you are going to take is not a virtual action; it's going to be an action

---

[1]According to Karatzogianni (2006), this involve online activism or electronic activism which takes two forms: when hackers attack virtually chosen political targets and when persons organise through the internet or carry through email a political message.

in real time. So you need also to spend some time in real time preparing for that' (Interviewee 5, 6 January 2014, Abuja).

Castells (2001) in the *Networks of Outrage and Hope* asserts that 'the public space of the social movement is constructed as a hybrid space between internet and social networks and the occupied urban space: connecting cyberspace and urban space in relentless interactions, constituting technologically and culturally instant communities of transformative practice' (p. 11). Essentially, the challenge arises when participants involved in contestation replace real-life occupations for cyber-activism or other forms of technological protests: 'It is easy for you (participants) to sit in the comfort of your home punching keys, sending out ideas, but the physical organisation and mobilisation of people exist outside the virtual. It lies in the streets' (Interviewee 3, 20 December 2013, Abuja). Although a large number of individuals trooped to the streets during the Occupy Nigeria protest, the consensus among some participants is that many more people were entangled in a web of networks Facebooking and Tweeting thereby negating the original intention of using the platform to mobilise people to join the protests on the streets. From a different point of view, it can also be argued that ICTs, however, provided a platform for individuals who may never have participated in the protest in person to get involved through online media.

While Interviewee 3 makes a crucial point earlier, at the same time, one cannot neglect the impact of online mobilisations and the role these play in the overall process, especially in terms of ensuring that the protests continued to gain an online presence through postings of political commentaries and perspectives on the protest by those who were engaged in blogging and similar activities online. Noting the point made by Interviewee 3, other interviewees argued that the benefits that were accrued in using the tools (ICTs) during the uprisings far outweighed the disadvantages since Nigerian dissidents came out to the streets in unprecedented numbers never witnessed in the Nigerian history of contentious activities. As the protest progressed, more people joined the movement due to exposure to the actions of Occupy Nigeria. For instance, one participant noted that 'people turned out partly because of ICTs and ease of communication of plans and ideas through social media' (Email interview, 29 April 2014).

Although in the current context Occupy Nigeria is an example of a hybrid movement combining both horizontal and vertical organisational structures, yet a common characteristic of most social movements is their spontaneity, leaderless character and lack of organisational structure, which fits succinctly into the horizontal network structure of the internet (low-power network effects notwithstanding). This structure has the potential for creating a gap between the online and offline components of the mobilisation process and further exposes the challenges of relying solely on cyberspace for activism. It was mentioned earlier how claims emerged that the government through its security personnel and media regulators shut down communication networks during the protests. Interviewee 3 suggested that Nigerian youths who had been at the forefront of the Occupy Nigeria mobilisations and had relied mainly on conducting their operation innovatively using computer-mediated communication especially through computers, IPads, smartphones and other online platforms were cut-off.

> There were instances handles particularly on Facebook were hijacked, by security forces […]. I had friends who were involved and were constantly complaining that they had been locked out from their Facebook account. For some of us that have been involved in protests for many years, we know how the security intelligence works in our country. […]. There were times within Abuja metropolises when protestors found it very difficult to upload protest materials to the net, and we have not been able to confirm, but there were suspicions, that the Nigerian security intelligence had jammed out web connectivity, so that […] limited the amount of work those young boys and girls could do.
>
> Interviewee 3, 20 December 2013, Abuja

According to him, this was unavoidable because this group of protesters neither had a physical platform to collapse their activities nor one to continue their online advocacy as it were. The short network episode affected dissidents using the tools for mobilisations. Another participant commented:

> That structure that needed to be on the ground to make sure that the large number of people on the streets can push the government to do what they wanted, that structure wasn't there.
>
> Interviewee 2, 17 December 2013, Abuja

To sum-up interviewees' opinions, protestors quickly resorted to other strategies and tactics to manage and minimise the limitations believed to have been imposed on communication networks by the government. Nonetheless, such occurrences can serve as a major challenge for contentious activities shaped around computer and media communications, the internet and online media as seen in the testimonials of Occupy Nigeria protestors. The government refuted the claims through its communication regulatory body, the NCC. In one press release, the organisation's Director, Public Affairs, Mr Tony Ojobo noted:

> The attention of the Nigerian Communications Commission (NCC) has been drawn to an information making rounds that the NCC had, at a meeting this morning agreed with CEOs of telecommunications networks to shut down Blackberry Services in order to deny Nigerians the use of that very important social network […] The Management hereby states categorically that there was never such a meeting held, nor was there ever a resolution to shut down Blackberry services. The Public is please advised to disregard such information.
>
> Nigerian Communication Commission (2012)

The press release was also published in a Nigerian newspaper online. While the government refutes the claims made by protestors, the plausibility of authorities shutting down the internet or mobile networks is undisputable in the digital age. Besides, other technical faults associated with the service or content provider could cause a breakdown, and by this token, users would be unable to communicate using ICTs. In recent years, the major social networks (FB and Twitter) have experienced such episodes. Other socio-political demobilising dynamics include of course government interference as in the context described and the gap between the online and offline components of the mobilising process due to lack of proper organisational structures. Also, inexperience on the part of protesters engaged in digital activism could also pose some complexities.

The point aforementioned is attendant to the previous observation that Occupy Nigeria was to a degree influenced by international trends of social movement activities across the globe which suggests that Nigerian protesters were inadequately equipped with the know-how capabilities of using digital tools for contentious activities. As one participant succinctly put it, 'the protests [Occupy Nigeria] was driven more by people I call the post June 12 generation' (Interviewee 3, 20 December 2013, Abuja), as in those who were born post 12 June 1993, a period that was characterised by mass protest and resistance following the annulment of the June 12 presidential election by the then military dictatorship. According to him, if one considers the 12 June 1993 to January 2012 period, there was no momentous national protest in Nigeria. As such, a large spectrum of youths who participated in the organisation of the January protests had no experience on how to organise, sustain and push protests from a certain level of demand to another level (Interviewee 3, 20 December 2013, Abuja). This participant's point of view is informed by the idea that with prior experience of organising protests at that level together with ICTs at the disposal of Occupy Nigeria dissidents, it would have been a lot easier to counter state interference. Nonetheless, a broader spectrum of veteran activists, with many years of experience participating in civil society action, were involved in the Occupy Nigeria protests.

4.2.5. ICT Uses and Impact Created

With regard to the impact of the Occupy Nigeria movement, especially in the context of whether or not the movement was successful in its uses of ICTs, participants had mixed reactions. Generally speaking, respondents did not believe that the Occupy Nigeria movement achieved its sole objective of returning the price of oil to the original price before the subsidy was removed; instead the NLC Coalitions and the Government agreed to a partial subsidy which reduced the increased petroleum pump price to 97 Naira (Emmanuel & Ezeamalu, 2013). As one participant argued, when the government came with its placatory reduction of the astronomical oil price, the movement collapsed. Another interviewee had this to say, 'personally; it wasn't a success, but it was a success on the trade unions side. It was a success because we were able to reduce the price of petroleum products' (Interviewee 4, 1 January 2014, Abuja). For another, no matter how minimal, the protests still forced a reduction.

> I have argued in several places that in the January 2012 protests, we won a partial victory, a number of people say it was a failure [...] without up turning the system, and building the world anew [...] 99% of our victories cannot but be partial victories. Even where and when we win what could seemingly be a full victory, the ruling elite go back [...] to their drawing table to take back with the right hand what they were forced to give with the left hand.
>
> Interviewee 8, 15 January 2014, Abuja

Another participant reflects the dichotomy evident in the belief of most members of the Occupy Nigeria movement:

> There were two objectives of the Occupy Nigeria movement. There was the conscious objective, and there was the unconscious objective. The conscious objective was captured in the slogan '65 Naira per litre or nothing'. The unconscious objective was that of change in the governance structure completely. In terms of those two objectives, you could say it was only partially successful because we did not get a reversal to 65 instead we got a partial reversal. In terms of changing the governance, we did not get a change in government rather; we compelled some changes in the processes [...] it was also partially successful.
>
> Interviewee 5, 6 January 2014, Abuja

Nonetheless, respondents also agreed on some parameters of success especially in connection to the uses of ICTs for protests in the Occupy Nigeria case. The success of using the ICTs goes beyond returning the oil prices to what it was before the subsidy was removed which was the main goal of the movement. The majority of the activists and members of the Occupy Nigeria movement interviewed agree that the movement was successful to the extent that digital media provided a platform for successfully engaging the government, building solidarity networks and creating a political belief in change. As one participant explained, 'for me, were total success, I mean 100% success was, in the fact that it completely transformed the consciousness of a generation of Nigerians, in the sense that it proved to them that they could engage with their government and that they could actually compel the government to make certain changes' (Interviewee 5, 6 January 2014, Abuja). So in that sense that it became a life-defining moment for a generation, it was extremely successful. Another participant also stated that the use of ICTs 'raised the "confidence of the people that when we unite in our fight, we can win", and it created ties of solidarity' among protestors which 'could be called upon for subsequent waves in a circle [...]. I gave example of Malik, we didn't know each other before in the physical sense, but now quite often now and then we sit down together to even discuss issues beyond the struggle, of family for instance' (Interviewee 8, 15 January 2014, Abuja), indicating another success in terms of development of ties and solidarity which was only made possible with social media.

Similarly, there is a shared belief among some interviewees that the Occupy Nigeria movement was successful in laying the foundation for subsequent movements that have emerged since Occupy Nigeria.

> I will say that the January 2012 Occupy Nigeria was the life-defining moment for this generation of activists and since then we have seen this influence in several ways, the cost of governance movement, the movement against child marriage […]. All the other movements that have evolved since then have gained their inspiration from that sustained demonstration and struggle of the January Uprising, and so you could see that.
>
> Interviewee 5, 6 January 2014, Abuja

Interviewee 5 explained that most of the protests that emerged in post-Occupy Nigerian had been youth-led. An *Aljazeera* report also corroborated this point demonstrating how in different parts protests were organised mainly through social media especially on Twitter (Aljazeera, July 22, 2013). The 'Child Not Bride' protest was entirely Twitter organised. The 'Child Not Bride' is a protest that was ignited online and inspired by a review of legislation, Section 29 4(b) of the Nigerian constitution, which would allow children under the age of 18 to get married. An outburst ensued online with protestors describing the failure of the authorities to amend a clause as exploitative. The protests were predominantly organised online around the hashtag #ChildNotBride. Organisers called for contacts and individuals who volunteered to coordinate in their cities. Everything was done via Twitter. They linked themselves up, held their first meeting and then started organising towards that. The rally to the National Assembly too was also largely mobilised on Twitter (Interviewee 5, 6 January 2014, Abuja). One of the major successes of the #ChildNotBride campaign was the global awareness campaigners create via online media, the protests and criticism that ensued. The uses of ICTs, the internet and social media exposed the level of corruption within the down-stream sector of the petroleum industry in Nigeria, which impelled radical reforms in the industry. One participant pointed out that:

> The series of probes into the financial recklessness, fraud and theft that emerged after the protests were also largely influenced by the protests and exposure of the illegal acts within the oil industry through the uses of ICTs.
>
> Interviewee 5, 6 January 2014, Abuja

In other words, the uses of ICTs, the internet and social media impels state actors and governments to act dutifully as in the present case, where failure to do so will affect the corporate image of the administration. Different committees had been set-up within the legislature to investigate alleged corrupt practices that had been going on for many years in the sector. Notable among this was the Ad Hoc Committee on Fuel Subsidy Management probe, which was supposed to scrutinise the industry but became entangled in corruption allegations.

Ultimately, the framing process is a crucial element of the mobilisation of political protests, and as seen earlier, both movement actors and the state understand the importance of controlling discourse emergent in the media and more precisely new media. From all indications, protesters were able to deploy ICTs, the internet and social media in the battle for the minds of the public both at home and across the globe. For the first time, ICTs have created an inclusive culture where formerly passive and suppressed voices can be heard. Individuals can participate in protests and engage the government through alternative platforms availed by the new communication tools.

The scenario aforementioned does not undermine the state's capacity to impede the uses of new media communication technologies as we have seen. The state still proves it can limit new media uses by restricting access and shutting down mobile networks as alleged by protestors and as seen in Maiduguri, where due to insurgents and terrorist-related activities (to be discussed in a subsequent section) the government shut down mobile and communication networks for months to disconnect communication amongst insurgents. Therefore, it is possible for the state to impede the free flow of communication offered by the decentralised nature of the internet. However, Morovoz (2011a, 2011b) explained that it is increasingly becoming difficult for the state to exercise such powers due to constant scrutiny of the global community on issues of media freedoms and civil liberties. The point is that state actions may be interpreted as an infringement on freedom of expression, thereby serving as a deterrent for both dictatorial and democratic governments.

Another critical shortfall in the success of the Occupy Nigeria movement is regarding the weakness in the organisational form and leadership structure. There was a conflict between the volunteered leadership provided by the Labour Civil Society Coalition and the majority of protesters. The conflict of interest arose in the area of the goals and demands of Occupy Nigeria protestors. Although the ultimate goal was to revert the price of petroleum to its original price, however, this demand had metamorphosed to other complexities, for instance, the issue of corruption, bad governance, infrastructural backwardness and security concerns. Also, there were the controversial issues among some protestors for a complete system change. 'The trade unions were calling a reversal in the price of fuel products, we were calling for a stop in the deregulation policy and such other things [...] but as the protests entered the second day, people were asking for a system change' (Interviewee 4, 1 January 2014, Abuja). This created a conflict and distrust in the leadership being provided by the civil society coalition and the traditional labour unions.

The conflict of interests is not a surprise given that there was no adequately articulated leadership structure where such issues including goals and objectives would have been deliberated upon at the initial stages of the protest. The movement was mostly amorphous, buttressing the point on the loose organisational form of the movement. This is characteristic of NSMs in the digital age. One could attribute the decentralised nature of Web 2.0 for facilitating conflict of interests as it relates to the mobilisation of political protests.

> I do know if the know what it takes to call for system change, system change is different from the change in government; it's different from the change in prices, change in whatever policies. System change is a more serious social thing and political thing that you are asking that capitalism should end that a particular system to end but we are not prepared for a replacement of that system because we did not even understand this other system that we are talking about […] that is why NLC, in particular, couldn't call for system change because we needed people to understand this current system, we needed to make people understand what system should replace it, we needed people to understand the painstaking implications struggling for that change and for that replacement. We didn't understand all that so we encouraged an ultimate theme for a minimum demand […] the ultimate response to the crisis […]. That's why I said it was anarchistic.
>
> Interviewee 4, 1 January 2014, Abuja

The conflict of interests and disconnect between the negotiators and the protestors lead to the collapse of Occupy Nigeria. In other words, once the government reduced the price of petroleum, and interviewees acceded to this, the Occupy Nigeria protests ended abruptly. An interviewee corroborated this. He observed that:

> As soon as NLC suspends the strike that is the end of the protest […] they went under; they were no longer existing, the save Nigeria group just *fizzled out*, Occupy Nigeria fizzled out. Those who didn't fizzle out are those who were existing before that day like UAD, Committee on Human Rights […] and such other groups.
>
> Interviewee 4, 1 January 2014, Abuja

Getting right the organisational and leadership structure of conflict movements is essential if success will be achieved. An illustrative example of how problems with the structure of leadership of conflict movements can worsen outcomes can be seen in the ousting of Hosni Mubarak the erstwhile ruler of Egypt in the Egyptian revolution of 2011. Although the Egyptians were successful in sending their leader into exile, the implication of such drastic change has meant instability in the country since then. Failure to evaluate the dangers and impact of regime change or to use a more nuanced attribution, leadership change, has cost Egyptians more than they bargained. The country has experienced more protests, insurgency and instability since then. The finding of El-Sherif (2014) suggests that Egyptians continue their struggles with the political system. For instance, in spite of the emergence and fall of the Muslim Brotherhood, totalitarian elements endured and continued to hold sway. In his words:

> Democratic alternatives have not capitalized on cracks in the system. Prospects for the Brotherhood's political reintegration and a democratization of political Islam are bleak. As long as credible alternatives fail to gain traction, the old state will persist, and Egypt's central challenges will remain unresolved.
>
> El-Sherif (2014)

4.3. Conflict Resolution and Digital Media

Participants interviewed explained that the government also used various online platforms in an attempt to shape public opinion during the protests. As Eyck (2001, p. 219) rightly pointed out, 'activists are not the only group capable of using technology to become more fluid and flexible'. The state is online too, promoting its ideas and limiting what the average user can see and do. Innovations in communications technology provide people with not only new sources of information and new opportunities to share ideas, but they also empower governments to manipulate the conversation and to monitor what people are saying (Ronfeldt & Varda, 2008, p. 12). In the Nigerian context, one interviewee noted that:

> You find that they on several websites [...] placing adverts trying to convince people about the policies. The pros and how it was going to change the lives of Nigerians. They also had their people working underground also on social media platforms, throwing comments here and there to trying to sell people the idea of the government.
>
> Interviewee 2, 17 December 2013, Abuja

However, other participants argue that the government hasn't been very responsive in utilising new communication technologies: 'the government has not been responsive to civil society, of taking advantage of social media to interact with citizens. So it is often citizens talking to the government, and the government may once in a while reply' (Interviewee 4, 1 January 2014, Abuja). In the present context, however, another activist explained that:

> The government also tried to use social media, but at that material time, the balance was in favour of the citizens [...] the government could not mount an effective counter-war in social media space. They knew they did not have that ground. Opposition forces dominated social media.
>
> Interviewee 5, 6 January 2014, Abuja

Although there are no data to backup these assertions made by participants and interviewees, the reality is that careful observation of the number of tweets and FB posts that emerged from different individuals during the protests suggests an overwhelming dominance of the social platforms by Nigerian dissidents. According to an ITrealms (2012) report, Nigerian tweets may have reached a record high of about 86,400 tweets per day during the first week of the protests. The IT realms (2012) report also indicated a continuous increase in the activities on the occupy Nigeria Twitter account from an initial 11,766 as on Friday 6 January to 14,955 on 15 January.

In the same vein, another interviewee stated that the government did not use the social platforms as much as the opposition.

> Although the government was on social media, we were using it effectively [...] they were not countering us, they were not writing anything, rather they were issuing press statements abusing the people.
>
> Interviewee 4, 1 January 2014, Abuja

By implication, one could suggest that for the state, the avenues provided by online media and ICTs were useful for getting their argument across regarding the removal of oil subsidy. The government tried to show that the policy was especially beneficial to only a few individuals in society. In this regard, the main issue the government attempted to address was corruption. In the address of President Jonathan during the protests, he argued that the deregulation policy was the most reliable approach to tackling the challenge (corruption) in the down-stream oil sector (CPAfrica, 8 January, 2012). The problem for the state, as one interviewee pointed out, is that as soon as the government is bombarded with social media counter advocacy, they give up. While ICTs, the internet and social media have become very useful for both sides in a conflict, the evidence suggests that civil society and social movement dissidents benefit extensively from the capacity these tools present especially for bypassing restrictions and asserting their voice and opinions on issues that affect them.

> The government is saying we would not allow this platform to be dominated by anti-government elements [...] that is why if you post anything now, you see many people coming in opposition using different names they purchased.
>
> Interviewee 7, 15 January 2014, Abuja

Essentially, there was no clear, direct communication between the government and the people using ICTs. Instead, what exists is a circle of an argument and counter-argument going on in cyberspace between protestors and what some respondents tagged 'sponsored handles' of the government. Further illuminating this point, Interviewee 7 explained that although the government is gaining some online presence, there has not been an interface between citizens and the government like you would have expected on social media. In his words, 'you don't have a minister of information engaging there neither is there a commissioner for information or special adviser engaging citizens'. So although there are government sponsored handles and designated offices for ICTs and social media, in the context of engaging citizens in contentious situations, it is not clear how the authorities deploy the medium.

Conclusively, the focus of this chapter was on the Occupy Nigeria protest as a contemporary case of socio-political movement using ICTs. The three interrelated dynamics, that is, mobilising structure, opportunity structure and framing process of the resource mobilisation model which are succinctly integrated into the CC theoretical framework, provided the lens used to evaluate the role played by of ICTs with regard to the different structures in the Occupy Nigeria movement. It was found that the removal of oil subsidy created a window of opportunity for political protests in January 2012. The activities of TSM also served as a stimulus. The movement started as a single-issue movement around the removal of subsidy but subsequently mutated into a multi-issue movement incorporating other, long-held, socio-economic and political grievances with corruption topping the list (others included issues relating to poverty, corruption, development, economy and the advocacy for system change).

The consensus among participants interviewed is that the success of the Occupy Nigeria lies in the fact that for the first time in the political history of modern Nigeria (under democratic rule), individual groups, independent activists, social movements and civil society organisations were able to, through contentious activities, impel the government to change its policy. Even though it was a partial success, they were still able to obtain some concessions through the reduction negotiated by the Labour Civil Society Coalition. The same principle applies to the other demands regarding poverty, corruption development and economy issues. The government was compelled to audit accounts and set-up panels and committees to investigate alleged oversight issues (see Ejiogu et al., 2013, p. 223). Also, programmes were set-up to cater to the needs of Nigerians using revenue generated from the petroleum industry. An illustrative example is the SURE-P projects, which is a subsidy re-investment programme to facilitate developments in rail, road, electricity, housing and education, among other projects. Ultimately, some of the veteran movement actors interviewed explained that neither movement actors nor indeed the government was prepared for a system or regime change.

Juxtaposing the CC framework and the perspectives of participants in the Occupy Nigeria protests about the mobilising structures, the evaluation that followed revealed some dimensions pointing in the direction that ICTs are influencing socio-political protests in Africa's most populous country. There was a definite response elicited from the data collected during the semi-structured interviews about the role of ICTs on the mobilisation of protests. In other words, the uses of ICTs by Occupy Nigeria dissidents played a significant facilitative role in increasing participation during the protests. These tools were handy and resourceful such that participants were able to use them innovatively to recruit more participants by making calls for political action using online media. Indeed, as the opinions of interviewees reflected, this resulted in more people participating in rallies and demonstrations. The uses of new media tools especially social media had led to the formation of various online groups or communities in pre-Occupy Nigeria and during the Occupy Nigeria action. These online networks that had been formed developed new trusts and friendship that subsequently transferred from online networks to real offline networks. As Interviewee 8 pointed out, some of the offline networks comprised individuals who met online through the Occupy Nigeria group page either on FB or Twitter. They subsequently mobilised and assembled in various physical occupations and participated in the daily activities of the Occupy Nigeria movement. Thus, in the context of facilitating participation in the protests, recruitment of members and online advocacy, the study found that the uses of ICTs and the internet were very resourceful and instrumental in the large turnout of protestors.

The study also found that the uses of ICTs, the internet and social media can fall short of the desired outcomes, especially in terms of getting people out to the streets in what Interviewee 3 described as the socio-political demobilising effect of ICTs. Three dynamics are crucial to our understanding of negative influence. The time spent on ICTs (convenience), the fear of state harassment and the reduced cost of participation that ICTs offer could serve as a demobilising factor. The point is that these dynamics have the potential of stopping potential participants from participating in rallies, demonstrations and protests (real-life occupations), thereby restricting such actors to the online space of advocacy. More so, as demonstrated by participants, state interference with digital and communications networks could cripple the activities of movement actors who rely heavily on technological forms of protest. While some participants identified state interference with ICTs as a challenge for dissident movements, the majority of the interviewees affirmed that the benefits of using the tools of new media for mobilisation far outweighed the shortfalls.

On the opportunity for conflict and protest to strive, the study found a mostly positive reaction among interviewed participants. For one, ICTs provided an alternative platform for mobilisation, communication, organisation and interaction during the January 2012 Occupy Nigeria protest. The findings corroborate the hypothesis that ICTs have in a positive direction affected the opportunity structure for movements engaged in conflict by providing several avenues to bypass state regulation and limitations. During the Occupy Nigeria protests, protesters relied mainly on social networks, blogs and other online media to propagate their cause, share information and mobilise support, telling their stories by themselves. The decentralised nature of the internet favours this approach and thus benefited protestors. As reflected in the opinions of respondents, the government is also on social media and uses ICTs. However, the deployment of the ICTs by the authorities is not as efficient as protestors. Interviewees pointed out that majority of government officials don't have the necessary technical know-how. Therefore, they employ 'sponsored handles'. ICTs have reduced the capacity of the state to impede mobilisation while empowering movement actors facilitating entry, inter-movement and civil society interaction as demonstrated in Occupy Nigeria protests. Besides the impact of ICTs on the political opportunity, another notable influence on the opportunity structure for contentious activities is the system of government in place. For instance, conflict will thrive more under a democratic system as opposed to a dictatorial/authoritarian system. This idea was implicit in participants' perspectives that the current democratic system and the reduced likelihood of an attack from the state also served as a motivation for participants.

On the framing, a positive reaction was elicited from interviewed participants. But of more crucial significance is the examination of individual texts on various online social media platforms. ICTs were instructive for shaping public perception of the movement both at home and abroad. Independent activists, social movement actors and ordinary Nigerians used the new media platforms to tell their stories to the world the way they wanted the world to view it, using FB, Twitter and Nairaland, to mention the notable social media used by participants.

The autonomy of the process meant that these actors were able also to shape public opinion and counter state, narratives and propaganda on the movement in both traditional and new media. Movement actors were able to influence the agenda for both local and global media since most of these media outlets relied on the materials emerging from the social network pages of the Occupy Nigeria movement in the initial stages of the protests and beyond to report the events and generate new content. These positively influenced how the movement framed issues, their strategies, goals and the level of sympathy and support they could garner around the globe. Ultimately, while recognising the increasing influence of the state on new technologies of communication in the digital age, in the present context, ICTs played an instrumental role by facilitating the entire action. The benefits of using the medium far outweigh the disadvantages.

Chapter 5

The Boko Haram Conflict

5.1. Evolution of Boko Haram

Over the years, varying perspectives have emerged in academia, national and international political commentary and media evaluation of the exact origins of the Boko Haram movement in Nigeria. One can trace the roots of the movement's struggles to similar conflicts dating back to the colonial and post-colonial era by making associations to the intra-communal jihadist conflict and inter-communal struggles. For instance, the Maitatsine uprising of the 1980s (discussed in subsequent paragraphs) is a crucial example of a jihadist ethnoreligious conflict that can be juxtaposed with the Boko Haram insurgency (Adesoji, 2011; Aghedo & Osumah, 2012). On the other hand, the revolt of the group is reminiscent of the ethnic and religious tensions that emerged as a result of the 1914 amalgamation of the northern and southern protectorates in what became Nigeria. Chapter 2 provided some context to the inter-religious and ethnic suspicions and tensions that gradually developed and continued in the post-1960 Nigerian independence. Mainly, Nigeria post-independence in 1960 has been characterised by struggles for ethnic, religious and political hegemony, especially among the dominant ethnic groups (Hausa, Yoruba and Igbo) in the country. Grievances and dissatisfaction among these groups and other ethnic minority groups provide useful insights into the origins and motivation of ethnoreligious conflicts in the country, as will be demonstrated in the Boko Haram case.

Boko Haram's origin as a conflict movement in Nigeria remains unclear. For instance, Ujah (2009) argues that Abubakar Lawan created the group which existed under various facades around 1995. Some commentators have linked the Boko Haram movement's activities to events that predate the group's revolt. For instance, Adesoji (2011) holds the view that the Boko Haram ideology was started by Mohammed Yusuf's father in the 1960s given his condemnation of western education. The lack of agreement on the emergence of the movement demonstrates the difficulty of understanding the dynamics of violent insurgency and conflict groups. The reason is that the activities of insurgency conflict movements are mostly covert due to the style of their warfare. Nonetheless, drawing on the varying opinions, perspectives (political and social commentary within the media) and scholarly studies on Boko Haram, one could trail the corpus of the movement's activities as a contemporary religious movement to 1995, nonetheless masked under various identities. For instance, the movement took on an identity of a religious youth organisation, *Ahlulsunna wal jamaah hijra*, in 1995 in Maiduguri Borno State, Nigeria, under the leadership of Abubakar Lawal, a

Muslim cleric (Aghedo & Osumah, 2012, p. 585). Mohammed Yusuf later took over the leadership of the religious organisation in 2002 (Adesoji, 2011, p. 9).

The Boko Haram movement was launched into the national and international limelight in 2009 following the arrest and subsequent extrajudicial murder of Mohammed Yusuf, the erstwhile leader and founder of the movement. After Yusuf took over the *Ahlulsuma wal'jama'ah hijra*, the movement experienced radical changes in its stance on Islam and politics in the years that followed. In particular, the movement took a strong stance on political Sharia, which in simple terms refers to the 'religious law of Islam' (An-Na'im, 2008, p. 1). In a political sense, Boko Haram actors seek to enforce the Sharia as the principal means of governance across the northern region of Nigeria and indeed other parts of the country. Radical insurgency tactics have chiefly accompanied their strong stance on Sharia. Suspicion of the group's secret jihadist plans and confrontation with security operatives at different times prompted a security onslaught on the group which included arrests of some of its members and a raid of the group's haven (see Walker, 2012, p. 3). For instance, in 2003, following a public disagreement concerning rights over a local fish pond, the group overpowered the police in a confrontation that ensued and confiscated the security weapons of the police. The threat the group now posed led to a security siege at the group's mosque that involved members of the police. Eventually, a shoot-out emerged which led to the group losing approximately 70 of its members. A similar security onslaught on the insurgents and reprisal attacks resulted in the capture and subsequent death of Mohammed Yusuf, the leader of Boko Haram, in 2009 (Adesoji, 2010; Bakare, Adedeji, & Shobiye, 2009; McConnell, 2009; Onuoha, 2010; Owuamanam, Falola, & Shobiye, 2009).

The movement has existed under different names including *Ahlulsunna wai'jama'ah hijra*, the 'Nigerian Taliban' and 'Yusufiyyah', to mention but a few. However, it was under Mohammed Yusuf's leadership that it became known as Boko Haram given its attacks on western education. Boko Haram is considered an ethnoreligious movement, given its predominant ethnic composition and religious affiliation. First, in the movement's original establishment, Mohammed Yusuf who was an Islamic cleric led the movement as a religious organisation. At the beginning of Yusuf's led Boko Haram, the objectives of the movement mainly included propagating what they considered as the true values of Islam as prescribed by Sharia. The group's leader challenged what he perceived as an encroachment on Islam by western values that contradicted the true practices of the religion and, as such, were inimical to the development of the religion. For example, in an interrogation by security officers posted on YouTube shortly before Yusuf's killing, he argued that 'any values or knowledge that contradicts the Quran, God forbid' (Saharatv, August 2009). Building on Yusuf's point, Shekau also made similar claims. For instance, in one of the Shekau's speeches posted on YouTube, speaking fluently in English, he argued that:

> We are Boko Haram, when they started, they planned, centuries ago on how to crush Islam. They sent one of their men to Egypt

> to study the secrets of the powers of the Muslim. The person returned with a copy of the Quran. The person stated that as long as the Muslim read and practised the injunctions in the Quran, they will be powerful. Therefore, they deliberated on how to tactically make the Quran insignificant and unimportant. At the end of the meeting, they outlined many programs which were centred on making Muslims occupied so that they had no time for the Quran. The programs include secular education, sport and music. As a result of this today, many Muslims lost their Islam, while others claim to be Muslim, but have no traces of Islam [...]. All in the name of being educated.
>
> TVC News (20 February 2014)

The ethnic component ties to the fact that the majority of the members of the group belong to the Kanuri tribe, most of whom also speak Hausa, the predominant language spoken throughout northern Nigeria (Agbiboa, 2013, p. 72). Also, these tribes account for a dominant proportion of the ethnic groups in its Maiduguri stronghold (Agbiboa, 2013, p. 72). Members of the group are drawn from across this tribe, exclusively Muslim in their religious orientation and largely composed of youths between 18 years and their late 30s, as well as those perhaps in their early 40s. This analysis is based on a careful evaluation of videos of the groups and media reports. For instance, a *Vanguard* 2011 report reveals that the erstwhile leader of the group was born in 1970 and died in 2009 which suggests he was in his late 30s when he led the sect (Onuoha, 2010, p. 56). Similarly, the report indicated that the mastermind of the bombing of the United Nations building in Abuja was a 27-year-old Nigerian, Mohammed Abul Barra; another leader of the group, Nur, was believed to be 35 years old. Nur was also supposed to be one of the two second in command to the late Yusuf. The other is Abubakar Shekau, the current and the reigning leader of the Islamic sect. According to a BBC 2014 report, Shekau is also believed to be in his late 30s or mid-40s. While there is no stated official report on the age demographics of the group, one can on the basis of the media reports and careful evaluation of videos produced by the movement show that the movement is predominantly composed of youth. Onuoha (2012a, 2012b) also pointed out the involvement of children in the activities of Boko Haram. This mostly involves the Almajiri (street children), which includes those children 'sent to live and study under renowned Islamic teachers in some cities in northern Nigeria' (Onuoha, 2012b, p. 2). Omonobi (2014) explained that such children are indoctrinated and groomed to participate in the activities of Boko Haram. Nonetheless, children's involvement is due to coercion and co-option in line with the group's propagandist agenda. The subsequent involvement of children has made it difficult for the security agencies to effectively combat the insurgents for fear of the safety of the children. Omonobi cites a military source:

> We have lost our men in the battle-field while we tried to avoid shooting children and teenagers who are forced to confront us.

> How do you expect us to arrest a child with a gun? Do we accord such an armed under-age combatant with the status of a child deserving of protection under the rules of engagement?
>
> Omonobi (2014)

5.1.1. *Boko Haram's Hierarchical Leadership Structure*

There is no doubt that the Boko Haram movement has leadership and an existing leadership structure within the movement. Nonetheless, there are conflicting accounts on the structure of leadership the movement operates. Although loose in its orientation, Boko Haram operates within a hierarchical organisational structure (Onuoha, 2013; Whitlowzw, 2015). The group has presented a leadership structure (see Adesoji, 2010; Aghedo & Osumah, 2012; Zenn, Barkindo, & Heras, 2013; Cook, 2011; Onuoha, 2010; Rogers, 2012). At each stage of the group's development, the group has presented one precise identity of the leadership of the movement, usually the head of the movement. Conversely, the identity of other members of the leadership has remained unclear, thereby making it difficult to ascertain the full composition of the movement. For instance, during the early days of the group's formation, only the identity of the movement's late leader (Yusuf) was made public in videos produced by the movement, while other members of the movement wear masks and other militarised apparel to disguise their identity. Consequently, this style continued in the second phase of the movement which followed the death of Yusuf. The approach to masking the identity of its members is no surprise given that the group uses a radical militant approach. For instance, in a 2014 video produced by the group and posted on Youtube, Shekau makes claims for attacks in Lagos and Abuja. In a forest-like environment, the leader of the group is shown delivering a speech in military camouflage unmasked while surrounded by 14 masked commanders also wearing military uniforms and carrying ammunition and surrounded by a combination of SUVs and military armoured vehicles. As with other cases of insurgency movements (like MEND) in Nigeria, the reason for this approach is to avoid security operatives from recognising members and participants, which could lead to their arrest, torture and destruction of lives and properties.

Having succeeded Yusuf, Abubakar Shekau continues in a similar fashion of being the only recognisable figure within the leadership of the movement. The movement's hierarchical structure and faceless identity help to facilitate their activities especially for evading the state law enforcement agencies (Onuoha, 2013, p. 19). It has been argued that when Yusuf founded the Boko Haram movement, he appointed two deputies, Shekau and Nur (see Doukhan, 2012; Kalu, 2011; Onuoha, 2013; Whitlowzw, 2015). The latter is believed to have introduced the former to the erstwhile founder of the movement. In the event following the death of Yusuf in 2009, the two deputies contested each other's legitimacy to occupy the late Yusuf's position. Shekau subsequently declared himself the leader of the movement, following Nur's political exile due to the security onslaught on the group. A *Vanguard* 2011 article, which is based on investigations with the States Security Service (SSS) and other sources, captures the contention that emerged between Yusuf's deputies. According to the report:

> Sources claiming to have been sect members as well as those familiar with the group, Nur took over temporarily as a leader while Shekau recovered from gunshot wounds suffered during the uprising. Nur is thought to have left Nigeria for Chad [...] to escape arrest by security agents. From Chad, he is believed to have moved to Somalia along with some close allies, according to the sources [...]. Rumours have spread that there has been a power struggle between Nur and Shekau, with Nur and his faction of loyalists contending he was more competent to lead the sect [...].
>
> Kalu (2011)

This contention between the leaders of Boko Haram created factions within the movement. The ideals and loyalties of these factions may be different but are nonetheless bound by a common religious philosophy. For instance, factions including Yusufiya Islamic Movement (Yusufiya) and Ansaru evolved during the long campaign of the sect over various internal grievances, from the controversy over the leadership's tactical choices and strategy to internal issues relating to a power struggle. The emergence of factions within movements is not a new phenomenon. Hazen (2009) explained that competition could produce a negative effect on social movements. Consequently, competition within such movements would produce a negative effect of division and factions breaking away from the main group. In the present context, however, the primary source of the division has been the issue of intra-movement power struggle (as in the case following the death of Yusuf), a dispute over leadership roles and other issues related to tactical choices and differences. For instance, the less-prominent Yusufiya group, named after the erstwhile leader of the movement, preferred a less violent approach than what was mostly used by Yusuf (Zenn, 2014, p. 25). A more notable breakaway is the group known as 'Ansaru', which had a brief spell of significance due to its focus on kidnapping foreign expatriate workers in Nigeria and demanding ransom or some trade by barter. Unlike the Boko Haram movement, Ansaru's main target was expatriate workers in Nigeria, but the group also became popular for condemning Boko Haram's killings of Muslims and innocent citizens (see Zenn, 2013, pp. 3–7). Ansaru's breakaway and choice of modus operandi emerged as a result of disagreements within Boko Haram on its target, which included Muslims. Nonetheless, none of these groups has gained the level of media attention as in the case of the Boko Haram movement.

In the hierarchy of Boko Haram, Shekau's role as leader of the movement is perhaps the only visible office in the movement's organisational structure. While other individuals exist as part of the leadership, the role they play in the movement has remained unclear. Drawing on media reports, videos produced by the movement and existing literature on the movement (Adesoji, 2010; Cook, 2011; Udum, 2011; Walker, 2012), it could be argued that Boko Haram operates a top–down model structure of leadership. For instance, media reports and political commentary have indicated a leadership structure that includes what can be called a central leadership council (Chothia, 2015; Cook, 2011; Walker, 2012) which represents the leadership of the organisation. To further bolster the aforementioned point, the movement's media chats have revealed spokespersons who frequently speak for the movement. Notable among the spokespersons of the movement is Abul Qaqa, who Cook (2011, p. 13) described as being more visible since 2011. According to Cook, press releases issued by Qaqa are considered legitimate. While the group's media productions including audio-visuals suggest the existence of a media team, Boko Haram's extensive use of improvised explosive devices (IEDs) is also symptomatic of an existing training cell in making, operating and detonating such apparatus, which is reminiscent of a militarised establishment. Furthermore, Cook (2011) states that within Boko Haram, the central leadership council operates through a cell-like structure which enables the movement to work in different regions across Nigeria.

The aforementioned point echoes with what Doukhan (2012) referred to as 'a network of cells'. Indeed, the organisational disposition of the group which spreads mostly across the northern region and sporadic activities in other regions attest to Doukhan's theorisation. According to him, the present structure of the movement is led by Imam Abubakar Shekau, who handles the general operations of the movement. Also, Doukhan explained that Shekau's activities are complemented by 'a network of cells', which comprise a consultative forum (which represents the leadership) of 30 members who operate from different regions of the country (see also Walker, 2012, p. 8). Members handle an allocated cell (comprising groups within the different regions or states), with particular assignments set out for specific regions. In his words:

> The organisation's activities are discussed in the forum of the council, but sometimes Abubakar Shekau, the leader, makes operative decisions without consulting the members of the Shura [...]. A reliable and trustworthy person, is positioned in every state where the organization is active; local 'emirs', report to him, are the direct operations officers of the recruited jihadi.
>
> Walker (2012, p. 10)

On the one hand, the regionalisation of the movement or cell structure as Doukhan pointed out is crucial, especially when set against the backdrop of the Boko Haram's objectives and goal to spread across the country and Islamise the nation. Established structures across the country could facilitate more effortless execution of the movement's goals and aims across these regions or cells. While there is evidence to suggest the group's activities across all the areas, nonetheless, this is circumstantial. Across the six geopolitical regions (mentioned earlier) that make up the entire country, the movement's presence and activities have mainly concentrated in three regions, the north-east, north central and north-west areas. Other regions, including the south–south, south-west and south-east have experienced little or no Boko Haram-related activities since the movement commenced its insurgency.

5.1.2. Socio-political, Economic and Cultural Motivations

To fully understand Boko Haram as a movement, the issues, origins and motivation of the group's long campaign of insurgency, a discussion in context of the environment of conflict is crucial. The discourse on the environment of conflict in this regard falls into two broad categories. On the one hand, we have the socio-economic dimension while on the other hand is the political and cultural dimension. The environment of conflict is one of the first ports of call in the CC framework. Although some general discussion on the environment of conflict (Nigeria) was held in the mapping of the political economy of communication section in Chapter 1, nonetheless, this took a broad view of the overall Nigerian context. The analysis offered from now on reflects on the current state of the political environment in the north-east where Boko Haram mainly operates.

The socio-economic conditions within a given society can be a defining instrument for contentious activities, resistance and protest. A careful evaluation of the socio-economic conditions in the north-eastern part of Nigeria is crucial and provides useful insight into the roots, goals and motivations of the group. As media reports and political commentary on the movement have shown, this dynamic is particularly telling in the Boko Haram case and stands out in both local and global media discourse. The discussion here is streamlined to focus on the political economy of the north-east region of Nigeria to reflect the period of Boko Haram's development. This takes into context the geopolitical and economic differences between the six regions that make up present-day Nigeria and enables us to understand the motivations of the movement and its growth numerically. Although Boko Haram intends to spread and extend its campaign across all the regions (Cook, 2011; Hakeem Onapajo & Uzodike, 2012; Walker, 2012), to some extent, the north-eastern region and the entire northern region account for the movement's main operating base and headquarters.

Various scholarly works and media reports on Boko Haram have credited one of the primary causes of the movement's activities to displeasure, anger and dissent towards the poor conditions of living experienced in the northern region, or more specifically the north-eastern, which is the movement's headquarters. Proponents of this perspective link the rebellion of the Boko Haram movement to the largely weak economic conditions in the region epitomised by high levels of poverty and lack of development, to mention but a few (see Adesoji, 2010; Odamah, 2012; Onuoha, 2014; Rogers, 2012; Hakeem Onapajo & Uzodike, 2012; Walker, 2012). The implication of the weak economic conditions in this region includes disadvantaged upbringing, unemployment and rise in poverty levels which then serve as catalysts of insurgency in the region. Onuoha also identified the high levels of illiteracy in the region as a factor encouraging youth radicalisation. According to him, 'illiterate people can be more easily manipulated because their state of social deprivation denies them the capacity and knowledge to critically question the narratives and doctrines of extremist groups' (Walker, 2012, pp. 6–7).

Although the political elite of the region held power in much of the Nigerian political development stages after independence to date, with brief spells of leadership emerging from the other areas, very little was done by the political elite of the north to develop the region. As such, the region is perhaps the least developed in Nigeria with high levels of poverty. It is with this in mind that in an interview with the International Business Times, Obasanjo, an ex-president of Nigeria, observed that Boko Haram has legitimate grievances. According to him, 'we don't need anyone to tell us that that is a problem: a problem of disparity, a problem of marginalisation' (Isine, 2015). According to Obasanjo:

> Only 19 per cent of the population in Boko Haram's stronghold of North-East Nigeria are receiving education, [compared to 79 percent in the South-West and 77 percent in the South-East], there was no question that the area should feel marginalised [...], it's a problem because education is fundamental to your employability and your living conditions. If you are not educated, you are handicapped.
>
> Isine (2015)

Although the view expressed earlier captures the most current outlook of the problem in the region, the statistics are a reflection of many years of an unchanged phenomenon in the level of inequality and disparity across the geopolitical zones that make up Nigeria. The result of this is that the majority of the movement's membership belongs to a vulnerable, jobless, less educated section of the society within which they operate. Rogers (2012) found that the relative economic negligence in the predominantly Muslim north is a nationwide issue of huge scale divisions of wealth and poverty. Likewise, the problem of corruption, which confronts the entire political structure of the country, accounts for the movement's support (Rogers, 2012, p. 2). When queried on poverty data in Nigeria, the Research Director of the Nigerian Economic Summit Group, explained that increasing unemployment accompanies the increasing poverty in Nigeria. 'Unemployment is higher in the north than in the south. Mix this situation with radical Islam, which promises a better life for martyrs, and you can understand the growing violence in the north' (Rogers, 2012, p. 4). Data and information provided by the Nigerian authorities reveal that the northern region of the country houses the highest percentage of poverty (see Figures 5.1 and 5.2) which also translates into lack of jobs, high illiteracy levels and low standard of living for the majority. Consequently, this economic drawback and gap has served as one primary catalyst and incentive for resistance and is also responsible for the movement's constantly enlarging character. 'If you link a lack of education and attendant lack of opportunities to a high male youth population, you can imagine that some areas are a breeding ground for terrorism' (Rogers, 2012, p. 4). The significance of socio-economic drawbacks, such as poverty, marginalisation, inequality, unemployment and poor growth, as a catalyst for conflict are well established in other national contexts where insurgency is rife. For instance, in the 'rooted in poverty hypotheses', Piazza (2006, p. 160) explains that the general understanding is that terrorist activities are channels by which its actors express socio-economic discontent and

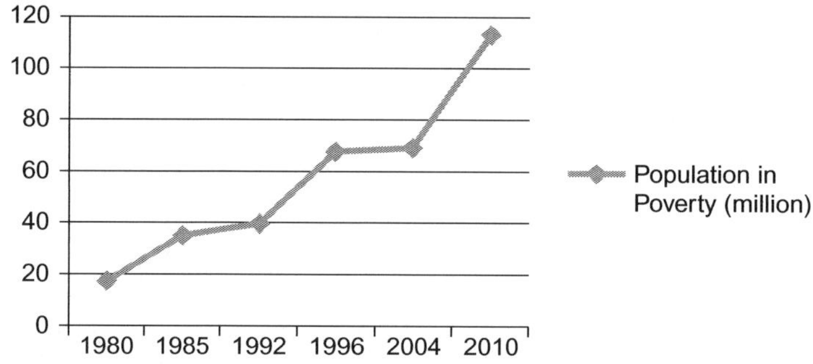

Figure 5.1. Rising Trend of Poverty in Nigeria from 1980 to 2010. *Source*: National Bureau of Statistics. Available at: http://www.nigerianstat.gov.ng/pdfuploads/Nigeria%20Poverty%20Profile%202010.pdf

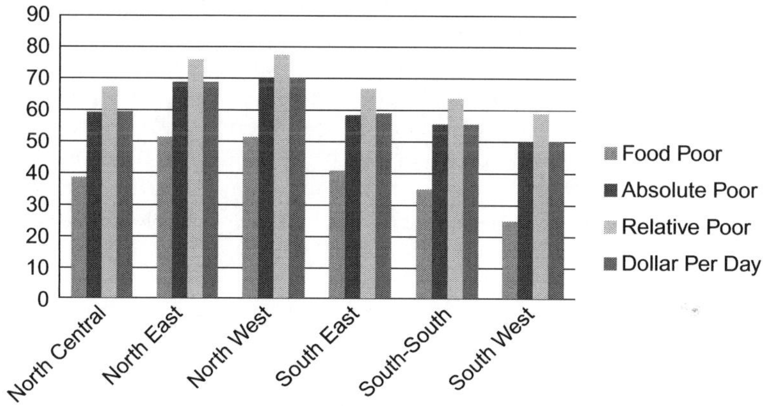

Figure 5.2. Poverty Levels across the Six Geopolitical Zones in Nigeria. *Source*: National Bureau of Statistics. Available at: http://www.nigerianstat.gov.ng/pdfuploads/Nigeria%20Poverty%20Profile%202010.pdf

desperation (see also Beall, Goodfellow, & Putzel, 2006; Krueger & Maleckova, 2002; Lichbach, 1989).

For instance, referring to the socio-economic conditions that the Maitatsine uprising in 1980 endured, Adesoji (2010) explained that the conditions at the time are no different to the situation experienced in the stronghold of the Boko Haram movement today. 'In some cases, the situation had got worse: There was mass poverty; inequality in educational, political and employment opportunities; ignorance due to limited educational opportunities; growing unemployment and governmental corruption, the misuse of resources by which the people repulsed' (Adesoji, 2010, p. 100). A sociologist of Nigerian origin in a video commentary on the Boko Haram sect explained that the north had been marginalised as a territory by its ruler. According to him, to fully grasp the problem:

> You have to trace it back to the way northern Nigeria is. Despite the fact that it has produced a dominant part of leadership that Nigeria has produced, the north has been marginalised as a territory by its rulers [...] the Northern ruling elite or ruling clique [...] has mobilised politics around northern privileged.
>
> Aina (2009)

Speaking further on the economic conditions in the Boko Haram stronghold, David, Asuelime and Onapajo (2015) also corroborated the point made by Adesoji. They explained that the lack of development has served as the motivation for individuals with a low standard of living. It is with this view that Imam Shekau the leader of the movement made his claim. While claiming responsibility for the attack on a military infrastructure (Giwa Barracks in Maiduguri) in 2014, he argued that Boko Haram has taken full responsibility for catering to the needs of their brethren (see TracNigeria, 19 April 2014). In his words, 'we brought them, we bought them clothes, we got them houses, we gave them cars, we gave them food, we gave them everything, we cleaned them up and put fragrances on them [...] today they are enjoying fresh air, and enjoy themselves, and all our brethren are enjoying good health' (TracNigeria, 19 April 2014). From Shekau's statement, one can see on the one hand an intrinsic motivation for individuals joining the movement. While on the other hand, it is clear that Boko Haram takes advantage of the weak economic conditions within its political environment as a means to win an already aggrieved and deprived population. In a video, political commentary on the movement, Aina (2009) explained that:

> Northern Nigeria used to be agriculturally productive, but today it leaves the oil of the delta. You have a situation where there are no industries, de-industrialization, no agricultural farms or plantations because the Nigerian government and elite went crazy for 20–30 years neglecting agriculture [...] you have millions of disinherited illiterate northern youths in the cities known Maiduguri, Bauchi [...]
>
> Aina (2009)

Corroborating the point made by Aina earlier, a recent finding of the Crisis Group Africa 2014 report suggests that a large fraction of youths living in the north are uneducated. The implication is that they are semi-skilled or unskilled and as such are almost not employable. The result of this is that such individuals remain unproductive. This is an interesting point, especially when one considers that majority of the adherents of this movement are usually young, poor and rural. As such, it is easy for the leadership of the movement to leverage on the plight of the people. So from this point of view, the government's continuous failure to cater to the needs of the people, promote economic development and provide an enabling environment is serving as a window of opportunity for the movement. In particular, movement actors use these pitfalls as a strategy to recruit members while offering them various incentives including monetary gains and shelter for their families in exchange for their commitments to jihad (a holy war).

The economic condition of targeted individuals determines whether or not they will become quickly co-opted by conflict movements. In the Boko Haram context, unemployment and poverty may not be direct causes of increasing youth participation, 'rather, privation and other frustrating conditions of life render youth highly vulnerable to manipulation by extremist ideologues' (Onuoha, 2014, p. 6). Komolafe (2012) argued that there are higher chances for societies defined by anguish and idleness to produce suicide bombers in contrast to those communities where the majority enjoy basic needs of food, education, health, housing and sanitation. In other words, the poor conditions of living become a recruitment factor as Shekau alluded to in the previous paragraph. Although there has been some level of economic growth, notably the Nigerian economy in 2015 was rebased and has now overtaken South African economy to be the largest economy in Africa. Nonetheless, the reality is that poverty levels have remained negative. In fact, poverty levels have increased. Over 70 percent of the population – are classified as poor, and Sokoto State in the North West has the highest poverty rate (86.4 percent), Niger State in North Central the lowest (43). The North East, Boko Haram's main operational field, has the worst poverty rate of the six official "zones"' (Crisis Group, 2014, p. 3).

It is within this milieu of increasingly worsening socio-economic conditions that the Boko Haram movement emerged. Other groups with similar grievances and perhaps unrelated to Boko Haram continue to surface in the region. The movements mainly draw support from amongst youths within the communities in the northern region. The guarantee of better welfare, monetary gains, food and shelter, job and other rewards including catering to the needs of their loved ones are rife within the movement's narratives and has served as a crucial means for attracting individuals to join and participate in the movement's activities (Anyadike, 2013; Silas, 2013; Track Nigeria, 19 April 2014; Walker, 2012). Issues relating to how the group funds itself have remained unclear. However, Boko Haram has made claims that its sponsors include some 'politicians and Islamic clerics. Three ex-governors and a serving governor of some northern states have been indicted for aiding Boko Haram' (Aghedo & Osumah, 2012, p. 863).

The socio-economic predicaments of the people of the region are not unconnected to the issue of endemic corruption in Nigeria, with authorities and political elite in the area mismanaging revenue and funds allocated for developing programmes and infrastructure; the result is little progress in the area. Walker (2012) explained that widespread corruption (a financial corruption of the government and the moral depravity of the religious establishment as perceived by Boko Haram), especially in this region, had had a positive influence on the group's activities. In a study conducted by Onuoha (2014) in two north-western states, namely Sokoto and Kano States, 70% and 67% (respectively) of the participants surveyed cited corruption as an essential factor in the Boko Haram conflict. Accordingly, 'widespread corruption in Nigeria has not only deprived communities of needed amenities and infrastructure, but also has created an environment conducive to recruitment and radicalisation' (Onuoha, 2014, p. 7).

The founder of the Boko Haram movement, Mohammed Yusuf, and Sheakau with regard to the development of the movement became very critical of the corrupt practices of the political elite of the north-eastern states (Onuoha, 2014, p. 7). Criticism of the leadership with regard to the of the issue of corruption (discussed further in the framing section) is not far from the truth, especially when juxtaposed against the backdrop of high levels of poverty, unemployment and low literacy levels experienced in the north-eastern region. The government failed in its attempt to sustain initial cooperation with the movement during the movement's earliest development. Boko Haram criticised the government for politicising sharia (Adesoji, 2010, p. 103), and members perceived the cooperation as another form of manipulation which led to disagreements and a fall out between the state and the movement.

The fall out between the insurgents and the state led to the witch-hunting of members of the movement. The brutality perpetrated by security forces in witch-hunting members of the movement is another factor Onuoha (2014) identified as a motive for individuals, particularly youths, joining and participating in the Boko Haram conflict. The belief is that a large section of the population who are innocent have been victims of the security onslaught on members of the Boko Haram movement. 'Allegations include unlawful killings, dragnet arrests, extortion, and intimidation. A section of the media, especially international media, has repeatedly mentioned that the excesses of the security forces are a crucial factor in youth radicalisation' (Onuoha, 2014, p. 7). Grievances as a result of the killing or detention and the destruction of properties by security operatives may become an incentive for joining the movement. Nonetheless, Onuoha (2014) further suggests the factor is less crucial for influencing dissidents to join the movement.

5.1.3. The Politics, Ethnicity and Religious Grievances

As demonstrated earlier, some commentators see the socio-economic shortfalls in the region and, indeed, Nigeria as one aspect responsible for the motivation for the Boko Haram conflict and how the movement exploits poverty, the lack of infrastructural development and corruption as a means for attracting dissidents in the region to join the movement. In addition to the socio-economic issue, there are also ethnic, religious and political undertones prevalent in the struggle of the Boko Haram movement. These conflicts have roots that go back as far as the 1940s when the protectorates under the then British colonialists amalgamated and the tensions that emerged following the Nigerian independence in 1960. This paradigm has received lesser attention within academic literature, media criticism and western political commentary, but can be useful for understanding the contemporary tensions and struggles of the movement.

Indeed, the socio-economic discourse is a crucial element in the evolution and development of Boko Haram. One thing the argument, which advocates socio-economic drawbacks as an incentive for the Boko Haram activities, pays less attention to is the existence of other ethnic (Igbos and Yoruba notably) and religious (Christians and other secular groups) groups within the same region.

These groups who are in the minority in the north-east and north-west are also subject to similar economic status. They have remained non-partisan in the activities of the insurgents. For instance, although Muslims are dominant in north-eastern Nigeria and in particular, the Kanuri, Hausa-Fulani clan, the minority Christian communities and other tribes who live side by side with their Boko Haram counterparts have nonetheless not been involved in the conflict. Similarly, while the movement has a broad northern appeal, sympathy and support (Olojo, 2013, p. 1), there is sufficient evidence to suggest that not all Muslims, Hausa-Fulani and Kanuri support Boko Haram's campaign. For instance, Jama'atu Nasril Islam (JNI), the umbrella Islamic organisation in the country based in Kaduna State, has criticised the activities of Boko Haram on numerous occasions (see Mshelizza, 2009)

In this regard, the economic argument exists alongside other contextual influences including the political struggles for hegemony. In short, the economic impacts live side by side with the conflicts between political, ethnic and religious communities as the earlier paragraph described. Conversely, for Nigerians (ethnic and religious groups) in the other geopolitical zones, Boko Haram's activities are seen as a political struggle for power to assert a northern political agenda and hegemony in contemporary Nigeria. This view is particularly telling, as careful observation of this line of thought exposes decades of ethnic, religious and political tension in Nigeria. The struggle has revolved around political dominance among the different ethnoreligious groups that make up the Nigerian society (see Adebola, 2013; Campbell, 2013). A political commentary asserts that:

> While many in the Muslim community in the North might blame the government for problems that led to Boko Haram. Relatively few in the South and Middle Belt share the same sentiments. In the South and many parts of the Middle Belt, Boko Haram is just seen as the latest manifestation of 'the North's grab for power'. In this narrative, control of the Military, political Sharia and now Boko Haram is attempting to advance the same cause: Northern domination […] Does poverty and lack of education make recruitment more likely? Yes, but we must also note that mass uprisings by charismatic Islamic preachers are not unknown in Northern Nigeria (Maitatsine & Kano, 1980, 4,000 dead).
>
> Chukudebelu cited in Campbell (2013)

Headed by Mohammed Marwa, the Maitatsine group was an ethnoreligious movement with an anti-modernist political perspective. The two movements (Boko Haram and the Maitatsine) share some characteristics. For instance, Marwa originated from the Bornu Empire in Maiduguri, the same region where the Boko Haram movement originated. The Maitatsine movement went on an Islamic jihad, in the premier city of Kano in 1980. According to Ayelabola (2013), the Maitatsine provides a classic comparable pair with Boko Haram, given that both movements share Islamist and radical ideologies. As the Boko Haram conflict is believed to have cost several thousand lives and destruction of property, the Maitatsine killed over 4,000, including the destruction of properties within days of the movement's rampage.

Both movements share and operate on an anti-modernist, anti-western and anti-establishment standpoint. Nonetheless, there are individual differences in the philosophy of both groups. For instance, the Maitatsine held a mixed view that combined anti-modernism by proscribing any western-related ideology and innovations; at the same time, the leader of the Maitatsine movement was known for contesting some beliefs in the Holy Quran and some practices of Prophet Mohammed (Adebola, 2013, p. 114). Falola (1998) explained that the leader of Boko Haram professed himself to be an 'annabi', meaning a prophet with divine power and mission to save the world. Boko Haram, however, holds a substantial anti-westernisation philosophy as well an anti-nationalist philosophy. But unlike the Maitatsine, Boko Haram holds a fully supportive and loyalist orientation to the Quran, in that it strives to follow and fulfil prescribed instructions to the letter. Hence, the movement's original designation *Jama'atu ahlis sunna lidda'awati wal-jihad* (people committed to the prophetic teachings and jihad). 'The Leadership of the movement has a penchant for using "Allah" as a means to justify their activities. "We are running our caliphate, our Islamic caliphate," Shekau said. "We follow the Koran [...]. We now practice the injunctions of the Koran in the land of Allah"'(Barrabi, 2014). The aforementioned quote is a standard narrative of Shekau, which he reiterates in several videos produced by the group. In fact, the group's longtime goal is to enforce a tradition of strict adherence to the precepts of the Quran; western civilisation is impeding the practice of which it believes. This perception arms us with an alternative lens through which the Boko Haram movement's activities can be understood.

In much of the Nigerian five decades of independence, much of the nation's political conflict has revolved around ethnic and religious politics. For one, the struggle for the control of political power has been a significant concern since the amalgamation of what is today Nigeria, a marriage of formerly distinct and independent protectorates (southern and northern territories) under the Lagos colony by the British government. Before the merger, the southern region was composed of Christians and different ethnic groups of which the Yoruba and Igbo tribe were predominant.

They strive to achieve a real Federal character, one which would reflect the ethnic and religious diversity of new Nigeria, with resources and power equally distributed between the ethnic and religious representations. However, this proved to be a significant challenge for successive governments. It is this perception that instructed the notion of an ethnoreligious political power struggle for dominance and hegemony. In the present context, it is argued that Boko Haram is an extension of such political strife in contemporary Nigeria. In other words, the struggle of the Boko Haram movement extends to include a dimension of a power struggle for political supremacy, dominance and conquest. This is embedded within the political discourse and narrative of Boko Haram, especially in its explicit goal to override the Nigerian constitution and enforce Sharia law as the legal blueprint for the Nigerian state in view to establishing an Islamic caliphate.

In one of the movement videos available on YouTube, Shekau is heard saying 'Nigeria was dead; her constitution is dead' following the burning of the Nigerian national flag.

5.1.4. Ideology, Framing Issues and Strategy

The concept of ideology is crucial to the success of political protest and resistance movements. For instance, scholarship within social movement studies has demonstrated the importance of ideology, especially as a resource employed by movement leaders in a conflict to garner support, participation and facilitate membership within a given movement (see Furseth, 2002, p. 91). In this regard, they are 'systems of belief that are elaborate, integrated, and coherent, that justify the exercise of power, explain and judge historical events, identify political right and wrong, set forth the interconnections (causal and moral) between politics and other spheres of activity' (McClosky, 1964, p. 362). For another, ideologies are 'sets of ideas by which men posit, explain and justify ends and means of organised social action, and specifically political action, irrespective of whether such action aims to preserve, amend, uproot or rebuild a given social order' (Seliger, 1976, p. 11). These perspectives share some essential attributes. The fact is that ideologies are a belief system deliberately and carefully crafted and used by actors to achieve specifically set out goals. In the present context, ideology is therefore used to refer to those underlying principles and norms that guide the core beliefs of a movement. In contrast to the goals or the aim of the movement, these beliefs serve as a crucial link, common denominator and unifying factor for members of the movement or a given movement or society. Furthermore, ideologies serve as a psychological tool deployed by movement actors as it binds members of the movements together. For instance, religion (Islam or Christianity) widespread in a society can become an ideological tool used by proponents of such culture. The idea here is that due to the all-encompassing nature of religion and colossal obeisance to them in a given society, movement actors can exploit the beliefs of the people during the conflict as instruments of propaganda to attract the sympathy and loyalty of individuals within such communities.

Furseth (2002) explained that such ideologies are then framed by movement leaders to reflect the structural and social conditions (socio-political and economic dynamic explained previously) within their environment of conflict. This point builds on the hypothesis of Obserschall (1973) who views ideologies as tools which link individual sufferings to social conditions, which then translate into grievances, and collective action (Furseth, 2002, p. 91). The processes involved in crafting such ideologies to fit into the particular repertoire of contention is described as a framing process. As discussed in Chapter 2, the framing process could involve several things, from intentional efforts to create narratives, publishing and challenging or countering the worldview of a movement circulated within the media, to political commentary. Garrett (2006) and Zald (1996) in separate accounts explained that the aim of the framing process is to justify the claims of actors involved in a conflict while also exploiting the platform to provoke action through the deployment of socially shared beliefs.

Drawing from these perspectives, media reports and video produced by Boko Haram, the study found that Boko Haram engages ideology as a means of propaganda. In this regard, the movement uses different frames and framing processes that are central to the activities. Boko Haram relies on Islamic religious ideology as a means to advance its cause, garner support and justify its actions. There are also socio-economic and political undertones in the groups' narrative which sheds insights into other grievances and motivations for their conflict and increasing membership (Waazin skekh Muhannnad Yusuf 1, 17 February 2011, pp. 1–5). With regard to the the environment of conflict, the study has identified socio-economic issues relating to decaying structural conditions, poverty, lack of education, unemployment, ethno-nationalist struggles for political hegemony and cultural tensions as the sum of the intrinsic motivation for the movement's insurrection. One would therefore reasonably expect that the ideology (which is discussed under the next heading) of the movement would resonate within some socio-political and economic deprivation model. The movement exploits a wholly religious ideology in its outlook.

The systemic use of religious ideology has proved resourceful for attracting sympathisers and numerically boosting the membership of the movement. For one, the north-eastern region that is the stronghold of the Boko Haram movement shares a strong Islamic religious identity, given that Muslims predominantly populate the area. Similarly, there is also an ethnic affiliation given that like the Boko Haram insurgents, the region and Maiduguri, in particular, are mainly dominated by the Hausa-Fulani/Kanuri tribe who are, again, predominantly Islamic in their religious orientation. With this, it is easy for the leadership of the Boko Haram movement to exploit religion, which it uses mostly as a means to appeal to Muslim adherents who have over the years become hugely divided between extreme and moderate views. The core belief which has been propagated since the reign of Yusuf and extended by Shekau is that God prohibits any knowledge that contradicts Islam. In an interview with Yusuf before his death posted on YouTube, he argued that:

> All knowledge that contradicts Islam is prohibited by the Almighty […] sihiri (sorcery or magic) is knowledge, but Allah hath forbidden it; shirk (Polytheism or sharing or associating partners to Allah) is knowledge, but Allah has forbidden it; astronomy is knowledge, but Allah has forbidden it.
>
> SaharaTv (3 August 2009)

They believe the system was, 'not only decidedly secular but had taken a position against God and made materialism and hedonism the ultimate in life' – subverted the north's traditional Islamic values, and replaced 'morality, that sense of right and wrong which only consciousness of God confers', with a kind of ruthless materialism (Ross, 2014).

The movement's continuous rhetoric on decaying Islamic values as a result of the secular state and influence of westernisation is an illustrative example of how religion is being used as a tool by the leadership of Boko Haram and epitomises the point made by Ross (2014) earlier. Muslims who hold moderate Islamic views and as a result object to the beliefs of Boko Haram are also considered as 'enemies' by Boko Haram. Boko Haram's use of religion is psychological, to grab the minds of its target audience using a shared belief system. Once the attention of adherents has been grabbed using religion, individuals become caught up in the ideology of the movement and subsequently become potential recruits and members of the movement.

To demonstrate how religion is used as a resource, since its inception, the Islamic centres' of worship were exploited by the leadership of the movement for propaganda and radicalisation (see Walker, 2012, pp. 1–15). Sermons preached by the leadership of the movement are a means through which such radical ideologies and manipulations were conveyed to its members, knowing well that adherents hold religion in high esteem. In essence, the group's leadership uses the pulpit and preaching podium within its religious centres' of worship to construct and propagate their radical narratives and propaganda. The original founding of the movement by the late Yusuf reflects this perception. According to a BBC (2015) report, Yusuf's first gesture was to create a religious complex that housed a mosque and an Islamic school. With these, many families flooded the school with their children, especially those belonging to the lower-income earning class in society within the immediate Muslim-dominated region. Subsequently, this became an avenue for recruiting disciples. Furthermore, some clerics in the region also promote and approve many of the issues that the Boko Haram uses to attract recruits. For instance, Yusuf was an Islamic cleric who was popular in the region. An examination of Yusuf's teachings and sermons posted on YouTube shows how the religious centres were used to teach anti-state, anti-nationalist and anti-western values, including creating hatred and further inter-faith divides (see Muhammad Bukar 17 Feb 2011, pp. 1–5). Subsequently, Shekau, an Islamic cleric too, also used the medium to advance propaganda and psychological manipulations similar to Yusuf (Sunnahization, 28 October 2011).

Other narratives which the movement affiliates to its struggles, especially about the socio-economic issues explained elsewhere, are also embedded within the movement's broader religious discourse. Whereas Boko Haram exploits religious frames to advance its goals and other objectives, the movement's sermons reveal embedded socio-political, economic and other grievances. These include issues relating to poverty and oppression, disparities, marginalisation and corruption, in concert with narratives on political hegemony and dominance which the group seeks to achieve by Islamising Nigeria. For instance, after Gwoza, a town in Maiduguri, was captured by Boko Haram, its leader declared the city an Islamic state in a video that circulated on YouTube (Channels Television, 2014). 'Thanks be to Allah who gave victory to our brethren in [the town of] Gwoza and made it part of the Islamic caliphate' (cited in The Telegraph, 24 August 2014), Abubakar Shekau said in the video. Shekau's allusion to Allah in the text earlier confirms the argument on how the leadership exploits religion as a means for legitimatising its activities and in doing so galvanising the support of adherents.

On one level, the injustice theme embedded in the socio-political grievances expressed in the narratives of the leadership of the movement echoes with western discourses on socio-economic inequality and marginalisation, as in the case of the anti-globalisation and anti-capitalist movement. In the present case, however, these grievances reflecting injustice are expressed under a religious narrative. However, Boko Haram's strong stance against western values in Nigeria could be interpreted as a take against neo-liberal agenda and imperialist ideas, which has been a significant concern for movements in post-colonial societies. The fear of completely losing Islamic values to western ideals has been central to the discourse of the leadership. In fact, this is a common attribute in countries where Islamic fundamentalism is prevalent (see Barber, 1996, pp. 205–216). The leadership of the Boko Haram believes that Islamic values are gradually eroding (MOHD Nur & Yusuf, 2011). Barbar (1996) argued that there is a conflict between democracy and jihad which is apparent in the Islamic world.

The struggle of jihad has been much more than a metaphor for tribalism or a worried antimodernism. It has been a literal war on the values, cultures and institutions that make up liberal society (Barbar, 1996, p. 206).

> They fight back, struggling reactively against the present in the name of the past; they fight for their religious conception of the world against secularism and relativism; they fight with weapons of every kind, sometimes borrowed from the enemy, carefully chosen to secure their identity; they fight against other who are agents of corruption; and they fight under God for a cause that because it is holy, cannot be lost even when it is not yet won.
>
> Barbar (1996, p. 206)

Besides the movement's inclination towards self-determination or conquest, which is the means through which the movement seeks to achieve the former, one key driver of the movement is its rejection of western values, taking on anti-western narratives. This has been particularly obvious in the movement's anti-education campaign, especially an anti-girl child education campaign. This has taken centre stage in the group's conflict. The group's dissent towards western education has had roots in the discourse of the leadership of the sect since the inception of the movement (MOHD Nur & Yusuf, p. 3, 28 October 2011). For instance, in one of the group's sermons, the founder of the movement, Yusuf, argued that Muslims, who had migrated to the west and obtained some form of education, returned with a misrepresentation of Islam (MOHD Nur & Yusuf, 2011). This group, according to him, were responsible for claims that democracy and Islam could operate side by side, including that jihad is only appropriate under self-defence. For Yusuf, the Boko Haram's jihad aims to end democracy, western education and any form of civilisation associated with to the West (MOHD Nur & Yusuf, 2011). In the same fashion, Nur, one of the alleged second in command of Yusuf, blamed the northern elite Muslim leaders for conceding to western values during the colonial era and beyond (MOHD Nur & Yusuf, 2011).

Given the criticism of the integrity of messages preached by Islamic clerics and other individuals of the same category who Boko Haram believes have a misrepresented view of Islam due to their exposure to Western values, the most prominent anti-western education protagonist has been the current leader of the sect Shekau. His position is particularly interesting as he takes a strong stance against girl child education, as well as women in politics and other areas of responsibility in society. In one of Shekau's sermons, he explains to his large youth congregation that western forms of education are meant to mislead and subjugate the individual (MOHD Nur & Yusuf, 2011). According to him, it's so bad that when these issues are mentioned, Muslims who have been schooled through western education are the first to condemn their Muslim counterparts who have not. The point about the perspectives offered in the rhetoric of the leadership of the movement is that such sermons become a form of doctrine for the followers that attend and listen to them. Add the anti-state, anti-western ideologies and other socio-economic and political undertones in their sermons with their exploitation of religious texts which followers are inclined to obey, such grounds become a fruitful avenue for breeding insurgents. The following paragraphs explain the framing activities of the Boko Haram actors considering the different frames (anti-western and anti-nationalist) used by the movement actors and how these build on its ideology.

5.1.5. Boko Haram's Core Framing Tasks

Benford and Snow's (2000) theorisation on framing explored in Chapter 3 is crucial for us to understand Boko Haram's core framing activities. Drawing on Benford and Snow's (2000, p. 615) insight, Boko Haram's framing activities mainly enable the movement to identify issues and conditions for which adherent desire change. As will become clear in this section, the movement engages with different frames to make claims about who andwhat is responsible for the situation, makes alternative plans to provide redress and urge adherents to act in line with the leadership vision to effect change. As such, the core of the groups framing activities could be classified following the Benford and Snows (2000, p. 615) thematisation of diagnostic framing, prognostic framing and motivation framing. The first two framing dynamics enable the leadership to make a case and form consensus while the latter is used to instigate response and action. The rest of this section attempts to engage with the frames used by Boko Haram in connection to the dynamics identified here.

Boko Haram's use of anti-western frames is one striking illustration of the group's demonstration of an anti-westernisation and a firm stance against imperialism which the teams see as a significant issue affecting Islam in Nigeria. Shekau argued that westerners introduced the idea of civilisation which imposes education. According to him, your inability to communicate in English amounts to anything but stupidity and such an individual is then classified an illiterate in contrast to individuals who have attained some western education who are considered civilised and wise (Sunnahization, 28 October 2011). According to Shekau, this is the philosophy of many who have attained western education (including Muslims). Consequently, this elitist group exploits such means they have acquired to mock and disrespect those not educated through western education. According to him, education (especially of western origin) is damaging and harmful to their children, families and relations (see Mallam Abubakar Shekau, 2011). Speaking further, Shekau argued that 'they have impressed on our values and a mentality that God forbids' (Mallam Abubakar Shekau, 2011).

In virtually all the broadcasts of the Boko Haram movement (offline and online), the movement has undeniably put forward an outlook of a religious movement, using religion as its ideological basis for conflict. In this regard, the movement holds a chauvinistic position that favours the establishment of an Islamic state or Islamic caliphate which Boko Haram projects as its ultimate goal – a society that would be rid from western values. In an interview with the erstwhile leader and founder of the Boko Haram movement and Nigerian security operatives, Yusuf demonstrates such affiliation by criticising practices which he considered anti-Islamic and proscribed by God. The following is the transcribed extracts from the interview:

> Q. So why do you think the law enforcement agencies are fighting you?
>
> MY. I don't know, but it may be to do with my belief in Islam
>
> Q. But I am also a Muslim.
>
> MY. That is why I don't know why you are fighting me
>
> Q. Is it true that you believe that Western education is a sin?
>
> MY. Of course, it is a sin.
>
> Q. How can you say it is a sin, the trousers you are wearing?
>
> MY. This are made from cotton that is one of Allah's materials.
>
> Q. But Allah said we should seek Knowledge, it is in the Quran
>
> MY. Yes, but not the sort of Knowledge that goes contrary to the teachings of Islam, any Knowledge that contradicts Islam is not allowed by Allah […].
>
> Saharatv (3 August 2010, YouTube)

Shakau takes a stronger stance against girl child education. Besides the apparent religious justification that the group has dwelt on since its formation, the anti-girl child narrative and dissent towards women in politics echoes with deeply seated patriarchal issues on gender inequality that is predominant within the Nigerian society (see Makama, 2013, pp. 115–140). This is reflected in the movement's discourse. Interestingly, this is not peculiar to Boko Haram or Islam. It is a political and cultural issue that cuts across all creed, culture and predates the era of colonisation in Nigeria (Makama, 2013, pp. 115–140). The problems of gender inequality are also evident in both developed and underdeveloped societies in other parts of the globe. While most groups and organisations across the globe claim to be working towards greater equality rather than subjugation of women, Boko Haram's approach to attacking women and girls is counter-intuitive and anti-modern. From murdering young girls wearing bikinis (Marama, Aliyu, & Balogun, 2012) to the abduction of girls and women from their schools, Boko Haram has demonstrated dissent to westernisation. Following the movement's attack on Giwa Barracks in Maiduguri, in 2014, the leader of the sect reflects the movement's stance on education. According to him:

> Glory is to Allah. The world has changed! Work has started. And for your information, Western education is forbidden. University is forbidden; you should vacate university! You should leave university, I hate university. You should quit university, I hate it [...]. Western education is totally forbidden. Girls, you should return to your homes. In Islam, it is allowed to take infidel women as slaves and in due course we will start taking women away and sell in the market.
>
> Audu (24 March 2014)

Moreover, Boko Haram also uses anti-nationalist frames. Besides embedding anti-western and anti-imperialist narratives, there is ample evidence to suggest that the group also draws on anti-nationalist narratives in its framing process (see Muhammad Bukar, 17 Feb, 2011, 1, 2, 3, 4 and 5; MOHD Nur & Yusuf, 2011). This is also evident in some of the video sermons produced by the movement. The discourse of the movement demonstrates, in this context, a seemingly anti-Nigerian viewpoint. First, the movement's goal to Islamise Nigeria is a classic indication of the perspective. The group has not made any specific provision indicating what will happen to other ethnic and religious groups within its catchment areas and more broadly the Nigerian society in its quest to Islamise Nigeria. The use of such frames fits within the movement's original goal. Another salient feature of the group's anti-nationalist narrative has been epitomised in the group's anti-establishment stand. For instance, Shekau has argued that Sharia law should replace the constitution of the Federal Republic of Nigeria, and likewise the system of government in preference for an Islamic caliphate (Ajayi, 2012; Cook, 2011; Maiangwa, Uzodike, Whetho, & Onapajo, 2012). Further, the group has expressed resentment towards the values enshrined in the National Anthem, and the National Pledge, which are symbols of the Nigerian national spirit. Whereas Nigerians pay obeisance through those symbols, Shakau preaches strict obeisance to Allah (see Mallam Abubakar Shekau, 2011).

In one of Shekau's sermons, the leader of the sect questioned why Nigerians should place constitutional principles and values in the national symbol above the beliefs in the Quran. 'They have created for us, laws that were not given by God' (see Mallam Abubakar Shekau, 2011). The sect appears to hold a penchant for picking certain tenets the group wants or feels uncomfortable with and reinterpreting such concepts to suit its objectives. Better still such concepts are picked up by the group and given a different version of their interpretation. Shekau's opposition to the National Pledge is a glaring illustration of this. In one of his speeches, Shekau recites an altered version of the National Anthem, thereby subjecting key concepts used in the national symbol for his interpretation.

For instance, where the clause describes 'I pledge to Nigeria my country', this becomes 'I pledge to Allah my God, to serve Nigeria with all my strength', the sect leader rejects this notion, arguing that the clause comes into conflict with the Islamic creed. According to him, the individual should only pledge to serve God. This also applies to the other clauses in the document. Where it states 'to defend her unity and uphold her honour and glory', he argues that such obeisance is only meant for God (see Mallam Abubakar Shekau, 2011). By and large, the movement's anti-national stance in favour of the supremacy of Islamic culture can be interpreted as antagonism towards the multi-ethnic and religious diversity that represents the character of the present Nigerian state. Again, this re-affirms the group's struggle for religious hegemony. Besides, the group's actions expose its true anti-modern character and objectives since nations are a modern phenomenon. The implication is that Boko Haram's activities threaten the features that bind Nigerians together, the territorial unity and sovereignty, mobility and civil and political rights of inhabitants of the northern region and indeed the entire nation (see Smith, 1995, p. 56). We can link the threat the movement poses to the current existence and unity of Nigeria to the tensions, conflict, suspicions and divides that followed the 1914 amalgamation of the northern and southern protectorates discussed briefly in Chapter 2. Nonetheless, the group's anti-modern stance is also reminiscent of its ideological underpinnings, which are discussed under the next heading.

On the whole, the Boko Haram movement operates on a hybrid identity. The Boko Haram movement can be considered as a network, given its extensive use of social media tools, ICTs and the internet as would be demonstrated later. Nonetheless, at the same time, a careful evaluation of the group's media narratives (contained in videos it broadcasts) shows that the movement adheres to hierarchical identities. Hierarchical identities are in the sense that Boko Haram discourse shows a proclivity towards discussions of religious, ethnic and cultural superiority and dominance. The movement's narratives adhere to hierarchical discourses of dominance and supremacy. For instance, the group holds a robust view of the supremacy of Islamic religion as against Christianity and non-believing groups in society that the movement tags infidels. So in regard to group membership, it won't be a surprise that religion and ethnicity will be a critical criterion to be fulfiled by individuals. The group mainly dwells on a shared and collective identity around Islam, which is similar to al-Qaeda. As explained by Karatzogianni (2006a, 2006b), al-Qaeda depends on shared religious affiliation and kinship (p. 381).

By their hierarchical identities and loyalties, these three movements enjoy increasing participation from the diverse ethnic and religious groups they claim to represent. For instance, in the Boko Haram context, there is an apparent ethnic opening epitomised in the predominantly Kanuri and Hausa-Fulani composition of the group and indeed other ethnic minorities in the region provided that they belong to the Islamic religion. So the only limitation on membership in this regard is religion. In fact, for Boko Haram, Christians and other non-believers (used to describe those who don't believe in the Boko Haram ideals, Muslims, Christians and others) who are willing to repent and join the movement will be welcomed. In a video posted on YouTube, Shekau, while claiming responsibility for attacks on two north-eastern states, advised the military and 'others' 'we call on you all to repent and come to the ways of Allah. Forget about the constitution and accept Shariah. We don't have socialism, we don't know communism, we don't want federalism, but we are Muslims [...] it is never too late for you to repent and join us on the path of righteousness' (see Audu, 12 August 2013).

5.1.6. Situating Boko Haram's Islamism

On the whole, as demonstrated, the group's extreme affiliation to a religious ideology reflects some level of chauvinism, meaning that the group held onto some unholy, illogical and inflated religious patriotism. Unholy, because, the movement's beliefs and actions are indictable and irrational because the goal of the movement to Islamise Nigeria is unachievable in a country evenly divided between Christians and Muslims. While the group's inflated religious patriotism is linked to the view they hold which pronounces Islam as the only real religion while discrediting 'others', such stance is not uncommon especially when similar movements across the globe share such chauvinistic beliefs. Nonetheless, to understand Boko Haram and other related groups in Africa, the Middle East and other regions across the globe, an attempt to situate the movement within a broader global jihadist discourse is crucial. In this regard, Boko Haram's ideology can be situated within a broader context of global jihadist philosophy that in many ways is linked to Wahhabism and Takfirism. The former, Wahhabism (also Salafism), is a term used to describe a revivalist movement dating as far back as the eighteenth century in the Arabian Peninsula. It is labelled after a popular cleric, Shaykh Ibn Abdul Wahhab, whose sermons have continued to impact on Islam and its followers in the last 200 years. Wahhab advocated a 'puritanical' version of Islam (Blanchard, 2006, p. 2). At the epicentre of the movement's core beliefs is an anti-western and anti-modernist view. The latter (Takfirism) also hold a puritanical Islamic view, but more specifically, the resistance to non-Islamic belief systems is what has set the movement that followed into the limelight. The two systems of beliefs are related in many ways, especially in their tendencies to explore extreme and radical conflict tactics. The rise and unprecedented growth of the Wahhabi ideology have been traced to its development in Saudi Arabia, which is believed to have been primarily responsible for funding the movement through civil society organisations as early as the 1970s (see Blanchard, 2006; Masoud, 1999; Sattar, 1995; Shipoli, 2009).

In its purest form, the Wahhabi movement has been described as an 'expansionist sect intolerant of Shi'ite Islam, Judaism, Christianity, and Hinduism; in fact, Wahhabis seeks to challenge and destroy these faiths' (Schwartz, 2003), a common practice with the Takfiri. According to a *PBS Frontline* (2014) report on Wahhabism, the document explains that the practice is a stringent form of Islam that contends for an accurate interpretation and strict adherence to the Quranic doctrine that is rooted in Sharia law. For Wahhabis, anyone who does not practice their form of religion is an adversary. This explains their justification for the targeting and killing of Christians and other faiths, including Muslim faithful (Shi'ism) who hold a much more moderate belief and do not propagate the Salafist ideology. Protagonists of Wahhabism include the late Osama bin Laden of the al-Qaeda organisation, the Taliban and more recently the Islamic state IS, also called ISIS, to mention but a few. While these movements claim that they seek to promote strict adherence to Quranic values, by attempting to enforce Sharia law, such resolve has created intra- and inter-religious divides. This is particularly true within the Islamic religion epitomised by divides between the moderate Shi'ites on the one hand, and the more radical Takfirists and Wahhabis on the other hand.

Consequently, coming down to the Nigerian context, one can safely suggest that the Boko Haram movement represents Wahhabism in its purest anti-modernist perspective, particularly since Boko Haram exhibits specific characteristics and ideals observable in Wahhabi ideologies. Following this paradigm, one could also argue that Boko Haram's philosophy draws from a post-national tradition of global jihad. Boko Haram has also advanced a puritanical Islamic view, alleging that Western values have encroached into Islamic values leading to the devaluing of the latter. In line with this, the movement holds a robust religious philosophy that facilitates its activities. For Boko Haram, they are carrying out the injunction of the Quran as prescribed by Allah. This practice conforms to the Wahhabi and Takfirist philosophy, both of which tie their activities to Islam. Like this global jihad philosophy, Boko Haram exploits the use of certain frames to create 'otherness' (with us or against us).

The 'other' (Christians, Shi'ite Muslims and other non-believing groups and ethnic groups) are considered enemies of the group, the Islamic religion and Allah. A BBC (2015) report, confirms this view, observing that Boko Haram's ideology is guided by the Quranic verse that states that 'Anyone who is not governed by what Allah has revealed is among the transgressors'. So there is the Sunni which influences Boko Haram's philosophy and the Shi'ite which is another denomination whose beliefs are being contested by Boko Haram. While the two share similar views on doctrine and other Islamic practices, the difference between the Sunni and the Shi'ite Muslim is wholly embedded in different understanding and interpretation of the Quran and the Hadith (Guidère, 2012, p. 319). For instance, while Shi'ites are more inclined to the meanings inferred by the Family of Prophet Mohammed, Sunnis follow strictly the interpretations offered by Prophet Mohammed himself (Guidère, 2012, p. 319). Thompson (2012) explained that, over recent years, Salafism, which is mostly associated with radical Islam, has been experiencing an upsurge on the African continent.

Boko Haram's religious affiliation is further demonstrated in a video, where the sect leader claimed responsibility for the attacks on the Giwa military barracks in Maiduguri by attributing the success of the invasion to Allah and justifying the movement's activities.

5.1.7. Modus Operandi and Targets

In the last two decades, empirical evidence has shown that the proponents of Wahhabism ideologies relied mainly on violence and other radical insurgency tactics to achieve their goals to create an Islamic state (Blanchard, 2006, p. 5). Boko Haram is not an exception in this regard. Different dynamics can account for why conflict movements use violence. For instance, the failure of other peaceful and non-radical tactics in a given struggle or confrontation by a supposedly superior authority (the state and its security apparatuses) could prompt a radical response from peaceful protestors. While the two dynamics highlighted earlier have at different stages influenced Boko Haram's activities, at the same time, the chauvinistic nature of the movement's goal means that only guerrilla-style warfare may yield the desired result for its proponents. The problem with Boko Haram's intent to Islamise Nigeria is that in societies such as Nigeria, where the country's population is seemingly equally distributed along religious lines, with ethnic diversity, the reality of such goals being achieved is slim or at best, impossible. The movement combines its religious belief (jihad) with use of force to guarantee its success. The movement's goal that seeks to overawe the Nigerian state and the movement's exploitation of violence is a treasonable offence in accordance to the Nigerian constitution. The consequence of this is a backlash against the state security apparatuses and the movement.

Over the years, influenced by both internal and external dynamics, the movement's strategy has gradually evolved. For instance, the abduction and kidnapping of young girls and women were never part of the group's strategy in its beginning. In fact, the group had previously advocated for the protection of girls and women during raids. This has left men as the prime target of Boko Haram attacks. Nonetheless, as the movement thrived, women became part of the group's target of assault. An illustrative example was demonstrated by the sect leaders who threatened in a video message to attack and kidnap girls if they failed to abstain from education. In the aftermath of the Giwa Barracks attack, the sect went on to abduct over 200 schoolgirls (Chiluwa & Ifukor, 2015, p. 2) from a local community in Maiduguri, which lead to the emergence of the #bringbackourgirls movement – a global movement with women serving as the face of the movement across the globe.

By contrast, in the movement's early days, the main target had been security apparatuses of the state. The reason has been that the activities of the insurgents had put the movement under the scrutiny of the state authorities, leading to a confrontation between the state and the insurgents. Consequently, the group, in retaliation for various arrests of their members, turned to attack the police and prisons while staging several jailbreaks, which saw the insurgents release their members and other criminals held by the police (Pham, 2016; Walker, 2012; Zenn et al., 2013). One can assert that it was at this level, the government, police officers and other security agencies became the prime targets of Boko Haram

(Walker, 2012; Zenn et al., 2013). Following the death of the erstwhile leader and founder of the movement, the sect became even more radical and widened the range of its targets. Besides security agencies, the group has moved to target commercial and public places, from markets and government buildings to civil society organisations including churches, mosques, schools, media houses, telecommunication installations, residential areas and kidnapping of foreign expatriate workers and public figures in Nigeria.

A major headline in the news in 2011 was the successfully staged suicide attack on the United Nations building in the Federal Capital Territory, Abuja, which left casualties, destruction of lives and properties. 'Boko Haram, a shadowy Nigerian Islamist insurgency group with possible links to Al Qaeda's affiliates in the region, claimed responsibility for the attack in a telephone call to the BBC's Hausa language broadcast service in northern Nigeria' (Murray & Nossiter, 26 August 2011). In the same manner, the group claimed responsibility for the bombing of the *Thisday* newspaper in Abuja, the Federal Capital Territory, in 2012 among other newspapers it targeted. The important thing to note, however, is how the group moved from attacks on security agencies and their installations to the bombing of commercial and other public infrastructures. The 2011 Christmas day bombing that killed 44 persons and wounded 75 others in St. Theresa's Catholic Church at Madalla, Niger State, is another illustrative example of the group's resolve to target places of worship.

Besides the noticeable impact of security onslaught on the group's changing and escalating strategy (Waazin shekh Muhammad Yusuf maiduguri, 5 February 17, 2011; see also Onuoha, 2014), there are also elements of global influences that impact on the strategy employed by the movement. There is evidence to suggest that the sect is exposed to global jihad strategies. As such, Boko Haram is continuously aligning its strategy with such jihadi organisations. Evidently, Boko Haram's style has since moved from the prison breaks and attack on security personnel to a more al-Qaida and ISIS style attacks which include the use of suicide bombers (IEDs and bombings (Adesoji, 2011; Onuoha, 2012a, 2012b; Thompson, 2012). More recently, following their allegiance to ISIS, the dreaded Islamic state of Iraq and ash-Sham, Boko Haram have become more inclined to slaughter their victims compared to the very sparing use of such techniques in the past (see Prince, 2015). The exposure to global jihadist styles and strategies in concert with evidence, which suggests that members of the Boko Haram movement receive training in foreign countries, all contribute to the diversification in the movement's modus operandi. This leads us to the discussion of the opportunity structure and tactical repertoire of the sect.

5.2. The Role of Information and Communication Technologies

5.2.1. *Bypassing State Limitations: Influence of ICTs on Boko Haram's Tactical Repertoires*

As the diversity of its modus operandi, there have also been mutations in the group's tactical repertoire. The opportunity structure are those dynamics that favour the activities of Boko Haram. According to McAdam et al. (1996), such dynamics could include the government's ability and tendency to subjugate and suppress dissent. In other words, the relative openness or closed nature of the political system could be an indication of whether conflicts will thrive within a given polity. Nonetheless, with the technological revolution, the discussion on the open or closed nature of the polity has become less significant, especially in the light of the multiple and alternative channels of communication. Indeed, the group has capitalised on various media strategies (Onuoha, 2012a, 2012b, p. 3), relying on the opportunities created by the ICTs, the media, the internet and social media to bypass the state repression.

Before the technological revolution, and in the group's initial formation, to pass across its radical doctrine to the public, the movement depended solely on face-to-face communication to advance the cause it sought to achieve. As demonstrated earlier, this was mostly carried out through sermons in the mosques where the leadership of the movement had direct control. However, raids by the security forces and backlash from non-radical Islamic communities meant that that approach was not sustainable. Similarly, due to the radical tactics subsequently employed by the sect, it meant that the group had to operate clandestinely to avoid the radar of the security forces in Nigeria. Constant raids made it difficult for the leadership of the movement to access the infrastructure (places of worship) and audience of its manipulation. This perhaps explains the reason behind the group's uses of other means to get across its messages, including the uses of pamphlets and the subsequent use of ICTs (mobile phone communication, media correspondence and eventually social media).

Based on the difficulties highlighted earlier, there have been constant mutations in the tactical approach of the movement, leaning towards ICTs in more recent times. These new technological forms have proven beneficial for the Boko Haram movement's overall tactical repertoire and strategy as will be discussed under the next heading. Nonetheless, it was in the light of the movement's uses of ICTs that the federal government instructed the shutting down of communication networks (especially mobile networks and the internet) through its security agencies. This decision was targeted at states where the Boko Haram movement have based their activities and thrived. As a *Premium Times* 2013 report revealed, 'on the telephone shut down, a top security official said the networks were put off as part of a strategy to demobilise the insurgents in the state […] the grounded GSM networks were part of the military strategy to slow down the communication of the Boko Haram who are spread in camps in the forest of Sambisa, Mafa, Wulgo and Kirenowa axis of Borno State' (Audu, 17 May 2013).

Consequently, since a majority of Nigerians depended on internet service from their mobile operators or better still, on the mobile phone, shutting down mobile phone networks also meant individuals lost the internet. The opportunity structure hypothesis is relevant here, given how ICTs (in this context, mobile phones) create an alternative platform for conflict to thrive. The Nigerian government recognised this opening and the impact of ICTs on the tactical repertoire of the movement and issued a directive to shut down the mobile internet in the Boko Haram hotspot areas. With the instruction, mobile telecommunication and network providers had shut-off their services in the three states affected in a roughly six-month period. The aim has been to impede their communication and access to the information highway. At the same time, the government's strategy was expected to aid the operation of the security agencies.

This strategy proved ineffective as the leadership of the movement found a way to bypass the limitation. In an informal discussion with some northern residents of the regions affected (the centre of Boko Haram activities) during a fieldwork trip in Nigeria, they argued that the insurgents reverted to using Thuraya mobile phone to communicate and forge interaction within the vast network of the movement. The Thuraya mobile is known to evade local networks with multimedia and internet capabilities. The use of Thuraya is further confirmed in a recent media report (see Alade & Kilete, 9 May 2015), which stated that the leader of the sect who is on the run had abandoned his Thuraya phone due to the capacity of the authorities to track his movements using his phone.

The aforementioned scenario is an interesting dynamic to take note of especially when juxtaposed with the group's clandestine tactics. Communication is only possible using ICTs since the militants can only operate from discrete and covert locations to avoid the military. Using traditional media that included radio and television could leave more visible traces to the location of the insurgents which could include their identities and covert operations. Following Hoskins and Loughlin (2009) and Awan (2007), the structure of the internet, ICTs and other online media forums, therefore, present a haven for such insurgents to facilitate their activities, from organising and recruiting members, to mobilising and coordinating its activities. They also theorised that the internet and ICTs disregard conventional modes of media and warfare.

Principally, the movement produced video messages that it delivered to media organisations. Such media organisations would then broadcast the videos to the public. Nonetheless, Boko Haram soon developed a lack of trust for the media organisations. However, in an exclusive interview with *Premium Times*, one of the leaders of the movement, Abu Qaqa, blamed media organisation for misleading the public, manipulating its messages and helping security operatives to trace the movement's activities (*Premium Times*, online, no date). In his words, 'we have repeatedly cautioned reporters and media houses to be professional and objective in their reports […] the media have not been objective and fair in their report of the ongoing war, they chose to take side […] they (media) go by the unsubstantiated view of government' (*Premium Times*, Online, no date). This informed the targeting and bombing movements of some media organisations, including *Thisday* newspaper, as mentioned earlier. The group became more selective about which media organisations to send its videos. According to a 2015 *Premium Times* report, the group subsequently moved from delivering its video messages to journalists through couriers to posting them on YouTube (*Premium Times*, Online, no date) Such videos were usually posted again using pseudonyms to avoid being tracked by security operatives. The problem, however, is that with YouTube videos, with YouTube's policy on violent or graphic content', such videos will normally be taken down, 'We also do not permit foreign terrorist organisations to use YouTube' (YouTube, 2015). This thereby impedes the goal of Boko Haram.

In 2014, the movement moved to set up social media accounts. The most striking of this was a Twitter account that has been linked to the sect. However, like YouTube, the social media organisation immediately suspended the account of the group. Before the media organisation suspended the account, the movement had published about 19 tweets before it was flagged and taken down. This is the only known attempt by the movement to be on Twitter. According to a *Premium Times* 2015 report, before the account was shut down, it was used to spread information about the group and its leader. Such messages were broadcast in English, Arabic and Hausa languages. The videos publicised by the group were hosted on sendvid, and images were hosted on Justpaste.it (Emmanuel, 2015). While these trends and mutations in the group's tactical repertoires indicate the desire to bypass state and mainstream public media, the clampdown by the state, media organisations and social media organisations have had a negative impact on the media strategy of the movement. Also, the move impedes the ethnographic study of the group's communication and objectives online. This connects us to the network style of the movement, considering their uses of ICTs.

5.2.2. Network Style of Boko Haram

As noted earlier, Boko Haram also uses ICTs, the internet and social media. Following the aforementioned point, which has demonstrated how Boko Haram's tactical repertoire has evolved over the years to incorporate various information technologies, the internet and social media platforms, it is also significant to understand the uses of these innovative technological platforms among Boko Haram actors, especially the leadership of the sect. It is noteworthy to mention that information warfare is absent in the Boko Haram conflict perhaps due to lack of the required technical know-how for such advance types of conflict. Nonetheless, it will be demonstrated that the movement, however, employs the ICTs and in particular the internet and accompanying applications as tools and resources to advance its goals and objectives. Undoubtedly, Boko Haram's seemingly faceless image in concert with the group's covert operations and guerrilla tactics will fit succinctly into the style and orientation of hacking and cyberterrorism which offers sufficient anonymisation for individuals and groups exploring such tactics during the conflict. Although the trajectory reveals Boko Haram's evolving tactical repertoire to include uses of ICTs in more recent times, an evaluation of the uses of ICTs among Boko Haram actors does not reveal any inclination towards information warfare (hacktivism and cyberterrorism) in the group's strategy. Their use of ICTs is discussed in the next section. Nonetheless, it could be argued in the present case that Boko Haram lacks the necessary technical know-how to exploit and incorporate elements of information warfare into their overall strategy.

This is particularly true especially when juxtaposed against the backdrop of the issue of lack of education and low literacy levels in the north-eastern region, where the Boko Haram movement holds sway. This type of information warfare often requires advanced computer skills. As demonstrated earlier, the level of literacy in the region and especially among the majority of the members of the group (excluding some of the leadership) suggests a predominantly semi-skilled or unskilled membership structure. The digital divide hypothesis is useful for understanding why Boko Haram and similar groups may not be able to exploit in full the benefits of ICTs for information warfare. For instance, there are technological distribution issues, including inequality of access and disparities in economic status. These are some factors that contribute to Boko Haram's inability to engage in hacktivism. The movement's seemingly anti-western, anti-modernist and anti-education stance also presents challenges to their appreciation of such innovations. What follows is a discussion on Boko Haram's uses of ICTs.

5.2.3. Digital Media: A Resource for Mobilisation and Propaganda

The use of ICTs, the internet and social media is a common practice of extremist groups. In fact, 'right-wing militias in the USA, Islamist opposition movements originating in the Middle East and single-issue pressure groups such as environmental activists or human rights campaigners' (cited from karatzogianni 2006 after Rathmell, 2000, p. 230) are illustrative examples of extremist movements using the internet and ICTs. Similarly, 'many insurgents, from the provisional IRA through Mexico's Zapatistas to Lebanon's Hizbollah, have incorporated ICTs into their more traditional propaganda and fund-raising activities' (Karatzogianni, 2006a, 2006b, p. 22). Regardless of the institutional, structural, national, philosophical and systemic differences that exist between such radical movements, Rathmell identifies uses of information and communication technologies among such groups. According to him, 'all of these groups have been quick to exploit ICTs for propaganda and psychological operations' (Rathmell, 2000, p. 230). These are two fundamental dynamics explored by insurgency and radical movements in contemporary times. Boko Haram is not an exception to this practice.

To start with, as demonstrated earlier, Boko Haram has incrementally developed in its tactical repertoire from old traditional media (face-to-face communication, the use of pamphlets and video recordings which are delivered to media houses) to new media tactics, from telephone conversations (teleconference) with media houses (as in the case of Abu Qaqa interview with *Premium Times*) to YouTube video postings and social media. As opposed to hacktivism which deploys the internet as a weapon, Boko Haram uses online media, mainly mobile phones, and YouTube, the online video sharing site which the movement employs mostly as a resource to advance its ideology and goals. The movement may also be using other technologies covertly. However, it would be a difficult task to establish other ICTs the group is exposed to though personal communication due to Boko Haram's ideological and violent stance. Media reports inform the assumption here and video postings of the movement, which help to shed light on the purpose and objectives of ICT use.

Indeed, the Boko Haram movement employs ICTs to mobilise and recruit its members. The use of ICTs in the latter case is less clear and perhaps not as useful as other mechanisms such as face-to-face recruitment and the use of coercion in enlisting child soldiers and youth. In an interrogation of some members of the group caught by the security operatives in the region, one of the members claimed he had been coerced to join the group (see ENDS.ng. 23 September 2015); yet new communication media have played an influential role in the group's mobilisation. In examining if Boko Haram was a foreign terrorist organisation, Connell's (2012) study revealed that over the years, the deployment of new media technologies surfaced in the Boko Haram's tactical repertoire. 'The insurgents started employing internet forums as a means for expansion and recruitment' (Connell, 2012, p. 89). It was these practices, in particular the uses of ICTs and online media among the leadership of the movement, that informed the Nigerian government's decision to shut down networks of communication.

The leader of the sect, Abubakar Shekau, has exploited several videos produced by the movement posted on the internet to call for support and action from loyalists both in Nigeria and abroad. For instance, in one video, the sect leader, towards the end of his speech, is heard issuing a call to action. According to him, 'my brethren wherever you are, in Abuja, Lagos, or the south-south, wherever you are, commence attacks. Even as an individual, take up your swords and slaughter anyone you come across in his sleep. My brethren, take up knives and start slaughtering people. Just pick up your knife and break into homes and kill' (Audu, 24 March 2014). Such calls to action have proven to be a call towards self-radicalisation especially for sympathisers across the country who may agree with the activities of the group, but (1) have no direct link to the leadership of the group and (2) lack the psychological motivation to participate in the conflict. In this regard, one could link some of the spontaneous attacks in different regions of the country to the chilling effect of such instructions for which the group has claimed responsibility. For instance, there have been recorded bomb blasts in Lagos State in south-western Nigeria. The belief is that not all cases of individual suicide attacks, bombings and kidnappings can be directly linked to Boko Haram since the movement's leadership does not have direct contact with individuals in the different regions.

We may only attribute to some unified ideology or shared goal among the Islamism which Boko Haram leverages in videos posted on the internet via YouTube and other channels to motivate, manipulate and encourage such groups to action. In other words, the video posting and messages being propagated in those videos by the leader of the sect can serve as a self-radicalising mechanism, since the ideologies expressed in them (religious) are meant to grab the attention of sympathisers and adherents of the religion. The chances are that if such sermons are listened to from the online handles sponsored by the group, some supporters could become caught up in the message. There is growing evidence to support the notion of self-radicalisation online (see von Behr, Reding, Edwards, & Gribbon, 2013, pp. 15–21). Although the previous point is difficult to verify, nonetheless, one can assert that as in the case of face-to-face radicalisation, the internet can replicate similar attributes. This is not an uncommon occurrence. Regarding the rise of ISIS since 2014, media commentary and political rhetoric demonstrate how the internet has become a haven for recruitment (see Gilsinan, 8 December 2015). This was another factor that informed the Nigerian government's decision to shut down mobile networks, including internet service in the region.

In a 2013 *Daily Times* report online, a top security official, while commenting on the telephone shut down, argued that the networks were suspended as part of an approach to demobilise the Boko Haram. While the belief was that shutting communication networks will slow down the activities of the movement, the strategy proved ineffective as movement actors found alternative ways to bypass the limitation (censorship) on ICT platforms. Following Hoskins and Loughlin (2009) and Awan (2007), the structure of the internet, ICTs and other online media forums present a haven for insurgents to facilitate their activities, from organising and recruiting members, to mobilising and coordination. For this school of thought, the internet and ICTs disregard conventional modes of media and warfare that can make insurgents' activities easily predictable and as such monitored by the state.

The internet, ICTs and social media have provided a window of influence in the circle of global jihad for Boko Haram insurgents over the years. In other words, one could safely assert that the movement is continuously exposed to the activities of other jihad movements across the globe. This has been only possible with modern technologies of communication, and there is a reason to believe that Boko Haram has leveraged such technologies. Besides self-radicalisation online, ICTs have helped Boko Haram to build networks with their contemporaries across the globe, training, especially as seen in the evolving tactical repertoire of the group that has metamorphosed over the years. Upon setting up its Twitter handle, some political analysts and commentators (BBC Monitoring, 4 March 2015; Cummings, 13 March 2015) were of the assumption that ISIS may be managing the Boko Haram public relations campaign, given the similarity between the group's latest drives to that of ISIS.

More specifically, the influence of global jihad movements on Boko Haram, given the impact of ICTs and the internet, has been consistently demonstrated by the aspiration of Boko Haram to carry out the objectives of the Taliban or al-Qaeda in Nigeria. As a result, some commentators have termed the group as the 'Taliban', or as some others have, 'the Al-Qaeda of Nigeria'. Following the death of Yusuf, the new leadership under Shekau vowed to carry out the goals and objectives of Osama Bin Laden in Nigeria (Vanguard, 14 August 2009). As suggested in the report of the US House of Representatives Committee on Homeland Security, Subcommittee on Counterterrorism and Intelligence, members of the insurgency movement (Boko Haram) use internet forums to lobby and garner the sympathy and support of global jihadist organisations that are structured in other countries (Taliban/al-Qaeda).

These global jihadist organisations have a track record of providing support to local and regional jihadist movements including training, funding and procurement and technical and tactical know-how. In this context, careful observation of Boko Haram's modus operandi, tactical repertoire and organisational set-up reveal a resemblance to popular jihadist and terrorist organisations across the globe. The movement operates using similar methods including kidnappings and the use of improvised explosive devices also known as IEDs in Afghanistan, suicide bombings, extra-judicial killings and hostage taking. Boko Haram has also targeted bombings at international diplomat buildings in Nigeria, which reflects the group's grievances towards western influence and presence in Nigeria.

In virtually, all online videos of Boko Haram in which Shekau has appeared over the years, the trail reveals a penchant for using ICTs for public relations and information sharing. The usual claims of responsibility for attacks carried out by the leaders of the insurgents are one classic example. For instance, in a recent video surrounding the abduction of over 200 girls from the school in a local community in Maiduguri, the leader of the movement is pictured in a video, where he, in his usual trend, claims responsibility for the abduction (see Saharatv, 5 May 2015). In the same video, the leader of the movement warns the public on the movement's next line of action and targets of its assault which include Christian and Muslim infidels. Furthermore, while justifying its initial attack on some media organisations, Shekau in another video circulated on YouTube promises to attack some other newspaper corporations in Nigeria (including an online media owned by a Nigerian in New York, *Sahara Reporters*). In the video, Shekau provides details regarding why the movement will attack the media organisations in addition to other targets, including Christians, and a Nigerian woman, who according to Shekau blasphemed against the prophet Mohammed in 2002. It would be recalled that in 2002, the country was thrown into conflict while hosting the Miss World beauty pageant following claims of blasphemy against the Prophet Mohammed by a Nigerian woman (see Isaacs & Butcher, 23 November 2002). The movement uses such avenues created by ICTs as a means for advancing their propaganda.

One of the significant dynamics of the debate on Boko Haram's public relations is that the movement in most cases fulfils their promises by attacking its targets, which suggest weakness on the part of the government to respond to such intelligence. For instance, a few weeks after making claims that schools will be attacked and that girls should withdraw from schools or risk being abducted in 2014 (see TRAC Nigeria, 19 April 2014), over 290 female students were kidnapped from their school in Chibok, a remote town in Maiduguri, while preparing for their senior secondary school examination; some of them remain missing at the time of writing. Subsequently, a new video was published by the movement, in which Shekau again claims responsibility for the abduction and restates his intention to sell the girls in the market (see Saharatv, 5 May 2014).

Besides sharing information, careful consideration of the messages in videos produced by the Boko Haram movement reveals how the information the insurgents share serves as an informative guide and instruction manual for members of the movement across the country. Following the point on mobilisation, it can be argued that the information contained in the speech of the sect leadership, published either by the media or by the group itself, provides its network with hints, such as the sect's next line of action, from instructions and strategies, to targets and in general their modus operandi. For instance, in the video where Shekau, the sect's leader, claimed responsibility for the attack on the Giwa

Barracks in Maiduguri, Shekau implores and instructs adherents of the movements across Nigeria to kill non-believers. In his words, 'Brethren, wherever you are, I pray this cassette meets you well. I give you the go ahead, whether you are two or three, take up your weapons and start killing them [...] kill kill kill, slaughter them, but do not eat, spare the old, women, children, the mentally unstable and those who repent. All those who refuse Allah kill. Not following the religion is a sin and against Allah [...] kill kill and kill that is the information for today' (Audu, March 2014). A few weeks later, there were two consecutive bombings in Abuja, the Federal Capital Territory, where it is believed that no less than about 70 lives were lost with severe damage to properties worth millions (*The Guardian*, 2 May 2014). In the usual tradition of the movement, Shekau in another video claimed responsibility for the attack.

In a 2015 African Independent Television report (AIT) a Nigerian Television Broadcaster with international reach corroborated the point that Boko Haram deploys the use of propaganda, media and psychological operation through ICTs, the Internet and social media. The report provides on the alleged arrest of the Boko Haram's ICT expert who is suggested to have been in charge of designing computer images, website and providing internet access for the group. The report also demonstrated that such expertise enhances the movement's media and psychological operations (AIT, 2015). The instrument of propaganda, media and psychological operations is crucial for the success of movements (radical and non-radical) and the opposition (usually the state, although in the present case it also involves other civil society organisations and individuals).

The competition between conflict movements and the state to project a superior image of dominance, in view to acquiring more power, is constructed through new media platforms. To achieve this, movements engage in psychological operations and propaganda by exploiting narratives that reflect the dynamics mentioned earlier (dominance and superiority especially in creating fear among the public). In the Boko Haram context, this strategy has been crucial in the group's narrative. The groups leverage on some ICTs (YouTube) to express and construct such dynamics has aided the message of the group particularly to adherents who have access to the internet. In other words, new media platforms, the internet and in particular YouTube, have become the principal instrument to convey the group's propaganda and psychological operations. For instance, the narratives of dominance and superiority have often manifested through the movement's video postings on YouTube, videos sent to media houses which are later published online and, recently, videos and images posted on the Twitter handle of the movement.

A video posted on YouTube by *SaharaTV* showing how the Boko Haram insurgents govern their captured territories is particularly telling of how the movement validates its superiority and dominance and creates fear in public using ICTs. In the video, an unidentified man is buried alive in a shallow grave and stoned to death; another unidentified man has his hands chopped off (Saharatv, 5 October 2014). These videos are carefully taken with gory details of the activities of the movement. Members are shown hoisting the flag of the Boko Haram sect and jubilant following decapitations and murder of their victims. Besides instilling fear in the territories in which the assailants hold sway, the publication of such videos creates fear in the Nigerian public domain. In the same video, other victims of the group's assault have received relentless attacks. This way the movement demonstrates how it's in control of its captured territories.

Having shot down a Nigerian fighter jet and captured the Nigerian Air Force pilot, another video emerged online. The video begins with the sounds of a gunshot in the background, music, a voice-over and video images of the wreckage of the jet. A few minutes into the video, surrounded by members of Boko Haram and the movement's flag hoisted in the background, the voice-over fades out, and the camera then shows an injured pilot kneeling before the camera introducing himself, his place of assignments and mission. This introduction is interrupted by the commander of the movement with a brief prayer that is followed by a speech. According to him, 'God has made a covenant with us that infidels will not have victory over us, and he has a covenant with us that we will always have victory over them, in spite of their strength and might [...] this is a message to the entire world. As he stated, he is a pilot of the Nigerian Air Force [...] God gave us victory, and we brought down their jet. Here also lies the pilot we captured'. This is followed by threats to global leaders and the Nigerian president (as at the time of writing) 'we would do to you what Allah has prescribed for you', and then the pilot is hacked to death (see Boko Haram Militants Behead a Nigerian Air Force Pilot, 2014). Similar beheadings of those considered infidels by the group have been posted online, especially on YouTube, by the group, the media and other individual actors.

There are reasons to believe that such postings have had a great deal of psychological effect on the Nigerian public and the Nigerian armed forces executing an offensive against the group. Media reports have revealed scenarios in which Nigerian troops had abandoned the fight, escaping the insurgents. For instance, in a 2014 Telegraph United Kingdom report online, key public figures in Nigeria had expressed disappointment over the failings of the military. The document, while quoting a top Islamic cleric in Nigeria, explained that 'Soldiers take to their heels and abandon their bases, arms, ammunition and other military hardware on the approach of the insurgents [...] Nigerian Security Forces only surface after the deadly attacks and terrorise an already terrorised people by installing roadblocks and searching homes' (The Telegraph, 25 November 2014). Shekau also made similar claims. Referring to weapons seised from the military, in a video, the sect leader claimed that 'this war equipment that you see being displayed on the screen are gotten from Baga and Doro. Your army kept deceiving the world that you can't fight us because you have no arms. Liars! You have all that it takes; you are just coward soldiers' (Audu, 24 March 2015). The propaganda and psychological operations of Boko Haram have also constituted a challenge for the Nigerian military confronting the insurgents. Other reasons for the low morale, as argued by some military officers, tie to issues of corruption within the military (misappropriation of funding meant for officers and lack of proper machinery to prosecute the battle, to mention but a few) (Ibekwe, 2015).

In addition to the idea that the leadership of the movement uses its sermons in mosques to construct anti-nationalist and anti-Western ideologies embedded in a religious guise, these messages have emerged on YouTube and have been instrumental in expressing the ideology and other propaganda of the movement. Besides videos that the group produces to claim responsibility for attacks including showcasing raids on public infrastructure, the Boko Haram leadership under its founder Yusuf and successor Shekau formed the habit of creating audio-visual documentation of their sermons in mosques which carried the groups propaganda, grievances and other messages (MOHD Nur & Yusuf, p. 3, 28 October 2011; Sunnahization, 28 October 2011; Waazin skekh Muhannnad Yusuf 1, 17 February 2011, pp. 1–5). In such videos, we can see how the sermons of the leadership stimulate anger and resentment among members who continuous chants and make comments in response to the statements of the leadership. The videos are greeted with mixed reactions among net citizens. For instance, comments on such videos on the YouTube platform show both sympathy and rejection for the doctrine preached by the leadership of the movement online once such sermons emerge on YouTube. For example, in response to a video posted in 2011, some comments read, 'this is real Islam [...] I like Sheikh Shekau', another 'Allah ya saka da Alheri, malam shekau' meaning May Allah bless you. Another argued that '[...] his preaching is so retrogressive; a throwback to the stone-age. That is why he sounds like an idiot to other folks' (Sunnahization, 28 October 2011). It is, however, difficult to ascertain the demographics of sympathisers in this case, since members holding a YouTube account can do so using pseudo-identities. A careful consideration of the Twitter handle of the group reveals a salient characteristic of the movement manipulation and psychological operation. For instance, there are images of child soldiers posted on the site. In reality, the use of child soldiers and women as shields can be seen as a tactic to slow down the military onslaught on the movement. This approach distracts the military and the government who know that the military's image had already been tainted with various human rights issues in their prosecution of the war against the insurgents. Boko Haram's forceful enlisting of children into the movement make it difficult for the Nigerian army to confront the sect in view to avoiding civilian casualties which could result in human rights backlash against the military. Also, the use of children demonstrates the reach and doggedness of the sect.

Boko Haram has also exploited other propaganda and psychological manipulations. For example, hoisting of the logo and flag of the organisation which is synonymous with images of the Islamic state on Twitter. The group in several videos has displayed weaponry and other military apparel and artillery (displays of cars, anti-aircraft weaponry, thousands of live ammunition and videos of operations against the military) it has succeeded in seising from the military during raids on army barracks. The display of such items can be attributed to the group's penchant for positioning itself as the stronger side, winning the battle against the state security apparatuses. The leader of the movement is fond of attributing such victories to the support of God, again embedding a religious philosophy to the support of the group's activity.

> We announce our allegiance to the caliph of the Muslims, Ibrahim ibn Awad ibn Ibrahim al-Husseini al-Qurashi and will hear and obey in times of difficulty and prosperity, in hardship and ease, and to endure being discriminated against, and not to dispute about rule with those in power, except in case of evident infidelity regarding that which there is proof from Allah.
>
> Tukur (8 March 2015)

Again, relying on the ideological propaganda of religion which the group has consistently exploited, the text earlier extracted from an audio message broadcasted on the internet from Boko Haram to ISIS demonstrates another salient feature of the group's propagandist and psychological operations, in its strides to connect with other jihadist movements across the globe. Shekau bases the movement's move towards allegiance on the Quranic provision that every Muslim must have a leader or risk dying, which implies that the movement was struggling with the conflict. Arguing that Shekau was exploiting religious texts for manipulative gains, a prominent rights campaigner explained that Boko Harams' message indicated a stronger ideological philosophy compared to previous messages and suggested that the government should exploit superior Islamic texts to counter the insurgent's psychological operation (World Bulletin, 2015).

This has been one striking feature of Boko Haram since its inception – its consistency in making efforts to link up with similar jihadist movements directly and indirectly. This drive may be interpreted given the group's quest to situate itself as a global player, especially within global jihadist circles. Before the evolution of ISIS, Boko Haram has made efforts in their (Shekau) speech to connect to other similar movements. For instance, in one of Shekau's statements, he pledges that Boko Haram will carry out Osama Bin Laden's goal in Nigeria. While such acts demonstrate Boko Haram's loyalty to global jihadist movements (from al-Qaeda and the Taliban to ISIS), it also paints a scenario indicating some working relationship between Boko Haram and al-Qaeda even though there is no sufficient evidence to suggest how (if at all) these groups work together. Following Boko Haram's declaration of allegiance to ISIS, the Islamic state through its spokesperson responded by accepting Boko Haram's loyalty in a similar audio message, which also circulated on the internet.

The tactic is of crucial significance to Boko Haram's struggle to assert hegemony, especially in the face of the ongoing onslaught on the movement. For instance, Boko Haram's most recent pledge of allegiance came in the face of the regional military onslaught on the group which has dislodged them from their haven. Besides establishing itself as a global jihad player, the move to ally with global jihad groups helps Boko Haram maintain a greater sense of meaning and relevance among its supporters, members and sympathisers at home and abroad. While in the face of conflict, morale among adherents may be gradually weakened; the global allegiance may serve as an instrument for attracting more members from the supporters and sympathisers of global jihad movements (Moftah, 2015). One point to note, however, is again how the movement uses religion as the basis for such alliance. Nonetheless, if successful in its propaganda, the assumption is that this tactic will be instrumental in recruiting more individuals into the group. Experts and political commentators have argued that Boko Haram uses global jihadi groups to boost its recruitment drive (Matfess, 13 March 2015; Moftah, 3 October 2015; News 24, 3 September 2015; Tisdall, 8 March 2015). The move could also have other positive effects on the Boko Haram movement, especially in terms of r global jihadist groups providing training and funding to support Boko Haram activities in Nigeria (Matfess, 13 March 2015).

According to a 2015 *World Bulletin* report, the alliance between Boko Haram and ISIS will pose further threats to a country already struggling to grapple with increasing insurgency activity. The report bases its assertions on the belief that with the more sophisticated and better-funded ISIS, Boko Haram stands to benefit from ISIS's strategic planning capacity, including a better public image from the movement's sympathisers across the globe. As it were, 'it appears that they are getting more recruits by the day [...] the alliance with ISIL had been expected since Boko Haram had in the past made veiled comments to this effect. The statement is a way of saying yes, we have expanded the scope of our operations and ideology and [...] foreign support' (World Bulletin Report, 10 Match 2015).

5.3. Conflict Resolution and Digital Media

Conversely, it is not only Boko Haram that exploits and uses propaganda and psychological operations, the authorities and other security agencies, prosecuting the war against the insurgents, have also demonstrated similar characteristics. A most recent example can be seen in the broadcasting of video images related to the ongoing onslaught of the Boko Haram insurgents. Such videos, captured with more sophisticated video capturing gadgets mounted on fighter jets, show the insurgents fleeing from their stronghold, while the military recovers certain territories the insurgents have claimed. Indeed, the use of media, especially traditional media, has been key to the military's propaganda. The military has also used social media, for instance Twitter, to issue and respond to statements. The Boko Haram sect nonetheless exploits the new media tools to make claims of winning the battle. Not all their videos are published online; some are sent through intermediaries to some private media organisations (before losing trust in mainstream media), knowing well that such videos will be broadcasted by the media houses concerned. This explains how numerous videos of the group surface online. It is also difficult to distinguish which video is published by the group, as opposed to those posted by individuals. For one, it is believed that the group operates under various pseudonyms in line with its tactics to avoid being recognised by the security apparatuses of the state.

Besides using ICTs to mobilise for public relations (spread information that also includes propaganda and psychological operations), the Boko Haram movement uses ICTs, the internet and social media to counter opposition narrative. Meaning that the insurgents use the platform to counter the views of the state, local and global media narratives and the public perception of the movement. As the media remains a battleground for conflicting groups and the state to try to assert legitimacy, power and dominance, the online media, especially the use of posting videos to online platforms, have enabled the Boko Haram group to shape public discourses relating to the group. For instance, in numerous videos produced by Boko Haram, claims made by the military in their prosecution of the conflict have been disputed by the leadership of the movement. The case is surrounding claims made by the army to have killed Abubakar Shekau, the defunct leader of the movement, is particularly telling. According to a 2014 *Premium Times* report, at the time, the military had declared it had killed Shekau. The security officials are confronting the insurgents made available pictures to support their claims to have killed Shekau (see Figure 5.3). The image of the allegedly dead Shekau is placed side by side with an original photo of Shekau as seen in Figure 5.3 to justify their assertions. It was not the first time the military would make such claims. The Cameroonian government made similar claims:

> Officially, the military insists the real Mr Shekau was killed by soldiers more than a year ago, but that another leader of the deadly group had assumed his character. The impersonator is the man who appeared in several Boko Haram propaganda videos, claiming he is Mr Shekau, the military said [...]. The troops captured some of the terrorists and their equipment. In the course of those encounters, one Mohammed Bashir who has been acting or posting videos as the deceased Abubakar Shekau, the eccentric character known as the leader of the group died.
>
> Ibeh (2014)

Figure 5.3. Alleged Dead Shekau, Leader of Boko Haram – Circulated Online. *Source*: *Premium Times* Nigeria online. L – alleged impersonator of purported dead Shekau; R – Shekau.

Following the military's statement, Shekau surfaces in another video online dismissing the alleged claim of the military. Again, this was not the first time Shekau will deny rumours of his death. The leader of the sect has used several videos in previous times to challenge similar statements made by the state. In this particular case, Shekau described his purported death as propaganda of the military (*Premium Times*, Online, 2014). In his words, Shekau stated, 'Here I am alive. I will only die the day Allah takes my breath [...]. Nothing will kill me until my days are over [...]. I'm still alive. Some people asked you if Shekau has two souls. No, I have one soul, by Allah. It is propaganda that is prevalent. I have one soul. I'm an Islamic student' (*Premium Times*, Online, 2014). In another scenario, Shekau denies claims made by the government indicating ongoing dialogue between the Boko Haram insurgents and the government towards a ceasefire. This is corroborated in a *Vanguard* 2013 report. According to the report, 'Shekau, in a video message, denied reaching any ceasefire agreement with or having a dialogue with the Federal Government' (Marama & Odiogor, 2013). This act demonstrates the group's resolve to use ICTs to counter state narratives on the movement in view to putting their viewpoint across. But more specifically, it also reveals the idea that the group is exposed to political and media discourse on the movement via old and new media platforms.

Further, careful consideration of the movement's online discourse epitomised by videos the sect releases on YouTube also reveals a dimension towards justifying and legitimising the group's action. Put differently, Boko Haram uses ICTs, the internet and online media to defend its operations and activities. This is particularly significant, especially when set against the backdrop of the initial point that the group embeds its operations within a religious ideology. This is also demonstrated in online videos either published by the insurgents or the media. Shekau while disputing the claims made by the government of some dialogue between the group and the state alluded to such acts being proscribed by Allah. This message was contained in a video available on YouTube that went viral (TVC News, 1 November 2014). Two things play out here. Besides the obvious exploitation of the platform to respond to and counter the claim of the state, there is also an apparent reference to Allah, which the leader of the movement uses to justify his claim. This is not peculiar to the current video; in fact, it is a trait that would be found in most of the videos produced and published online by the insurgents. The leader of the group has consistently justified all the groups' dreaded radical actions using a religious guise. In his words:

> This message is prepared by me and targeted towards clarifying the issue of the ceasefire. We have never had any dialogue with anyone. How would we have had a dialogue with the government when our members are being killed and detained in cells, both women and children? Do you call this dialogue? That is not dialogue or truce in Islam. In Islam, there is condition prescribed for us to go into the dialogue, and there are also the situation in which we cannot go into dialogue. What we are doing now is

> what is prescribed for us by Allah and his holy prophet. We are workers in the vineyard of Allah.
>
> Marama (2013)

This chapter's aim was to assess ethnoreligious movements in contemporary Nigeria in the light of the CC framework. Boko Haram provides a unique and illustrative example of such movements, especially within modern-day Nigeria. Given the theoretical premise, the findings in this section echo with the hypothesis of the CC framework. Beyond the ethnoreligious affiliation, the group has demonstrated significant levels of ethnic and religious chauvinism especially in its anti-establishment, anti-nationalist and anti-western struggle in favour of dominant Islamic culture. There is sufficient evidence in the narratives of the leadership of the movement.

Another salient feature is the impact of ICTs on the mobilisation and tactical repertoire of the movement. The use of ICTs has been instrumental in the movement's guerrilla-style warfare. In particular, the Boko Haram movement exploits ICTs, the internet and social media as a public relations and information sharing mechanism, for its propaganda and psychological operations, to defend and justify its activities and as a mobilisation resource. This activity may not have been possible entirely relying on traditional media. In fact, the framing processes engaged by the leadership which carries the propaganda and mobilisation attempts of the group couldn't have been efficient with the absence of the internet, social media and ICTs which the movement relies on to create and produce such messages. These technological platforms have served as a vector for carrying the movement's messages.

Although ethnoreligious movements are known for information warfare, in the current context, the uses of digital media platforms are restricted to propaganda and mobilisation, given the lack of technical know-how and the required educational knowledge prevalent among Boko Haram adherents. In other words, there are no elements of cyberwarfare or better still hacktivism in the group's tactical repertoire and strategy. The movement engages in a guerrilla warfare tactic that is aided by technology, especially on the communicative aspects. Ultimately, there is concentration on the motivation for the group's insurrection, which the study found to be both socio-political (issues of marginalisation, exclusion, poverty, infrastructural and developmental backwardness, high levels of unemployment and low literacy levels) and ethnoreligious (bordering on matters of ethnic and religious superiority and political power struggles for hegemony, to mention but a few). The two dynamics cannot be separated as these are intertwined in the movement's struggle. There is no doubt that access to ICTs aid the activities of Boko Haram. By extension, one can argue that ethnoreligious conflicts in future Nigeria will be more shaped around ICTs.

Chapter 6

The Movement for the Emancipation of the Niger Delta (MEND)

6.1. Evolution of MEND

The Movement for the Emancipation of the Niger Delta (MEND) emerged as a regionalised resistance movement and has remained so all through its development. This characteristic is what makes MEND stand out from the other movements examined. Occupy Nigeria emerged as a national movement, taking its cue from transnational movement activities. Boko Haram is also different. Although ethnic and religious in its outlook, Boko Haram's interests go beyond the northern region from where it mainly operates. The movement takes on a political conquest objective with its goals to overthrow the nation-state in favour of an Islamic caliphate. As the name 'Movement for the Emancipation of the Niger Delta' suggests, MEND emerged in the Niger Delta. The region is home to nine states (Abia, Akwa Ibom, Bayelsa, Cross-River, Delta, Edo, Imo, Ondo and Rivers), with a rough estimate of over 30 million inhabitants (see National Population Commission, Nigeria, 2010).

The region is also home to roughly 5,000 communities, 185 local municipal authorities and about 40 different ethnic groups. In no particular order, the Igbos, Icons (Ijaws), Ogonis and the Itsekiris account for the dominant section out of the over 250 dialects spoken among the diverse ethnic groups that make up the region (Akujuru, 2014, p. 12). The region is made up of one of the world's densest swamps just like the North American Mississippi and the South American Amazon Basin. The Niger Delta is home to Nigeria's burgeoning oil and gas industry that accounts for Nigerian wealth. According to a 2014 International Monetary Fund (IMF) report, Nigeria's oil and natural gas industry accounts for 75% of internal government revenue and 95% of total export revenue. The land surrounding the Niger Delta is arable and has been very beneficial for agricultural production and commercial agricultural activities. The farming of palm oil, rubber, cocoa, coconut and a wide range of other aquatic resources for commercial purpose is notable in the region (see Ikein, Alamieyeseigha, & Azaiki, 2008, pp. 49–53).

Despite the enormous resources prevalent in the Niger Delta regions, this area has been at the epicentre of conflict and with insurgency movements leading different struggles. Mapping conflicts and resistance within the region could go as far back as the colonial era to the period of independence, through the various dictatorial regimes to the current age of democratisation. As will be seen, the opening and closure of political opportunities, especially regarding issues of access to and exclusion from the polity, are particularly significant for understanding the political resistance that has emerged from a historical perspective and beyond. However, the scope of this thesis focuses on the current period of democratisation.

In the last two decades, various conflict movements have emerged to oppose and challenge the government and multinational oil companies operating in the region. Such movements have drawn on socio-political, economic and developmental issues that spurred protests and resistance through the four decades of the Nigerian political development since independence in 1960. Owugah (1999) succinctly summarised the struggles of various movements who have engaged the government and multinational companies through both peaceful protests and violent insurgency conflict activities. According to him, the initial struggle dates back to the early and mid-1980s. During this time, dissenters used legal means as a principal strategy to express their grievances against oil companies in the region. They demanded the firms provide payment for damages to their possessions mainly through land pollution. Failure to realise their goals from the government and multinational oil companies led to the second stage in the early 1990s.

During the first stage, the conflicts did not get the attention of the authorities as the legal approach and peaceful protests employed by dissidents did not negatively impact oil exploration activities (see Ibaba & Okolo, 2009, p. 5). The second phase was characterised by non-violent protests and various occupations that were staged in view to getting the oil companies to pay compensation and 'fulfil their promises to provide certain amenities and to employ indigenes of the community' (Ibaba & Okolo, 2009, p. 5). Rather than engage protesters, the security apparatuses of the state were deployed to combat dissident movements. For instance, Ken Saro-wiwa, an ethnic minority rights activist, led the Movement for the Survival of the Ogoni people (MASOP) in the region to challenges through peaceful non-violent protests the multinational oil companies in the region, in particular Shell Petroleum Development Company (SPDC), and successfully stopped the activities of the organisation in Ogoniland in their mass action in 1993 (Courson, 2009, p. 13). However, the military regime under General Sani Abacha used military force to repress the mass action led by Saro-wiwa. Many MOSOP leaders and Ogoni people suffered during the military repression and 'some fled into exile or went underground. This culminated in the arrest, torture, detention, trial and the widely condemned execution by hanging of Ken Saro-Wiwa' (Courson, 2009, p. 13). With constant interference of the state security forces, damages were recorded including to lives and property. At this stage, the conflict took a different dimension which was confrontational in style. This was the third phase of the struggle between the

'mid-1990s to 1998 [...] characterised by the militant strategy of forceful occupation and shutting down of flow stations, kidnapping of oil workers, seizure of tug boats and other vessels belonging to the oil companies [...] The fourth phase is the demand for resource ownership and control' (Owugah, 1999, pp. 5–8).

However, since mapping the history of political protest in the Niger Delta goes beyond the scope of the present study, the focus in this section is on the period following the current dispensation of democracy that was heralded in 1999. In this regard, MEND's activities provide a classic example of the most recent resistance in the region. A crucial feature of MEND, especially when juxtaposed with the two other movements discussed in earlier sections, would appear to be the fact that the movement emerged as a direct response to the socio-political and economic issues. Similar factors underpin the motivation for protests that have developed in other parts of the country over the years.

Despite the Niger Delta's wealth of resources, there are alarming levels of poverty in the region, in concert with high rates of unemployment, low standards of living, lack of infrastructure and land pollution owing to oil exploration activities. These factors have been the catalyst for mobilisation, collective action and insurgency in the region. The hypothesis is that the wealth generated from the region arguably rests in the hands of a few well-to-do in society and those who occupy public offices, and these few exploit the broader population. It is noteworthy to state that this problem is not limited to the Niger Delta, but the problem in this region aptly reflects the condition of Nigerians in a broader scale. A Vanguard Nigerian 2014 report explained that over 120 million Nigerians survive on less than £2 dollars a day (Vanguard Nigeria, 15 July 2014).

In the Niger Delta, a UNDP (2006) survey revealed that for the roughly over 30 million inhabitants living in the region, there are very few economic opportunities, in concert with the appalling state of infrastructure and hugely insufficient social services. The deficiency of these structural dynamics means that there is a high rate of poverty in the Niger Delta. Using a self-assessment tool, the document places poverty levels in the region at an alarming rate of 74.8%. The report further reveals that the inhabitants of this region do not enjoy the benefits of the oil wealth it produces. Furthermore, high unemployment levels are prevalent in this area either due to lack of technical know-how or the means to engage in the oil industry. Thus, despite the oil produced from the region, which 'accounts for about 95% of Nigeria's foreign exchange earnings and 80 percent of [...] revenues [...] its impact is not felt within the region, a situation that is further worsened by the deleterious impact of the oil industry on the region's fragile ecosystem and wetland' (Courson, 2009, p. 9).

It is within this political environment that the MEND and other resistance movements in the region emerged. MEND, however, stands out as the most recent and notable of such political groups. Various media reports (local and international) and research have described MEND as an umbrella for several resistance groups in the area (BBC, 2007; Ezeamalu, 2014). Courson (2009) explained that MEND represents a loose assemblage of insurgency groups in the region. Simply put, the movement has produced several factions and allies in its struggles, which has made studying the movement more difficult. In addition to the multiplicity of resistance movements in the region, the guerrilla-style warfare adopted by such movements makes it difficult to ascertain which movements are directly connected or not to MEND. This is a crucial concern with conflict movements that use guerrilla-style warfare tactics.

Nonetheless, drawing on media reports and official sources, including designated spokespersons of the movement and government officials, notable figures within the ranks of the movement have been identified. Notable names include Asari Dokubo (who has denied the existence of MEND) who has been alluded to as the leader of the Ijaw Youths Council (IYC) including the Niger Delta Volunteer Force (NDVC), Victor Ben Ebikabowei who is believed to use the alias General Boylof, Chief Government Ekpemukpolo (Tompolo) and Henry Okah who is described as the central leader of MEND. The others are presumed to have led factions under MEND or other similar resistance movements in the region with some alliance with MEND. In an interview with Boyloaf, who claimed to be the second in command, he confirmed Okah (who had been arrested) as the leader of the movement (Visser, 2009a, 2009b, 2009c, p. 3). The movement's predominant use of pseudonyms and aliases together with its loose structure can be attributed to the leadership's tactical strides to evade Nigerian security forces combating the insurgents. This is not a surprise given that movements that preceded MEND in the region (MOSOP, NDPVP and EBA) were subjected to harassment and assault from security apparatuses of the state.

The continuous state confrontation, harassments and arrests of local activists in the region by security forces is another factor that arguably influenced the insurgency dimension and form of conflict MEND developed. For instance, the conflicts that ensued in the third phase of the struggle (described previously) were predominantly non-violent and mostly peaceful. Courson (2009) explained that the detention of prominent leaders of the movement ended in creating more tensions in the region, which then, inspired the fundamental dimensions that the protest took, especially within the top ranks of the predominantly Ijaw dissidents. According to Courson (2009), the armed tendencies that emerged were instigated by the belief that the non-violent approach to the struggle for political autonomy had failed to get the federal government and oil companies to change their attitude towards the plight of the people of the Niger Delta. Boylof, the alleged second in command to Henry Okah, in a 2009 video documentary posted on YouTube on the movement's activities corroborated this point. According to him, 'back in the days, our people would use traditional forms of protests including, placards, sit-ins and dialogue. But you see, it doesn't work. So we had to change our ways. I think this is the only way you can tackle the Nigerian state because the Nigerian state understands the trigger play (referring to exchange of gun firepower) more than dialogue' (Visser, 2009a, 2009b, 2009c, p. 3). The failure of peaceful protests arguably instigated infinite resistance and militia groups to which MEND later became the umbrella body.

6.1.1. Membership and Ethnic Affiliation

Although the group attempts to conceal and shroud its identity in secrecy due to their guerrilla-style warfare, nonetheless, drawing from videos and media reports on the movement, one could safely argue that the majority of the members of the movement are roughly between 18 and the 50s . As per age demography, the youth account for a large segment of the population in the region and it further suggests that a large population of the youth are disadvantaged socio-economically (further discussed later). Members of the movement, including both men and women, are belonging to the aforementioned age group as videos of the movement reveal, although men are portrayed as custodians of the movement. In particular, in most of the videos of the movement, only men are represented. They are also depicted as occupying critical positions, as seen in their communications with the media. Besides, the group also enjoyed widespread support from inhabitants of the Niger Delta region, irrespective of age, class or creed (see Maweni Farm Documentaries, 15 July 2008). The broad support and sympathy that MEND enjoys in the region is one of the reasons for the vast success of the group. This is perhaps because of the commonality of the problem and deeply seated socio-economic and political grievance across the region. It is within such grievances that MEND established itself as the mouthpiece of the people of these regions in the struggle to liberate the people from decades of marginalisation and oppression. This strategy has been crucial to the success of the movement, especially for garnering momentum, sympathy and support across the entire region. The high rates of unemployment in the region in concert with the low standard of living meant that partakers in the struggle had something to keep them busy.

Regarding identity, a 2007 Jamestown Foundation document explained that majority of the members of the movement are drawn from across the ethnic groups in the region. While membership of the movement is drawn from ethnic groups in the region 'with volunteers from Ijaw, Urhoho, Itsekiri, Ikwerre and other ethnic groups in the region' (Vanguard, 2009), the Ijaws account for a significant section of the movement. This is not a surprise given that the Ijaws are the largest ethnic group within the region of conflict (Council on Foreign Relations, 22 Mar, 2007). To corroborate the point mentioned earlier, media reports have alluded to the movement as an Ijaw group (Daily Trust, 23 May 2009; The Guardian, 21 Mar 2006).

The leadership of the movement is believed to be in the hands of someone who has attained some level of education, at least upto university level (Hanson, 2007, p. 3), while other members belong to the lower skill and unskilled class. Interestingly, despite their education, many of this skilled youths like their unskilled contemporaries remained unemployed, with a low standard of living (Francis, LaPin, & Rossiasco, 2011, pp. 30–34). The movement represents a fusion of different and diverse groups and individuals who had been in the struggles for autonomy, participation and better socio-economic and political standards before MEND. Within the MEND ranks, there are those groups who are genuinely fighting the cause, student groups, cult groups and some groups that emerged to exploit the existence of a legitimate organisation to perpetrate criminal activities (Francis, LaPin, & Rossiasco, 2011, p. 55.).

With several groups fusing into MEND and coming under the umbrella of the movement, there is more considerable difficulty in fully articulating the structure of membership. For example, who occupies what position in the leadership? Different figures (Jomo Gbomo, Brutus Ebipadei, Major-General Godswill Tamuno and Asari Dokubo) within the ranks of the movement have communicated with the media as leaders of the movement without defining the roles they play specifically. They mostly use pseudonyms and wear masks. 'The core leadership of MEND [...] explained to him they remain undercover to protect themselves. "They have to work in such a way that the government does not get into their working structure", [...] the leadership of MEND maintains anonymity due to Asari's arrest' (Hanson, 2007, p. 3). One thing is sure, however, that the movement is largely composed of the Ijaws and other minority groups in the region. This is based on careful examination of videos, media reports and images and is also supported by scholarly perceptions of the movement. For instance, Hanson (2007) in an article for Council on Foreign Relations suggested that the size of the group can be roughly placed around the low hundreds to the low thousands. 'Like other Delta militant groups, MEND is largely made up of young Ijaw men in their twenties [...] Its leaders are educated, some at the university level, and they have learned from militant movements in other parts of the world' (Hanson, 2007, p. 3).

6.2. The Role of Information and Communication Technologies

6.2.1. Impact of ICTs on Framing Issues, Ideology and Strategy in MEND

A core activity of conflict movements is in relation to how they frame their issues. This takes us to the notion of framing process which in MEND is a crucial component of the movement's struggles. Framing processes are vital to how a movement is perceived and could have a tremendous impact on membership in numerical terms. Framing entails purposeful strides by members of a group, more specifically, the leadership of the group ,to systematically craft its issues, objectives and goals in ways that make them attractive and boost the impact and success of the movement significantly. While there are different types and categories of framing (Benford & Snow, 1988; Snow & Benford, 1992) which have been demonstrated in the discussion part in Chapter 3, in the current context, it will become apparent how MEND engages different frames as a crucial tool for boosting local and global support intrinsic to its objective to force a global consciousness towards the plight of the people of the Niger Delta. The consideration here is how MEND engages the framing process and in particular the effect of the ICTs on the process.

As observed earlier, the motivations of MEND have revolved around socio-economic and political grievances, and since the goal of the framing process is to win support and increase membership of a movement, the leadership of MEND has taken care to creatively engage with frames which resonate with the predominantly shared characteristics in the region. At the same time, MEND also innovatively uses frames that reflect the endemic socio-economic/political issues (marginalisation, poverty, exclusion, deficit development, power, political autonomy and their penchant for self-determination) in the region. This projects the movement as a pressure group representing the interest of the people of the region. The group's efforts at framing are largely aimed at justifying its activities, garnering local and international support and identity construction. MEND's framing process to construct meaning and legitimatise the actions of the group has benefited from their access to the internet and ICTs. As will become evident in succeeding paragraphs, MEND succinctly engages with the different framing processes described by Snow and Brendford (2000, p. 615) to form assemblages and drive action in its attempt to legitimate its activities and win support. To demonstrate how MEND engages with the two dynamics spelt out by Benford and Snow, what follows is a discussion of each concept in relation to MEND's activities.

6.2.2. MEND's Core Framing Task

A starting point for MENDs framing is their use of diagnostic framing. As the term suggests, it involves MEND's use of different frames in its narratives to identify and attribute the main problem and issues motivating their grievance and insurgency tactics to the socio-economic and political drawbacks in the area. Environmental pollution, endemic poverty in the region, marginalisation and neglect are the main issues that the group has defined as their major grievance (Courson, 2009; Hanson, 2007; Obi, 2009a, 2009b, 2010). Indeed, several media reports and videos produced by the group, other media (local and international) and email correspondence of the group with the media corroborate this point. MEND takes advantage of the shared commonality and endemic scale of the problem within the region to build its resistance and justify its activities. In view of the marginalisation in the region, Courson (2009) explained that the goals of MEND include seeking autonomy over oil producing communities, 'securing benefits – royalties, employment, infrastructure, and compensation for the degraded environment caused by oil production activities – from the federal government and oil companies' (p. 9). A resident of the region aptly reflects the issue MEND seeks to resolve. According to her:

> This fuel that you use comes from our area; we handle Nigeria's wealth, but if you come to the Niger Delta, you cannot see anything […] we don't have where to live, no good hospitals, we don't have anything. You can see my present condition in spite of the much oil explorations in my area. I am an illiterate; I didn't go to school because of school fees.
>
> Maweni Farm Documentaries (15 July 2008)

Essentially, the diagnostic dynamics of the framing process are an attribution method employed by movement actors for making a distinction between the good and evil as it relates to their condition, while also identifying movement protagonists and antagonists (Benford & Snow, 2000, p. 616). Following the earlier point, MEND's leadership, evidently recognises the movement as the main protagonist in the struggle, while mapping its principal antagonist as the government and multinational oil companies operating in the region (Visser,

2009a, 2009b, 2009c, pp. 1–2). In other words, MEND and indeed the communities in the Niger Delta blame their circumstances on the government and oil companies in the region (see Trip to the MEND Headquarters part 1: 2009; Trip to the MEND Headquarters part 2: 2009; Trip to the MEND Headquarters part 3: 2009; Delta – oil's dirty business, 2007). To demonstrate this, the leadership of the movement has often employed various adjectives to qualify the government and multinational organisations in the region. For instance, in an interview with Boyloaf, in a 2009 video posted on YouTube, he uses terms 'oppressors and tyrants' to describe the antagonist (the authorities and multinational companies) in the conflict. Besides the movement's direct attribution to the government and multinational oil companies in the region, the movement's numerous assaults on multinational oil companies, their installations and various kidnappings of government personnel and infrastructure also clearly demonstrate the movement's opponents.

The movement's exploitation of themes relating to marginalisation, neglect, exclusion and environmental pollution are means by which the groups argue regarding the injustice and unfair treatment by the state and multinational companies in the region. This can be interpreted as the major frame exploited by MEND to propagate their issues and the general problem being encountered by the people. MEND's acknowledged second in command's narrative was particularly telling. In response to questions about the goals of the movement, Boyloaf stated that the movement emerged as a response to the marginalisation and the brutality of the Nigerian state. According to him, 'it is the Niger Delta people that feed the nation, but nothing is being paid back to the people [...]. If you look into the Niger Delta, the people are suffering, in total abject poverty [...] we are the host community producing oil, yet at the end of the day, everything goes back to the politicians' (Visser, 2009a, 2009b, 2009c, p. 2).

Similarly, another example of the movement, engaging with the injustice frame, can be seen in a 2007 video documentary 'Delta-Oil's Dirty Business', produced by a Greek journalist (Yorgos Avegeroropoulos). In this video, a masked member of the group, who acted as a spokesperson or leader of that particular group, told the foreign journalists to carefully observe the environment as this should give the journalists the much-needed idea of the current situation of things. The camera pans to the right tracking the environmental degradation caused by oil exploration activities of the multinational corporations in the area. The unidentifiable spokesperson then continued, 'we don't lie, look at the villages, look [...] they have polluted the area. We have no good water, we cannot fish here, this is the water we drink, and this is the water we have. We have even lost most of our young boys, due to the pollution in the area' (Delta-Oil's Dirty Business, 4 September 2007). Again, these narratives echo with the point of injustice, although, unlike in the previous case study involving Occupy Nigeria, the blame for injustice and unfair treatment is put on the multinational companies operating in the oil industry.

The two aforementioned excerpts are illustrative examples of how the leadership of the movement uses different frames to paint a picture of exploitation and discrimination by the government and multinational oil companies, thereby engaging with 'injustice frames'. This shows that injustice frames are typical across movements engaged in contentious activities. Indeed, the idea of injustice proved very useful for MEND, who employed such injustice frames as a means to validate their claims and generate sympathy for the cause of the movements. Injustice frames in the MEND context enable the movement to identify inhabitants of the region as sufferers of injustice and also employ this frame, given their plight, to unveil such prejudice, unfairness and inequality within their immediate society. 'Injustice frames appear to be fairly ubiquitous across movements advocating some form of political and economic change' (Benford & Snow, 2000, p. 615).

Indeed, one could point to other types of frames used in the narratives of the movement. Nonetheless, it all comes down to the issue of injustice. For instance, the movement's argument on environmental degradation and pollution is used to depict the paralysing of significant commercial activities and means of livelihood of the people of the region by multinational companies. This argument could be set as an environmental discourse frame (see also International Crisis Group Report, 2006, p. i). Such discourse is framed within the context of negligence, exploitation and marginalization to show their exclusion from the benefits, rights, and privileges that come from the enormous wealth generated from the region's oil industry. Boyloaf identified four cardinal issues as part of the grievance of the movement: (1) that the Niger Delta is less developed, (2) the imposing of the law on the people of the region, epitomised by their ethnic minority classification by the Nigerian state (even though they are the majority in the region), (3) denial of the people's economic rights (benefits and dividends from oil wealth) and (4) a deficit in the Nigerian federalism system. Consequently, one could safely suggest that the issues argued by the insurgents go back to the problem of injustice especially when juxtaposed against the backdrop of reluctance and failure of oil companies in the region and the government to attend to developing infrastructure and providing compensation for affected businesses, individuals and communities.

Having identified the movement's issues and identified the state and multinational companies as the cause of the problem, the next thing is to determine a cause of action. This is what has been termed prognostic framing (Benford & Snow, 2000, p. 615). The prognostic framing involves the articulation of a proposed solution to the problem, or at least a plan of attack, and the strategies for carrying out the plan (Benford & Snow, 2000, p. 616). These dynamics involve the framing of the movement's approach to resolving the perceived problem. In this regard, two dynamics are notable in the movement's narrative. First, the leadership of the movement believes that the only way to redress their problem is to get political autonomy over the means of production that include the multinational companies in the region.

Following the aforementioned point, Courson (2009) explained that the movement's activities could be contextualised as a struggle for resource control, given MEND's drive for greater control of the resources in the region. The idea has been that the more opportunity individuals from the region have to manage their resources, the better the system would be for indigenes. As a result, the subject of marginalisation would have been reduced. This explains why the insurgents, through their usual channels of spokespeople have argued that multinationals should leave or face assault in the region. According to Henry Okah, the purported leader of MEND, 'the oil companies are on our land if somebody comes to our land without our consent, it our business to get rid of them. If somebody takes control of your house or your car, what you want is your house or your car back from him' (Al Jazeera's exclusive interview with Nigeria's rebel leader, 1 November 2009). Boylof also argued that 'if you ask the multinational companies to go they will never leave [...] they are addicted to the oil. So the best thing to do is to chase them off' (Trip to the MEND Headquarters part 3, 2009).

Although a latent resolve, other members of the movement and ordinary individuals in the region have also identified self-determination (Osaghae, Ikelegbe, Olarinmoye, & Okhonmina, 2007, pp. 17–111) as another alternative way to resolve the problem which tallies with the point on resource control cited earlier. This group had argued that the region should break away from the current structure of the Nigerian state to determine their faith, in the hope that they will be able to manage their resources and empower the people of the region. This is not a surprise given the endemic lack of trust in the Nigerian government due to the problem of corruption, failing institutions of governance and lack of development.

To achieve their goals, however, rather than pursue a legal strategy, including peaceful protests and litigation, the leadership of MEND chose wholly radical and violent tactics as the principal approach. The choice of an extreme militancy tactic has been predicated on the hypothesis that a non-radical approach previously employed by preceding movements in the region failed to get the attention of government and multinational companies operating in the area. More so, the choice of a radical tactic by the leadership is noted by the belief that since oil is responsible for running the Nigerian economy, attacking and bombing oil installations and expatriate workers will invariably hamper the excavation of petroleum. A further implication is the adverse effects on the economy with a similar impact on all other sectors of the Nigerian economy. As a consequence, the objective is that a failing and unstable economy will put pressure on the Nigerian government, thereby impelling developmental reforms in the region. The same applies to the multinational oil companies in the area whom, as a result of the approach taken by the insurgents, are expected to act in line with the desire of the people of the region.

MEND also engages in 'motivational framing', another dynamic Benford and Snow (2000) described earlier in Chapter 3. This has to do with narratives used by movement leaders to motivate members of the movement and spectators in the conflict region to act on the concerns identified by the movement. Benford and Snow argued that this third phase 'provides a "call to arms" or rationale for engaging in ameliorative collective action, including the construction of appropriate vocabularies of motive' (Benford and Snow, 2000, p. 617). MEND has deployed elements efficiently from the lexical components of motives (severity, urgency, efficacy and propriety) pointed out by Benford (1993) to successfully gain the support of indigenes of the region, Nigerians in other parts of the country and indeed the international community. Its narratives revealing the severity of the harsh conditions of living as a result of oil exploration is one example. The group and locals in the region, through spokespersons and other comrades within the ranks and file of the movement, have consistently painted pictures indicating and revealing the damage and loss of arable land due to oil spillages and the loss of aquatic life and livelihood of the people. The danger of this is the loss of commercial activities, which increases poverty amidst government negligence in the region leading to growing social vices and conflict.

An unidentified leader of the group, in an interview with Avgeropoulos, a Greek journalist, demonstrating the danger inhabitants in the region are subjected to revealed how inhabitants have lost their young boys due to environmental pollution caused by the oil companies (Delta-Oil's Dirty Business, 2009). This is some of the extreme scenarios put forward by the movement in view to give some justification for resistance. This has been instrumental in garnering local and international sympathy and support for MEND. Furthermore, the severity of the issue and failure of the parties involved to provide redress is used to inspire some sense of urgency about what action is to be taken by the affected population to correct the problem. In this regard, the leadership carefully chooses frames arguing that the only way out of their predicaments was through a fight for political autonomy to using radical conflict and guerrilla warfare strategies.

This takes us to the idea of the dynamic of efficacy. According to Benford (1993), the desire to partake in contentious activities is usually predicated upon the participant's assurance of a positive result. In other words, optimism about the outcome of an event can serve as a catalyst enhancing participation (Snow et al., 1986, p. 470). As such, the onus rests hugely on the leadership of the movement to provide such confidence for would-be members and bystanders. In this regard, the importance of framing cannot be underestimated. If harnessed effectively, such framing processes could yield positive results regarding mobilisation. There are elements of this framing activity in MEND's narratives. A particularly notable example can be seen in the interview with Boyloaf, the alleged second in command to the leader of the movement, where he argued that before the emergence of MEND, individuals engaged in political protest using placards and dialogue. Nonetheless, according to him, 'it doesn't work' [...] referring to the efficacy of violence, he stated, 'I think this is the only way you have to tackle the Nigerian state because the Nigerian state only understands the trigger play more than dialogue' (Visser, 2009a, 2009b, 2009c).

6.2.3. *MEND's Religious Undertones*

> We have a belief that the air, water space here is occupied by the gods. I used to go to the river, to meditate most mornings, but now you cannot. Because gas oil exploration has driven away these gods so far away, it is also believed by our people that because these gods are angry, they now possessed these boys to fight back. All these kidnappings were attributed to the fact that these boys are possessed by angry gods.
>
> Maweni Farm Documentaries (15 July 2008)

Besides the radical ideology, the multi-ethnic identity and the commonality of the socio-economic and political issues, an interesting dynamic that the movement dwells on regards the group's religious belief. The religious belief is another shared identity and ideology the group employs in its struggles. The above quotation from a social activist and indigene of the Niger Delta is very telling of the general religious philosophy and practices in the region. The anger of the gods and rage is widely believed to be the reason for the conflict dimension. For the insurgents, however, their religious belief is both an instrument and a resource in their struggles for autonomy. Egbesu 'refers to a local deity within the 40 or so Ijaw clans associated with warfare but it has, as one might expect (and here a parallel with jihad is instructive), a complex set of shifting meanings (including a sense of personal or interior truth or purity)' (Watts, 2007, p. 658). In an interview with the alleged second in command to the leader of the movement, Boyloaf argued that the military was scared to battle the insurgents for fear of their Gods. According to him:

> We believe we have the god of war and Egbesu is behind us. That is our belief. Egbesu is a symbol of the goddess in Ijaw land and most parts of the Niger Delta [...] Egbesu strictly believes in war [...] Egbesu rises during the war season; Egbesu is not scared of anybody, no matter who you are. You can go with a little number and confront a crowd, which is where you will see the performance of Egbesu. So we believe in Egbesu badly.
>
> Visser, Trip to MEND Headquarters Part 2 (1 April 2009)

As an Ijaw traditional deity and 'God of war', obeisance to this deity is a common practice in the Niger Delta region. Nonetheless, the origin of the practice could be traced as far back as the origin of the Ijaw ethnic group. To play out as a resource and instrument in the ideological context of the group's struggle, the Egbesu deity is popularly believed among the group to provide some divine protection for members of the ethnic group. For MEND, the movement believes it is protected, defended and empowered by this deity to win the battle against the security apparatuses of the state confronting the militants. In essence, Egbesu is a source of strength for members of the group. This presents one contrast to Boko Haram's religious ideology and how the movement operates. For instance, Boko Haram typically believes carrying out God's instructions and defending the religion, but in the present case study, the 'God of war' is primarily a source of inspiration and defence for MEND (Obi, 2010, p. 228).

The group also uses the deity 'God of war' to rationalise their violent activities. Customary practices for joining Egbesu by Ijaw traditional priests were adopted by the leaders of MEND to stimulate Ijaw youths who volunteered to partake in MENDs activities. MEND like other movements before it also held the confidence that Egbesu could provide supernatural power to be invincible in a battlefield, thereby placing them in an advantageous position (Obi, 2010, p. 229). The movement's adoption of Egbesu into the group's struggles is by no means a miscalculation. The leadership of the movement can inspire and sustain the interest of members through the use of religious beliefs that are shared by adherents and indeed across the region (Obi, 2010, p. 228). In a country where religious beliefs are held in high esteem and have often served as a catalyst for conflict (e.g. the Boko Haram conflict and other notable inter-communal Christian versus Muslim clashes in Jos and Kaduna), trust in the efficacy of metaphysical powers becomes an incentive for conflict and a shield. This is not peculiar to the Niger Delta; such forms of beliefs have been central in struggles across communities in the region and indeed in the broader Nigerian society.

Finally, 'propriety', the fourth element of the motivational vocabulary, is described as that moral duty or sense of responsibility that stimulates contentious activities or protests. 'It follows that movements must attend to a fourth motivational framing task: the social construction and amplification of beliefs about the propriety of taking action to alleviate the identified problem' (Benford, 1993, p. 206). In the present context, the failure of the government and lack of trust in the institution are exploited by the leadership of the insurgents who believe that they have to take charge of their destiny to fix the problem. The leadership of MEND stimulates such sense by creating the belief that if they (inhabitants of the region) do not take action about their predicament, the chances are that things would only get worse. In this sense, the moral sense of responsibility is built around government negligence and the idea Boylof and Henry Okah held that the only way out is to force the companies out of the region.

6.2.4. Situating MEND in a Global Resistance

MEND's struggles can be located within the classic demands and struggles of anti-globalisation and the anti-capitalist movements. The anti-globalisation movement is an issue-based movement whose collective actions have revolved around issues of local and national implications of neo-liberal strategies. Prime examples of such movements that have emerged over the years include 'trade unionists, environmentalists, anarchists, land rights and indigenous rights activists, organisations promoting human rights and sustainable development, opponents of privatisation, and anti-sweatshop campaigners' (Engler, 2007). Engler further argued that such movements believe that the programmes of corporate globalisation and capitalism have made worse the issues of poverty and inequality across the globe.

This point succinctly echoes MEND's grievances and demands. For instance, about gas flaring activities of multinational oil companies in the region and the environmental consequence that resulted from such actions including oil spillage, a social activist in one of the communities argued that 'the oil companies don't come to the Niger Delta to develop the Niger Delta. They are Businessmen. They come here to make their profit and go away' (Maweni Farm Documentaries, 15 July 2008). According to him, the oil companies are to blame for the restiveness and violent conflict in the region, while government's failure to correct the situation also aggravated the conflict. The widespread dissent and anger of members of the region highlight what MEND's goals represent. The shared commonality of the issue in the region aids the success of the movement in the struggle, especially as the group enjoys the sympathy and support of the locals (International Crisis Group report, 2006) who also advocate for a higher level of participation (inclusion), control of their wealth, democracy and power.

6.2.5. *Digital Media: Resource for Mobilisation and Recruitment*

Beyond deploying radical insurgency tactics to forcing the government and multinational companies to act, an essential attribute of MEND is in relation to the networked style of the movement, including how it combines both traditional media and new media strategies to achieve its goals. This is particularly important for a movement that operates in secrecy. How are movement actors able to organise themselves, plan for action and efficiently mobilise? This is one crucial aspect of the MEND's struggle that has not received sufficient consideration in the literature. The group employs ICTs and the internet in its struggle as tools and resources. As will become clear, the movement like Boko Haram enjoys the benefits of the video sharing site YouTube, the use of email and teleconferencing using mobile phones as mediums to communicate and disseminate its messages. Although out of the three the movement's leadership mostly employs email in contrast to the other tools, most videos of the movement on YouTube have been made available by third parties that include local and international media organisations. The question, however, is whether ICTs and the internet have been particularly useful for recruitment and mobilisation considering the large workforce and membership of MEND.

As noted in the beginning, the political opportunity structure could be useful for understanding the movement from various angles; nonetheless, in this context, the political opportunity structure is considered by the accessibility to alternative platforms that the internet and ICTs have provided. What this means is that activists, individuals and movement actors can more readily gain access to state actors and the media, thereby facilitating inter- and intra-movement interactivity as in the present context of MEND. Due to the movement's covert operation style, ICTs and the internet have been instrumental for the group's communication, thereby helping them to bypass the limitations of going to the media directly, which could jeopardise their campaign. As in the previous socio-political and ethnoreligious cases considered, MEND's approach is similar. The movement exploits the avenue of Web 2.0 as a means to facilitate its activities. But, unlike in the case of Occupy Nigeria, MEND and Boko Haram employ identical tools (email and YouTube videos) in particular due to its covert-style guerrilla warfare.

As a focal point, the framing process described earlier would be inconsequential without the movement's deployment of ICTs and the internet, since a reasonable percentage of the movement's communication either through its designated spokespersons or other channels have emerged via email, telephone conversation and audio-visual images on YouTube. For instance, Oriola (2013) in 'Criminal Resistance? The Politics of Kidnapping Oil Workers' distinguished between what is a legitimate protest on the one hand and the other 'criminal expropriation' in the Niger Delta MEND conflict on the other hand. Oriola obtained 30 official emails from the period between 2009 and 2010 from the recognised spokesperson of MEND. The emails were principally correspondence between MEND and media organisations and individuals in Nigeria and the diaspora. 'The Listserve include media organisations such as Aljazeera, the Financial Times of London, South African Broadcasting Corporation (SABC), Bergen Risk Solutions, Sahara Reporters, Reuters, Bloomberg News, Newswatch, the Daily Trust and Next Newspapers of Nigeria among others' (Oriola, 2013, p. 20). Although, beyond ICTs and the internet, the socio-economic plight of the people in the region made it significantly easier for individuals in the region to subscribed to the goal and vision of MEND. Their economic conditions became the catalyst for young men and women joining the movement while also enjoying the widespread support of the old generation (elders) in their communities. As such the International Crisis Group 2006 report pointed out that the way to redress the conflict in the region is through infrastructural development, as well as training and employment of locals in the region to be able to work for oil companies. This will produce a general benefit for individuals in the region, especially with regard to improvement in their conditions of living.

Although the majority of the members of the movement, especially the leadership, attained some level of education (from undergraduate to master's degree), nevertheless, the technicalities of cyberwarfare or better still hacking as an essential component of the tactical repertoire of contemporary ethnoreligious movements engaged in CC meant that MEND could not participate in cyberwarfare. In essence, the group did not consider it as the best tactic to prosecute a strictly internet-based conflict in their struggle with the companies and the Nigerian government. Consequently, in concert with the group's radical approach, ICTs and the internet were solely exploited as a resource to facilitate their activities and goals. In a 2008 video created by an advocacy group within the region, a social activist argued that 'since we can't fight, we don't have guns, the only voice we have been […] video editing […] if we can make a small film about what is happening to us, it will go to the internet, and the whole world would see it' (Maweni Farm Documentaries, 15 July 2008). Her statement is particularly telling of similar practices among civil society organisations and insurgency movements in the region. Drawing from her narrative, ICTs and the internet are tools used by such movements as an alternative means to get their message across to their target public. In particular, to create global awareness and consciousness of the plight of the people of the region.

> The use of emails, photographs, and hostage taking by MEND is a strategy aimed at focusing 'the attention of Western governments and the world's media on the Niger Delta, exploiting the blaze of publicity generated by hostage-taking to Structuring Transnational Spaces of Identity, Rights and Power in the Niger Delta press their grievances and demands'.
>
> Obi (2009a, 2009b, p. 478)

The aforementioned scenario succinctly fits into MEND's uses of ICTs. Principally, the movement uses online avenues including emails and YouTube videos as a means to communicate their grievances to the public at home and abroad for raising awareness and putting pressure on the Nigerian government and multinational companies in the region. Like several advocacy groups in the region, MEND harnesses the tools provided by ICTs both to produce and broadcast audio and visual images that reflect their struggle and the plight of the people in the region. For instance, videos are produced to show the extent of damage caused by oil excavation activities of multinational companies in the region in concert with visual images revealing the socio-economic plight of the people (the lack of decent infrastructure; interview with residents show anger and outrage). This video is then broadcast on the internet using video sharing websites like YouTube. Such videos are a means to showcase the deeply seated grievances (socio-political and economic) in the region. What is crucial is that such videos are, in themselves, capable of generating sympathy and support for the movement locally and internationally.

Another strategy of the movement included providing physical access to global media actors. The group's exposure to global media is crucial particularly for the group's goals to create awareness of the plight of the Niger Delta's people. This is crucial as a strategy associated with ICTs and the group's goals to create awareness of the plight of the Niger Delta's people. Essentially, access provided to local and international journalisls help the movement to gain an online presence since such videos are broadcast on online platforms especially on YouTube. For instance, the part 1–3 of the Trip to MEND Headquarters available on YouTube together have an aggregate view of over 156,000 as at the time of writing. Such videos receive very few comments which are in most cases masked using pseudo-names. Ascertaining the demographics of the viewers is difficult. Nonetheless, a considerable viewership can be seen as a means that the leadership employs to further its objectives of creating global awareness on their plight while also trying to give credence and legitimacy to their activities. An illustrative example of movement actors justifying their conflict activities can be seen in a 2006 video documentary in which a masked member of the group, who acted as a spokesperson or leader of that particular section, explained that careful observation of the environment should give an idea of the problem. The camera then pans to the right tracking the environmental degradation caused by oil exploration activities of the multinational corporations in the area. In his words, 'we don't lie, look at the villages, look [...] they have polluted the area. We have no good water, we cannot fish here, this is the water we drink, and this is the water we have. We have even lost most of our young boys, due to the pollution in the area' (Delta-Oil's Dirty Business, 4 September 2007). The spokesperson for MEND in the narrative mentioned earlier makes an effort to point to the problems they face in the region, associating the issue with environmental degradation and negligence. The video provides proper documentation of the plight of the people of the region. As the journalist explained when asked what their mission was in the Niger Delta, 'our mission is to show what is happening in the Delta'. The video is then broadcast through the internet on YouTube (Delta-Oil's Dirty Business, 4 September 2007) for a global audience to understand the conflict in the region. Over the years, such videos have become a mechanism for revealing deeply entrenched issues in society while serving as a form of checks and balance on the government and multinational corporations. This could also have the effect of urging reforms to transpire.

Given the guerrilla approach that the movement relied on, ICTs and in particular the use of email and mobile communication are crucial for networking both within and outside the movement. In other words, the only way communication and interaction have been possible within the movement and between diverse factions of MEND is through the use of ICTs, in particular mobile phones. Movements like MEND, which engages in guerrilla-style warfare and have to operate covertly, benefit immensely from the networked and borderless structure of mobile communications (SMS and email communication), which offer multiple access points and serve as alternative platforms providing free flow of information and communication. Both peaceful and violent conflict groups benefit from these, but the latter's success hinges on these innovations. MEND uses the internet and mobile phones in particular to communicate with its members, multiple groups and ordinary individuals in the region who support the activities of the insurgents.

MEND also used ICTs and the internet as a resource for public communication. For instance, email communication and telephone conversation were two principal techniques used by MEND to converse with the state and traditional media organisations. The group is known for sending email messages to local and international media organisations where it either makes claims for the bombing of oil installation facilities or of public infrastructure. Several media reports will go on to corroborate this point. For instance, following the 2010 Independence Day bombing, a 2010 Reuter report explained that MEND had issued a warning in an email to journalists of the impending attack. 'Several explosive devices have been successfully planted in and around the venue by our operatives working inside the government security services', (Oriola, 2013, p. 135) said the warning email, which was signed by MEND spokesman Jomo Gbomo.

Similarly, the group has used email to advise oil companies and expatriate workers in the region to leave the region. Having taken responsibility for some raids with casualties and property destruction, the group, according to *The Independent* report in 2006 issued an email statement, 'It must be clear that the Nigerian government cannot protect your workers or assets. Leave our land while you can or die in it' (Oriola, 2013). In another 2013 *Vanguard* report, the group advised the public of impending attacks, noting that the idea of notifying security and media organisations is to warn the public to minimise casualties. 'The general public is again advised to take very seriously, any warnings of impending bombings. Such warnings will always precede a bombing, providing sufficient time for evacuation. Specific members of the security services and the media will in addition to email, receive notification of the impending attacks by SMS in order to minimise the possibility of civilian casualties' (Mamah & Amaize, 2012). Besides warning the public, state and multinational companies of its planned attack (Obi, 2009a, 2009b, 2010; Okonta, 2006; Osaghae et al., 2007), this email communication has been used by the movement to communicate the plight of the people of the region. This has attracted international attention to the suffering of the people (Obi, 2010, p. 13). As noted previously, the movement engages media organisations at home and abroad and individuals via email; such email messages become a threshold for media outfits who engage investigative reporting tactics to unravel the issues surrounding the conflict in the region. It is a benefit for the movement since, through the activities of the media, increasing awareness of the movement is created while the issues for which it struggles gain reception across the globe.

Furthermore, careful consideration of some of the email messages of the group also reveals a trajectory towards countering the state narrative on the movement. In essence, the group has used email as a means to respond to and refute claims made by opponents of MEND, which they consider misleading. For instance, in an email message to the media, MEND advises the Nigerian public to disregard threats and statements attributed to other resistance groups and the government (Mamah & Amaize, 2012). 'By sending emails and pictures to the world's leading news agencies and local newspapers, and by taking journalists to its camps in the swamps of the Niger Delta [...] MEND has tried to distance itself from, and has criticised, the [...] the ruling elite' (Obi, 2010, p. 13). Also, the group has, by the same token, challenged other groups in the region battling to assert legitimacy, dominance and relevance using the media (Obi, 2010, p. 13). The battle over new media space echoes with the hypothesis of Castells, who argued that the medium is a contested terrain, where struggles for freedom in the technological age is being battled (Castells, 2002, p. 171), only that this time, the struggles are for legitimacy and justification of the activities of MEND.

6.3. Conflict Resolution and Digital Media

The government's response to MEND's activities can be classified into two categories. The first being the use of coercion and, the other, applying conflict resolution tactics. In the first scenario, at the early development stage of the conflict, the government responded with repression and coercion (see Obi, 2009a, 2009b, 2010; Okonta, 2006; Osaghae et al., 2007). This approach meant deploying the military and a joint task force comprising the army and the police to confront and combat the insurgents. This led to various arrests and torture of insurgents, which further escalated the conflict in the region. 'For example, the heightened insurgency after December 2005, has been associated with the arrest, incarceration and trial of Asari-Dokubo, the "flag bearer of the Niger Delta and leading light of the Ijaw nation" for a treasonable felony in September 2005' (Osaghae et al., 2007, p. 16). Another notable example is the arrest of Henry Okah, the purported leader of MEND in 2007. Okah's 'incarceration and trial by the Nigerian government further jeopardised the peace process in the region leading to the declaration of armed campaigns [...] in the region by MEND and other groups calling for his immediate and unconditional release' (Courson, 2009, p. 23). The failure of the use of force led to a change in the strategy of the government, when in 2010, through conflict resolution strategy, the government employed mediation and dialogue to co-opt members of the movement into some agreement.

The agreement came in the form of an amnesty programme for the insurgents. The strategy that was widely welcomed by the leadership of the movement included a deal that saw the insurgents letting down their weapons in exchange for some contracts and other benefits. According to the Office of the Special Adviser to the President on Niger Delta (OSAPND), on the amnesty programme, the scheme was designed to benefit the insurgents and provided a platform for knowledge and skills acquisition, financial empowerment which included placement programmes and provision of micro-credit and benefit from education programmes via government sponsorship. First, members of MEND had to voluntarily go through demilitarisation epitomised in the turning in of their weapons in exchange for amnesty. The programme is designed to equip members of the movement with skills and funds to empower them to be self-sufficient.

Although the offer was welcomed by the leadership and indeed the majority of the members of the movement, yet some media reports indicated some mixed reactions within the ranks of the movement. For instance, a 2009 France international (RFI) report explained that Henry Okah, one of the purported leaders of the movement, accepted the offer of amnesty; yet in the same report, other members of the movement distanced themselves from the leader's actions. A *Daily Independent* 2009 report explained that midway into the amnesty programme some insurgents had turned in their weapons while others refused. Another report, a 2009 Jamestown Foundation research found that most of the critical leaders of MEND (not all) had come to terms with the amnesty programme of the federal government. The mixed reaction among members of the movement is by no means a surprise, given that MEND had several factions, which shared the central identity and ideology of the MEND, and nonetheless pursued slightly different goals.

For some of these disgruntled members of the MEND, their grievance was motivated by irregularities in the governments' implementation of the amnesty programme. 'Disagreements arose between former militants and the government concerning who qualified for the amnesty program, the number of cash payments, the availability of vocational training, and continued possession of arms by former militants' (Globalsecurity.org). The disagreement that ensued explains among other reasons why some factions of the movement continued their hostilities in the post-amnesty period. For instance, in 2012, Jomo Gbomo, a purported spokesman for MEND, announced in a email statement on 5 February 2012 that the group was responsible for attacks that destroyed an oil trunk line in Bayelsa State in the Niger Delta region and promised further attacks (Amaize, 2012).

> Rather than address serious issues facing the nation and its citizens, Goodluck Jonathan squanders public funds on tribalistic sycophants and thugs calling themselves ex-militants [...]. The general public is again advised to take very seriously, any warnings of impending bombings. Such warnings will always precede

> a bombing, providing sufficient time for evacuation. 'Specific members of the security services and the media will in addition to email, receive notification of an impending attack, by SMS in order to minimize the possibility of civilian casualties'.
>
> Amaize (2012)

To sum up, this chapter has demonstrated that the MEND is an ethnic movement with regional interest. It identified socio-economic, political and ethnic factors as the primary motivation for grievances and resistance in the region. Using the CC theoretical framework to understand MEND, this study set out to determine the impact of ICTs and the internet on the movement's mobilisation of political protests. This demonstrates MEND's innovative engagement with the different elements of the framework. The framing process showed how the movement deploys various frames both to justify its activities but more specifically to garner support and sympathy from residents in the region and other parts of the country to the international community, in view to putting pressure on its antagonists (the government and multinational companies).

The political opportunity structure both in terms of the political system that is favourable for civil society action and insurgency activity provided the platform for contentious activities to thrive in the region. More specifically, the success of the group hinged on the political opportunity availed by new media technologies which provided the insurgents with an alternative access point and a means to bypass the government and security operatives to conceal the faceless identity of the movement. The study has gone some way towards enhancing our understanding of these processes. However, of specific significance is the extended consideration of the networked style (uses of ICTs) of the movement.

Chapter 7

The Use of Information and Communication Technologies in Conflicts: A Reappraisal

This book gives a comprehensive look at the role of ICTs in contemporary conflict movement activities by looking at the uses of digital media by dissident movements. The analysis sits within a period of intense conflict across the globe, between 2006 and 2014. The African-centred context and, in particular, the Nigerian case provided the basis for an analysis of digital activism and CCs from a developing non-western context. The innovative study identified empirical instances of conflict and highlighted an evolving digital culture in the uses of media by non-state actors in society. The findings of the study show continuities in the use of modern ICTs (the internet and social media to mobile phones) during mobilisation of dissident movements in Nigeria as in the case of traditional mainstream media.

Two types of conflict movement, socio-political and ethnoreligious, were identified as the unit of analysis for this study. The first case involving Occupy Nigeria provided a classic example of a socio-political social movement using ICTs, while Boko Haram and MEND both provided examples of ethnoreligious movements in the most contemporary sense of violent militancy and insurgency conflicts in modern-day Nigeria. The activities of the conflict groups continue as at the time of writing except for the Occupy Nigeria movement. The analysis in this book followed the structure of Karatzogianni's (2006a, 2006b) CC theoretical framework. The CC framework (Karatzogianni, 2006a, 2006b) which synthesises the features of resource mobilisation, conflict and media theories provided a lens for examining the three conflict movements vis-à-vis the role of ICTs. It is the first time that any study in this specific context is used to assess through a comparative approach the three distinct movements in Nigeria.

As seen in Chapter 1, the focus of the discussion was on the environment of conflict which is the starting point for any analysis of CCs and digital activism. This is especially crucial for articulating the inherent dynamic that makes conflict thrive in society. Such features differ from one national context to the other and therefore create different effects and results for conflict movements. In the discussion on the environment of conflict, the Karatzogianni (2006a, 2006b) framework allows for an examination of the virtual and offline infrastructure that aid movement activities. The debate that emerged demonstrated that the media landscape has evolved with critical developments in ICT infrastructure

(The Internet, corresponding applications and mobile telephony, with the mobile phones becoming the main access point for the Internet). Developments in ICTs and other digital media subsequently shed insights into the widespread uses of the tools by conflict movements in Nigeria.

The following chapter engages a discussion on the CC framework and explained the different elements against the backdrop of ICTs and the broader literature on digital activism. In the last few decades, sub-Saharan Africa like other parts of the globe has also seen an increasingly growing wave of conflict with ICTs serving as tools for dissident youth movements and civil society action. The discussion in this section relied on empirical evidence to highlight how different movements on the Africa continent are employing ICTs in recent struggles for social reform and change. It also considered other movements using the tools of new media across the globe. It is argued that expansive developments in ICT infrastructure in Africa has engendered shifts in digital cultures especially in the uses of the tools to advance daily living, communication and interaction. The tools are mostly instrumental in disseminating information which aid mobilisation and widespread dissent. There are even more extensive uses for ICTs across the globe. Crucial to state is the developing battle over ICTs between protestors and the authorities in various countries in Africa. Authorities continue to seek ways to limit the influence of such technologies through various means including the shutting down of networks and ICT infrastructures as seen in the Congo and Burkina Faso. This point leads us to the established debate on whether ICT technologies hold the potential to serve as emancipatory technologies. Morovoz (2011a, 2011b) and Meier (2011), in separate incidents, have demonstrated the states' ever-increasing ability and capacity to curb the benefits of ICTs for dissident movement activities. Besides, other contextual dynamics (digital divide, literacy and technological know-how) which are peculiar to each national context pose more significant issues for access to ICTs. Correspondingly, issues related to access create a problematic situation for dissident movements trying to reach a wider audience via digital media. For instance, there is a wide gap between internet coverage among rural areas and urban areas and, as such one would expect, different results in ICT uses.

The following discussion compares the socio-political (Occupy Nigeria) and ethnoreligious movements (Boko Haram and MEND) in the light of the elements of the theoretical framework, in particular, mobilising structures, opportunity structures and framing process and the literature on digital activism. This will help to situate the current study within broader academic discourse and also harness the analysis into one conclusion by identifying the critical contribution made by this book.

Research on the conflict movements in Nigeria has been mostly restricted to a focus on the emergence, motivation and demise of the different movements in Nigeria (Abimbola, 2011; Cook, 2012; Elkaim, 2012; Ezeamalu, 2014; Ikein et al., 2008; Luqman & Lawal, 2011; Nitya, 2011; Obi, 2010; Walker, 2012). Only a limited amount of scholarship in this area considered the structural dynamics and tactical repertoire of such movements to which ICTs are playing a crucial role. Consequently, explanations of the digital and organisational aspects of mobilisation of dissident movements in the Nigerian context were necessary to extend and complement existing literature on computer-mediated forms of conflicts. Considering that conflict has been an integral part of the Nigerian political system, one that has kept the government and political elite under constant check, the identified conflict movements are novel for some reasons. Besides being illustrative examples of contemporary conflict movements in Nigeria, Occupy Nigeria case study, for example, involved protests on a scale never witnessed in Nigerian political history. In a country divided along ethnic and religious lines, the government's decision and the subsequent response of millions of Nigerians who attended various protests and occupations raised interests and triggered discussions on the power of a single issue to unite Nigerians. For the first time in a long time, the protests that evolved blurred the ethnic and religious divides that had permeated Nigerian society. The use of ICTs among Occupy Nigeria protestors was a hallmark event and demonstrated how the tools can influence political outcomes, social change and reform within a given polity.

As with the Occupy Nigerian case, Boko Haram and MEND also provide comparative studies of sustained ethnoreligious conflicts in contemporary Nigeria, providing useful insights into the role ICTs play in violent militancy and insurgency mobilisations. Boko Haram and MEND's classification as ethnoreligious movements are based on their overarching loyalties to ethnic and religious ideologies and identities, which also conforms to the ethnoreligious component of the CC framework. The structure of MEND and Boko Haram revealed a mostly ethnic composition in the Ijaws in the MEND case and Hausa/Fulani/Kanuri in the case of Boko Haram, in addition to its Islamist membership orientation. This is a stark contrast to Occupy Nigeria, which was all-encompassing and open to all, irrespective of creed, religion, identity or ethnicity. The consideration of the role of ICTs in mobilisation was the research focus.

7.1. Applying the Cyberconflict Framework to the Three Case Studies

On the notion of mobilising structures, the argument that the current structure of Web 2.0 and the widespread innovation of ICTs, especially mobile phones and other social media applications, have significantly enhanced conflict movement activities (Garrett, 2006; Karatzogianni, 2009, 2013, 2015; Kavada, 2006, 2013, 2015; Lui, 2012; Meier, 2011; Morovoz, 2011a, 2011b) is consistent with the finding in this study. The findings revealed that ICTs served mostly as a vector providing alternative channels for contentious activities, communication and interaction to thrive among actors in both socio-political and ethnoreligious movements. The argument offered here does not suggest that ICTs are responsible for conflicts in the sense that new technologies of communication serve as the primary motivating dynamic. Instead, as demonstrated in the ethnoreligious and socio-political case studies, the thesis advances the view that ICTs are primarily influencing conflict by serving as tools and resources facilitating organisation and mobilisation conforming to the Karatzogianni CC framework.

Sharing and broadcasting information was a common trend across the socio-political and ethnoreligious movements, as a result of which, we have seen increases in participation levels, a boost in recruitment, variance in tactical repertoire and goals of the movements which are in line with the theorisation of both Karatzogianni (2006a, 2006b) and Garrett (2006) and indeed the wider literature on digital activism. It is evident that the more messages and information were made available to dissidents and residents, the more involved they became. In the Occupy Nigeria case study, one crucial point for this chapter is the widespread use of ICTs during the January 2012 protests. While protests in Nigeria is a common event and has a long history that can be traced as far back as in pre-colonisation era, a distinction in the Occupy Nigeria context is the widespread use of ICTs which include the internet, mobile phones and social media applications. Before the January 2012 uprising, speculation was rife on the possibility of any mass resistance and protests in the country. The doubt was as a result of the hugely repressive and suppressive culture which was predominant towards media, political and civil liberties in much of the political history of the country (see discussions in Chapter 2). Using the socio-political parameters of the CC, the findings in this chapter show that ICTs had a positive influence on the Occupy Nigeria protests. ICTs were used innovatively by dissidents to mobilise, plan and coordinate the entire protests.

Interviewees explained that ICTs were principally responsible for increasing and boosting participation levels, owing to the cost reduction, affordability and multimedia capabilities of the platforms. More people had access to specific ICTs. Mainly, ICTs were used to create global awareness and consciousness on the plight of the people by putting out information on social media, blogs and audio-visual materials on the internet. As a result of the awareness that was created, more individuals joined the protest, and the protests eventually became multinational and transnational. During the Occupy Nigeria protest, the findings revealed that different ICTs, mobile phones, FB, Twitter, blogs, YouTube and similar online mediums were harnessed by dissidents to further their objectives of broadcasting information to the global community and Nigerians at home. In the ethnoreligious contexts involving Boko Haram and MEND, the study also found a similar attribute in the role played by ICTs. Again, across the two case studies, ICTs mainly served as a platform for sharing information and interaction between insurgents, the media and state authorities. In both movements, we see a penchant for email communication and extensive use of the video sharing platform (YouTube). While information dissemination and communication was a vital feature of the three movements, striking observation showed a disparity in the kind or type of ICTs used by the different conflict movements for some reasons.

For the socio-political movements, dissidents used a plethora of ICTs during the protests in concert with physical occupations of strategic locations. For instance, for the Occupy Nigeria protests, we saw a synthesis in the uses of different ICTs including the internet, social media, blogs, mobile phones, IPad and computers. Together, these tools were crucial for the activities of the movement to achieve their goal of creating global awareness and mobilisation. In the ethnoreligious context, the uses of ICTs were limited. For instance, at the beginning of the Boko Haram conflict, the movement depended on flyers and letters to traditional media to broadcast its messages. Subsequently, the groups deployed its messages to the media via email and videos and then came to the social media phase which included the use of YouTube to self-direct its messages. Although an attempt was made by Boko Haram to lunch a social media campaign on Twitter, it, however, failed due to the policies of Twitter.

MEND and Boko Haram have some similarities in their choice of ICT. In addition to MEND's use of emailing and the access the group offers local and global media outlets, the two movements relied heavily on YouTube and SMS to propagate their cause. Both groups also used teleconferencing as a means to communicate with media organisations. Despite the differences in the choice of ICTs, a characteristic feature of the three case studies can be seen in their uses of traditional mainstream media. Even though the medium played a limited role, it raises questions on the dialectical correlation between old and new media and whether the old can replace the new. The disparity in use of ICTs can be attributed to the choice of their tactical repertoire exploited by the different movements. For the ethnoreligious groups (MEND and Boko Haram), the choice of ICTs is particularly crucial as the mediums fit largely within their covert violent militancy and insurgency approach to the conflict. In other words, ICTs allow conflict movements to operate clandestinely. This ensures that members of such movements and their families avoid the onslaught of the joint security operatives confronting the insurgents. Socio-political movements also benefit from the anonymisation afforded by new ICTs. In the Occupy Nigeria case study, some participants had more than one FB page under different pseudonyms. As suggested by Interviewee 4, this was to cushion the effect of one social media handle being targeted by the authorities.

In the MEND case, the crucial role played by ICTs in getting information between dissident movements led to similar reactions from state authorities across the socio-political and ethnoreligious movements. For instance, dissidents in the Occupy Nigeria case study including media reports made claims that the government shut down internet communications during the Occupy Nigeria protests which affected communication and interaction during the protests. Although the government denied allegations attributed to dissidents, the complete shutdown of mobile networks in three states where Boko Harams activities where rife demonstrates the capacity of the authorities to shut down computer-mediated communication. Although the shutdown was meant to curtail Boko Haram's communication and interaction, the government's approach failed to stem the tide of the movement's activities. The group continued to use alternative ICTs, especially for their communication. Morovoz's (2011a, 2011b) book, *The Net Delusion: How Not to Liberate the World,* succinctly captures the debate on how states and their allies can use ICTs to interrupt the activities of media movements during the conflict. In the socio-political context, the study found that using ICTs or overly depending on the tools could result in socio-political demobilisation. This means that dissidents in conflict could be caught up online as a distraction to real-life occupations. Moreover, the digital divide could also pose limitations on particular sections of the public due to lack of access or literacy issues, to mention but a few.

With regard to opportunity structures, three observations are notable. First, the current democratisation in Nigeria which was heralded in 1999 opened the political activities; as a result, contentious activities can thrive albeit with some limitations, such as state interference. This point was alluded to by some Occupy Nigeria activists interviewed; this was in contrast to mobilisation during the military dictatorships which were difficult. The political system in a given state can be a determining factor in conflict. Second, the main opportunity structure is the increase in the price of petroleum occasioned by the removal of petroleum subsidy. This was the primary motivation that triggered the outburst and spontaneous outpouring to the streets on 1 January 2012. The third dynamic echoes with the findings of Karatzogianni (2006a, 2006b) and Garrett (2006) ICTs provided an alternative platform to bypass the usual state limitations and restrictions on the media across the three case studies. It has become increasingly difficult for state authorities to limit the free flow of communication and autonomy availed by ICTs and the internet. Besides the removal of the subsidy, the momentum that was built before the emergence of the Occupy Nigeria January 2012 protest was influenced by an opening in political opportunity at the global level that the Arab uprising and Occupy Wall Street (OWS) offered. With exposure to the conflicts earlier, there was a general perception in Nigeria that such protests could be replicated at home. Therefore, Occupy Nigeria actors took a cue from the global Occupy movement with the understanding that protests were possible in Nigeria. Their rhetoric revolved around the subject of exploitation of the poor in society similar to the 'we are the 99%' frame and anti-capitalist discourse evident in Occupy Wall Street OWS. The same attribute is seen in the Boko Haram's context with the movement's constant affiliation to radical Islamist organisations that include al-Qaida and more recently ISIS. The movement also demonstrates attributes of such Islamist organisations. The argument here is that ICTs created the window of opportunity for the Boko Haram conflict to thrive.

Framing is another dynamic that is central to the activities of conflict movements (Garrett, 2006; Karatzogianni, 2006a, 2006b; McAdam et al.). In this study, a crucial connection was found between ICTs and the framing processes of both socio-political and ethnoreligious movements which conforms to the theorisation of Karatzogianni (2006a, 2006b) and Garrett (2006) regarding the importance of ICTs, the internet and social media for framing movement issues, goals and a means for bypassing state interference. Gaining access to the media to shape public opinion is a crucial characteristic of movement leaders and actors especially when the media is seen as a vector for legitimating the cause while also providing impetus and justification for movement activities. However, the significance of the media means that movement actors and the state will have to contend for space that usually falls in favour of the state given its ability to exact hegemony either through legal instruments or coercion.

In the current context, the window of opportunity offered by ICTs meant that movement actors in both socio-political and ethnoreligious contexts could influence public opinion through their framing activities online. ICTs mainly served as an alternative platform in line with the notion of bypassing traditional mainstream media. The multimodal nature of ICTs and the autonomy they afford makes them suitable for actors engaged in online activities. For example, in the Occupy Nigeria case, movement actors and dissidents turned to online spaces to engage the issues that matter most to them by blogs, vlogs and postings commentaries and press releases on various social media platforms especially Twitter and FB and audio-visual materials on videos sites as in the case of YouTube. We also saw how the ethnoreligious movements also used mainly emailing and YouTube as a means to get across their messages.

A salient characteristic across the three cases studies is demonstrated in the use of injustice frames to enhance and communicate their grievances. Audio-visual and textual materials produced by the different conflict movements echoed issues of marginalisation, exploitation of the poor by the rich and socio-economic inequality, poverty and corruption, to mention but a few. Besides these frames, the study found that Boko Haram demonstrated momentous levels of ethnic and religious chauvinism particularly in its anti-establishment, anti-nationalist, anti-western struggle which surfaces in the frames of the leadership in their struggle for dominant Islamic culture. These narratives served as a means for carrying the movements 'propaganda and psychological operations'. More crucial is the fact that the narratives were mostly expressed via online media platforms, from Twitter and FB to Nairaland as in the case of Occupy Nigeria, to YouTube videos and online commentaries on local and global media sources taking advantage of by Boko Haram and MEND. The limited filters on online media and its unhindered flow were particularly crucial for Boko Haram and MEND due to their covert structure. Clearly, in the Occupy Nigeria context, framing online produced significant results as indicated in the quick spread of the movement across the globe, and the global awareness and publicity the process generated across the three case studies.

The videos, social media commentary and other online media activities of the groups available on the internet via YouTube helped in internationalising their operations. In this context, the three movements exploited ICTs for public relations. For instance, MEND's documentaries and access to foreign media helped to spread information on the plight of the people of the region to other parts of the globe. This strategy generated support for the movement, even though their guerrilla-style warfare has been criticised. Boko Haram also employed a similar approach and was able to form alliances with similar movements with Islamist ideologies across the globe (al-Qaeda, ISIS and AQIM). While in the Occupy Nigeria case study, besides the spread of the movement to other countries, alliances were created with OWS protestors given their shared ideology struggle and similar goals. In spite of the global publicity generated by Boko Haram, it failed to gain broader global support to win legitimacy for its course. Instead, the awareness and global consciousness that resulted from the group's activities urged the state and political actors across the globe to take action, from policy initiatives to security coalitions, to combat the situation. In the Occupy Nigeria case, the activities of the movement forced the carrying out of several probes and implementation of policies to deal with the problem of corruption in the oil sector.

Presumably, the future of protest in Nigeria will be intertwined with and connected to the use of the social media and ICT infrastructure. The more developed ICT infrastructure becomes in Africa's most populous nation and largest economy, the more advanced and sophisticated the uses of ICTs will be for mobilisation, going forward to the next few decades. Karatzogianni (2006a, 2006b) makes an astute point that it is essential for socio-political movements involved in technological forms of protest to engage in more organised and innovative ways in their general operational and tactical repertoire. This will help socio-political movements relate better to the present political system and benefit from components of the system.

7.2. Beyond the Framework: The Specificity of the Nigerian Context

Another crucial feature of the socio-political and ethnoreligious movements, which also adds to CC, draws attention to the specificity of the Nigeria context of the conflict, thereby adding to the conflict elements. Specifically, the study found that the present socio-political and ethnoreligious conflicts in Nigeria, epitomised by Occupy Nigeria, Boko Haram and MEND, are a resultant effect of historical issues and long-held grievances reinventing themselves in modern-day Nigeria. Such concerns have a deep root that can be traced back to the colonial era and have incrementally developed through the post-colonial era (civilian to dictatorial regimes) to the present democratisation. These issues are contextualised in view of the traditional grievance models, and rational choice described in Chapter 2 of this study is classified into two broad categories: (1) political and socio-economic grievances and (2) ethnic and religious divides. In the framing activities of the socio-political and ethnoreligious movements, the thesis identified different dynamics, including corruption, poverty, poor infrastructural development, lack of education, failing institutions of governance, repression towards civil and political rights and low levels of employment, to mention but a few dynamics that represent the political and socio-economic issues. As a typical feature, the problems above opened the window of opportunity for conflict in the socio-political and ethnoreligious movements examined. Even more crucial is the fact that the same issues (as demonstrated in Chapter 1) also formed the basis for civil society struggles through the dictatorial and civilian regimes since the country gained its independence in 1960.

On the ethnic and religious issue, the current ethnoreligious conflicts in Nigeria can be seen as an extension of the ethnic and religious tensions and struggles for political hegemony among the different ethnic and religious groups. The amalgamation of the southern and northern protectorates in 1914 which led to what is today Nigeria created a political rivalry, ethnic tensions and conflicts that ensued after independence in 1960. Such conflicts emerged mainly against the backdrop of struggles for political power (see discussions on this in Chapter 1), equality and issues of inclusion and exclusion in the polity by minority ethnic groups under-represented or not represented at all at the federal level of governance. The ethnoreligious movements, Boko Haram and MEND, can be said to be reinventing similar concerns. This is aptly demonstrated in the narratives of the two groups. For instance, a standard feature in the narrative of both groups is their demand for self-determination, autonomy and grievances over marginalisation even though in the Boko Haram context such demands are masked under its religious narratives. Boko Haram and MEND's grievances are symbolic of long-standing displeasures held by the ethnoreligious groups in Nigeria for secession. It further reveals the tensions between different ethnic and religious groups living side by side with each other. At the same time, the conflicts reflect the issue of ethnic/religious tension mentioned earlier in the empirical discussions in Chapter 1. Boko Haram takes it further in its goal to Islamise Nigeria through conquest, which is also a reflection of the Christian–Muslim divide that has long constituted a crisis in Nigeria. As noted in Chapter 1 of the study, the Nigerian nation had never really unified along ethnic and religious lines.

In post-colonial societies, as in the Nigerian context, where there is increasing development of ICT and other digital infrastructures of communication, these events have encouraged a political culture of citizen participation. The innovative use of ICTs allows dissidents to compete for space and show objection to the policies of the government in concert with occupations and street protests. The study found that both socio-political and ethnoreligious movements are increasingly employing ICTs during protests and conflict, and these movements principally use ICTs as a tool and resource to disseminate their propaganda and psychological operations.

Summarily, conflicts in Nigeria, whether socio-political or ethnoreligious, are tied to issues around the environment of conflict (poverty, development and economic pitfalls, infrastructural drawbacks and corruption, political struggle for power and tensions among Nigerian ethnic and religious groups centred on minority rights and marginalisation, to mention but a few) that characterise this environment. ICTs are playing a significant role in both dimensions of conflict in Nigeria. Even so, it is more difficult to fully understand the general workings of ethnoreligious movements given their guerrilla-style warfare and covert orientation.

7.3. Future Directions and Developments for Research

As with empirical research of this nature, the focus of the study was developed incrementally and modified in relation to the research design as well as the analysis of data collected during fieldwork. There are areas of interest that are crucial for future directions in the broad field of media, culture and society, digital activism and CC. For one, the research here is the first study to explore in a single research socio-political and ethnoreligious movements through a cross-comparison of three case studies, Occupy Nigeria, Boko Haram and MEND. It is also novel for employing the CC theoretical framework to understand the role of ICTs in mobilisations in an African context. By addressing the role of ICTs in conflict mobilisation among socio-political and ethnoreligious movements in Nigerian society, this study highlights the significance of new ICTs, the internet and social media (FB and Twitter) for new forms of dissent in both virtual and real-life public spheres, as well as the capacity for such dissent to influence the democratic development, give voice to the voiceless and impel social change and reform in the Nigerian society.

Accordingly, there is scope for future research to focus on the interconnection between ICTs and policy reform. In particular, how digitalised forms of conflict are instigating targeted ICT reforms which could have positive or negative consequences for the media industry, civil society and dissident movements using ICTs. This will include broader discussions on how governments are responding to digitalised forms of conflict in both developed and developing non-western contexts. Moreover, while it has been established that ICTs play a crucial role in mobilisations, there is still more scope for a closer consideration of those inherent and overt cultural dynamics that motivate and influence dissent. Understanding these dynamics could be useful for shaping government policy initiatives which could minimise conflict in society. In addition, future studies can pay attention to understanding the uses of ICTs in other everyday contexts of political communication in the Nigerian society. For instance, research into the digital and organisational aspects of political campaigning and elections in developing countries as we witness a growing social media presence of political figures and party stalwarts not just in Nigeria but across the globe. In addition, there has been little discussion about the intersection between ICTs and fake news, trolling, bullying, online nationalism/authoritarianism, surveillance, censorship and algorithmic politics, to mention but a few emerging concepts in an African-centred context. The rapid developments in media on the continent make these issues timely and crucial for discussions especially when we consider how such issues could contribute to democratic development and digital democracy.

Bibliography

Abimbola, O. A. (2011). Between Maitatsine and Boko Haram: Islamic fundamentalism and the response of the Nigerian State. *Africa Today*, *57*(4), 98–119. Retrieved from http://muse.jhu.edu/journals/africa_today/v057/57.4.adesoji.pdf

Adebanwi, W., & Obadare, E. (2010). Introducing Nigeria at fifty: The nation in narration. *Journal of Contemporary African Studies*, *28*(4), 379–405.

Adebola, B. A. (2013). Limits of the Game of Masks: Class, ethno-religious identities, and the rise of Salafi-Jihadism in Northern Nigeria. *Socialism and Democracy*, *27*(3), 104–128.

Adejumobi, S. (Ed.). (2011). *State, economy, and society in post-military Nigeria*. New York, NY: Palgrave Macmillan.

Adeleke, A. A., & Habila, J. (2012). Awareness, ownership and use of weblogs by librarians in Nigeria. *Electronic Library*, *30*(4), 507–515.

Adeleke, T. (1988). The political economy of mass communication in Nigeria. In M. N. Alkali (Ed.), *Mass communication in Africa: A book of readings*. Enugu: DeltaPublications.

Adesina, J. O. (2000). Adjustment and the transformation of labour identity: What's new and does it matter? In A. Jega (Ed.), *Identity transformation and identity politics under structural adjustment in Nigeria* (pp. 134–160). Uppsala and Kano: Nordic Africa Institute and Centre for Research and Documentation.

Adesoji, A. (2010). The Boko Haram uprising and Islamic revivalism in Nigeria. *Africa Spectrum. [E-journal]*, *45*(2), 95–108. Retrieved from http://www.jstor.org/stable/pdf/25798918.pdf?acceptTC=true

Adesoji, O. A. (2011). Between Maitatsine and Boko Haram: Islamic fundamentalism and the response of the Nigerian State. *Africa Today*, *57*(4), 98–119.

Adeyanju, A. M., & Okwori, J. Z. (2006). *African media initiative: Nigeria*. United Kingdom: BBC World Service Trust. Retrieved from http://africanmediainitiative.org/wp-content/uploads/2015/10/AMDI-Report-Nigeria.pdf

Adichie, C. N. (2011). *A Nigerian revolution. Guardian Newspaper* (online), 16 March. Retrieved from http://www.guardian.co.uk/commentisfree/2011/mar/16/nigerian-revolution-young-people-democracy (Accessed on 6 January 2012).

AFP. (2016). Dr Congo block social networks as Kabila mandate experience. *Daily Mail* (online). Retrieved from http://www.dailymail.co.uk/wires/afp/article-4036958/DR-Congo-block-social-networks-Kabila-mandate-expires.html

AFPBB News. (2014). ボコ・ハラム、連続爆破で犯行声明 *Boko Haram chief claims Lagos, Abuja attacks in new video*. Retrieved from https://www.youtube.com/watch?v=ZAuvRDS6kg8 (Accessed on 13 November 2016).

Agbaje, A. A. B. (1992). *The Nigerian Press, Hegemony, and the social construction of legitimacy: 1960-1983*. New York, NY: Lewiston, The Edwin Mellon Press.

Agbese, A. (2013). *The role of the press and communication technology in democratization*. NewYork, NY: Routledge.

Agbiboa, D. E. (2013b). The Nigerian burden: Religious identity, conflict and the current terrorism of Boko Haram. *Conflict, Security and Development*, *13*(1), 1–29. doi:10.1080/14678802.2013.770257

Agbiboa, E. D. (2013a). Why Boko Haram exists: The relative deprivation perspective. *African Conflict and Peacebuilding Review*, *3*(1), 144–157.

Agence France-Presse (AFP). (2010, May 15). Jonathan tend la main aux rebelles du delta. (*Jeune Afrique*). Retrieved from http://www.jeuneafrique.com/Article/DEPAFP20100515115714/petrole-nigeria-rebellion-umaru-yar-aduajonathan-tend-la-main-aux-rebelles-du-delta.html (Accessed on15 May 2015).

Agence France-Presse (AFP). (2011, May 16). Delta du Niger: un groupe armé dit arrêter la lutte, l'armée pas au courant. (*Romandie News*). Retrieved from http://www.romandie.com/news/n/_Delta_du_Niger_un_groupe_arme_dit_arreter_la_lutte_l_armee_pas_au_courant160520112005.asp> [10/06/205].

Aghedo, I., & Osumah, O. (2012). The Boko Haram uprising: How should Nigeria respond? *Third World Quarterly*, *33*(5), 853–869. Retrieved from http://www.tandfonline.com/doi/pdf/10.1080/01436597.2012.674701

Ahmed, I., & Costa, K. (2011). Nigeria: IMF pushing the Country to end subsidy report. Retrieved from http://allafrica.com/stories/201112300791.html

Aina. Commentary on boko Haram. (2009). (Video File). Retrieved from https://www.youtube.com/watch?v=ohd0aLa4oGE (Accessed on 10 June 2015).

AIT. (2015). Boko Haram's ICT expert arrested. *African Independent Television* (online). Retrieved from http://aitonline.tv/post-boko_haram___s_ict_expert_arrested (Accessed on 1 November 2015).

Ajayi, A. I. (2012). 'Boko Haram' and terrorism in Nigeria: Exploratory and explanatory notes. *Global Advanced Research Journal of History, Political Science and International Relations*, *1*(5), 103–107. Retrieved from http://garj.org/garjhpsir/index.htm

Akinfeleye, R. (2003). *Fourth estate of the realm or fourth estate of the wreck: Imperative of social responsibility of the press*. Lagos: University of Lagos Press.

Akinfeleye, R., & Okoye, I. (Eds.). (2003). *Issues in Nigerian media history: 1900–2000 AD*. Lagos: Malthouse Press.

Akoh, B., Jagun, A., Odufuwa, F., & Akanni, A. (2012). Mapping digital media: Nigeria. In M. Dragomir & M. Thompson (Eds), *A report by the Open Society Foundation*, 21 June, 2012. Retrieved from http://www.opensocietyfoundations.org/sites/default/files/mapping-digial-medianigeria-20120813.pdf

Akresh, R., Bhalotra, S., Leone, M., & Osili, U. (2012). War and stature: Growing up during the Nigerian Civil War. *The American Economic Review*, *102*(3), 273–277. 2012, *JSTOR*, JSTOR. Retrieved from www.jstor.org/stable/23245541

Alade, A., & Kilete, M. (no date). Shekau flees Nigeria. *The Sun* (online). Retrieved from http://sunnewsonline.com/new/shekau-flees-nigeria/ (Accessed on 1 June 2015).

Alohan, J. (2013). Fuel subsidy removal: Should FG heed IMF warnings. *Leadership Newspaper*. Retrieved from http://leadershipeditors.com/news/130613/fuel-subsidy-removal-should-fg-heed-imf-warnings (Accessed 25 September 2012).

Amaefule, E. (2012, January 15). Rage as Nigerians fuel protests on social media. *The Punch*, (online). Retrieved from http://www.punchng.com/business/close-up-on-ict/rage-as-nigerians-fuel-protests-on-social-media/ (Accessed on 4 March 2013).

Amaize, E. (2012). MEND: Directions of a new upsurge. *Vanguard Nigeria* (online), 11 February. Retrieved from https://www.vanguardngr.com/2012/02/mend-directions-of-a-new-upsurge/ (Accessed 12 September 2015).

Amerson, R. (2011). Making a case for the case study. *Journal of Nursing Education, 50*(8), 427–428. Retrieved from https://doi.org/10.3928/01484834-20110719-01

Aminzade, R. (2001). *Silence and voice in the study of contentious politics.* New York, NY: Cambridge University Press.

Amuwo, K., Bach, D. C., & Lebeau, Y. (2001). Nigeria during the Abacha years (1993–1998). Institut français de recherche en Afrique. Open Edition Books. Retrieved from http://books.openedition.org/ifra/632?lang=en

An-Na'im. (2008). *Islam and the secular state: Negotiating the future of Sharia.* Cambridge, MA: Harvard University Press.

Anderson, G., & Arsenault, N. (1998). *Fundamentals of educational research* (2nd ed.). London: Falmer Press.

Ani, O. E. (2010). Internet access and use: A study of undergraduate students in three Nigerian universities. *Electronic Library, 28*(4), 555–567.

Anugwom, E. E. (2000). Ethnic conflict and democracy in Nigeria: The marginalisation question. *Journal of Social Development in Africa, 15*(1), 61–78. Retrieved from http://pdfproc.lib.msu.edu/?file=/DMC/African%20Journals/pdfs/social%20development/vol15no1/jsda015001007.pdf

Anyadike, N. O. (2013). Boko Haram and national security challenges in Nigeria; causes and solution. *Journal of Economics and Sustainable Development, 4*(5), 12–23.

Arab Social Media Report. (2011). Retrieved from http://www.dsg.ae/en/ASMR2/ASMRHome2.aspx?Aspx

Archer, J. E. (2000). *Social unrest and popular protest in England, 1780–1840.* United Kingdom: Cambridge University Press.

Aremu, F. A., & Omotola, J. S. (2007). Violence as threats to democracy in Nigeria under the fourth republic, 1999–2005. *African & Asian Studies, 6*(1), 53–79.

Ariye, C. E. (2010). The impact of private broadcasting in Nigeria. *Pakistan Journal of Social Science, 7*(6), 415–423.

Arksey, H., & Knight, P. (1999). *Interviewing for social scientists: An introductory resource with examples.* London: Sage Publication.

Arquilla, J., & Ronfeldt, D. F. (2001). Networks and netwars and the fight for the future. *Peer Reviewed Journal on the Internet, 6*(10). Retrieved from http://www.firstmonday.dk/ojs/index.php/fm/article/view/889/798 (Accessed on 9 December 14).

Arthur, C. (2011). Egypt blocks social media websites in attempted clampdown on unrest. *The Guardian* (online), 26 January. Retrieved from http://www.theguardian.com/world/2011/jan/26/egypt-blocks-social-media-websites (Accessed on 2 October 2015).

Associated Press. (2014). Death toll rises from car bomb in Nigerian capital Abuja. *The Guardian*, 02 June. Retrieved from http://www.theguardian.com/world/2014/may/02/car-bomb-nigerian-capital-abuja (Accessed on 20 December 2014).

Attoh, N. R. (2015). Biafran self-determination and Radio Biafra: Legal issues arising (1). *Premuim Times* (online), 10 November. Retrieved from http://blogs.premiumtimesng.com/2015/11/10/biafran-self-determination-and-radio-biafra-legal-issues-1-by-nonso-robert-attoh/

Audu, O. (2013). Boko Haram leader laughs in new video, claims sect winning war against Nigerian military. (Online) 12 August. Retrieved from http://www.premiumtimesng.com/news/142626-boko-haram-leader-laughs-in-new-video-claims-sect-winning-war-against-nigerian-military.html (Accessed on 9 September 2014).

Audu, O. (2014). Boko Haram: Shekau claims responsibility for attack on Giwa Barracks, threatens to attack universities, Civilian-JTF. *The Guardian*, 24 March. Retrieved from http://www.premiumtimesng.com/news/157374-boko-haram-shekau-claims-responsibility-attack-giwa-barracks-threatens-attack-universities-civilian-jtf.html (Accessed on 21 December 2014).

Audu, O. (2015). 'Boko Haram leader, Shekau, brands Nigerian soldiers cowards; says Baga weapons enough to win war'. *Premium Time* (online), 21 January. Retrieved from http://www.premiumtimesng.com/news/headlines/175372-boko-haram-leader-shekau-brands-nigerian-soldiers-cowards-says-baga-weapons-enough-win-war.html [10/06/15].

Awan, A. N. (2007). Virtual Jihadist media: Function, legitimacy and radicalizing efficacy. *In European Journal of Cultural Studies*, *10*(3), 389–408.

Aye, B. (2012). *Era of crises and revolt: Perspectives for workers and youths*. Nigeria: Solaf Publishers.

Ayelabola, B. A. (2013). Limits of the Game of Masks: Class, ethno-religious identities, and the rise of Salafi-Jihadism in Northern Nigeria. *Socialism and Democracy*, *27*(3), 104–128. doi:10.1080/08854300.2013.833770. Retrieved from http://www.tandfonline.com/doi/pdf/10.1080/08854300.2013.833770 (Accessed on 12 December 2014).

Ayres, J. (1999). From the streets to the internet: The cyber-diffusion of contention. *Annals of the American Academy of Political and Social Science*, *566*, 132–143.

Bakare, W., Adedeji, A., & Shobiye, H. (2009). Islamic Militant leader Killed—Borno government. *The Punch* (lagos), 31 July, p. 5.

Baldwin, T. (2010). High principles and a great orator. *The Times*, 4 March. Retrieved from http://global.factiva.com/ha/default.aspx (Accessed on 4 March 2010).

Barber, B. (1996). *Jihad vs McWorld: Terrorism's challenges to democracy*. London: Corgi Books.

Barrabi. (2014). Abubakar Shekau alive? Boko Haram leader dismisses death claims in new propaganda video. (Online) 2 October. Retrieved from https://www.ibtimes.com/abubakar-shekau-alive-boko-haram-leader-dismisses-death-claims-new-propaganda-video-1698354 (Accessed on 12 October 2015).

Baxter, P., & Jack, S. (2008). Qualitative case study methodology: Study design and implementation for novice researchers. [E-Journal]. *The Qualitative Report*, *13*(4). Retrieved from http://www.nova.edu/ssss/QR/QR13-4/baxter.pdf

Bazeley, P., & Richards, L. (2000). *The Nvivo qualitative project book*. London: Sage Publications.

BBC. (1998). War of words on the internet. (Online) 25 October. Retrieved from http://news.bbc.co.uk/1/hi/world/monitoring/200708.stm (Accessed on 12 December 2014).

BBC. (2007). The Shadowy Militants in Nigeria's Delta. (online 10 May). Available at: http://news.bbc.co.uk/1/hi/world/africa/6644097.stm

BBC Monitoring. (2015). Is Islamic State shaping Boko Haram media? *BBC* (online), 4 March. Retrieved from http://www.bbc.co.uk/news/world-africa-31522469 (Accessed on 23 December 15).

BBC News. (2014). Nigerian army raids newspaper depots. (Online) 7 June. Retrieved from https://www.bbc.co.uk/news/world-africa-27749024 (Accessed on 9 October 2015).

BBC report. (2012). Nigerians living in poverty rise to nearly 61%. (Online). Retrieved from http://www.bbc.co.uk/news/world-africa-17015873

BBC report. (2013). Vietnam internet restrictions come into effect. BBC (online), 1 September. Retrieved from http://www.bbc.co.uk/news/world-asia-23920541 (Accessed on 2 October 2015).

Beall, J., Goodfellow, T., & Putzel, J. (2006). Introductory article: On the discourse of terrorism, security and development. *Journal of International Development*, *18*(1), 51–67. doi:10.1002/jid.1262

Beaumont, P. (2011). The truth about Twitter, Facebook and the uprisings in the Arab world. (Online). Retrieved from http://www.theguardian.com/world/2011/feb/25/twitter-facebook-uprisings-arab-libya

Becker, T. (2001). Rating the impact of new technologies on democracy. *Communications of the ACM*, *44*(1), 39–43.

Behr, P., & Witt, A. (2002, July 28). Visionary's dream led to risky business. *Washington Post* (online). Retrieved from http://www.washingtonpost.com/wp-dyn/content/article/2005/06/10/AR2005061000709.html (Accessed on 20 April 2013).

Benford, R. D. (1993). You could be the hundredth monkey": Collective action frames and vocabularies of motive within the nuclear disarmament movement. *The Sociological Quarterly*, *34*(2), 195–216.

Benford, R. D., & Snow, D. A. (2000). Framing processes and social movements: An overview and assessment. *Annual Review of Sociology*, *26*, 611–639.

Bennett, W. L. (2004). Communicating global activism. In W. Van de Donk, B. Loader, P. Nixon, & D. Rucht (Eds.), *Cyberprotest: New media, citizens and social movements*. London and New York: Routledge.Van de Donk, 2004.

Berg, L. B. (1989). *Qualitative research methods for social sciences* (4th ed.). USA: California Stole University.

Berg, L. B. (2001). *Qualitative research methods for the social sciences*. California State University, Long Beach: Allyn and Bacon.

Best, M., & Wade, K. (2009). The internet and democracy: Global catalyst or democratic dud? *Bulletin of Science, Technology & Society*, *29*(4), 255–271.

Black, I. (2011). Egypt protest leaflets distributed in Cairo give blueprint for mass action. *The Guardian*, 27 January. Retrieved from http://www.theguardian.com/world/2011/jan/27/egypt-protest-leaflets-mass-action. [19 February 2014].

Blake, R. (1989). Integrating quantitative and qualitative methods in family research. *Families Systems and Health*, *7*, 411–427.

Blanchard, C. M. (2006). *The Islamic traditions of Wahhabism and Salafiyya*. USA: United States Congressional Research Service. Retrieved from http://www.investigativeproject.org/documents/testimony/47.pdf

Block, J. H., Haan, N., & Smith, B. M. (1968). Activism and apathy in contemporary adolescents. In J. F. Adams (Ed.), *Understanding adolescence: Current developments in adolescent psychology* (pp. 198–231). Boston, MA: Allyn & Bacon.

Boko Haram Militants Behead A Nigerian Air Force Pilot. (2014). (Video File). Retrieved from https://www.youtube.com/watch?v=bNq0DIqgR5A&bpctr=1431962232 [10.06.2015].

Bonchek, M. S. (1997). *From broadcast to netcast: The internet and the flow of political information*. Ph.D. dissertation, Harvard University.

Bosch, T. (2017). Twitter activism and youth in South Africa: The case of #RhodesMustFall. *Information, Communication & Society*, *20*(2), 221–232. doi:10.1080/1369118X.2016.1162829. Retrieved from https://doi.org/10.1080/1369118X.2016.1162829

Boyatzis, R. E. (1998). *Transforming qualitative information:Thematic analysis and code development*. Thousand Oaks, CA: Sage.

Boyle, M. P., & Schmierbach, M. (2009). Media use and protest: The role of mainstream and alternative media use in predicting traditional and protest participation. *Communication Quarterly*, *57*(1), 1–17.

Bratton, M. (1989). Beyond the state: Civil society and associational life in Africa. *World Politics*, *51*(3), 407–430.

Bratton, M. (1992). Civil society and political transitions in Africa. *Institute for Development Research*, *11*(6), 6. Retrieved from https://www.issuelab.org/resources/19673/19673.pdf (see also) in Harbeson *et al.*, *Civil Society and the State in Africa:* 33–50.

Bratton, M. (1994). *Civil society and political transition in Africa*. Boston, MA: Institute for Development Research.

Bratton, M., & Walle, N. (1997). *Democratic experiments in Africa: Regime transitions in comparative perspective*. Cambridge: Cambridge University Press.

Braungart, R. G. (1971). Family status, socialization, and student politics: A multivariate analysis. *American Journal of Sociology*, *77*(1), 108–129.

Brenner, M. Brown, J., & Canter, D. (Eds.). (1985). *The research interview: Uses and approaches*. London: Academic Press International.

Breuer, A. (2012). The role of social media in mobilizing political protest: Evidence from the Tunisian revolution. Discussion Paper No. 10/2012. German Development Institute. Retrieved from https://www.die-gdi.de/uploads/media/DP_10.2012.pdf

Bryman, A. (2002). *Qualitative data Analysis: Explorations with Nvivo*. Philadelphia, PA: Open University Press.

Bryman, A. (2012). *Social research methods* (4th ed.). Oxford: Oxford University Press.

Bukar, M., (2011). waazin shekh muhammad yusuf maiduguri 3. *YouTube* (online), 17 Febuary. Retrieved from https://www.youtube.com/watch?v=9nYGyYEA1Y8 Accessed on 12 June 2015].

Bush, G. W. (2008, May 5). Statement on world press freedom day. *Weekly Compilation of Presidential Documents*, *44*, 636–637.

Campbell, J. (2013). Boko Haram recruitment strategies. *Africa in Transition*. N.p., 2013. Web. 15 May 2015. Retrieved from http://blogs.cfr.org/campbell/2013/04/16/boko-haram-recruitment-strategies/

Caramani, D. (2014). *Comparative politics* (3rd ed.). Oxford: Oxford University Press.

Carter, M. S., & Little, M. (2007). Justifying knowledge, justifying method, taking action: Epistemologies, methodologies, and methods in qualitative research. *Qualitative Health Research*, *17*(10), 1316–1328.

Castells, M. (2000). *The rise of the network society, the information age: Economy, society and culture* (2nd ed., Vol. 1). Oxford: Blackwell.

Castells, M. (2001). *The internet galaxy: Reflections on the internet, business, and society*. Oxford: Oxford University Press.

Castells, M. (2002). *The information society and the welfare state*. USA: Oxford University Press.

Castells, M. (2011). *Communication power*. Oxford: Oxford University Press.

Chabal, P., & Daloz, J. (1999). *Africa works: Disorder as a political instrument*. USA: Indiana University Press.

Channel 4. (2011). Arab revolt: Social media and the people's revolution. (Online) 25 February 2011. Retrieved from http://www.channel4.com/news/arab-revolt-social-media-and-the-peoples-revolution (Accessed on 1 December 2013).

Channels television. (2014). Shekau declares Gwoza Boko Haram State. (Video online). Retrieved from https://www.youtube.com/watch?v=LQ9bCMgt9jI (Accessed on 23 November 2014).

Chiluwa, I. (2009). The discourse of digital deceptions and '419' emails. *Discourse Studies*, *11*(6), 635–660.

Chiluwa, I. (2012). Social media networks and the discourse of resistance: A sociolinguistic CDA of Biafra online discourses. *Discourse & Society*, *23*(3), 217–244.

Chiluwa, I., & Ifukor, P. (2015). 'War against our children': Stance and evaluation in #BringBackOurGirls campaign discourse on Twitter and Facebook. *Discourse and Society*, *26*(3), 267–296.

Chothia, F. (2015). Who are Nigeria's Boko Haram Islamists? BBC, 4 May 2015. Accessed on 1 December 2015.

Christensen, H. S. (2011). Political activities on the internet: Slacktivism or political participation by other means? *Peer-Reviewed Journal on the Internet* [*Online*], *16*(2). Retrieved from http://firstmonday.org/article/view/3336/2767 (Accessed on 21 October 2015).

COI, S. (2013, June 14). *Nigeria: Country of origin information (COI) report*. Home Office UK Border Agency (online). Retrieved from http://www.ukba.homeoffice.gov.uk/sitecontent/documents/policyandlaw/coi/nigeria/report-06-1121.pdf?view=Binary

Connell, S. (2012). To be or not to be: Is Boko Haram a foreign terrorist organization? *Global Security Studies*, *3*(3), 87–93.

Cook, D. (2011a). 'Boko Haram: A prognosis.' James A. Baker III Institute for Public Policy. Retrieved from http://bakerinstitute.org/publications/REL-pubCookBoko Haram-121611.pdf (Accessed on 17 April 2012).

Cook, D. (2011b). 'The rise of Boko Haram in Nigeria.' *CTC Sentinel*, 26 September 2011. Retrieved from http://www.ctc.usma.edu/posts/the-rise-of-boko-haram-in-nigeria (Accessed on 14 June 2012).

Costigan, S. S., & Perry, J. (Eds.). (2012). *Cyberspaces and global affairs*. Farnham: Ashgate Publishing Limited.

Council on Foreign Relations, & Hanson, S. (2007). MEND: The Niger Delta's umbrella militant group. (Online) 21 March. Retrieved from https://www.cfr.org/backgrounder/mend-niger-deltas-umbrella-militant-group (Accessed on 15 December 2015).

Courson, E. (2009). *Movement for the emancipation of the Niger Delta (MEND): Political marginalization, repression and petro-insurgency in the Niger Delta.*

Discussion Paper 47. Nordiska Afrikainstitutet, Sweden. Retrieved from http://www.diva-portal.org/smash/get/diva2%3A280470/FULLTEXT01.pdf

CPAfrica. (no date). Interview with Seun Osewa, founder, Nairaland Forum. Retrieved from http://www.cp-africa.com/2011/03/17/cp-africas-interview-with-seun-osewa-founder-of-nairaland/ (Accessed on 1 May 2016).

Creswell, J., Fetters, M., & Ivankova, N. (2004). Designing a mixed methods study in: Primary care. *Annals of Family Medicine*, *2*, 7–12.

Creswell, J. W., & Plano Clark, V. L. (2007). *Designing and conducting mixed methods research*. Thousand Oaks, CA: Sage Publications.

Creswell, J. W., Plano Clark, V. L., Gutmann, M., & Hanson, W. (2003). Advanced mixed methods research designs. In A. Tashakkori & C. Teddlie (Eds.), *Handbook of mixed methods in social and behavioral research* (pp. 619–637). Thousand Oaks, CA: Sage.

Creswell, W. J. (2014). *Research design: Qualitative, quantitative and mixed methods approaches* (4th ed.). London: Sage publication.

Crisis Group. (2014). Curbing violence in Nigeria (II): The Boko Haram insurgency. Report 216 (online), 3 April. Retrieved from https://www.crisisgroup.org/africa/west-africa/nigeria/curbing-violence-nigeria-ii-boko-haram-insurgency

Crisis Group Africa Briefing. (2006) N°115, The swamps of insurgency: Nigeria's Delta unrest. International Crisis Group (online), 3 August. Retrieved from http://justiceinnigerianow.org/lppy/2008/10/118_fuelling_the_niger_delta_crisis.pdf

Crowel, S., Cresswell, K., Robertson, A., Huby, G., Avery, A., & Sheikh, A. (2011). The case study approach. *BMC Medical Research Methodology*, *11*(1), 100. Retrieved from https://doi.org/10.1186/1471-2288-11-100

Crumm, R. (1996, June). Information warfare: An air force policy for the role of public affairs. IWS-The information warfare site. Retrieved from http://www.iwar.org.uk/psyops/resources/iw-pa/crumm.pdf (Accessed on 12 May 2015).

Cummings, B. (2014). Burkina Faso revolution 2.0. *The Guardian* (online). Retrieved from https://www.theguardian.com/world/2014/oct/30/burkina-faso-protests-president-constitution-power (Accessed on 12 October 2016).

Cummings, R. (2015). Boko Haram's pledge to ISIS: Public relations or reality? *IPI GlobalObservatory* (online), 13 March. Retrieved from https://theglobalobservatory.org/2015/03/boko-haram-pledge-allegiance-isis/ (Accessed on 23 December 2015).

Curbing Violence in Nigeria (II): The Boko Haram Insurgency. (2014). Crisis Group Africa Report. Retrieved from http://www.crisisgroup.org/~/media/Files/africa/west-africa/nigeria/216-curbing-violence-in-nigeria-ii-the-boko-haram-insurgency.pdf (Accessed on 10 June 2014).

Dabbs, Jr, J. M. (1982). *Making things visible. Varieties of qualitative research*. Beverly Hills, CA: Sage.

Daily Mail Online. (2016). DRC orders social networks shut as Kabila's term expires. *The East African* (online), December 15. Retrieved from http://www.theeastafrican.co.ke/news/ea/DR-Congo-orders-social-networks-shut-as-Kabila-term-expires/4552908-3488600-7vvmhe/index.html (Accessed on12 December 2017).

Daily Trust [Nigeria]. (2009, May 23). Muhammad Bello. "Nigeria: 12 missing soldiers – Tension mounts as JTF, militants square off." Retrieved from https://allafrica.com/stories/200905250679.html (Accessed on 10 June 2015).

Dalton, R. J., & van Sickle, A. (2005). *The resource, structural, and cultural bases of protest*. Center for the Study of Democracy Working Paper. Irvine, CA.

David, O., Asuelime, L. E., & Onapajo, H. (2015). *Boko Haram: The socio-economic drivers*. [*E-book*]. London: Springer.

Della Porta, D., & Mosca, L. (2005). Global-net for global movements? A network of networks for a movement of movements. *Journal of Public Policy*, *25*(1), 165–190. Retrieved from https://www.cambridge.org/core/journals/journal-of-public-policy/article/globalnet-for-global-movements-a-network-of-networks-for-a-movement-of-movements/3178775B428C682D85E1C4E55495DE9F

Delong-Bas, N. J. (2004). *Wahhabi Islam: From revival and reform to global Jihad*. New York, NY: Oxford University Press.

Deme, M. (2005). *Law, morality, and international armed intervention: The United Nations and ECOWAS in Liberia*. London and New York: Routledge.

Denning, D. (2001). 'Is cyberterrorism next?' Wired.com. Online. Retrieved from http://essays.ssrc.org/sept11/essays/denning.htm

Denzin, N. K., & Lincoln, S. Y. (Eds.). (2003). *Collecting and interpreting qualitative materials*. California: Sage.

Diamond, L. (1983). Class, ethnicity, and the democratic state: Nigeria, 1950-1966. *Comparative Studies in Society and History*, *25*(03), 457–489.

Diamond, L. (1997). Prospects for democratic development in Africa. Paper presented at the Democratic Governance Project, Department of Political and Administrative Studies, University of Zimbabwe, Harare.

Diamond, L. (2010). "Liberation technology." *Journal of Democracy*, *21*(3), 69–83.

Diamond, L. J. (1988). *Class, ethnicity and democracy in Nigeria: The failure of the first republic* (1st ed.). USA: Syracuse University Press.

Diani, M. (1999, September 16–17). 'Social Movement networks virtual and real'. Paper presented at Conference 'A New Politics?' CCSS, University of Birmingham. Online. Retrieved from http://www.nd.edu/~dmyers/cbsm/vol2/bgham99.pdf

Diani, M. (2000). Social movement networks virtual and real. *Information, Communication and Society*, *3*(3), 386–401.

Dibua, J. I. (2005). Citizenship and resource control in Nigeria: The case of minority communities in the Niger Delta. *Africa Spectrum*, *40*(1), 5–28.

Donatella, P. (2009). *Democracy in social movements*. Basingstoke: Palgrave Macmillan.

Doukhan, D. (2012). Who are you, Boko Haram? International institute for counter terrorism. (Online). Retrieved from \\data.adir.hull.ac.uk\home4\448\448593 \Desktop\ICTBoko Haram.htm (Accessed on 9 September 2009).

Drezner, D. (2010). Weighing the scales: The internet's effect on state-society relations. *Brown Journal of World Affairs*, *16*(2), 31–44.

Dzirutwe, M. (2016). From Tweets to streets, Zimbabwe social media anger erupts into anti-Mugabe protests. Reuters (online). Retrieved from https://www.reuters.com/article/us-zimbabwe-protests/from-tweets-to-streets-zimbabwe-social-media-anger-erupts-into-anti-mugabe-protests-idUSKCN0ZN1E3

Earle, L. (2011). *Literature review on the dynamics of social movements in fragile and conflict-affected states*. Birmingham, UK: Governance and Social Development Resource Centre University of Birmingham.

Edetaen, O. (2008). Media and governance in Nigeria. In R. Islam (Ed.), *Information and public choice: From media markets to policy makings*. Washington, DC: The World Bank Washington D. C.

Edwards, P. N. (1998). Y2K: Millennial reflections on computers as infrastructure. *History and Technology*, *15*, 7–29.

Egbejule, E. (2015). Nigeria must own up to the blood shed for oil. *The Guardian* (online), 10 November. Retrieved from http://www.theguardian.com/world/2015/nov/10/nigeria-ken-saro-wiwa-20-years-niger-delta-crisis (Accessed on 17 November 2015).

Ejiogu, C., Adejumo, L. O., & Szczygiel, A. (2013). Social networks, social media and dispersed leadership: Critical perspectives on emergent leadership in African networks and social movements. *Journal of Sustainable Development in Africa*, *14*(4), 206–241.

Ekanade, O., & Odoemene, A. (2012). Challenges of democracy and the (de)memorialisation of June 12, 1993, elections in Nigeria. *International Journal of African Renaissance Studies*, *7*(1), 73–93.

Ekiert, G., & Kubik, J. (2001). *Rebellious civil society: Popular protest and democratic consolidation in Poland 1989-1993*. Ann Arbor, MI: The University of Michigan Press.

Elin, L. (2003). The radicalization of Zeke Spier: How the internet contributes to civic engagement and new forms of social capital. In M. Mccaughey & M. Ayers (Eds.), *Cyberactivism: Online activism in theory and practice* (pp. 97–114). New York, NY: Routledge.

Elkaim, Z. (2012). *Boko Haram: The rise, success and continued efficacy of insurgency in Nigeria*. The International Institute for Counter-Terrorism (online). Retrieved from http://www.ict.org.il/Article/53/Boko-Haram-The%20Rise-Success-and-Continued-Efficacy (Accessed on 10 October 2014).

Eltantawy, N., & Wiest, B. J. (2011). Social media in the Egyptian revolution: Reconsidering resource mobilization theory. *International Journal of Communication*, *5*(Feature), 1207–1224. Retrieved from file://data.adir.hull.ac.uk/home4/448/448593/1242-5202-1-PB.pdf

Email interview (2014 April 29). (personal communication online).

Emmanuel, O. (2015). "Boko Haram Twitter account suspended. *Premium Times* (online), 8 June. Retrieved from https://allafrica.com/stories/201502250116.html (Accessed on 5 September 2016).

Ends.ng. (2015). Captured Boko Haram (ISIS) leader can't pray or read Quran. Retrieved from https://www.youtube.com/watch?v=Ex0mHy5TTBI (Accessed on 5 December 2015).

Enemaku, S. (2003). The deregulation of the Nigerian broadcast industry and the ensuing challenges and opportunities. In R. A. Akinfeleye & I. Okoye (Eds.), *Issues in Nigerian media history 1960–2000AD* (2003, pp. 47–61). Lagos: Malthouse Press Limited.

Engler, M. (2007). Defining the anti-globalization movement. Retrieved from http://www.democracyuprising.com/2007/04/anti-globalization-movement/ (Accessed on 10 June 2015).

Ernest Harsch. (2015). 'Citizens' revolt in Burkina Faso, *African Futures*, *Social Science Research Council*, New York. Retrieved from http://forums.ssrc.org/african-futures/2014/12/09/citizens-revolt-in-burkina-faso/; Firoze Manji, 'Burkina Faso: Liberation not looting', *Red Pepper*, March 2015.

Exandas Documentaries. (2007). 'Delta – Oil's dirty business'. (Online video file). Retrieved from https://www.youtube.com/watch?v=ZGMB9Z4t5Xc [10/06/2015].

Ezeamalu, B. (2014). 'MEND declares ceasefire, demands release of Okah brothers as condition for dialogue' 30 May. Retrieved from http://www.premiumtimesng.com/news/161732-mend-declares-ceasefire-demands-release-okah-brothers-condition-dialogue.html ([10/06/2015]

Fabiyi, M. (2014). Rethinking the amalgamation of 1914 by Malcolm Fabiyi. Retrieved from http://saharareporters.com/2014/01/06/rethinking-amalgamation-1914-malcolm-fabiyi (Accessed on 10 October 2014).

Falola, T. (1998). *Violence in Nigeria: The crisis of religious politics and secular ideologies*. Rochester, NY: Rochester Press.

Fast Facts, United Nations Development Programme. (2011). 11 October 2011-last update, *Fast Facts: e-governance and access to information* [Homepage of United Nations Development Programme], (online). Retrieved from http://www.undp.org/content/dam/undp/library/corporate/fast-facts/english/FF-eGovernance.pdf (Accessed on 10 June 2013).

Fayemi, K. (1998). *No. 1169: Radio and democracy*. Retrieved from https://www.laits.utexas.edu/africa/ads/1169.html (Accessed on 13 November 15).

Fendrich, J., & Krauss, E. S. (1978). Student activism and adult left-wing politics: A causal model of political socialization for black, white and Japanese students of the 1960's generation. In L. Kriesberg (Ed.), *Research in social movements, conflicts, and change* (pp. 231–255). Greenwich, CT: JAI Press.

Flick, U. (2002). *An introduction to qualitative research* (2nd ed.). London: Sage Publications.

Fowler, A., Campbell, P., & Platt, B. (1992). Institutional Development and Nongovernmental in Africa: Policy Perspectives for Europe. Development Agencies, INTRAC NGO Management Series, No. 1. Oxford.

Francis, P., LaPin, D., & Rossiasco, P. (2011). *Securing development and peace in the Niger Delta: A social and conflict analysis for change*. USA: Woodrow Wilson International Center for Scholars.

Freedom House. (2009). Nigeria: Freedom in the world. Retrieved from https://freedomhouse.org/report/freedom-world/2009/nigeria (Accessed on 1 December 2015).

Freedom House. (2011). Nigeria: Freedom in the world. Retrieved from https://freedomhouse.org/report/freedom-world/2011/nigeria (Accessed on 1 December 2015).

Freedom House. (2012). Nigeria: Freedom on the net. Freedom House (online). Retrieved from http://www.freedomhouse.org/report/freedom-net/2012/nigeria (Accessed on 17 December 2012).

Freedom House. (2013). Key developments: May 2012 – April 2013. (Online). Retrieved from https://freedomhouse.org/sites/default/files/resources/FOTN%202013_Full%20Report_0.pdf

Freedom House. (2013). Democratic breakthrough in the balance: Selected data from Freedom House's annual survey of political rights and civil liberties. (Online). Retrieved from https://www.freedomhouse.org/sites/default/files/FIW%202013%20Booklet.pdf

Freedom House. (2014). Freedom of the press: Nigeria. (Online). Retrieved from https://freedomhouse.org/report/freedom-press/2014/nigeria

Freedom of Information Coalition. (no date). Retrieved from http://www.foicoalition.org/about.htm (Accessed on 12 March 2011).

Furseth, I. (2002). *A comparative study of social and religious movements in Norway 1780s-1905*. Lewiston, NY: The Edwin Mellen Press.

Gabriel, O., Ogwuda, A., Muhammad, A., Mosadomi, W., Akannam, T., Dangida, A., ... Moses, T. (2015). Nigeria loses N50trn annually from untapped natural resources. *Vanguard Nigeria*, (online), 29 June 2015. Retrieved from http://www.vanguardngr.com/2015/06/nigeria-loses-n50trn-annually-from-untapped-natural-resources/ (Accessed on 9 September 2015).

Gamson, W., & Meyer, D. (1996). Framing political opportunity. In D. McAdam, J. McCarthy, & M. Zald (Eds.), *Comparative perspectives on social movements: Political opportunities, mobilizing structures, and structural framings*. Cambridge: Cambridge University Press.

Garner, R. T. (1999). Virtual social movements. Paper prepared for the Zaldfest: A conference in honor of Mayer Zald, University of Michigan, Ann Arbor, MI.

Garrett, K. (2006). Protest in an information society: A review of the literature on social movements and new ICTs. *Information, Communication and Society*, *9*(2), 202–224.

General John Togo. (2010). The new face of the Niger Delta insurgency. Speaks to SaharaReporters (online) 28 December. Retrieved from https://www.youtube.com/watch?v=4ntmT6QZdaA (Accessed on 10 June 2015).

Gerring, J. (1997). Ideology: A definitional analysis. *Political Research Quarterly*, *50*(4), 957–994. Retrieved from http://www.jstor.org/stable/pdf/448995.pdf?acceptTC=true

Gilbert, N. (2008). *Researching social life* (3rd ed.). London: Sage Publications Ltd.

Gillan, K., Pickerill, J., & Webster, F. (2008). *Anti-war activism: New media and protest in the information age, Palgrave*. Basingstoke: Macmillan.

Gillham, B. (2005). *The research interviewing: The range of techniques*. Berkshire: Open University Press.

Gilsinan, K. (2015). ISIS and the 'internet radicalization' trope. *The Atlantic,* 8 December. Retrieved from http://www.theatlantic.com/international/archive/2015/12/isis-internet-radicalization/419148/ (Accessed on 5 December 2015).

Gisler, M., G, M., #252, nter and Spahni, D. (2001). eGovernment. *Proceedings of the 34th Annual Hawaii International Conference on System Sciences (HICSS-34) – Volume 5 – Volume* 5 IEEE Computer Society, p. 5002.

Gitlin, T. (1980). *The whole world is watching: Mass media in the making and unmaking of the new left*. Berkeley, CA: University of California Press.

Gladwell, M. (2010). Small change: Why the revolution will not be tweeted. *The New Yorker*, October 4, 2010.

Global security.org. (no date). Nigeria – Niger Delta. Retrieved from http://www.globalsecurity.org/military/world/war/nigeria-2.htm

Gold, T. B. (1990). The resurgence of civil society in China. *Journal of Democracy*, *1*(1), 18–31.

Goodwin, J. Jasper, J. M., & Polletta, F. (Eds.). (2001). *Passionate politics: Emotions and social movements*. Chicago, IL: University of Chicago Press.

Gould, M. (2012). *The struggle for modern Nigeria: The Biafran war 1967–1970*. New York, NY: Palgrave McMillan.

Greene, C. J., Caracelli, V. J., & Graham, F. W. (1989). Towards a conceptual framework for mixed method evaluation designs. *Sage Journals*, *11*(3). Retrieved from http://journals.sagepub.com/doi/10.3102/01623737011003255.

Groshek, J. (2010). A time-series, multinational analysis of democratic forecasts and internet diffusion. *International Journal of Communication*, *4*, 142–174.

GSMA. (2016). The mobile economy Africa 2016. (Online). Retrieved from https://www.gsma.com/mobileeconomy/africa/ (Accessed on 17 February 2017).

Guardian African Network. (2014). Burkina Faso's revolution 2.0. *The Guardian* (online), October 30. Retrieved from https://www.theguardian.com/world/2014/oct/30/burkina-faso-protests-president-constitution-power (Accessed on 10 February 2017).

Guest, G., & Macqueen, N. (2012). *Applied thematic analysis*. Los Angeles, CA: Sage Publication.

Guidère, M. (2012). *Historical dictionary of Islamic fundamentalism*. United Kingdom: The Scarecrow Press Inc. Lanham.

Gupta, J. N. D. (2009). *Handbook of research on information security and assurance*. USA: IGI Global.

Gurr, T. R. (1970). *Why men rebel*. Princeton, NJ: Princeton University Press.

Gustafson, T. (1989). 'A Civil Society in the Soviet Union' in SOVSET News, The Economic Newsletter of Soviet Studies, 5, October 2. In M. Bratton (Ed.), *1994 Civil society and political transition in Africa*. Institute for Development Research. IDR Reports volume 11, Number 6. Retrieved from https://www.issuelab.org/resources/19673/19673.pdf

Hakeem Onapajo, H., & Uzodike, O. U. (2012). Boko Haram terrorism in Nigeria. *African Security Review*, *21*(3), 24–39. doi:10.1080/10246029.2012.687693

Hammersley, M., & Atkinson, P. (1995). *Ethnography: Principles in practice* (2nd ed.). London: Routledge.

Hampton, K. N. (2003). Grieving for a lost network: Collective action in a wired suburb. *The Information Society*, *19*(5), 1–13.

Hancock, L. (2000). Going around the houses: Researching in high crime areas. In R. King & E. Wincup (Eds.), *Doing research on crime and justice*. Oxford: Oxford University Press.

Hands, J. (2011). *@ id for activism: Dissent, resistance and rebellion in a digital culture*. London: Pluto Press.

Hanson, S. (2007). MEND: The Niger Delta's umbrella militant group. Council on Foreign Relations (online), 22 March. Retrieved from http://integritynigeria.org/wp-content/uploads/2012/07/MEND-The-Niger-Deltas-Umbrella-Militant.pdf

Harbeson, J., Rothchild, D., & Chazan, N. (Eds.). (1994). *Civil society and the state in Africa*. London: Lynne Rienner Publishers.

Hargattai, E. (2000). Radio's lessons for the internet: Will the government's inevitable regulation reflect the Net's historic egalitarian, democratic, all-welcoming view of information? *Communications of the ACM*, *43*(1), 51–57.

Hari, I. S. (2014). The evolution of social protest in Nigeria: The role of social media in the "#OccupyNigeria" protest. *International Journal of Humanities and Social Science Invention*, *3*(9), 33–39.

Harnisch, C. (2011, March). *'Al Qaeda's operating environments: A new approach to the war on terror'* (p. 10). Washington DC: The American Enterprise Institute. Retrieved from http://www.youtube.com/watch?v=umkj50SUzck (Accessed on 9 September 2013).

Hassan, K. (2014). The role of private electronic media in radicalising Pakistan. *The Commonwealth Journal of International Affairs, 103*(1), 65–81. [Online].

Retrieved from http://www.tandfonline.com/doi/pdf/10.1080/00358533.2013.874164 (Accessed on 2 February 2015).

Hassani, S. N. (2006). Locating digital divides at home, work, and everywhere else. *Poetics*, *34*, 250–272. Retrieved from http://ac.els-cdn.com/S0304422X06000209/1-s2.0-S0304422X06000209-main.pdf?_tid=6d0842e0-b930-11e5-9795-00000aab0f6b&acdnat=1452605514_5c8435e17eed49e638420e9b1ac08068 (Accessed on 12 December 2015).

Hazen, J. (2009). From social movement to armed group: A case study from Nigeria. *Contemporary Security Policy*, *30*(2), 281–300.

Heckathorn, D. D. (1997). Respondent-driven sampling: A new approach to the study of hidden populations. *Social Problems*, *44*(2), 174–199.

Heckathorn, D. D. (2002). Respondent-driven sampling II: Deriving valid population estimates from chain-referral samples of hidden populations. *Social Problems*, *49*(1), 11–34.

Heckathorn, D. D. (2007). Extensions of respondent-driven sampling: Analyzing continuous variables and controlling for differential recruitment. *Sociological Methodology*, *6*, 151–208.

Heimer, M., & Thøgersen, S. (2006). *Doing fieldwork in China*. North America: University of Hawai'i Press.

Hennink, M. M. (2007). *International focus groups research: A handbook for the health and social sciences*. Atlanta: Cambridge University Press.

Hermida, A. (2002). Behind China's Internet Red Firewall. *BBC News* (online), 3 September. Retrieved from http://news.bbc.co.uk/1/hi/technology/2234154.stm (Accessed on 1 September 2014).

Herskovits, J. (1979). Democracy in Nigeria. *Foreign Affairs*, *58*(2), 314–335.

Herskovits, J. (2007). Nigeria's rigged democracy. *Foreign Affairs*, *86*(4), 115–130.

Hilbert, M. (2010). When is cheap, cheap enough to bridge the digital divide? Modeling income related structural challenges of technology diffusion in Latin America (PDF). *World Development*, *38*(5), 756–770. doi:10.1016/j.worlddev.2009.11.019

Hilbert, M. (2013). Technological information inequality as an incessantly moving target: The redistribution of information and communication capacities between 1989 and 2010. *Journal of the Association for Information Science and Technology*. Retrieved from http://onlinelibrary.wiley.com/doi/10.1002/asi.23020/epdf (Accessed on 9 April 2015).

Hine, C. (2000). *Virtual ethnography*. London: Sage.

Hoffman, A. (1995). Nigeria: The policy conundrum. *Foreign Policy*, *101*, 146–158. doi:10.2307/1149414

Holloway, I., & Todres, L. (2003). The status of method: Flexibility, consistency and coherence. *Sage Journals*, *3*(3), 345–357.

Holstein, J. A., & Gubrium, J. F. (Eds.). (2003). *Inside interviewing: New lenses, new concerns*. Thousand Oaks, CA: Sage Publications.

Hope in Nigeria: Hail the useful chief." *The Economist*, 26 May 2011. Retrieved from http://www.economist.com/node/18744065 (Accessed 20 February 2012).

Hoskins, A., & Loughlin, B. (2009). Media and the myth of radicalization. *Media, War and Conflict*, *2(2)*, 107–110. 107.

How Boko Haram Militants Brutally Govern Captured Territories in Northeastern Nigeria, 2014 (video File), Available at: https://www.youtube.com/watch?v=L1dc1OiWuNA [10.06.1015].

Howard, P. (2010). *The digital origins of dictatorship and democracy: Information technology and political Islam*. New York, NY: Oxford University Press.

Howard, P., Duffy, A., Freelon, D., Hussain, M. M., Mari, W., & Mazaid, M. (2011). Opening closed regimes: What was the role of social media during the Arab Spring? (Online). Retrieved from https://papers.ssrn.com/sol3/papers.cfm?abstract_id=2595096 (Accessed on 9 December 2013).

Huang, C. (2011). 'Facebook and Twitter key to Arab Spring uprisings: Report'. *The National*, June 6. Retrieved from http://www.thenational.ae/news/uae-news/facebook-and-twitter-key-to-arab-spring-uprisings-report (Accessed on 1 September 2015).

Hughes, J. (2000). The virtual objects of ethnography. In C. Hine (Ed.), *Virtual ethnography*. London: Sage Publications.

Human Rights Watch. (2003). Nigeria: Renewed crackdown on freedom of expression. (Online). Human Rights Watch. [[01/11/2014]. Volume 15, No. 19(A). Retrieved from https://www.hrw.org/reports/2003/nigeria1203/nigeria1203.pdf

Human Rights Watch. (2003). *Nigeria: Renewed crackdown on freedom of expression*. NewYork, NY: Human Rights Watch.

Human Rights Watch. (2007). Criminal politics: Violence, "Godfathers" and corruption in Nigeria. (Online). Human Rights Watch. [[01/11/2014]. Volume 19, No. 16(A). Retrieved from https://www.hrw.org/sites/default/files/reports/nigeria1007webwcover_0.pdf

Human Rights Watch. (2008). World report. (Online). United States of America. Human Rights Watch. [01/11/2014]. Retrieved from https://www.hrw.org/legacy/wr2k8/pdfs/wr2k8_web.pdf

Human Rights Watch. (2010). 2009 Human Rights Report: Nigeria. (Online). Retrieved from http://www.state.gov/j/drl/rls/hrrpt/2009/af/135970.htm. Human Rights Watch.

Huntington, S. P. (1968). *Political order in changing societies.* New Haven and London: Yale University Press.

Ibaba, S. I., & Okolo, P. O. (2009). Resolving militia conflicts in the Niger delta: The role and strategies of mediation (online) Martins papers. Retrieved from http://www.class.uidaho.edu/martin_archives/Martin%20Papers.html (Accessed on 21 October 2015).

Ibeh, N. (2014). 'We have killed Boko Haram leader, Abubakar Shekau — Nigerian military'. *Premium Times* 24 September. Retrieved from http://www.premiumtimesng.com/news/headlines/168622-we-have-killed-boko-haram-leader-abubakar-shekau-nigerian-military.html (Accessed on 10 June 2015).

Ibekwe, N. (2015). Full text and video of NSA Sambo Dasuki's famous presentation at Chatham house, London. *Premium Times* (online) 24 January Retrieved from http://www.premiumtimesng.com/news/headlines/175497-full-text-video-nsa-sambo-dasukis-famous-presentation-chatham-house-london.html

Ibrahim, J. (1997). *'The military and the programme of transition to democratic rule' expanding Nigerian democratic space*. Dakar: CODESRIA.

Igwe, K. (2010). 'Eight killed by Nigeria independence day bombs, *Reuters* (online) 1 October. Retrieved from http://uk.reuters.com/article/2010/10/01/us-nigeria-idUSTRE6901Y320101001 (Accessed on 10 June 2015].

Ihonvbere, J., & Vaughan, O. (1995). Nigeria: Democracy and civil society. In J. Wiseman (Ed.), *Democracy and political change in sub-saharan Africa* (pp. 71–91). London: Routledge.

Ikein, A. A., Alamieyeseigha, D. S. P., & Azaiki, S. (2008). *Oil, democracy, and the promise of the federalism in Nigeria*. Lanham: University Press of America.

Ikelegbe, A. (2001). The perverse manifestation of civil society: Evidence from Nigeria. *Journal of Modern African Studies*, *39*(1), 1–24.

Immigration and Refugee Board of Canada. (2009). Nigeria: Movement for the emancipation of the Niger Delta (MEND); whether it forcibly recruits its members and, if so, how; whether members are only from the Ijaw ethnic group (online) May 2009. Retrieved from http://www.refworld.org/docid/4b20f032a.html (Accessed on 10 June 2015).

Immigration and refugee board of Canada. (2011). *Responses to information requests*. Retrieved from http://irb-cisr.gc.ca/Eng/ResRec/RirRdi/Pages/index.aspx?doc=453565 (Accessed on 10 June 2015). INTRAC NGO Management Series, No. 1.

Innocent, E. O., & Jide, I. (2012). The cost of Boko Haram activities in Nigeria. *Arabian Journal of Business and Management Review (OMAN Chapter.)*, *2*(2). Retrieved from http://eprints.covenantuniversity.edu.ng/3754/1/Eme%26Ibietan.pdf

International Crisis Group. (2006). Fuelling the Niger delta crisis. (Africa Report No. 118). (Online) 28 September Retrieved from https://www.crisisgroup.org/africa/west-africa/nigeria/fuelling-niger-delta-crisis (Accessed on 06 January 2015).

International Monetary Fund. *Nigeria*, IMF Country Report No. 14/103, (Online) April 2014. Retrieved from https://www.imf.org/en/Publications/CR/Issues/2016/12/31/Nigeria-Staff-Report-for-the-2013-Article-IV-Consultation-41496 pp. 10–25.

Interview 2, 17 December 2013, Abuja.

Interviewee 1, 11 December 2013, Abuja.

Interviewee 3, 20 December 2013, Abuja.

Interviewee 5, 6 January 2014, Abuja.

Interviewee 6, 11 January 2014, Abuja.

Interviewee 7, 15 January 2014, Abuja.

Interviewee 8, 15 January 2014, Abuja.

Interviwee 4, 1 January 2014, Abuja.

Isaacs, D., & Butcher, T. (2002). How Miss World 'blasphemy' led to carnage. *The Telegraph* 23 November. Retrieved from http://www.telegraph.co.uk/news/worldnews/africaandindianocean/nigeria/1414111/How-Miss-World-blasphemy-led-to-carnage.html (Accessed on 20 October 2015).

Isine, I. (2015). 'Again, Obasanjo seeks dialogue with Boko Haram; says sect has legitimate grievances'. *Premium Times* 17 March. Retrieved from http://www.premiumtimesng.com/news/headlines/178601-again-obasanjo-seeks-dialogue-with-boko-haram-says-sect-has-legitimate-grievances.html (Accessed on 10 June 2015).

Iskhandar, A. (2010). Reclaiming silence in Egypt. (Online). 22 July. (Accessed on 2 October 2015). Retrieved from http://www.egyptindependent.com/opinion/reclaiming-silence-egypt

Janićijević, N. (2011). Methodological approaches in the research of organizational culture. *Ekonomski Anali/Economic Annals*, *56*(189), 69–99. doi:10.2298/EKA1189069J

Jankowski, N. W., & Wester, F. (1991). The qualitative tradition in social science inquiry: Contributions to mass communication research. In K. B. Jensen & N. W. Jankowski (Eds.), *A handbook of qualitative methodologies for mass communication research* (pp. 44–74). London: Routledge.

Jasper, J. M. (1998). The emotions of protest: Affective and reactive emotions in and around social movements. *Sociological Forum*, *13*(3), 397–424.

Jasper, J. M., & Poulsen, J. D. (1995). Recruiting strangers and friends: Moral shocks and social networks in animal rights and anti-nuclear protests. *Social Problems*, *42*(4), 493–512.

Jega, A. (2015). Towards effective electoral processes in Nigeria. *IT Telecom Digest* (Online) (Accessed on 01 January 2016). Retrieved from http://www.ittelecomdigest.com/towards-effective-electoral-processes-in-nigeria/

Joseph, R. (1997). Democratisation under military rule and repression. In P. Beckett & C. Young (Eds.), *Dilemmas of democracy in Nigeria* (p. 13). Rochester, NY: University of Rochester press.

Juris, J. S. (2005). The new digital media and activist networking within anti-corporate globalization movements. *Annals of the American Academy of Political and Social Science*, *597*(1), 189–208.

Kalu, U. (2011). How Nur, Shekau run Boko Haram. Vanguard Nigeria (online) 3 September. Retrieved from https://www.vanguardngr.com/2011/09/how-nur-shekau-run-boko-haram/ (Accessed on 15 November 15).

Kaplan, A. (1964). *The conduct of inquiry: Methodology for behavioural science*. SF: Chandler publication.

Karatzogianni, A. (2004). The politics of cyberconflict. *Journal of Politics*, *24*(1), 46–55.

Karatzogianni, A. (2006a). *Cyber conflict and global politics*. London and New York: Routledge.

Karatzogianni, A. (2006b). *The politics of cyberconflict, Routledge research on Internet and society*. Oxon: Routledge.

Karatzogianni, A. (2009) (ed.). *Cyber conflict and global politics*. London and New York: Routledge.

Karatzogianni, A. (2012a). WikiLeaks affects: Ideology, conflict and the revolutionary virtual. In A. Karatzogianni & A. Kunstman (Eds.), *Digital cultures and the politics of emotion: feelings, Affect and technological change*. Basingstoke: Palgrave MacMillan.

Karatzogianni, A. (2012b). Blame it on the Russians: Tracking the portrayal of Russian hackers during cyber conflict incidents. In A. Karatzogianni (ed.), Violence and war in the media: Five disciplinary lenses. London and New York: Routledge.

Karatzogianni, A. (2012c). Cyberconflict and the future of warfare. In H. Gardner & O. Kobtzeff (Eds.), *The Ashgate reseach companion to war: Origins and prevention* (p. 491). Ashgate. Surrey: Ashgate Publishing Limited.

Karatzogianni, A. (2013). A cyberconflict analysis of the 2011 Arab Spring uprisings'. In G. Youngs (Ed.), *Digital world: Connectivity, creativity and rights*. London and New York: Routledge.

Karatzogianni, A. (2015). *Firebrand waves of digital activism 1994-2014: The rise and spread of hacktivism and cyberconflict*. Basingstoke: Palgrave MacMillan.

Karatzogianni, A., Nguyen, D., & Serafinelli, E. (Eds.). (forthcoming). *The digital transformation of the public sphere: Conflict, migration, crisis and culture in digital networks*. Basingstoke: Palgrave Macmillan.

Karatzogianni, A., & Robinson, A. (2014). Digital prometheus: WikiLeaks, the state-network dichotomy and the antinomies of academic reason. *International Journal of Communication*. (Online) Retrieved from https://lra.le.ac.uk/bitstream/2381/32086/1/2879-12852-1-PB.pdf

Karen Mossberger. (2003). *Virtual inequality: Beyond the digital divide*. Georgetown University Press.

Kassim, S. (2012). Twitter revolution: How social media helped the Arabs spring. Mic Network Inc (online). Retrieved from https://mic.com/articles/10642/twitter-revolution-how-the-arab-spring-was-helped-by-social-media#.2iGYp3ORQ (Accessed on 12 December 2014).

Kavada, A. (2010). Between individuality and collectiveness: Email lists and face-to-face contact in the global justice movement. *International Journal of E-Politics*, *1*(1), 41–56. ISSN 1947–9131.

Kavada, A. (2010). Email list and participatory democracy in the European Social Forum. *Media Culture and Society*, *32*(3), 355–372.

Kavada, A. (2012). Engagement, bonding, and identity across multiple platforms: Avaaz on Facebook, YouTube, and MySpace. *Journal of Media and Communication Research*, *28*(52), 28–48.

Kavada, A. (2013). Internet cultures and protest movements: the cultural lins between strategy, organizing and online communications. In B. Cammaerts, A. Mattoni, & P. McCurdy, (Eds.), *Mediation and protest movements London intellect* (pp. 75–94).

Kavada, A. (2015). Creating the collective: Social media, the Occupy movement and its constitution as a collective actor. *Information, Communication & Society*, *18*(8), 872–886.

Kennedy, M. (2016). Congo to block social media sites ahead of protests against the president. National Public Radio (online) Retrieved from https://www.npr.org/sections/thetwo-way/2016/12/16/505854670/congo-to-block-social-media-sites-ahead-of-protests-against-the-president

Khondker, H. H. (2011). Role of the new media in the Arab Spring. *Globalizations*, *8*(5), 675–679.

Kidd, D. (2003). The independent media center: A new model. (Accessed on 17 February 2004). Indymedia. Global. ImcBrochure.

Klandermans, B. (1984). Mobilisation and participation: Social psychological expansions of resource mobilization theory. *American Sociological Review*, *49*(5), 583–600.

Kolawole, S. (2010). Power rotation and its presumptions. *Thisday Online*, (online) July 25. Retrieved from http://www.thisdaylive.com/articles/power-rotation-and-its-presumptions/82529/ (Accessed on 02 February 2016).

Komolafe, K. (2012). "Boko Haram: A Crisis in Search of Strategy," *Thisday*, (online) 25, 2012 . Retrieved from https://allafrica.com/stories/201201250649.html

Korieh, C. J. (Ed). (2012). *The Nigerian Biafran war: Genocide and the politics of memory*. New York: Cambria Press.

Krueger, A. B., & Maleckova, J. (2002). Does poverty cause terrorism?: The economics and the education of suicide bombers. *The New Republic*, 24 June.

Kumar, R. (2008). *Research methodology*. New Delhi: APH Publishing Corporation.

Laclau, E. (Ed). (1994). *The making of political identities*. London and New York: Verso.

Lado, C. (2000). The state and civil society: Transition and prospects of labour geographies in an era of economic globalisation in Nigeria and South Africa. *Singapore Journal of Tropical Geography*, *21*(3), 295–315.

Laer, V. J., & Aelst, V. P. (2010). Internet and social movement action repertoires. *Information, Communication and Society*, *13*(8), 1146–1171. Retrieved from http://www.ciberdemocracia.net/victorsampedro/wp-content/uploads/2012/12/Internet_social_movement_action.pdf (Accessed on 12 December 2014).

Langa, M. (2017). # Hashtag: An Analysis of the #feesmustfall movement at South African Universities. Center for the Study of Violence and Reconciliation. Johannesburg and Cape Town. (Online). Retrieved from file:///D:/An_analysis_of_the_FeesMustFall_Movement.pdf (Accessed 21 February 2018).

Leslie, C. (2012). Book review: Guobin Yang, The power of the internet in China: Citizen activism online and Susan L. Shirk (Ed.), Changing media, changing China and David Kurt Herol and Peter Marolt (Eds), Online Society in China. *Media, Culture & Society*, 34(8), 1059–1063.

Levan, C., & Ukata, P. (2012). *Countries at Crossroads 2012*. USA: Nigeria, Freedom House.

Lewis, J. (2010). *Crisis in the global mediasphere: Desire, displeasure and cultural transformation*. Basingstoke: Palgrave Macmillan.

Lewis, M. P. (1994). Endgame in Nigeria: The politics of a failed democratic transition. *African Afairs*, *93(372)*, 323–340.

Lewis, P. (1996). Prebendalism to predation: The political economy of decline in Nigeria. *The Journal of Modern African Studies*, *34*(1), 79–103.

Lewis, S. H., & Kraut, R. E. (1972). Correlates of student political activism and ideology. *Journal of Social Issues*, *28*(4), 131–149.

Lichbach, M. I. (1989). ‘An evaluation of “does inequality breed political conflict?’ Studies”. *World Politics*, *41*(July), 431–470.

Lui, J. (2012). Mobilized by mobile media: How Chinese people use mobile phones to change politics and demoncracy. Doctor of Philosophy. University of Copenhagen, Copenhagen. Retrieved from https://tel.archives-ouvertes.fr/tel-00797157/document

Luqman, S., & Lawal, F. M. (2011). The political economy of oil and the reform process in Nigeris’s fourth republic: Sucesses and continue challenges”. *Journal of Arts, Science & Commerce*, *2*(2), 59–76.

Lussier, R. N. (2009). *Management fundamentals: concepts, applications, skill development* (4th ed.). USA: South-Western Cengage Learning.

Maiangwa, B., Uzodike, U. O., Whetho, A., & Onapajo, H. (2012). “Baptism by fire”: Boko Haram and the reign of terror in Nigeria. *Africa Today*, *59*(2). Retrieved from http://muse.jhu.edu/article/494431/pdf

Makama, G. A. (2013). Patriarchy and gender inequality in Nigeria: The way forward. *European Scientific Journal*, *9*(17), 115–144.

Makumbe, J. (1998). Is there a civil society in Africa? *International Affairs*, *74*(2), 305–317.

Mamah, E., & Amaize, E. (2012). 'MEND resumes hostilities'. *Vanguard*, 06 February Retrieved from http://www.vanguardngr.com/2012/02/mend-resumes-hostilities-2/ (Acessed on 10 June 2015).

Mani, A. (2012). Sako game da hari kan jaridar Thisday.flv. Retrieved from https://www.youtube.com/watch?v=xDqv6srmol4 (Accessed on 02 February 2014)

Mano, W. (2017). Without social media many Zimbabwe would have died in the Mugabe Crisis. *i News* (online). Retrieved from https://inews.co.uk/opinion/without-social-media-many-zimbabweans-died-mugabe-crisis/

Mantel. (2011). Terrorism and the internet: Should websites that promote terrorism be shut down. In C.Q. Researcher (Ed.), *Issues in terrorism and homeland security* (2nd ed.). California: Sage publication.

Marama, N. (2013). Boko Haram: We did not cease fire-Shekau. *Vanguard Nigeria* (online), 4 March. Retrieved from https://www.vanguardngr.com/2013/03/20-gunmen-killed-in-borno-army-barracks-attack-2/ (Accessed on 12 July 2015).

Marama, N., Aliyu, A., & Balogun, I. (2012). '20 mini-skirt ladies massacred in Maiduguri, JTF places bounty on Boko Haram leaders' 24 November. Retrieved from http://www.vanguardngr.com/2012/11/20-mini-skirt-ladies-massacre-in-maiduguri-jtf-place-bounty-on-boko-haram-leaders/#sthash.JSPuswjq.dpuf (Accessed on 10 June 2015).

Marama, N., & Odiogor, H. (2013). Nigeria: Boko Haram:We did not declare ceasefire−Shekau. *Vanguard Nigeria* (online). Retrieved from https://allafrica.com/stories/201303040255.html (Accessed on 12 July 2015).

Maringira, G., & Gukurume, S. (2017). Being Black' in #FeesMustFall and #FreeDecolonisedEducation: Student Protests at the University of the Western Cape. In Langa, M. (Eds.), # Hashtag: An Analysis of the #feesmustfall movement at South African Universities. (Online). Retrieved from file:///D:/An_analysis_of_the_FeesMustFall_Movement.pdf. Accessed on 21 February 2018).

Mark, F. M. (2010). *Research methods in sport*. Exeter: Learning Matters Ltd.

Marples, D. R. (2006). Color revolutions: The Belarus case. *Communist and Post-Communist Studies*. Retrieved from http://ac.els-cdn.com/S0967067X06000274/1-s2.0-S0967067X06000274-main.pdf?_tid=6efbced4-be15-11e5-b37a-00000aacb361&acdnat=1453143677_e5e8c72032c6f13036dc1b816e52fda8 (Accessed on 18 January 2014). pp. 351−364.

Masoud, E. T. (1999). The Arabs and Islam: The troubled search for legitimacy. *The Next Generation*, *128*(2), pp. 127. Retrieved from http://www.jstor.org/stable/pdf/20027557.pdf

Matfess, H. (2015). How the ISIS-Boko Haram alliance will alter Nigeria's future, defense one, (online) 13 March. Retrieved from http://www.defenseone.com/threats/2015/03/how-isis-boko-haram-alliance-will-alter-nigerias-future/107484/ (Accessed on 23 December 2015).

Matfess, H. (2016). More African countries are blocking internet access during elections. *QuartzAFRICA*. (Online) 01 June. Retrieved from https://qz.com/696552/more-african-countries-are-blocking-internet-access-during-elections/ (Accessed on 17 March 2017).

Maweni Farm Documentaries. (2009). Poison Fire (Video File). Retrieved from https://www.youtube.com/watch?t=679&v=bq2TBOHWFRc [10/06/2015].

Maykut, P., & Morehouse, R. (1994). *Beginning qualitative research: A philosophic and practical guide*. London: Falmer.

McAdam, D. (1996a). Conceptual origins, current problems, future directions. In D. McAdam J. D. McCarthy, & M. N. Zald (Eds.), *Comparative perspectives on social movements: Political opportunities, mobilizing structures, and cultural framings* (pp. 23–40). New York, NY: Cambridge University Press.

McAdam, D. (1996b). The framing function of movement tactics: Strategic dramaturgy in the American civil rights movement. In McAdam & et al. (Eds.), *Comparative perspectives on social movements: Political opportunities, mobilizing structures, and structural framings*. Cambridge: Cambridge University Press.

McAdam, D., McCarthy, J. D., & Zald, M. N. (Eds.). (1996). *Comparative perspectives on social movements: Political opportunities, mobilizing structures, and cultural fgramings*. New York: Cambridge University Press.

McCarthy, J. D. (1996). Constraints and opportunities in adopting, adapting, and inventing'. In D. McAdam J. D. McCarthy, & M. N. Zald (Eds.), *Comparative perspectives on social movements: Political opportunities, mobilizing structures, snd cultural framings* (pp. 141–151). New York, NY: Cambridge University Press.

Mccaughey, M., & Ayers, M. (2003). *Cyberactivism: Online activism in theory and practice*. New York and London: Routledge.

McClosky, H. (1964). Consensus and ideology in American politics. *American Political Science Review*, *58*(June), 361–382.

McConnell, T. (2009). Islamist Sect leader shot dead after 600 killed in Nigeria siege, in: *The London Times*, (online) 31 July. Retrieved from http://www.timesonline.co.uk/tol/news/world/africa/article6734046.ece (Accessed on 10 February 2014).

McCracken, G. (1988). *The long interview*. Thousand Oaks, CA: Sage.

MediaShift. (2013). The rise of global free speech in the digital age: How blogs, forums, Facebook, Twitter, YouTube boost freedom of expression around the world 2006 to 2013. PBS.

Meier, P. P. (2011). *Do "liberation technologies" change the balance of power between repressive states and civil society?* Medford, MA: Tufts University.

Merton, K. R. (1948). The self-fulfilling prophecy. *The Antioch Review [E-Journal]*, *8*(2), 193–210. Retrieved from http://entrepreneurscommunicate.pbworks.com/f/Merton.+Self+Fulfilling+Profecy.pdf

Merton, K. R. (1972). Insiders and outsiders: A chapter in the sociology of knowledge. *American Journal of Sociology*, *78*(1), 9–47. [E-journal]. Retrieved from http://www.d.umn.edu/cla/faculty/jhamlin/4111/Readings/MertonKnowledge.pdf

Middle East Forum. (2003). Saudi Arabia and the rise of the Wahhabi threat. Retrieved from http://www.meforum.org/535/saudi-arabia-and-the-rise-of-the-wahhabi-threat (Accessed on 10.June.2015).

Mochizuki, K. (2009). Opposition movements and the youth in Nigeria's oil-producing area: an inquiry into framing. In S. Shigetomi & K. Makino (Eds.), *Protest and social movements in the developing world*. Cheltenham: Edward Elgar.

Moftah, L. (2015). 'Boko Haram ISIS Pledge: Possible alliance would reap limited victories for militant groups', *International BusinessTimes* (online), 10 March. Retrieved from http://www.ibtimes.com/boko-haram-isis-pledge-possible-alliance-would-reap-limited-victories-militant-groups-1842568 (Accessed on 12 December 2015).

Mogbejume, O. (1991). Constraints on mass media policies in Nigeria. *African Media Review*, *5*(2), 47.

Mohammed, J. B. (2000). *The crisis of hegemony in Nigeria: State-press relations in the Babangida years*, PhD edn, Ahmadu Bello University, Nigeria.

MOHD Nur & Yusuf. (2011). Sunnahization. YouTube.com (Online) 28 October. Retrieved from https://www.youtube.com/watch?v=cUot3BrT0FE (Accessed on 12 June 2015).

Momoh, A. (1996). Popular struggles in Nigeria 1960–1982. *African Journal of Political Science*, *1*(2), 154–175.

Moore, K. (1996). Organizing integrity: American science and the creation of public interest organizations, 1955–1975. *American Journal of Sociology*, *101*(6), 1592–1627.

Moore, K. (2008). *Disrupting science: social movements, American scientists, and the politics of the military, 1945–1975*. Princeton, NJ: Princeton University Press.

Morovoz, E. (2011). *The net delusion: The dark side of the internet*. New York: Penguin Group.

Mshelizza, I. (2009). More than 700 killed in Nigeria clashes the supreme muslim body denouncing boko haram. Reuters (online). Retrieved from http://www.reuters.com/article/us-nigeria-sect-idUSTRE5710AV20090802 (Accessed on 01 August 2014).

Muller, E. N., & Jukam, T. O. (1983). Discontent and aggressive political participation. *British Journal of Political Science*, *13*(2), 159–179.

Murray, S., & Nossiter, A. (2011). Suicide bomber attacks U.N. building in Nigeria. *The New YorkTimes* (online), 26 August. Retrieved from https://www.nytimes.com/2011/08/27/world/africa/27nigeria.html (Accessed on 15 September 2015).

Musa, M., & Mohammed, J. (2004). The political economy of media ownership in Nigeria. In P. Thomas & Z. Nain (Eds.), *Who owns the media? Global trends and local resistance* (pp. 227–247). London: Zed Books.

Mutsvairo, B. (2016). Can Robert Mugabe be tweeted out of power. *The Guardian* (online). Retrieved from https://www.theguardian.com/global-development-professionals-network/2016/jul/26/robert-mugabe-grassroots-protest-zimbabwe-social-media (Accessed on 01 February 2017).

Mutsvairo, B.(Ed). (2016). *Digital activism in the social media era: Critical reflections on emerging trends in sub-Saharan Africa*. London: Palgrave Macmillan.

Nairaland User 1, January 14 2012.

Nairaland User 2, January 14 2012.

Nairaland User 3, January 14 2012.

Nairaland User 4, January 14 2012.

Nairaland User 5, January 14 2012.

National Bureau of Statistics. (2015). State information. Retrieved from http://nigerianstat.gov.ng/information#! (Accessed on 05 May 2013).

National Population Commission. (2002). Retrieved from http://africanmediainitiative.org/wp-content/uploads/2015/10/AMDI-Report-Nigeria.pdf

National Population Commission. (2006). Population of Nigeria by state and sext 1991 and 2006. Retrieved from http://istmat.info/files/uploads/53129/annual_abstract_of_statistics_2011.pdf. (Accessed on 22 July 2018).

National Public Broadcasting Inc. (2011). The Arab spring: A year of revolution. (Online) December 17. Retrieved from https://www.npr.org/2011/12/17/143897126/the-arab-spring-a-year-of-revolution (Accessed on 12 December 2017).

National Public Radio. (2011). The Arab spring: A year of revolution. (Online) 17 December. Retrieved from https://www.npr.org/2011/12/17/143897126/the-arab-spring-a-year-of-revolution

National Public Radio. (2016). Congo to block social media sites ahead of protests against the president. (Online) 16 December. Retrieved from https://www.npr.org/sections/thetwo-way/2016/12/16/505854670/congo-to-block-social-media-sites-ahead-of-protests-against-the-president?t=1532294920427 (Accessed on 12 December 2017).

News24. (2015). Boko Haram bid to join ISIS a propaganda boost. *News24,* (Online) 9 March. Retrieved from http://www.news24.com/Africa/News/Boko-Haram-bid-to-join-ISIS-a-propaganda-boost-20150309 (Accessed on 02 September 2015).

Nigel, F. (Ed.). (2003). *Interviewing* (2nd ed). London: Sage Publications.

Nigeria, Central Intelligence Agency. (2013). (Online) 14 January. Retrieved from https://www.cia.gov/library/publications/the-world-factbook/geos/ni.html (Accessed on 14 January 2013).

Nigeria: Seizing the Moment in the Niger Delta. (2009). International Crisis Group report. Retrieved from http://www.crisisgroup.org/~/media/Files/africa/west-africa/nigeria/B060%20Nigeria%20Seizing%20the%20Moment%20in%20the%20Niger%20Delta.pdf (Accessed on 10 June 2015).

Nigerian National Petroluem Corporation. (2015). Oil production (Online). Retrieved from http://www.nnpcgroup.com/nnpcbusiness/upstreamventures/oilproduction.aspx (Accessed on 12 November 2015).

Nigerian Population Commission. (2006). Populations and housing census of the federal republic of Nigeria .NPC report. (Online). Retrieved from http://www.population.gov.ng/images/Priority%20Tables%0Volume%20I-update.pdf (Accessed on 19 September 2015).

Nigerian Poverty Profile. (2010). Nigerian Bureau of Statistics. NBS report (online). Retrieved from http://www.nigerianstat.gov.ng/pdfuploads/Nigeria%20Poverty%20Profile%202010.pdf (Accessed on 20 May 2014).

Nikolayenko, O. (2009). Youth movements in post-communist societies: A model of nonviolent resistance. Paper prepared for the Annual Meeting of the American Political Science Association, September 2 – September 6, 2009. Retrieved from https://irevolution.files.wordpress.com/2009/09/nikolayenko-apsa2009.pdf

Nitya, S. (2011). Nigeria's elusive quest for democracy: Multinational corporations and sustenance of authoritarianism. *African and Asian Studies*, *10*(2–3), 209–233.

Nolle, E. (2016). Social media and its influence on democratization in Africa. *International Policy Digest* (online). Retrieved from https://intpolicydigest.org/2016/08/11/social-media-influence-democratization-africa/

Nolutshungu, S. C. (1990). Fragments of a democracy: Reflections on class and politics in Nigeria. *Third World Quarterly*, *12*(1), 86–115.

Nossiter, A. (2011). Islamic group says it was behind fatal Nigeria attack. (Online) 28 August. *New York Times*. (Accessed on 12 April 2014).

Nsehe, M. (2013). 30 under 30: Africa's best young entrepreneurs. *Forbes*. (Online). Retrieved from https://www.forbes.com/sites/mfonobongnsehe/2013/02/23/30-under-30-africas-best-young-entrepreneurs/#339365391cf8 (Accessed on 01 February 2014).

Nwoko, K. C. (2009). Trade unionism and governance in Nigeria: A paradigm shift from labour activism to political opposition. *Information, Society and Justice*, *2*, 139–152 2, June ISSN 1756–1078. http://repository.londonmet.ac.uk/70/1/InformationSocietyAndJustice%20v2%2Cn2%20p139-152.pdf

Nworzor, A. (2014). Power rotation, ethnic politics and the challenges of democratization in contemporary Nigeria. *African Study Monographs*, *35*(1), 1–18 (online). Retrieved from http://jambo.africa.kyoto-u.ac.jp/kiroku/asm_normal/abstracts/pdf/35-1/13-23-3.pdf (Accessed on 14 September 2015.

Obadare, E. (1999). The press and democratic transition in Nigeria: Comparative notes on the Abacha and Abubakar transition programs. *A Journal of Opinion*, *27*(1), 38–40.

Obadare, E. (2004). In search of a public sphere: The fundamentalist challenge to civil society in Nigeria. *Patterns of Prejudice*, *38*(2), 177–198.

Obadare, E. (2006). Breakdown and reconstitution democracy, the nation-state, and ethnicity in Nigeria. *Journal of Political and Military Sociology*, *34*(2), 394–396.

Obadare, E. (2007). A culture of corruption: Everyday deception and popular discontent in Nigeria. *International Affairs*, *83*(4), 820–821.

Obadare, E., & Willems, W. (2014). *Civic agency in Africa: Arts of resistance in the 21st century*. Oxford: James Currey.

Obi, C. (2009a). Nigeria's Niger Delta: Understanding the complex drivers of violent oil-related conflict. *Africa Development*, *XXXIV*(2), 103–128.

Obi, C. (2009b). Structuring transnational spaces of identity, rights and power in the Niger Delta of Nigeria. *Globalizations*, *6*(4), 467–481.

Obi, C. (2010). Oil extraction, dispossession, resistance, and conflict in Nigeria's oil-rich Niger Delta. *Canadian Journal of Development Studies/Revue canadienne d'études du développement*, *30*(1–2), 219–236.

Obserschall, A. (1973). *Social conflict and social movements*. Eagglewood Cliff.: Prentice Hall.

Occupy Nigeria. (2012). *Social networking group*, (Facebook), 6 January. Retrieved from <https://www.facebook.com/pages/Occupy-Nigeria/160388144055585>. [29 October 2013].

Occupy Wall Street. (2011). Retrieved from http://occupywallst.org/about/. [12 January 2014].

Odamah, A. M. (2012). Socio-economic incentives, new media and the Boko Haram campaign of violence in Northern Nigeria. *Journal of African Media Studies*, *4*(1), 111–124. doi:10.1386/jams.4.1.111_1

Odugbemi, S. & Norris, P. (2009). Do the news media act as watchdogs, agenda-setters and gate-keepers? In P. Norris (Ed.), *Public sentinel: News media & governance reform. (Online)*. Washington, DC: The World Bank.

Oduko, S. (1987). From indigenous communication to modern television: A reflection of political development in Nigeria. *African Media Review*, *1*(3), 1–10.

Ogunleshi, T. (2014). Have over 13,000 people been killed in Nigeria's insurgency? The claim is broadly correct. African Check. (Online). Retrieved from https://africacheck.org/reports/have-13000-people-been-killed-in-nigerias-insurgency-the-claim-is-broadly-correct/ (Accessed 09 November 2015).

Ogunlesi, T. (2012). *The fuel subsidy crisis has woken Nigerians up. The Guardian* (online), 11 January 2012. Retrieved from http://www.guardian.co.uk/

commentisfree/2012/jan/11/fuel-subsidy-crisis-nigerians?INTCMP=SRCH (Accessed on 6 January 2013).

Ojakorotu, V. (2008). Environmental activism and the struggle for justice by the non-governmental organisations in the Niger Delta of Nigeria. *International Journal of Regional and Local Studies*, *4*(2), 40–55.

Ojo, E. (2009). Can Nigeria's nascent democracy survive? *Journal of Sustainable Development in Africa*, *11*(1), 1–26.

Ojo, E., & Adebayo, F. P. (2009). Can Nigeria's nascent democracy survive? *Journal of Sustainable Development in Africa (Online)*, *11*(1) Retrieved from https://www.researchgate.net/publication/265497883_CAN_NIGERIA'S_NASCENT_DEMOCRACY_SURVIVE (Accessed on 21 October 2015).

Oketunmbi, E. (2006 & 2007). Gains and pains of liberalization of broadcasting in Nigeria: A critical assessment. *Journal of communication and society*, *1*(2 &3), 51–62.

Okonta, I. (2006). *Behind the mask: Explaining the emergence of the MEND militia in Nigeria's oil-bearing Niger Delta*. Working Paper No.11. Institute of Inter) Accessed [31/04/15].

Okpaku, J. (1972). Nigeria: Dilemma of nationhood: an African analysis of the Biafran conflict (No. 49). Greenwood Press.

Okpi, A. (2012). The many intrigues of fuel price protests, online ed. *The Punch*. Retrieved from http://www.punchng.com/politics/the-many-intrigues-of-fuel-price-protests/ (Accessed on 14 February 2013).

Olabode, S. (2016). Veterans of diaspora activism: An overview of ICTs use among Nigerian migrant networks'. In A. Karatzogianni D. Nguyen, & E. Serafinelli (Eds.), *The digital transformation of the public sphere: Conflict, migration, crisis and culture in digital networks*. London: Palgrave Macmillan.

Olajide, O. T., Ojo Akinlabi, B. H., & Ojo Tijani, A. A. (2012). Agriculture resource and economic growth in Nigeria. *European Scientific Journal*, *8*(22), 103–115 October edition Retrieved from http://eujournal.org/index.php/esj/article/viewFile/422/570

Olayiwola, R. O. (1991). Political communications: Press and politics in Nigeria's second republic. *Africa Media Review*, *5*, 31–35.

Oliver, P., & Johnston, H. (2000). What a good idea: Frames and ideology in social movement research; online: http://ssc.wisc.edu/~oliver/PROTESTS/ArticleCopies/Frames.2.29.00.pdf (Accessed 30 August 2012).

Olojo, A. (2013). *Nigeria's Troubled North: Interrogating the drivers of public support for Boko Haram* International. In: ICCCT Research paper. Centre for Counter-Terrorism - The Hague, The Netherlands: Web. Retrieved from https://www.icct.nl/download/file/ICCT-Olojo-Nigerias-Troubled-North-October-2013.pdf (Accessed on 26 May 2015).

Olson, M. (1965). *The logic of collective action: Public goods and the theory of groups*. Harvard: Havard University Press.

Olukotun, A. (2000b, December). The 1999 Nigerian transition and the media. *African Journal of Political Science*, *5*(2), 33–44.

Olukotun, A. (2002a). Authoritarian state, crisis of democratization and the underground media in Nigeria. *African Affairs*, *101*(404), 317–342.

Olukotun, A. (2002b). Traditional protest media and anti-military struggle in Nigeria 1988–1999. *African Affairs*, *101*(403), 193.

Olukoyun, A. (2004). Media accountability and democracy in Nigeria, 1999-2003. *African Studies Review*, *47*(3), 69–90. doi:10.2307/1514943

Olusegun, A., & David, A. (2010). The implications of British colonial economic policies on Nigeria's development. *International Journal of Advanced Research in Management and Social Sciences*, *1*(2), 1–16. Retrieved from http://www.garph.co.uk/IJARMSS/Aug2012/1.pdf

Omavich. (2014). Nigerian government under fire for expansion of surveillance programs, Retrieved from https://www.privacyinternational.org/node/372 (Accessed on 02 December 2014).

Omonobi, K. (2014). Boko Haram: Military raises fresh alarm. *Vanguard* Nigeria, (12 November). Retrieved from Read more at: http://www.vanguardngr.com/2014/11/boko-haram-military-raises-fresh-alarm/ (Accessed on 01 February 2015).

Onigbinde, O. (2015). Nigeria's dire finances show it cannot grease the economy with fickle oil alone. (Online) 21 July. Retrieved from http://www.theguardian.com/global-development/2015/jul/21/nigeria-dire-finances-show-it-cannot-grease-economy-fickle-oil-alone (Accessed on 13 October 2015).

Onuoha, F. C. (2010). The Islamist challenge: Nigeria's Boko Haram crisis explained. *African Security Review,* [*E-journal*], *19*(2), 54–67 Retrieved from http://www.tandfonline.com/doi/pdf/10.1080/10246029.2010.503061.

Onuoha, F. C. (2012a). Boko Haram: Nigeria's extremist Islamic sect. Aljazera's report (online). Retrieved from http://studies.aljazeera.net/ResourceGallery/media/Documents/2012/2/29/2012229113341793734BOKO%20HARAM%20NIGERIAS%20EXTREMIST%20ISLAMIC%20SECT.pdf. (Accessed on 09 December 2015)

Onuoha, F. C. (2012b). The audacity of the Boko Haram: Background, analysis and emerging trend. *Security Journal*, *25*, 134–15. Retrieved from http://www.palgrave-journals.com/sj/journal/v25/n2/abs/sj201115a.html

Onuoha, F. C. (2013). Jamaátu Ansarul Musilmina Fi Biladis Sudan: Nigeria´s evolving terrorist group in Al-Jazeera centre for studies report, 14 March 2013, pp. 1–8.

Onuoha, F. C. (2014a). A danger not to Nigeria alone – Boko Haram´s transnational reach and regional responses, FES peace and security studies No. 17 Abuja, Nigeria: Friedrich Ebert Stiftung.

Onuoha, F. C. (2014b). Why do youth join Boko Haram? United States Institute for Peace Special Report no. 348, June 2014 Usip.org: Washington, DC.

Oriola, B. T. (2013). *Criminal resistance?: The politics of kidnapping oil workers* (p. 243). Farnham, Surrey, UK: Ashgate Publishing Limited.

Osaghae, E., Ikelegbe, A., Olarinmoye, O., & Okhonmina, S. (2007). Youth militias, selfdetermination and resource control struggles in the Niger-Delta of Nigeria. (Online). Retrieved from http://www.ascleiden.nl/Pdf/cdpnigeriaRevisedOsaghae%5B1%5D2.pdf. (Accessed on 15 May 2014).

Oseni, T. (1995). Government-media relations: A case of mutual exclusivity? Paper presented at the Quarterly Forum of the Nigerian Television Authority, lbadan, July 27.

Oso, L., & Pate, U. (2012). *Mass media and society in Nigeria*. Nigeria: Malthouse Publishing.

Oso, L., Soola, O., & Pate, U. (2012). *Media, governance and development in Nigeria: Issues and trends*. KG, Saarbrucken, Germany: LAP LAMBERT Academic.

Owuamanam, J., Falola, F., & Shobiye, H. (2009). The rise, threat and fall of Boko Haram. *Saturday Punch* (Lagos), 1 August, pp. 2–3.

Owugah, L. (1999). Local resistance and the state. Paper presented at Oil Watch African General Assembly, Port Harcourt, February 9–14, 1999.

Oyclere, M. (2014). Political developments, trade union and social movement unionism: A case of Nigeria labour congress. Regent's University London http://www.regents.ac.uk/media/989223/RWPBM1404-Oyelere-M.pdf

Page, J. (2011). China leaders laud 'red' campaign. *Wall Street Journal*. (Online). June 20. (Accessed on 2 February 2013). Retrieved from http://www.wsj.com/articles/SB10001424052702303936704576395621087173648

Pandey, T. (2009). Qualitative methods and sociology. *Nepalese Journal of Qualitative Research Methods*, *3*, 31–27.

Participant 1. 6 January 2012, Occupy Nigeria Facebook.

Participant 2. 6 January 2012, Occupy Nigeria Facebook.

Participant 3. 11 January 2012, Occupy Nigeria Facebook.

Participant 4. 16 January 2012, Occupy Nigeria Facebook.

Participant 5. 16 January 2012, Occupy Nigeria Facebook.

Participant 6. 11 January 2012, Occupy Nigeria Facebook.

Participant 7. 11 January 2012, Save Nigeria Group Facebook.

Participant 8. 12 January 2012, Save Nigeria Group Facebook.

Participant 9. 12 January 2012, Save Nigeria Group Facebook.

Participant 10. 12 January 2012, Save Nigeria Group Facebook.

Participant 11. 4 January 2012, Occupy Nigeria Facebook.

Participant 12. 4 January 2012, Occupy Nigeria Facebook.

Participant 13. 3 January 2012, Occupy Nigeria Facebook.

Participant 14. 11 January 2012, Occupy Nigeria Facebook.

Participant 15. 22 January 2012, Occupy Nigeria Facebook.

Participant 16. 13 January 2012, Occupy Nigeria Facebook.

Participant 17. 13 January 2012, Occupy Nigeria Facebook.

Participant 18. 13 January 2012, Occupy Nigeria Facebook.

PBS. (no date). Analysis Wahhabism. (Online) 10 June. Retrieved from http://www.pbs.org/wgbh/pages/frontline/shows/saudi/analyses/wahhabism.html (Accessed on 10June 2015).

PBS Frontline. (2014). Analysis Wahhabism. (Online). Retrieved from: https://www.pbs.org/wgbh/pages/frontline/shows/saudi/analyses/wahhabism.html [Accessed on 12 December 2015].

PBS MediaShift. (2013). The rise of global free speech in the digital age: How blogs, forums, Facebook, Twitter, YouTube boost freedom of expression around the world 2006 to 2013. Public Broadcasting Service MediaShift. San Bernardino, California.

Penfold-Mounce, R. (2010). *Celebrity culture and crime: The joy of transgression*. Basingstoke: Palgrave Macmillan.

Perham, M. (1970). Reflections on the Nigerian civil war. *International Affairs* (Royal Institute of International Affairs 1944), *46*(2), (Apr., 1970), 231–246. Retrieved from http://www.jstor.org/stable/pdf/2613824.pdf

Persell, C. H., Green, A., & Gurevich, L. (2001). Civil society, economic distress and social tolerance. *Sociological Forum*, *16*(2), 203–230.

Pham, J. P. (2016). Boko Haram: The strategic evolution of the Islamic State's West Africa Province. *The Journal of the Middle East and Africa*, *7*(1), 1–18.

Piazza, A. J. (2006). Rooted in poverty?: Terrorism, poor economic development, and social cleavages. *Terrorism and Political Violence*, *18*(1), 159–177. doi:10.1080/095465590944578

Pound, W. D. (1977). *The Marxist conception of ideology: A critical essay*. Cambridge: Cambridge University Press.

Premium Time Report. (2015). ISIS accepts Boko Haram's pledge of allegiance. *Premium Times* 13 March. Retrieved from http://www.premiumtimesng.com/news/top-news/178405-isis-accepts-boko-harams-pledge-of-allegiance.html (Accessed on 10 June 2015).

Premium Times Online. (2014). Controversy trails new video claiming Boko Haram leader, Abubakar Shekau, is alive. (Online) 2 October. Retrieved from https://www.premiumtimesng.com/news/headlines/168948-controversy-trails-new-video-claiming-boko-haram-leader-abubakar-shekau-is-alive.html?cat=1 (Accessed on 13 September 2015).

Press Reference. (no date). Nigeria. (Online). Retrieved from http://www.pressreference.com/Ma-No/Nigeria.html (Accessed on 20 December 2015).

Prince, S. (2015). Watch: ISIS Boko Haram beheads Nigerian soldier in Borno, Nigeria. Heavy (online) October 12. Retrieved from http://heavy.com/news/2015/10/new-isis-islamic-state-boko-haram-news-videos-pictures-west-africa-province-wilayat-gharb-ifriqiyyah-beheads-nigerian-soldier-beheaded-beheading-full-uncensored-youtube/

Quiggiz, T. (2009). Understanding al-Qaeda's ideology for counter-narrative work. *Terrorism Analysts*, *3*(2). Retrieved from http://www.terrorismanalysts.com/pt/index.php/pot/article/view/67/html [10.06.2015].

Quintal, G. (2015). What you need to know about #feesmustfall. *Mail and Guardian* (online). Retrieved from https://mg.co.za/article/2015-10-19-four-things-you-need-to-know-about-feesmustfall (Accessed on 19 December 2017).

Reilly, P. (2003). Civil society, the internet and terrorism: Two case studies from Northern Ireland. Paper prepared for the European Consortium for political research joint sessions of workshops, Edinburgh.

Remi, C. (2017). A history of opposition: Africa's contested election. France 24 (online) http://www.france24.com/en/20170814-africa-elections-contested-kenya-gambia-gabon-sao-tome-principe-democratic-republic-congo

Rheingold, H. (2003). *Smart mobs: The next social revolution*. Cambridge: Basic Books.

Rogers, P. (2012). Nigeria: The generic context of the Boko Haram violence. Oxford research group. 30 April. Retrieved from http://www.oxfordresearchgroup.org.uk/sites/default/files/AprEn12.pdf (Accessed on 05 May 2013).

Ronfeldt, D., Arquilla, J., Fuller, G. E., & Fuller, M. (1998). *The Zapatista social netwar in Mexico*. CA: Rand.

Ronfeldt, D., & Varda, D. (2008). The prospects for cyberocracy (Revisited). Southern Illinois University Carbondale, OpenSIUC. Retrieved from http://opensiuc.lib.siu.edu/cgi/viewcontent.cgi?article=1024&context=pn_wp

Rose, R. M., & Auwal, M. I. (2014). Ethnic minorities and the Nigerian state. *An International Journal of Arts and Humanities*, *3*(3), S/No11, 89–101.

Ross, K. (2014). Why Boko Haram wages war against western education. USNI (online). Retrieved from https://news.usni.org/2014/05/16/boko-haram-wages-war-western-education (Accessed on 05 October 2015).

Rossman, G., & Wilson, B. (1991). Numbers and words revisited: Being "shamelessly eclectic". *Evaluation Review*, *9*(5), 627–643.

Roughneen, S. (2010). Vietnam pushes Facebook clone to control online speech. Media Shift. (Online). 21. (Accessed on 2 October 2013). Retrieved from http://mediashift.org/2010/12/vietnam-pushes-facebook-clone-to-control-online-speech355

Ryan, C. (1991). *Prime time activism: Media strategies for grassroots organizing*. Boston: South End Press.

Ryan, G. W., & Bernard, H. R. (2000). Data management and analysis methods. In N. Denzin & Y. Lincoln (Eds.), *Handbook of qualitative research* (2nd ed., pp. 769–802). Thousand Oaks, CA: Sage.

Sahara Reporters. (2011). Occupy Nigeria: civil society, labour unions to engage in series of mass action in January 2012. Sahara reporters. (Online). Retrieved from http://saharareporters.com/2011/12/01/occupy-nigeria-civil-society-labour-unions-engage-series-mass-action-january-2012 (Accessed on 01December 2011).

Saharatv. (2014). Boko Haram leader Shekau releases video on abduction of Chibok girls. *The Guardian*, 05 05, p. Retrievedfrom https://www.youtube.com/watch?v=wrfWS_vL0D4

Saharatv, August. (2009). Boko Haram leader Mohammed Yusuf interrogation before his execution by Nigerian security agents. Saharatv YouTube (Online) 3 August. Retrieved from https://www.youtube.com/watch?v=ePpUvfTXY7w (Accessed on 12 September 2015).

Saletan, W. (2011). Springtime for Twitter: Is the internet driving the revolutions of the Arab Spring? Retrieved (online) from http://www.slate.com/articles/technology/future_tense/2011/07/springtime_for_twitter.html. (Accessed on 10 January 2012).

Salganik, M. J., & Heckathorn, D. D. (2004). Sampling and estimation in hidden populations using respondent-driven sampling. *Sociological Methodology*, *34*(1), 193–239.

Sall, E. (2004). Social movements in the renegotiation of the bases for citizenship in West Africa. *Current sociology*, *52*(4), 595–614.

Sani, A. A. (2014). Press freedom: Analyzing the portrayal of Nigerian-state on national dailies cover-page headlines. *Journal of Yasar University*, *9*(35), (online). Retrieved from http://journal.yasar.edu.tr/wp-content/uploads/2014/08/13_Vol_9_35.pdf (Accessed on 01 December 2015).

Sattar, N. (1995). Al Ikhwam Al Muslimi (Society of Muslim Brotherhood) aims and ideology, role and impact (online). *48*(2), 7–30. Retrieved from http://www.jstor.org/stable/pdf/41393514.pdf?acceptTC=true

Schradie, J. (2011). "The digital production gap: The digital divide and Web 2.0 collide" (PDF). *Poetics*, *39*(2), 145–168. doi:10.1016/j.poetic.2011.02.003

Schudson, M. (1999). *The good citizen: A history of American civic life*. Cambridge, MA: Harvard University Press.

Schulz, M. S. (1998). Collective action across boarders: Opportunity structures, network capacities, and communicative praxis in the age of advance globalization. *Sociological Perspective*, *41*(3), 587–616.

Schwandt, T. A. (2001). *Dictionary of qualitative inquiry*. (2nd ed). California: Sage Publications.

Schwartz, S. (2003). Saudi Arabia and the rise of the Wahhabi threat. Middle East Forum (Online). Retrieved from https://www.meforum.org/articles/2003/saudi-arabia-and-the-rise-of-the-wahhabi-threat (Accessed on 12 March 2015).

Scott, A., & John Street. (2000). From media politics to e-protest. *Information, Communication and Society*, *3*(2), 215–240.

Searcey, D., & Barry, Y. J. (2016). Violence after Gabon elections leaves one dead. *New York Times* (online). Retrieved from https://www.nytimes.com/2016/09/02/world/africa/gabon-election-protests.html?_r=0

Seddon, D. From junta to popular protest: Zimbabwe at the crossroads. *Review of African Political Economy*. (Online). Retrieved from http://roape.net/2017/11/24/junta-popular-protest-zimbabwe-crossroads/ (Accessed on 01 November 2018).

Seddon, D. (Nd). Popular protest & social movements – Part 1. *Review of African Political Economy* (online). Retrieved from http://roape.net/2015/09/30/popular-protest-social-movements-class-struggle-in-africa-a-roape-project/

Seliger, M. (1976). *Ideology and Politics*. London: George Allen & Unwin.

Seo, H., Kim, J. Y., & Yang, S. (2009). Global activism and new media: A study of transnational NGOs' online public relations. *Public Relations Review*, *35*(2), 123–126.

Shearlaw, M. (2016). Egypt five years on: Was it ever a 'social media revolution'? *The Guardian* (online). Retrieved from https://www.theguardian.com/world/2016/jan/25/egypt-5-years-on-was-it-ever-a-social-media-revolution (Accessed on 05 July 2017).

Shekau, M. A. (2011). Sunnahization (Online) 28 October video File. Retrieved from https://www.youtube.com/watch?v=eQY4GLtzLdU (Accessed on 10 June 2015)_.

Shenton, A. K. (2004). Strategies for ensuring trustworthiness in qualitative research projects. *Education for Information*, *22*, 63–75. Retrieved from http://www.crec.co.uk/docs/Trustworthypaper.pdf

Shepherd, M., & Shanade, B. (2016). Citizen journalism andmoral panics: A consideration of ethics in the 2015 South African xenophobic attacks. *Digital African Review: A special issue of African Journalism Studies*, *37*(4), 115–136.

Shigetomi, S., & Makino, K. (Eds.). (2009). *Protest and social movements in the developing world*. Cheltenham: Edward Edgar publishing Limited.

Shipoli, E. A. (2009). Is Wahhabism a security challenge for Kosova, or not? *European Journal of Economic and Political Studies*, *2*(2), 85–95. (Online). Retrieved from http://www.ejeps.com/index.php/ejeps/article/view/23/23 (Accessed on 20 December 2015).

Shirky, C. (2008). *Here comes everybody: The power of organizing without organization*. London: Penguin Press.

Shirky, C. (2010a). *Cognitive surplus: Creativity and generosity in a connected age*. New York: Penguin Press.

Shirky, C. (2010b). The Twitter Revolution: More than just a slogan. *Prospect Magazine* (online) 6 January. Retrieved from https://www.prospectmagazine.co.uk/magazine/the-twitter-revolution-more-than-just-a-slogan (Accessed on 10 October 2014).

Shirky, C. (2011). The political power of social media: Technology, the public sphere, and political change. *Foreign Affairs*, (online). Retrieved from https://www.foreignaffairs.com/articles/2010-12-20/political-power-social-media (Accessed on 20 October 2013).

Sigho. (2012). *CNN* ireport, (online) 26 April. Retrieved from http://ireport.cnn.com/docs/DOC-781372 (Accessed on 22 March 2013).

Silas, A. E. (2013). The effects of Boko Haram insurgency and the school system: A case study of selected states in Northern Nigeria. *Science Journal of Sociology and Anthropology*, *2013*(2013), 1–5. Retrieved from http://www.sjpub.org/sjsa/sjsa-137.pdf (Accessed on 01 May 2014).

Singh, N. (2011). Nigeria's Elusive quest for democracy: Multinational corporations and sustenance of authoritarianism*. *African and Asian Studies*, *10*(2), 209–233.

Smith, D. A. (1995). *Nations and nationalism in a global era*. Cambridge. Blackwell Publisher International.

Snow, A. D., Soule, A. S., & Kriesi, H. (Eds.). (2004). *The blackwell companion to social movements*. MA: Blackwell Publishing Ltd.

Snow, D. A., & Benford, R. D. (1988). Ideology, frame, resonance, and participant mobilization. *International Social Movement Research*, *1*(1), (1988), 197–217.

Snow, D. A., Rochford, E. B. Jr., Worden, S. K., & Benford, R. D. (1986). Frame alignment processes, micromobilization, and movement participation. *American Sociological Review*, *51*(4), 464–481.

Soludo, C. (2005). The Political Economy of Sustainable Democracy in Nigeria. *AllAfrica.com*.

Somide, A. (2001). Federalism, state creation and ethnic management in Nigeria. In A. B. Ojo (Ed.), (2001) *Problems and prospects of sustaining democracy in Nigeria*. New York. Nova Science Publisher Inc.

Soola, E. O. (Ed.). (2002). *Communicating for development purposes*. Ibadan: Kraft Books.

Sowore, O. (2013). Opinion: Nigerians still waiting for their 'African Spring'. *CNN* (Online). Retrieved from http://edition.cnn.com/2013/01/12/world/africa/nigeria-protests-african-spring/index.html (Accessed on 1 February 2014).

Spinelli, M. (1996). Radio lessons for the internet. *Postmodern Culture*, *6*(2), 32–43. Oxford University Press.

Stepanova, E. (2011). The role of information communication technologies in the "Arab Spring": Implications beyond the region. Ponars Eurasia Policy Memo No. 159. Retrieved from http://www.ponarseurasia.org/sites/default/files/policy-memos-pdf/pepm_159.pdf (Accessed on 10 December 2015).

Sternberg, I. D. (2014). Influence of social media in stages of democratization. University of Nevada Las Vegas. Theses, Dissertations (online). Retrieved from https://digitalscholarship.unlv.edu/cgi/viewcontent.cgi?article=3301&context=thesesdissertations (Accessed on 15 February 2017).

Stone, B., & Cohen, N. (2009). Social networks spread Defiance online. (Online) 15 June, Retrieved from www.nytimes.com/2009/06/16/world/middleeast/16media.html (Accessed on 22 July 2013).

Suberu, R. T. (1996). *Ethnic minority conflicts and governance in Nigeria*. Ibadan: Institut français de recherche en Afrique..

Taiwo, R. (2007). Language, ideology and power relations in Nigerian newspaper headlines. Retrieved from https://www.atria.nl/ezines/IAV_607294/IAV_607294_2010_4/Taiwo2.pdf (Accessed on 04 June 2016).

Tapscott, D., & Williams, A. (2010). *Macrowikinomics: Rebooting business and the world*. London: Portfolio Hardcover.

Tar, U. (2009). Organised labour and democratic struggles in Nigeria. *Information, Society and Justice*, *2*(2), 165–181.

Taylor, A. P. (1999). *Hackers: Crime in the digital sublime*. London and New York: Routledge.

The Economist. (1999). Can Obasanjo save Nigeria? *The Economist*. (Online) (Accessed on 01 November 2014). Retrieved from http://www.economist.com/node/188396

The Economist. (2011). Terrorism in Nigeria: A dangerous new level. *The Economist*, 3 September 2011. Retrieved from http://www.economist.com/node/21528307 (Accessed on 09 September 2013).

The Guardian. (2014). *The Guardian*. (Online) 2 May. Retrieved from https://www.theguardian.com/world/2014/may/02/car-bomb-nigerian-capital-abuja (Accessed on 13 December 2015).

The Guardian. (no date). Breaking news: Boko Haram threatens to attack *VOA*, *Guardian*, *Daily Trust* others. (Online, no date). Retrieved from http://www.premiumtimesng.com/news/4895-boko_haram_releases_video_on_thisday_bombing.html (Accessed on 09 December 2012).

The Guardian Nigeria. (2006). Orere. O. Hostage-takers deny interest in Nigeria's break up. (Online) 21 March. Retrieved from http://odili.net/news/source/2006/mar/21/65.html (Accessed on20 June 2015).

The information warfare site. (no date). Psychological operations. IWS-The Information Warfare Site. (online no date). Retrieved from http://www.iwar.org.uk/psyops/

The Stream. (2013). Nigerians rally around #ChildNotBride. *Aljazeera* (online). Retrieved from http://stream.aljazeera.com/story/201307222236-0022924 (Accessed on 01 February 2014).

The Telegraph. (2014). Nigerian town seized by Boko Haram 'part of Islamic caliphate'. Leader says. (Online) 24 August. Retrieved from https://www.telegraph.co.uk/news/worldnews/africaandindianocean/nigeria/11054219/Nigerian-town-seized-by-Boko-Haram-part-of-Islamic-caliphate-leader-says.html (Accessed on 12 October 12).

The Telegraphs report. (2014). Nigeria's top Muslim leader accuses military of running away from Boko Haram. 25 November. Retrieved from http://www.telegraph.co.uk/news/worldnews/africaandindianocean/nigeria/11251843/Nigerias-top-Muslim-leader-accuses-military-of-running-away-from-Boko-Haram.html [10.06.2015].

Thomas, L. E. (1971): Family correlates of student political activism. *Developmental Psychology*, *4*(2), 206–214.

Thompson, V. (2012). Boko Haram and Islamic fundamentalism in Nigeria. *Global Security Studies*, *3*(3). Retrieved from http://globalsecuritystudies.com/Thomson%20Boko%20Haram.pdf

Tilly, C. (1978). *From mobilization to revolution*. Reading, Mass: Addison-Wesley.

Tisdall, S. (2015). Boko Haram-Isis alliance is nothing but superficial propaganda. *The Guardian*, 8 03, p. Retrieved from http://www.theguardian.com/world/2015/mar/08/boko-haram-isis-alliance-is-nothing-but-superficial-propaganda.

Tolly, D.:.M. K. (2007). *Digital stories as tools for change: A study of the dynamics of technology use in social change and activism*, University of Pretoria.

Tormey, S. (2004). *Anti-capitalism: A beginner's guide*. Oxford: Oneworld.

TRAC Nigeria. (2014). Boko Haram Leader, Abubakar Shekau claims responsibility on Barracks attack https://www.youtube.com/watch?v=Pba8uvuf9Is (Accessed on 09 December 2014).

Tsagarousianou, R. (1998). *Cyberdemocracy, technologies, cities and civic networks*. London and New York: Routledge.

Tsagarousianou, R., Tambini, D., & Bryan, C. (Eds.). (1998). *Cyberdemocracy: Technology, cities and civic networks*. London and New York: Routledge.

Tukur, S. (2015). Boko Haram pledges allegiance to ISIS. *Premium Times,* 8 March. Retrieved from http://www.premiumtimesng.com/news/top-news/178135-boko-haram-pledges-allegiance-to-isis.html (Accessed on 10 June 2015).

Tullock, G. (1971). The paradox of revolution. *Public Choice*, *11*(Fall), 89–99.

Tuman, J. (1994). Organised labour under military rule: The Nigerian labour movement, 1985–1992. *Studies in comparative international development*, *29*(3), 26–44.

Tvc News. (2014). Boko Haram releases new video, more threats made. (Online). Retrieved from https://www.youtube.com/watch?v=sLz0U6E-iT4 (Accessed on 20 December 2014).

Twitter. (2012). Social networking group, (Twitter), 2 January. Retrieved from https://twitter.com/occupynigeria [29 October 2013].

Uche, C. (2008). Oil, British interests and the Nigerian civil war. *Journal of African History*, *49*(1), 111–135. Retrieved from https://www.jstor.org/stable/pdf/40206616.pdf?refreqid=excelsior%3Ae6849e1c22aa32c9b3255a9687341171

Udum, K. (2011). How Nur Shekau run Boko Haram. *Vanguard Nigeria*, 03 September. Retrieved from www.Vanguardngr.com/2011/09/how-nur-shekau-run-boko-haram/

Ujah, M. (2009). Yaradua orders probe of Boko Haram's leaders' killing. *Vanguard* (online), 4 August. Retrieved from http://www.vanguardngr.com/2009/08/yaradua-orders-probe-of-boko-haram-leaders-killing/ (Accessed on 03 May 2014).

Ukiwo, U. (2007). From 'Pirates' To 'Militants': A historical perspective on anti-state and anti-oil company mobilization among the Ijaw of Warri, Western Niger Delta. *African Affairs*, *106*(425), 587–610.

United Nations. l'amnistie dans le Delta risque d'être mise à mal – analyse. (2010) Integrated Regional Information Networks IRIN. (Online) 26 April. Retrieved from http://www.irinnews.org/fr/ReportFrench.aspx?ReportID=88924 (Accessed on 17 June 2013).

United Nations development program. (2006). *Niger Delta human development report*. Lagos: Perfect Printers Ltd, Web (Accessed on 10 June 2015).

Uzokwe, O. A. (2003). Surviving in Biafra: The Story of the Nigerian Civil War: Over Two Million Died. Writers Advantage iUniverse. Lincoln.

Van de Donk. (2004). Van de Donk, W., Loader, B., Nixon, P., Rucht, D.: *Cyberprotest: New Media, Citizens and Social Movements*, London and New York: Routledge.

van Eeden Taljaard & Borchardt. (2013). Democracy and the media go hand in hand. Voices of the World. (Online). Retrieved from http://www.voices-of-the-world.org/politics-and-economy/democracy-and-the-media-go-hand-in-hand/ (Accessed on 05 September 2017).

VanDigk, T. (2001). Critical discourse analysis. In D. Tannen, D. Schiffrin, & H. Hamilton (Eds.), *Handbook of discourse analysis*. USA: Blackwell Publishing Ltd.

Vanguard. (2009). Boko Haram ressurects, declares total Jihad. *Vanguard* (online), 14 August. Retrieved from http://www.vanguardngr.com/2009/08/boko-haram-ressurects-declares-total-jihad/

Nigeria, V. (2014). Over 120 million Nigerians live on less than two dollars per day. (Online) 15 July. Retrieved from https://www.vanguardngr.com/2014/07/over-120-million-nigerians-live-on-less-than-two-dollars-per-day/ (Accessed on 12 August 2015).

Vanguard Report. (2015). 83m internet users in Nigeria – NCC'. *Vanguard* (online). Retrieved from http://www.vanguardngr.com/2015/05/83m-internet-users-in-nigeria-ncc/ (Accessed on 01 October 2015).

Vegh, S. (2003). *Classifying forms of online activism: The case of cyberprotest against the World Bank*. New York: Routledge.

Virginia, B., & Victoria, C. (2006). Using thematic analysis in psychology. *Qualitative Research in Psychology*, *3*(2), 77–101. Retrieved from http://dx.doi.org/10.1191/1478088706qp063oa See all articles by this author.

Visser, P. (2009a). *Trip |To M.E.N.D Headquarters Part 1*. [Online Video]. 01 April. Retrieved from: https://www.youtube.com/watch?v=kJSVFnJruxM (Accessed on 10 July 2015).

Visser, P. (2009b). *Trip |To M.E.N.D Headquarters Part 2*. [Online Video]. 01 April. Available from: https://www.youtube.com/watch?v=BlXbY_lpk7g (Accessed on 10 July 2015).

Visser, P. (2009c). *Trip |To M.E.N.D Headquarters Part 3*. [Online Video]. 01 April. Retrieved from https://www.youtube.com/watch?v=p5iksguI3ZM (Accessed on 10 July 2015).

von Behr, I., Reding, A., Edwards, C., & Gribbon, L. (2013). Radicalisation in the digital era: The use of the internet in 15 cases of terrorism and extremism. RAND Corporation research report series. Europe. Retrieved from https://www.rand.org/pubs/research_reports/RR453.html

waazin shekh muhammad yusuf maiduguri 2. (2011). Youtube.com (online) 17, February. Retrieved from https://www.youtube.com/watch?v=elVjD7znMik

waazin shekh muhammad yusuf maiduguri 3. (2011). Youtube.com (Online) 17, February. Retrieved from https://www.youtube.com/watch?v=9nYGyYEA1Y8

waazin shekh muhammad yusuf maiduguri 4. (2011). Youtube.com (Online) 17, February. Retrieved from https://www.youtube.com/watch?v=yU7eVc-NOyE

Waazin skekh Muhannnad Yusuf 1. (2011). Youtube.com (Online) 17, February. Retrieved from https://www.youtube.com/watch?v=f89PvcpWSRg

Walker, A. (2012). What is Boko Haram? United States institute of peace. (Online). Retrieved) from http://www.usip.org/sites/default/files/SR308.pdf (Accessed on 23 November 2013).

Walker, A. (2014). Why Nigeria has not defeated Boko Haram. *BBC,* 14 May. Retrieved from http://www.bbc.co.uk/news/world-africa-27396702 (Accessed on 10 June 2015).

Walker, C. (2007). An ICT policy dilemma: Ramifications on strategic nonviolent social movements and the global Islamist insurgency. MA thesis, The Fletcher School at Tufts University.

Wasserman, H. (2017). The social is political: Media, protest and change in Africa. (Online) Retrieved from https://hermanwasserman.wordpress.com/2017/05/31/the-social-is-political-media-protest-and-change-in-africa/ (Accessed on 31 May 2017).

Watts, M. (2007) Petro-insurgency or criminal syndicate? conflict & violence in the Niger Delta. *Review of African Political Economy*, *34*(114), 637–660. doi:10.1080/03056240701819517

Webb, S. (2014). Junkie Jihadi John? Expert claims slurred speech of ISIS executioner in beheading video of Brit hostage David Haines could have been down to drugs. *Daily mail*, 18 November. Retrieved from http://www.dailymail.co.uk/news/article-2760354/Junkie-Jihadi-John-Expert-claims-slurred-speech-ISIS-executioner-beheading-video-Brit-hostage-David-Haines-drugs.html (Accessed on 5 February 2015).

Wejnert, C. (2009). An empirical test of respondent-driven sampling: Point estimates, variance, degree measures, and out-of-equilibrium data. *Sociological Methodology*, *39*(1), 73–116.

Wejnert, C., & Heckathorn, D. D. (2008). Web-based network sampling: Efficiency and efficacy of respondent-driven sampling for online research. *Sociological Methods and Research*, *37*(1), 105–134.

Whitlowzw. (2015). Strategy, targets, and methods of operation. Boko Haram terrorism group project. (Online) 27 July). Retrieved from https://rampages.us/boko-haram/2015/07/27/strategy-targets-and-methods-of-operation/ (Accessed on 10 December 2015).

Williams, W., & Mano, W. (2017). *Everyday media culture in Africa: Audience and users*. London and New York. Routledge.

World Bulletin Report. (2015). Experts: Boko Haram uses ISIL to recruit. World Bulletin, 10 March. Retrieved from http://www.worldbulletin.net/news/156375/experts-boko-haram-uses-isil-to-recruit (Accessed on 10 June 2015).

Yang, G. (2009). *The power of the internet in China: Citizen activism online*. New York: Columbia University Press.

Yin, R. (1994). *Case study research: Design and methods*. (2nd ed.). Thousand Oaks, CA: Sage Publishing.

Yin, R. K. (1994). *Case study research: Design and methods*. (2nd ed.). London: Sage Publication.

Yin, R. K. (2003). *Case study research: Design and methods* (3rd ed.). California. Sage Publications.

Yin, R. K. (2009). *Case study research: Design and methods* (4th ed.). London: SAGE.

Yin, R., & Moore, G. (1987). The use of advanced technologies in special education.

Yusuf, M. (2015). Burundi journalists protest closing of radio station. *VOA News* (Online) Retrieved from https://www.voanews.com/a/burundi-journalists-protest-closing-of-radio-station/2746796.html.(Accessed [12/02/17].

Zachary, E. (2012). Boko Haram: The rise, success, and continued efficacy of the insurgency in Nigeria. International institute for counter-terrorism. Retrieved from http://www.ict.org.il/Article/53/Boko-Haram-The%20Rise-Success-and-Continued-Efficacy

Zald, M. (2006). Culture, ideology and strategic framing. In D. McAdam, J. McCarthy, & M. Zald (Eds.), *Comparative perspectives on social movements:*

Political opportunities, mobilizing structures, and structural framings. Cambridge: Cambridge University Press.

Zayani, M. (2008). The challenges and limits of universalist concepts: Problematizing public opinion and a mediated Arab public sphere. *The Middle East Journal of Communication and Culture*, *1*(1), 60–79.

Zenn, J. (2013). Cooperation or competition: Boko Haram and Ansaru after Mali intervention. *CTC Sentinel*, 27 March 2013, 1–4.

Zenn, J. (2014). Boko Haram: Recruitment, financing, and arms trafficking in the Lake Chad region. *CCT.USMA*, *7*(10). Retrieved from https://ctc.usma.edu/boko-haram-recruitment-financing-and-arms-trafficking-in-the-lake-chad-region/

Zenn, J., Barkindo, A., & Heras, A. N. (2013) The ideological evolution of Boko Haram in Nigeria. *The RUSI Journal*, *158*(4), 46–53. doi:10.1080/03071847.2013.826506

Žydžiumaite, V. (2007). Methodological considerations: Sequential linking of qualitative and quantitative research. *Social Sciences*, *55*(1), 7–14.

Index